NGOs in Contemporary Britain

NGOs in Contemporary Britain

Non-state Actors in Society and Politics Since 1945

Edited By

Nick Crowson
Reader in Contemporary British History, University of Birmingham

Matthew Hilton
Professor of Social History, University of Birmingham

James McKay
Postdoctoral Research Fellow, University of Birmingham

First published 2009 by
PALGRAVE MACMILLAN

Palgrave Macmillan in the UK is an imprint of Macmillan Publishers Limited,
registered in England, company number 785998, of Houndmills, Basingstoke,
Hampshire RG21 6XS.

Palgrave Macmillan in the US is a division of St Martin's Press LLC,
175 Fifth Avenue, New York, NY 10010.

Palgrave Macmillan is the global academic imprint of the above companies
and has companies and representatives throughout the world.

Palgrave® and Macmillan® are registered trademarks in the United States,
the United Kingdom, Europe and other countries

ISBN-13: 978–0–230–22109–3   hardback
ISBN-10: 0–230–22109–2   hardback

This book is printed on paper suitable for recycling and made from fully
managed and sustained forest sources. Logging, pulping and manufacturing
processes are expected to conform to the environmental regulations of the
country of origin.

A catalogue record for this book is available from the British Library.

A catalogue record for this book is available from the Library of Congress.

10   9   8   7   6   5   4   3   2   1
18 17 16 15 14 13 12 11 10 09

Printed and bound in Great Britain by
CPI Antony Rowe, Chippenham and Eastbourne

Contents

List of Tables

Notes on Contributors

Matthew Anderson recently completed his PhD at the University of Birmingham. He has published articles on the history of co-operation and fair trade and is currently working on a book-length treatment of the fair trade movement in Britain.

Caitriona Beaumont is Senior Lecturer in Social History at London South Bank University. She is currently working on a new book entitled *Housewives and Citizens: Domesticity and the Women's Movement in England 1928–1964*.

Lawrence Black is Senior Lecturer in modern British history at Durham University. He works on the history of political culture and has published on topics including TV, consumerism, party activism and cultural politics in post-1945 Britain.

Stephen Brooke is Associate Professor of History, York University, Toronto. He is the author of *Labour's War* (1992), *Sexual Politics: Sexuality and the British Left, 1880s to the Present Day* (forthcoming), and articles in the *American Historical Review*, *Past and Present* and *Journal of Social History*.

Tom Buchanan is Reader in Modern History at the University of Oxford Department for Continuing Education, and a Fellow of Kellogg College. His publications include *Britain and the Spanish Civil War* (1997), *Europe's Troubled Peace, 1945–2000* (2005) and *The Impact of the Spanish Civil War on Britain: War, Loss and Memory* (2006).

Jodi Burkett is a PhD candidate at York University, Canada. She is particularly interested in articulations of national identity within social movements of the left. Her work compares ideas of Britishness within organisations including CND, the Anti-Apartheid Movement, the National Union of Students and the Northern Ireland Civil Rights Association.

Nick Crowson is Reader in Contemporary British History at the University of Birmingham. His past research has concentrated on aspects of British politics, particularly the Conservative party. His most recent book is *The Conservative Party and European Integration* (2006).

Tanya Evans is a Research Fellow at Macquarie University, Sydney. She was a Research Fellow at the Centre for Contemporary British History, Institute of Historical Research from 2004–2008 where she worked on a project 'Unmarried Motherhood in England and Wales, 1918–1995' led by Pat Thane. *Sinners? Scroungers? Saints? Unmarried Motherhood in Modern England* will be published in 2009.

Darren Halpin is Reader in the Department of Public Policy at The Robert Gordon University in Aberdeen. His research focusses on the engagement of interest groups in the policy process and with the contribution of groups to representation and democracy.

Matthew Hilton is Professor of Social History at the University of Birmingham. He has published widely on the history of consumer society and social activism. His most recent book is *Prosperity for All: Consumer Activism in an Era of Globalisation* (2008).

James McKay is a Postdoctoral Research Fellow at the University of Birmingham. He was awarded his PhD in 2006, on the topic of British Labour party attitudes to European integration.

Audra Mitchell is a PhD candidate at the Queen's University of Belfast. She holds doctoral fellowships from the Social Sciences and Humanities Research Council of Canada and Queen's University, and is co-editing the forthcoming book *Transformation and the Dynamics of (Radical) Change: Insights from Political Theory and Philosophy*.

Alex Mold is Lecturer in History at the Centre for History in Public Health, London School of Hygiene and Tropical Medicine. Her publications include *Heroin: The Treatment of Addiction in Twentieth Century Britain* (2008).

Christopher Rootes is Professor of Environmental Politics and Political Sociology, University of Kent. He edits *Environmental Politics* and has also edited: *The Green Challenge: the Development of Green Parties in Europe* (1995); *Environmental Movements: Local, National and Global* (1999); *Environmental Protest in Western Europe* (2003); and *Acting Locally: Local Environmental Mobilisations and Campaigns* (2008).

Clare Saunders is a Lecturer/RCUK Fellow in Politics at the University of Southampton. She works mostly on social movements and protest. She has authored and co-authored book chapters on the global justice movement and published articles in the *British Journal of Sociology*, *Environmental Politics*, and *Social Movement Studies*.

Rob Skinner currently teaches in the Department of Historical Studies at the University of Bristol. He has published work exploring the emergence of anti-apartheid activism as in Britain during the 1950s, and is currently writing a full-length study of the roots of anti-apartheid in Britain and the United States.

Matthew Waites is Lecturer in Sociology at the University of Glasgow. He is author of *The Age of Consent: Young People, Sexuality and Citizenship* (2005); and co-editor, with Jeffrey Weeks and Janet Holland, of *Sexualities and Society: A Reader* (2003).

Acknowledgements

This volume emerged out of the Non-Governmental Organisations and Politics in Contemporary Britain conference, held at Birmingham's Midland Institute in July 2007. The conference was organised by the DANGO project (Database of Archives of UK Non-Governmental Organisations since 1945), and as such we gratefully acknowledge the support of the Arts and Humanities Research Council under the Resource Enhancement Scheme, for funding both the conference, and the wider DANGO project, with a grant of £194,467 (Grant no. 112181).

Through their comments and ideas, all those who contributed to, and participated in, the DANGO conference helped influence the chapters in this book, and as such we would like to thank those contributors whose work could unfortunately not be featured in this collection: Anna Cento Bull, Nandini Deo, Nandita Dogra, Liza Filby, Shane Fudge, Tim Jackson, Bryn Jones, Morag McDermont, Yacob Mulugetta and Susan Trouvé Finding. Particular thanks are also due to Pat Thane, for her closing remarks to the conference.

We would also like to thank the Advisory Panel to the DANGO project: Chris Cook, Melinda Haunton, Christine Penney and Dick Sargent, as well as our colleague on DANGO, Jean-François Mouhot, whose help in making the conference a success was greatly appreciated.

We further gratefully acknowledge the kind permission of Dave Brown, and the assistance of the British Cartoon Archive, in allowing us to use his work as this volume's cover image.

Finally, the conference, and therefore this volume, could not have happened without the hard work of the DANGO project's administrator, Sarah Davies, to whom we are indebted.

Introduction

James McKay and Matthew Hilton

Contemporary Britain can only be properly understood with reference to the phenomenon of non-governmental organisations (NGOs). Their influence can be detected at the heart of every major socio-political initiative of the post-war period: from environmentalism to consumerism; from international aid to human rights; on identity issues such as age, gender, race, religion, disability and sexuality; and on social policy issues such as homelessness, education, child protection and mental health. NGOs as a sector have transcended the rigid categorisations of left and right, progressive and reactionary, and have constructed networks of activism that reach from the face-to-face work of awareness raising groups, to major international lobbying organisations. If one looks to any significant issue of the last 60 years, NGOs will have been involved: in mobilising supporters; in shaping the terms of debate; and in influencing policy outcomes.

This process can be seen, for example, in the field of gay rights. We can first witness the journey from the discreet, post-Wolfenden lobbying of the Homosexual Law Reform Society (HLRS), leading to the partial decriminalisation of homosexual acts in the 1960s. This was followed by later measures relating to the equalisation of the gay age of consent, the introduction of civil partnerships for gay couples and the outlawing of discrimination on grounds of sexuality. Such progress would have been inconceivable without the work of not only the HLRS, but also the Gay Liberation Front, the Campaign for Homosexual Equality, Stonewall and Outrage, to name just the most prominent. Similar stories could be told across the whole range of socio-political issues. The point is that wherever politics has gone, NGOs have been there first, signposting and shaping the issues of the future.[1]

The scale of the sector alone demands attention. Although there is a debate regarding what exactly constitutes an NGO, whatever proxy one uses, the vibrancy of social and socio-political action in Britain is clear. In round figures, there are 170,000 charities in the UK, up from 100,000 15 years ago. These charities have an income of £26 billion and assets of £66 billion, while a paid workforce of over 600,000 is complemented by a volunteer army twice that size.[2] On the alternative measure of voluntary associations, nearly 5,500 are (paying) members of the National Council for Voluntary Organisations (NCVO), the sector's umbrella body for England.[3] To take specific examples, by 1995 the environmental sector alone consisted of 18,000 paid workers and 44,000 volunteers. International agencies operating from Britain employed 54,000 people and the number of people volunteering in issues of health, social services and housing amounted to well over half a million.[4] If one looks to the individual level, 29 per cent of us formally volunteer every month, rising to 44 per cent every year. Moreover, every year 38 per cent of us contact an elected represent-ative or government official, attend a public meeting or rally, take part in a demonstration, or sign a petition.[5] Further evidence of social action can be gained from the huge demonstrations of recent years: 250,000 in Edinburgh in 2005 in support of Make Poverty History; 400,000 in 2002 backing the Countryside Alliance in its defence of fox hunting; and anywhere between one and two million turning out in 2003 to oppose the impending war in Iraq.[6]

Given the vibrancy of socio-political action, one faces the problem of why the sector is relatively neglected by historians. It is a develop-ing field, certainly: a rudimentary survey of scholarly articles dealing with NGOs and new social movements, conducted in 2005, discovered just 38 essays published in the period 1985–89; from 1995–99 this increased to 318, with a further 400 published up to 2004. Never-theless, in order to be a significant element within British historio-graphy, it still has a long way to go. A review of the topics of recently completed history doctorates will, it is true, reveal the occasional thesis addressing the ideas and institutions addressed in this volume (and here we present the exciting work of a number of younger scholars), but these examples are literally swamped by the more established areas and topics of war and the military, political parties and political ideo-logies (the background of two of the three editors of this volume), and diplomatic/international affairs.

These topics are of course hugely significant. However, there is an imbalance towards them in British historiography, and it is this imbalance that we seek to address. A new historical paradigm is needed, which is able to embrace the contribution of NGOs to the British socio-political realm, within wider, more mutually inclusive conceptions of social and political history. We need a history that appreciates the scale and diversity of the sector, and how it has changed, and been changed by, society more generally. We need to better understand the power of NGOs, not simply in terms of influencing legislative change, but also as forces impacting upon the way society perceives itself, conceptualises its problems, and selects the solutions with which to address them. We need to appreciate and analyse the great themes that are played out within the stories of NGOs: professionalisation; secularisation; identity politics and the equality agenda; the expansion of the democratic realm; the proper role of government; and the role of the citizen. All of these themes are considered through the chapters in this volume, and between them they have a real contribution to make to the emerging field of NGO history.

In order to properly advance that field, an attempt first needs to be made to define its subject. Although the term NGO came to prominence in the context of those bodies affiliated to the Economic and Social Committee of the United Nations, and has long been used to describe non-state actors in international development, the NGO is a breed that is increasingly being identified in the sphere of national politics.[7] Unlike in the international arena, however, here the term competes with other, longer established, labels, such as charity, civil society organisation, and voluntary association. These definitions overlap widely, and some suffer from a lack of clarity. Charity, in this sense, is thankfully straightforward, and can simply be assumed to mean (in England and Wales) those organisations registered with the Charity Commission (notwithstanding periodic tinkering with the precise definition of charitable objectives).[8] When one discusses the voluntary sector, or voluntary organisations, however, things begin to get problematic, as demonstrated by the categorical awkwardness of 'social enterprise' (given its existence on a border-line between business and philanthropy), and the considerable and continuing confusion caused by the word 'voluntary'. Civil society, meanwhile, is truly a term for all seasons. Resurgent since the fall of the Communist regimes in Eastern Europe, its precise usage is nevertheless subject to cultural and historical specificity.[9] What combines all of these terms is a descriptive focus on form, rather than function. Together, the chapters in this collection reflect a need to move beyond form-oriented labels, as part of a wider goal to broaden out the concept of the political in British political history, and build bridges, not only between the artificially-divided disciplines of political and social history, but also between history and the wider social science community.

NGOs, then, are those bodies seeking or exerting socio-political influence, while belonging to neither the government nor the business sectors. They exist in the overlap between the voluntary sector and the public sphere. While the form-oriented definitions discussed above would embrace hundreds of thousands of organisations, we believe the focus should be on those organisations that are socio-political actors. The Sunday league football team, although no-doubt important to its members, and certainly interesting in terms of the condition of voluntary association in Britain, cannot (and would not wish to) claim comparable socio-political influence to the major environmental pressure group, or the national road-safety campaign. This discrimination between the politically active and the politically passive is not arbitrary, but rooted in the reality of what is it to be an NGO. The term was popularised as a means of identification for those groups that would be awarded consultative status at the United Nations. Voice, consultation and influence have therefore always been recognised as key characteristics of NGOs. They belong to the third or voluntary sector, but they are not synonymous with it. Instead, they are its players, and that is why they should be of such interest to socio-political historians.

Equally problematic, at first glance, is our focus on a post-1945 chronology. 1945 can seem an incongruous starting point, when one considers that a recent survey of British civil society (in the voluntary sector sense of the term), took as its starting point the Glorious Revolution.[10] Nevertheless, the post-Second World War period is clearly distinctive, and there are factors specific to the post-1945 period, which warrant closer and independent scrutiny. 1945 did not simply mark the end of the war. In the British socio-political realm, it saw the birth of a new era. The implementation of universal, collectivist welfare was a fundamental 'shift in the external environment' for the voluntary sector, which had hitherto been primarily concerned with the provision of social services.[11] That this shift removed the sector's *raison d'être* has been lamented by Frank Prochaska.[12] Demonstrating the sheer scale of Christian social service from the Victorian period up to the mid-twentieth century, Prochaska outlines how the rise of the welfare state displaced this activity, alongside chronicling with bemusement the acquiescence of the Christian establishment in this process. As Prochaska eloquently puts it, 'rarely has a British institution so willingly participated in its own undoing. The bishops blew out the candles to see better in the dark.'[13] The elegiac tone is misplaced. The sector was not killed off by the Attlee reforms; it was, however, fundamentally transformed.

In place of service provision, the sector became more engaged with its longstanding interest in the shaping of the broader socio-political agenda. Social action was thereby reformulated as socio-political action. The analysis here takes its cue from 'post-materialism'. We adopt the insight that the affluence and improving social conditions of the post-war decades, provided by Keynesian capitalism, led to people (and therefore politics) turning away from the now-gratified material needs of work, diet, and housing to, instead, the exploration of personal belief and identity as a path to fulfilment.[14] Post-materialism thus builds on the psychological work of Abraham Maslow, with his conceptualisation of a hierarchy of needs, each needing to be met before the next could be addressed: starting from basic physiological needs, Maslow worked up through successive stages, before reaching the highest need, self-actualisation.[15] While we accept the widespread criticism of post-materialism that its assumptions rather jar with the forward march of consumer capitalism and acquisitive individualism, it is nevertheless the case that the focus of socio-political action changed dramatically. In the post-war decades, within the context of universal state provision of medical and social services, the voluntary sector joined the rest of society in climbing Maslow's ladder, and NGOs flourished, enabled to explore concerns beyond the here and now of service provision. We have put this provocatively, exaggerating in the hope of illuminating, and accept that much service provision continued as before. Dr Barnardo's still provided children's homes and the Salvation Army still provided shelter and accommodation, but the social context had changed in a fundamental way, and the sector changed with it.

Alongside the post-materialist turn, the post-war decades have also seen a demographic revolution. The UK population has grown significantly over the period, rising from c.50 million in 1951, to c.60 million today, and predicted to rise further to 77 million by 2051.[16] But the demographic revolution is not simply a case of raw numbers. The details of where we live, how we live, how long we live, and who we are have all undergone radical change. Following on from the post-war baby-boom, there has been since the early 1970s a clear downward trend in the number of under-16 year olds, and a steady rise in those over 65, with the latter group predicted to exceed the former by 2014.[17] Despite ever more restrictive immigration law, starting with the 1962 Commonwealth Immigrants Act, net immigration now accounts for two-thirds of population growth, as against only 2 per cent in the 1950s.[18] Mass urbanisation, originally a by-product of the industrial revolution, has continued apace. In 1901, the only areas on the British mainland with a population within the range of 555–15,000 people/ km² were to be found in London, central Scotland and Lancashire; today, other prominent examples include the Midlands, the North East, the West Riding of Yorkshire, and south Wales, with numerous other points scattered across the map.[19] We have also witnessed the collapse of the large/extended family and the rise of individual living. Marriage rates, which reached a peak of 480,000 in 1970, slumped to 284,000 in 2005, while the annual divorce figures jumped from 24,000 to 155,000 between 1958 and 2005. The proportion of children in lone-parent households rose from 7 per cent in 1972, to 24 per cent in 2006, while the proportion of one-person households rose 9 percentage points to 27 per cent between 1971 and 1991.[20] The demographic revolution directly led to both the formation and reinvigoration of NGOs, as new ways of living demanded new forms of representation. The organisation that forms the centrepiece of Tanya Evan's chapter in this volume, One Parent Families, had originally been formed as the National Council for the Unmarried Mother and Her Child in 1918. Then, as Evans shows, the new social conditions of the 1960s and 1970s drove the increasing professionalisation of the anti-poverty sector. Accordingly, new organisations such as the Child Poverty Action Group and Gingerbread (for one-parent families) were born.

There were also indirect manifestations of social change. The postwar decades saw the rise and exploration of new social and individual identities, and the development of political beliefs stemming from these. These were fuelled by the affluence, welfarism and mass education of the post-war decades, facilitating and generating the politicisation of an increasingly critical and empowered citizenry, thus again expanding the possibilities of self-identification. Recent decades have seen a phenomenal expansion of higher education, which catered for 2.5 million students in 2004/5, representing a ten-fold rise over the early 1960s, and including a huge increase in the participation of women.[21] These educated, affluent citizens then looked around for new means of self-expression. As Matthew Waites' chapter shows, one of the outcomes of this was the diverse gay rights movement, facilitating not only the exploration of sexual identity, but also showcasing the tensions inherent between forms of political and democratic expression, as activists found different solutions to the same problems. The same tensions can be seen in Jodi Burkett's chapter on the Campaign for Nuclear Disarmament (CND), which explores the conflict between hierarchical and conventional organisational forms, as against more chaotic, and individually-expressive, direct action.

But such self-expression was by no means the preserve of the radical or the new: Caitriona Beaumont's chapter shows how the feminist agenda was not only pursued by eye-catching organisations such as the Women's Liberation Movement, but also, in different ways, by longer-standing groups such as the Mothers' Union, the Townswomen's Guilds, and the Women's Institute. At the same time, social action took on its own dynamic, as an inspirational and practical lead was given by clear examples of the efficacy of socio-political action in influencing political agendas and effecting change. The inspiration provided by US civil rights activists to Western social movements in the 1960s is often cited. Another example can be seen in the use of liberationist terminology, as the language of anti-colonialism was taken up firstly by the Women's Liberation Movement, and then subsequently, by the Gay Liberation Front, and the Animal Liberation Movement.[22]

The assertion of individual identities feeds into a broader critique of the functionality of formal politics. A recent Commission funded by the Rowntree Foundation contended that Britain is labouring under an industrial political structure in a post-industrial age.[23] According to this view, one sees in the post-war years the relative inability of established (worker versus bourgeois) political parties, to meet the concerns of a post-industrial society and citizenry and, further, the fact that where such concerns were adopted, they were done so through being absorbed into, and therefore diluted by, existing ideologies and policy preferences. The collapsing voter turnout of the last 15 years was, they contended, not a result of apathy, but of a failure of formal politics to keep up with the socio-economic changes of the latter half of the twentieth century.[24] If this is the case, what role might there be for NGOs in shoring-up democracy?

This question is the point of departure for Darren Halpin's chapter. In unpicking the idea that NGOs might have a role to play in solving the problem of 'democratic deficit', that government is not sufficiently responsive to citizens, Halpin considers the importance of internal democratic structures to such a function. He highlights the problem that such structures are impossible when the NGO's approach is principally one of solidarity (advocating on behalf of non-human constituencies, such as the environment, or for future generations), and are often absent even when the approach taken is (theoretically) representative, when those being advocated for could indeed be consulted. Although Halpin's chapter concludes that these issues do not necessarily exclude a role for NGOs in reinforcing democracy, his analysis clearly problematises the assumption that they represent a potential solution to falling levels of democratic participation.

Alongside questions of identity and democracy, the chapters in this volume also speak to the debate over the shape and extent of British secularisation.[25] Regardless of the long-term decline in religious observance (a picture complicated, of course, once one looks beyond the pews of Anglican Christianity), there is evidence here that the religious motive for social action, lamented by Prochaska, lives on. As can be seen in Jodi Burkett's examination of CND, as much as in Rob Skinner's study of the Anti-Apartheid Movement (AAM), religious sentiment has been vital. Matthew Anderson's chapter on the development of fair-trade, meanwhile, reinterprets this modern-day phenomenon from being principally a manifestation of consumer power, into a demonstration of how religious groups such as Tearfund, Catholic Agency for Overseas Development (CAFOD) and Christian Aid developed new forms of assisting the developing world, not in an overtly Christian way, but with a Christian motivation none-the-less. None of these causes are explicitly religious, let alone explicitly Christian, but all have been sustained by people of faith, and all therefore demonstrate the continuing relevance of faith to British social action. Somewhat ironically, given the progressive nature of these causes, the most explicit example of Christian-inspired social action in the volume is that of the social reactionary Mary Whitehouse, and her National Viewers and Listeners Association (NVALA), examined by Lawrence Black. For NVALA, the fight against blasphemy was a key one, a battle against the perceived gulf between what they saw on their television screens, and the BBC's dedication to 'Almighty God', as proclaimed on the wall of Broadcasting House.

Another common theme deserving particular comment, as it goes to the heart of what is meant by an NGO, is the question of independence from the state. In her study of the Northern Ireland peace process, Audra Mitchell tells the story of a state bureaucracy keen to instil itself with the values of dynamism typical to emergent grassroots groups, such as the women's movement and the prisoners' movement. Through the provision of funding, however, the state instead inadvertently engendered in such groups the values of the bureaucracy. Alex Mold's chapter on drug user groups makes a similar point about how the Thatcherite 'rolling back the state' of the 1980s entailed the co-option of the voluntary sector in service provision, and thus the adoption of bureaucracy and formalisation where this had not existed before.

The significance of this trend, of course, is not merely organisational; when the state becomes a major (perhaps even the sole) funder of an organisation, tendencies that might have existed towards campaigning and confrontation with government will almost inevitably be tempered. If one looks at the international development field as an example, one can see that government (be it national, European, or international) funding is a hugely significant component of an organisation's income streams. For Oxfam, £48 million of a 2005/6 income of £310.5 million came from government and other public authorities.[26] For Save the Children, the comparable figures are £54.6 million, from a 2006/7 income of £148.4 million.[27] On top of this, one also needs to consider that many NGOs are charities, and are thus bound by campaigning restrictions set out in charity law. The far-reaching effect of this burden is examined in Clare Saunders' chapter on the history of the international development sector. Non-governmental clearly does not mean free from governmental control.

In the new, post-war world, the essence of voluntary sector power developed from being primarily applied, to primarily discursive. Instead of being concerned principally with providing essential services, a burden now carried by the state, organisations now focussed more exclusively on the task of identifying and conceptualising society's ills, drawing up the agenda for future reform. While such a view could be characterised as state-centric, placing voluntary activity at the peripheries of society, it is in fact recognising an important truth, that social action concentrates on areas that are either felt to have been neglected, or else have yet to be constructed as appropriate socio-political fora. This is the story told in Stephen Brooke's chapter, which recounts how the Abortion Law Reform Association (ALRA) defined and redefined the issue of abortion, in order to further the cause of reform, highlighting as a key NGO function the establishment of 'meaning in the public sphere about issues that are eschewed by political parties on grounds of controversy or indifference.' In this sense, this volume aligns itself with the recent discursive emphasis of political historians of earlier periods of British history, who have sought to explore and expand the nature of 'the political'.[28]

Two qualifications should perhaps be made, in order to clarify the perspective offered here. Firstly, given the stress placed upon the ALRA example above, it might seem perverse to argue that legislative impact is not within the capacity of NGOs. This is not the point being made. Clearly, NGOs and their ancestors have long campaigned for legislative change, from the abolition of the slave trade to the call for measures to curb greenhouse gas emissions. The point is not to privilege wider cultural meanings to a degree that legislative change is no longer a key goal, but rather to emphasise the process by which NGOs engage with, and ultimately achieve, such change. Each of the permissive society reforms in the late 1960s, for example, was championed by an NGO: ALRA for abortion law; the HLRS for the partial decriminalisation of homosexual acts, and so on. However, the NGOs in question successfully engaged with these issues as part of a coalition of action and persuasion, a coalition which also included Cabinet ministers and willing backbenchers.[29] In such coalitions, their goal was not only the implementation of change, but also (as an initial and arguably more significant task) the redefinition of the boundaries and meanings within and beneath which change is conceptualised.

Secondly, it is important to emphasise that, whilst NGO power is primarily discursive, it is by no means exclusively so. Conceptualising NGOs as pioneers not just of language, but also of service provision, allows a way around the potential theoretical dead-end that a focus on socio-political action creates, that it privileges campaigning bodies over innovative service providers (a problem particularly raised by Alex Mold's chapter on the rise of drug user groups). In fact, as shown by Mold's work, by Matthew Anderson's examination of the role of international development NGOs in the establishment of fair trade, and by Tanya Evans' reflections on the contributions of the sector to the 1960s 'rediscovery of poverty', pioneering and innovation takes place at many levels: culturally, linguistically, and practically. NGOs thus emerge as Shelley's unacknowledged legislators of the world, not simply in terms of pushing for legislative reform, but in the much wider sense of carving out spheres of action and thought where new concepts are tested and developed, often to then be absorbed, and implemented, by 'mainstream' politics.

When examining the NGO sector, there is a great temptation to search for chronologies, or development models, for the sector as a whole, a super-model that would render explicable the varied history of non-governmental action. What form do groups take when they first emerge? What do they merge into? How does their relationship with the State, with stakeholders, and with wider society develop? And how does the nature and form of the activity they undertake, interact with these other factors? These are difficult questions with complex answers. One could, for example, take from the environmental sector an impression of increasing radicalisation and biocentrism, usurping human-centred conceptions of conservation and land-management, in favour of a recognition of the importance of the biosphere in its own right. In the post-war decades, the dominance of the Victorian conservation bodies such as the Royal Society for the Protection of Birds, the National Trust, and the Royal Society for the Prevention of Cruelty to Animals gave way to a paradigm shift heralded, intellectually, by such seminal texts as *Silent Spring* and *The Limits to Growth*, and, organisationally, by North American imports like Friends of the Earth and Greenpeace.[30] The 1990s, according to this view, saw a further radicalisation, with the rise of the so-called 'disorganisations', often centred in Britain around anti-road protests, and with strong links to the broader anti-capitalist movement, epitomised by the 1999 Seattle protests. Such an interpretation, however useful in highlighting the biocentric trend in environmentalism, fails to explain not only the continuing relevance of (and enormous public support for) 'traditional' conservation bodies, but also, in privileging radicalism, fails to adequately address the increasing centrality of environmental concerns in the governing sphere. To take another example, Rob Skinner's chapter on the AAM sets out how it developed from being a formal organisation, an NGO, into a much more diverse network of action and activism, analogous to a social movement. This turns on its head the accepted 'logical' progression from grassroots activism to more hierarchical and formalised organisational forms, a trajectory often assumed in social movement literature. Diversity and particularism are the essence of NGO activity. The confusion is dizzying, and yet it is precisely the confusion, the variation, the cacophony of voices and perspectives and the infinite flexibility that such diversity brings, that allows the NGO sector to fulfil its pioneering function.

This diversity does not mean that generalisations cannot be sought or made. However, what does emerge from the chapters in this volume is the significance of both specific events and more general periods as triggers for particular types of action. Generic factors encouraging social action have already been mentioned, but the chapters provide a constant reminder of the importance of specificity: witness the rolling reinvention of the Lesbian, Gay and Bisexual (LGB) sector in the light of legislative developments; the way in which fair trade emerged to meet the perceived failure of state-directed international development; the way in which the Northern Ireland conflict acted as a catalyst for the formation of peace and reconciliation groups; the spur of the 'rediscovery of poverty', even of the specific television film *Cathy Come Home*, to the creation of poverty and social care groups in the 1960s; and how the British peace movement was triggered by the successful testing of a British Hydrogen bomb in 1958. It is not a question of the details of particular contexts taking primacy, but rather that specificity requires acknowledgement within more general narratives. This is why the case-study approach adopted by this volume is such an appropriate one.

Questions of context and chronology cannot be left without a comment on the significance of the 1960s. Writers drawn by the ground-breaking nature of the civil rights movement, environmentalism, the peace movement, and second-wave feminism, have awarded the 1960s pride of place in the histories of social activism. For Arthur Marwick, they formed nothing less than a Western cultural revolution; for Adam Lent, meanwhile, the 1960s mark the beginning of a 'long explosion' of activism, which only faded in the 1980s.[31] The reputation of the 1960s as a period of social innovation is secure enough to criticise the excesses of such a view, without being thought to question its essential validity. Whilst the Sixties were undoubtedly a hugely significant time for social activism, there are certain problems with their primacy.[32] In the first instance, the 1960s fetish has allowed the decade to unfairly overshadow its near (and not-so-near) neighbours. That this is the case can be illustrated with reference to the international development sector. The 1960s saw the foundation of CAFOD, the Disasters Emergency Committee, Voluntary Service Overseas, and the World Development Movement (only the last of which is an explicitly campaigning organisation.) Prior to the 1960s, giants such as Oxfam, the Red Cross, Christian Aid and Save the Children were already well-established. Since the 1960s, meanwhile, one can find a wide variety of bodies, many of which indicate an increase in radicalism, such as the Jubilee Debt campaign and Baby Milk Action, alongside organisations such as the Fairtrade Foundation and Comic Relief.

Such a point can be made for the entire NGO sector. As can be seen from Table 1.1, new agendas, and new organisations, were constantly emerging. Some clearly jump out. Service provision and social care is still a major factor in the 1940s, with the establishment of groups like the National Association for Parents of Backward Children (later MENCAP), the National Association for Mental Health (MIND), and Alcoholics Anonymous. In the 1950s, one can see the emergence of the politics of identity with the Homosexual Law Reform Society and the Institute of Race Relations. The 1960s rediscovery of poverty is clearly

Table 1.1   Prominent NGOs, with year of formation

MIND	1946
MENCAP	1946
Soil Association	1946
Alcoholics Anonymous	1947
European Movement	1948
Samaritans	1953
Spastics Society	1953
Indian Workers' Association	1954
Institute of Economic Affairs	1955
Consumers' Association	1957
Homosexual Law Reform Society	1958
Campaign for Nuclear Disarmament	1958
Institute of Race Relations	1958
Cruse Bereavement Care	1959
Amnesty International	1961
British Heart Foundation	1961
World Wildlife Fund	1961
Help the Aged	1961
National Viewers' and Listeners' Association	1964
Child Poverty Action Group	1965
Shelter	1966
Society for the Protection of Unborn Children	1966
Joint Council for the Welfare of Immigrants	1967
Campaign for Homosexual Equality	1969
Festival of Light	1971
Friends of the Earth	1971
Campaign for Better Transport (Transport 2000)	1973
Life Style Movement	1974
Low Pay Unit	1974
Centre for Policy Studies	1974
Campaign Against the Arms Trade	1974
Advisory Service for Squatters	1975
International Fund for Animal Welfare	1976
Peace People	1976
Greenpeace	1977
Sustrans	1977
Adam Smith Institute	1977
Muslim Aid	1981
Neighbourhood Watch	1982
Terrence Higgins Trust	1982
Afghan Aid	1983
Re-Solv, the Society for the Prevention of Solvent Abuse	1984
Islamic Relief	1984
Pesticides Action Network	1986
Rainforest Foundation	1989
Earth First!	1991
Fairtrade Foundation	1992
Big Issue	1995
Reclaim the Streets	1995
Countryside Alliance	1997
Muslim Council of Britain	1997

visible with Shelter and Child Poverty Action Group, but there are also less progressive, more conservative groups being formed then, such as the National Viewers' and Listeners' Association, and the Society for the Protection of Unborn Children. In the 1970s, both environment-alism (Greenpeace, Friends of the Earth, Transport 2000) and the right-wing resurgence (the Adam Smith Institute, the Centre for Policy Studies, Festival of Light) stand out, while the 1980s and 1990s see new agendas and new issues coming to the fore again, with the formation of Islamic Relief and the Muslim Council of Britain, the Fairtrade Foundation, and the Terrence Higgins Trust. The point is not that each decade has a coherent 'story' to tell, but that there are many such stories. To privilege one distorts the whole.

Perhaps more generally, another problem with the 1960s approach is that it can obscure what is really driving this wave of self-actualising activism it seeks to celebrate. In highlighting the chronological decade, it obscures attention from the real cause of all this post-material acti-vity, the golden age of Keynesian capitalism, and the long economic boom it generated (a point acknowledged by Marwick's proposition of a 'long sixties', grinding to a halt with the oil-led economic crisis of the early 1970s).[33] The particular economic and demographic conditions of the 1960s lent themselves to certain manifestations of social action. These were fascinating, certainly, but by no means exclusively so. With the grim economic crises of the 1970s and 1980s, for example, differ-ent groups, different agendas, and different forms of action emerged (and re-emerged). Confrontation and social strife could be seen with the rise of the National Front, challenged in turn by the Anti-Nazi League, but also through the dramatic return of class-based politics after years of consensus and growth (however limp, in both cases). This trend reached its climax in the two great political confrontations of the 1980s, the miners' strike and the anti-poll tax movement. But even by the 1980s, trends were already moving in other directions. During that decade, an annual average of 7.2 million working days were lost through strike action (a figure buoyed up by a tally of 27 million for 1984); however, this was in itself a dramatic fall over the 1970s average (12.9 million), and would tumble to just 660,000 in the 1990s.[34] With the triumph of Thatcherism, not only strike action, but unionisation itself, withered, with union membership falling 40 per cent in the 20 years after 1979.[35] The broader point is that social change is con-stant, and constantly changing social conditions inevitably throw up constantly changing agendas and organisations. The 1960s, then, were indeed unique, but not in the sense that other decades are uniform in comparison. Rather, the activity of each decade (or whatever other arbitrary division one wishes to choose) reflects, in part, the unique alignment of socio-economic forces particular to that time.

A point related to that about the 1960s is that, in this volume, we adapt an approach distinct from the sociological literature dealing with 'new social movements'. This has tended to focus on the higher profile movements often associated with the new forms of protest in the 1960s, alongside an essential focus upon confrontation over conciliatory forms of action. In many of the historical and sociological surveys, attention is rightly given to such developments as feminism, civil rights, environmentalism, the peace movement and human rights activism, but movements propounded by other NGOs are often over-looked.[36] The new social movement literature has little space for reform-oriented single issue pressure groups which merely seek to change their bit of the world, and are reasonably comfortable with the state of society and politics as they find them – surely the operating rationale of so many voluntary organisations? Within this literature, therefore, little has been written of the organised consumer movement, nor of the influence of faith-based organisations on questions of inter-national development.[37] Assumptions are made about what is new in these forms of socio-political action, such that organisations associated with second wave feminism are afforded a higher priority than those women's groups advocating less fundamental change.[38] Likewise, in accounts of environmentalism, the development of radical ecology has been emphasised despite the fact that questions about pollution and resource allocation have involved networks of Greenpeace and Friends of the Earth activists alongside older and more socially conservative institutions such as the British Ecological Society or the Council for the Protection of Rural England.[39] In human rights, it is Amnesty that has attracted more attention, and it is only now that we are beginning to hear accounts of the longer established, but less glamorous, National Council for Civil Liberties (NCCL).[40] The normative assumptions about what constitutes radicalism have resulted in the absence of attention to moral reform organisations, despite the fact that these groups flourished as much as more seemingly radical organisations at the same time and often from socio-economic groups precisely the same as those which provided the membership to the new social movements.

Similar assumptions have been made in the historical treatment of new social movements. In his overview of *The Sixties*, Arthur Marwick's 16 point definition of the characteristics of the decade begins with the observation that this was indeed the era of new social movements. Here he tries to convey the entrepreneurialism and experimentalism of the sixties by including in his list sub-cultural theatre, architectural think-tanks, the New Left, civil rights, feminism and environmentalism. Crucial to his definition, though, is the insistence that to be so identified these movements had to be 'generally critical of, or in opposition to, one or more aspects of established society.'[41] Again, the groups that are missing are those NGOs with less radical agendas, despite proliferating at the same time and despite coming from a social background similar to that of the more visible protestors.[42] There is clearly a rather basic gap in the historical record, perhaps the natural consequence of the political proclivities which direct much of our research as historians. What is needed is an account of NGOs at a much broader level, one which sees the rise of Christian development organisations – in bodies such as Christian Aid and in the influence on groups such as the World Development Movement, Jubilee 2000, and the Fairtrade Foundation – as part of a social process similar to that which gave rise to the Animal Liberation Front and Reclaim the Streets. What we seek to highlight is not a simple bifurcation between those NGOs we might wish to identify as radical and those which we see as conservative, between those which can be included under the category, 'new social movement', and those which must be understood according to some other historical development. Instead, we would emphasise the existence of a spectrum of social and political perspectives in which one could conceptually move from the Mothers' Union, to Christian Aid, to Oxfam, to War on Want, to Amnesty, to CND, to Greenpeace, to Friends of the Earth, to Fair Trade, to ethical consumerism, to anti-globalisation. There is something that unites all these groups, all these activists, and to do them justice we cannot simply pick and choose which of them we wish to include in our notions of social and political activism.

The intention of this introduction is not to leave the reader with the impression that diversity overwhelms analysis of the NGO sector. Within the sector, certainly, there has been an enormous range of activity, with the broadest range of causes, analyses and approaches all being advanced. The chapters in this volume attest to the fact that alongside the politics of gender, sexuality, and race, there sat issues of poverty and morality, international development and environmentalism, as well as democracy, human rights, peace, and consumption. The diversity of the volume thereby gives a sense of the diversity of the sector as a whole.

Stepping back, however, one can detect a deeper coherence to all this activity. There is a distinctiveness to the NGO sector, which justifies the full attention of contemporary British historians. NGOs are the post-material form of social and socio-political action, emerging out of the fundamental changes that took place in the post-war decades: the adoption by the state of responsibility for the provision of universal health and social care; the demographic revolution and the rise of the individual; and unprecedented levels of both mass affluence and mass education. Given this distinctiveness, the existing terminologies of civil society, charity and voluntary sector are insufficient. NGOs are drawn from all of these areas, but are further defined by the quest for influence. It is the deliberate intention to be socio-political actors that distinguishes the NGO from these other forms, as it has done since the term was conceived at the birth of the United Nations.

Equally, however, the terminology of social movements cannot adequately capture the NGO phenomenon, with its connotations of radicalism and confrontation. Many of these groups were neither radical nor confrontational, yet they still sought to be, and were, shapers of society. In this, their tools were primarily discursive. Of course service provision continued, as did campaigning for specific measures in the law, but the principal contribution of NGOs to the socio-political sphere comes in terms of how issues are conceptualised and discussed: the setting of new agendas, and the shaping of new ideas. The proper understanding of this process, of this power, is a task to which contemporary British historians, both social and political, should turn.

Notes

1 The volume emerged out of an academic conference in July 2007, organised by the DANGO project, Database of Archives of UK Non-Governmental Organisations since 1945. DANGO was an AHRC-funded project providing information on the availability of records relating to non-governmental organisations and pressure groups active in the UK since 1945, with the intention of encouraging the historical (and more general academic) study of the role of NGOs in British socio-political life. The database, which is free to use, can be found here: www.dango.bham.ac.uk.

2 NCVO *The UK Voluntary Sector Almanac 2006: The State of the Sector* http://www.ncvo-vol.org.uk/research/index.asp?id=2380&fID=158, (accessed 20 Aug 2008).

3 www.ncvo.org.uk; the comparable bodies for the rest of the United Kingdom are: NICVA (Northern Ireland Council for Voluntary Action); SCVO (Scottish Council for Voluntary Organisations); and WCVA (Welsh Council for Voluntary Action).

4   J. Kendall *The Voluntary Sector: Comparative Perspectives in the UK* (London: Routledge, 2003), p. 23.

5   Home Office *Early findings from the 2005 Home Office Citizenship Survey* http://www.homeoffice.gov.uk/rds/pdfs05/rdsolr4905.pdf, pp. 6–7 (accessed 20 Aug 2008).

6   http://www.makepovertyhistory.org/2005/index.shtml, *Power to the People*, p. 43.

7   See B. Seary, 'The Early History: From the Congress of Vienna to the San Francisco Conference', in P. Willetts (ed.), *'The Conscience of the World': The Influence of Non-Governmental Organisations in the UN System* (London: Hurst 1995), p. 27.

8   In Scotland, the relevant body is the Office of the Scottish Charity Regulator; in Northern Ireland, the Department for Social Development.

9   See J. Harris, 'Introduction' in J. Harris (ed.), *Civil Society in British History: Ideas, Identities, Institutions* (Oxford: Oxford University Press 2003), pp. 1–12; see also N. Deakin, *In Search of Civil Society* (Basingstoke: Palgrave 2001), pp. 4–11.

10 Deakin, *Civil Society*, p. 26.

11 The term is taken from Deakin, *Civil Society*, p. 16.

12 F. Prochaska, *Christianity and Social Service in Modern Britain: the Disinherited Spirit* (Oxford: Oxford University Press, 2006).

13 Prochaska, *Christianity and Social Service,* p. 152.

14 See, for example: R. Inglehart, *The Silent Revolution: Changing Values and Political Styles among Western Publics* (Princeton NJ; Guildford: Princeton University Press, 1977), chapter 1; R. Inglehart, *Culture Shift in Advanced Industrial Society* (Princeton NJ; Guildford: Princeton University Press, 1977), chapter 2; F. Parkin, *Middle-Class Radicalism: The Social Bases of the British Campaign for Nuclear Disarmament* (Manchester: Manchester University Press, 1968), chapter 8.

15 A. Maslow, 'A Theory of Human Motivation', *Psychological Review*, 50(4) 1943, pp. 370–96. For an acknowledgement of the debt to Maslow, see Inglehart, *Silent Revolution*, pp. 22–3.

16 A. Self & L. Zealey (eds), *Social Trends 37* (Office of National Statistics; Basingstoke: Palgrave Macmillan, 2007), p. 6; http://news.bbc.co.uk/1/hi/uk/7057765.stm.

17 *Social Trends 37*, p. 3.

18 *Social Trends 37*, p. 5.

19 *Social Trends 37*, p. 9.

20 *Social Trends 37*, pp. 14–19.

21 *Social Trends 37*, p. 35; N. Timmins, *The Five Giants: A Biography of the Welfare State* (London: HarperCollins, 2001), p. 202.

22 For a discussion of the intentions behind this deliberate adoption of the term, see P. Singer, *Animal Liberation: Towards an End to Man's Inhumanity to Animals* (London: Paladin, 1977), p. x.

23 *Power to the People: The Report of Power: An Independent Inquiry into Britain's Democracy*, March 2006, pp. 18–19.

24 Turnout was 77.7 per cent in 1992, 71.4 per cent in 1997, 59.4 per cent in 2001, and 61.5 per cent in 2005. Source: *Power to the People*, pp. 46, 118–22.

25 For the secularisation debate, see: C. Brown, *The Death of Christian Britain: Understanding Secularisation, 1800–2000* (London: Routledge, 2001); G. Davie, *Religion in Britain since 1945: Believing without Belonging* (Oxford: Blackwell, 1994); H. McLeod, *Religion and the People of Western Europe, 1789–1989* 2nd edn. (Oxford: Oxford University Press, 1997).

26 Oxfam Annual Report 2005/6, http://www.oxfam.org.uk/resources/downloads/reports/complete_oxfamreport05-06.pdf, pp. 17–18 (accessed 20 August 2008).

27 Save the Children Annual Report 2006/7, http://www.savethechildren. org.uk/en/54_3249.htm, pp. 2–3 (accessed 20 August 2008).

28 See, for example: J. Epstein, *In Practice: Studies in the Language and Culture of Popular Politics in Modern Britain* (Stanford: Stanford University Press, 2003); J. Vernon, *Politics and the People: A Study in English Political Culture, 1815–1867* (Cambridge: Cambridge University Press, 1993); J. Lawrence and M. Taylor (eds) *Party, State and Society: Electoral Behaviour in Britain since 1920* (Aldershot: Scolar Press, 1997); J. Lawrence *Speaking for the People: Party, Language and Popular Politics in England, 1867–1914* (Cambridge: Cambridge University Press, 1998); S. Brooke, 'Evan Durbin: Reassessing a Labour "Revisionist"', *Twentieth-Century British History*, 7(1) 1996.

29 J. Green, *All Dressed Up: The Sixties and the Counterculture* (London: Jonathon Cape 1988), p. 57.

30 R. Carson, *Silent Spring* (London: Hamish Hamilton, 1963); D.H. Meadows *et al*, *The Limits to Growth: A Report for the Club of Rome's Project on the Predicament of Mankind* (London: Earth Island, 1972).

31 A. Lent, *British Social Movements since 1945: Sex, Colour, Peace and Power* (Basingstoke: Palgrave Macmillan, 2001), chapters 3 and 4.

32 That such enthusiasm shows no sign of running dry can be seen by the 2008 launch of a new British academic journal, *The Sixties: A Journal of History, Politics and Culture*.

33 See, for example, E. Hobsbawm, *Age of Extremes: The Short Twentieth Century, 1914–1991* (London: Michael Joseph, 1994), pp. 257–63.

34 *Social Trends 37*, p. 54.

35 *Economist*, 16 Sept 1999.

36 H. Kriesi, R. Koopmans, I. Willem Dyvendak & M.G. Giugni, *New Social Movements in Western Europe: A Comparative Analysis* (Minneapolis: University of Minnesota Press, 1995); E. Laraña, H. Johnston & J. Gusfield (eds), *New Social Movements: From Ideology to Identity* (Philadelphia, PA: Temple University Press, 1994); D.S. Meyer & S. Tarrow (eds), *The Social Movement Society: Contentious Politics for a New Century* (Lanham, Maryland: Rowman & Littlefield, 1998); D. McAdam, J.D. McCarthy & M.N. Zald (eds), *Comparative Perspective on Social Movements: Political Opportunities, Mobilising Structures, and Cultural Framings* (Cambridge: Cambridge University Press, 1996); S. Tarrow, *Power in Movement: Social Movement and Contentious Politics* (Cambridge: Cambridge University Press, 1998).

37 M. Hilton, 'Social Activism in an Age of Consumption: The Organised Consumer Movement', *Social History*, 32(2), 2007, pp. 121–43.

38 A. Coote & B. Campbell, *Sweet Freedom. The Struggle for Women's Liberation*, 2nd ed. (Oxford: Blackwell, 1987); J. Lewis, *Women in Britain since 1945* (Oxford: Blackwell, 1992).

39   For example, see Lent, *British Social Movements*, pp. 100–5.
40   A. Clark, *Diplomacy of Conscience: Amnesty International and Changing Human Rights Norms* (Princeton N.J.: Princeton University Press 2001); S. Hopgood, *Keepers of the Flame: Understanding Amnesty International* (Ithaca, NY: Cornell University Press, 2006). For the NCCL, see the ongoing PhD work of Christopher Moores, at the University of Birmingham.
41   A. Marwick, *The Sixties: Cultural Revolution in Britain, France, Italy and the United States, c.1958–1974* (Oxford: Oxford University Press, 1998), p. 17.
42   See, for example, the collected oral histories in H. Curtis & M. Sanderson, *The Unsung Sixties: Memoirs of Social Innovation* (London: Whiting & Birch 2004).

1
Direct Action and the Campaign for Nuclear Disarmament, 1958–62

Jodi Burkett

The simplicity of the message 'Ban the Bomb' was the Campaign for Nuclear Disarmament's (CND) greatest asset and greatest liability. It enabled the organisation to attract a wide variety of people, but it also meant that they needed to undertake actions which would not alienate any of these disparate people. As the 1960s progressed CND, and its adherence to moderate activities, was increasingly marginalised within the radical left. As Adam Lent argues, 'more than anything else' the distinction between CND's respectful lobbying strategy and the more urgent, rebellious approach of direct action 'encapsulated the shift in movement politics during the 1960s.'[1] Focussing on the first four years of the CND, from its inaugural meeting in February 1958 through the passing of its first constitution in April 1962, we see an organisation at the vanguard, but also one fraught with tension over methodology. CND called for Britain to unilaterally renounce nuclear weapons, appealing to the morality of both politicians and the public. But it was not the only group making this demand. The Direct Action Committee Against Nuclear War (DAC) also used moral arguments to call for British unilateral nuclear disarmament. The two groups diverged in their belief about the best way to accomplish this goal. While the CND hoped to use the pressure of mass public support to sway politicians to adopt unilateralism, the DAC thought that politicians could only be forced into this attitude through the use of direct action.

Extra-parliamentary organisations, or social movements, have consistently grappled with the question of which tactics to employ. Researchers have found that the public recognises a number of levels of extremity in social movement activity. As activists move from conventional to unconventional politics, through direct action and non-violence, they tend to lose support.[2] The desire for large-scale support tends therefore to push organisations towards moderate activity. Yet, it is not just public opinion to which these organisations need to appeal. The type of activity they engage in also needs to galvanise their own supporters and provide internal cohesion and a sense of collective identity. Leaders therefore tread a fine line between advocating radical action to maintain rank-and-file support without alienating potential allies.[3] The tension that these questions create within a movement was visible in the early part of the twentieth century within the women's suffrage campaign in Britain. Moderate suffragists worked to galvanise large sections of the public, while the militant suffragettes employed more radical tactics hoping to pressure those in power to create change more quickly.[4]

It was not just in Britain that these were important issues. Around the same time that the anti-nuclear movement was struggling with these questions, they were also being discussed within independence movements throughout the former British Empire. The argument for non-violent direct action was famously won by Gandhi in India where he used it to successfully gain his country's independence.[5] This was not the only means of successfully fighting for independence as we can see by the examples of both Ghana and Tanganyika (later Tanzania) where moderate leaders worked with the British government to secure their countries' independence.[6] Moderation versus militancy continued to be a major issue throughout the 1960s. It was of vital importance in the United States civil rights movement where Dr. Martin Luther King Jr. famously took up Gandhi's example.[7]

The anti-nuclear movement also drew on longstanding traditions of British pacifism. One of the reactions to the violence of the First World War had been to define Britain as a 'peaceable kingdom' thereby privileging peaceful, respectable, law-abiding protest.[8] The Peace Pledge Union was the primary pacifist organisation from the early part of the century and became the 'source of the most extreme forms of protest against nuclear armament' after the Second World War. In 1950 they put forward a programme very similar to that advocated by the CND eight years later.[9] From the middle of the 1950s small, local anti-nuclear groups were being formed throughout the country.[10] The increase in nuclear tests also served to galvanise opposition and resulted in the formation of the first national anti-nuclear organisation, the National Council for the Abolition of Nuclear Weapons Tests in early 1957.[11]

Though not without tension, the CND and the DAC enjoyed a working relationship and an overlapping membership for more than two years. But by late 1960 questions of tactics had resulted in the division of the anti-nuclear movement. The creation of the Committee of 100, which advocated civil disobedience, and the resignation of Bertrand Russell as President of CND was, according to its chairman, 'a serious blow to the Campaign, and one from which it never fully recovered.'[12] This division was ostensibly about tactics, but the ability of CND and DAC to work together, shows that it was not that simple. The situation surrounding the formation of the Committee of 100, the personalities involved and their inability to work together, was equally important in causing the split in the movement.

The groups: CND, DAC and the Committee of 100

The Campaign for Nuclear Disarmament was the largest mass movement in Britain since the war. It is extremely difficult to gauge levels of support as there was no mechanism for individual membership throughout this period, but we do know that mere weeks after their inaugural meeting in February 1958 there were more than 100 local CND groups.[13] CND also took on symbolic importance and it was believed that 'identification with CND could be taken to be a capsule statement of a distinctive moral and political outlook.'[14] While this statement is oversimplified, assuming much greater unity than existed in the campaign, it is how CND was viewed by contemporaries.

The structure of CND was rigidly hierarchical with the Executive making all decisions for the organisation. In fact, in the early years the vast majority of CND's actions were the direct initiative of its Chairman Canon Collins.[15] The leadership of the CND was a self-selected group of well off, well known, politically important white men quite different from the rank and file of the organisation. A mass-based movement had not been Collins' objective[16] He was convinced that the way forward was to keep the Executive small and in control of all major decisions as this would enable it to take action quickly.[17] Throughout his tenure as Chairman, Collins resisted demands from the rank and file for representation at the level of decision-making. The creations of the Co-ordinating committee, made up of representatives of all affiliated groups to advise the Executive, and annual conference, were stop gap measures designed to placate the rank and file while preserving the existing Executive structure and power.[18] A democratic constitution was finally agreed by the Executive in 1961 and passed at the 1962 annual conference. It included the election of Executive members but not individual membership.

In 1957 Sheila and Harold Steele attempted to prevent Britain's testing of its first hydrogen bomb off Christmas Island by sailing a boat into the test area. Although failing to do so, they gained worldwide publicity and were supported in Britain by an Emergency Committee for Direct Action Against Nuclear War.[19] As this group transformed into the Direct Action Committee they did not lose their temporary nature saying that they did not intend 'to continue for years or to become an alternative political party.'[20] The DAC policy of direct action rested on a belief in personal responsibility. They thought that 'Britain should give up unilaterally all nuclear weapons and policies based upon them, without waiting for agreement between other countries' and that since they were asking this of their country they too should be prepared to act independently.[21] They also held that direct action should be undertaken 'to focus public attention on the issues involved.'[22] The success of their actions therefore relied on receiving media coverage and making a clear statement.

The organisation of the DAC was not dissimilar to that of the CND, but it managed to avoid many of their problems by being much smaller and more tightly knit. The biggest organisational difference between the two groups was their stance on the relationship of local and regional groups to the Executive. Whereas the CND Executive was determined to keep local groups under control, the DAC actively encouraged local groups to be independent. They thought that 'if direct action is to succeed it must go on independently of any particular group or persons. We hope that many other groups all over the country will initiate action.'[23] The preoccupation of the CND leadership with creating and maintaining an image of respectability by strictly controlling what was done in their name and avoiding controversy, was not present in the DAC. The leadership of the DAC expected their activities to be controversial. With the caveat that they hoped to get widespread support for their plans, they took pains to say that they did 'not immediately abandon any [plans] simply because they are controversial or unpopular in some quarters. Indeed one of [our] purposes is to initiate new types of action which, because they are unusual, are liable to arouse controversy.'[24]

The Committee of 100 was, according to Richard Taylor and Colin Pritchard 'a disparate coalition, united only in its belief in the primacy of the nuclear issue, its conviction that civil disobedience was the correct method, and its deep antipathy towards the CND leadership.'[25] The Committee was the brainchild of Ralph Schoenman, a young American member of the CND.[26] When Schoenman first pitched the idea of a new group to Bertrand Russell he was told that he 'should be able to work as part of the [existing] Direct Action Movement'.[27] Schoenman, however, succeeded in convincing Russell that a new organisation dedicated to civil disobedience was necessary.

The Committee of 100 consciously designed its structure to be different than that of the CND. In particular they tried to counter the hierarchical nature of CND, holding Quaker style meetings with members seated in a circle, each having the same authority to speak, and striving for consensus.[28] The Committee, like both the CND and DAC, was originally understood as temporary. Each of the three groups thought that they would be able to accomplish their objectives quickly and then disband. This proved not to be the case and they were forced to co-exist and, increasingly, compete for supporters within the movement.

What were direct action, civil disobedience and the alternative?

All three groups existed outside of traditional political circles. Of the three, CND took the constraints of the political system most seriously when planning their actions. The official CND line was that British unilateral nuclear disarmament would only come about through a Labour government. They, therefore, advocated more traditional methods, trying to convince the Labour Party to adopt unilateralism, while the DAC and Committee of 100 employed a tactical militancy which made the Labour party uneasy. The model of direct action to which members of the anti-nuclear movement turned was that of Gandhi and Martin Luther King. This included 'obstruction, occupations, boycotts, tax refusal, industrial action, [and] illegal leafleting.'[29]

One of the reasons direct action was so much debated and so divisive was that its relationship with non-violence and civil disobedience was unclear. The majority of those who propounded direct action agreed that it should be non-violent, but did not necessarily agree on what that meant.[30] In their 1959 policy statement the DAC used an extremely broad definition of non-violence. Not only did they argue that it required a complete absence of physical violence but also that it involved 'complete openness with the authorities.' This, they argued, was required because the purpose of non-violent demonstrations was 'not to score points off the authorities but to win public support and to protest in an effective and dramatic way.'[31] To use violence would be 'tragically inconsistent' with their purpose. If they 'lapsed into secrecy, sabotage and violence' it was argued, the Committee 'would inevitably lose all its moral power and defeat its own purpose.'[32]

Direct action and civil disobedience were often conflated. In the 1980s Pat Arrowsmith, a member of the DAC Executive, remembered the debates about direct action as being about civil disobedience. As she says

> many and prolonged were the wrangles about direct action by nuclear disarmers twenty years ago. Breaking democratically passed laws was undemocratic argued the constitutionalists. No it wasn't, the direct actionists countered – not when something so utterly undemocratic as planned genocide was involved.[33]

Her assumption that direct action meant 'breaking democratically passed laws' illustrates this confusion. It was this confusion which often resulted in the rejection of direct action by more moderate supporters. For the DAC civil disobedience was only one of its many forms of activity in 1959. The creation of the Committee of 100 itself points to a clear distinction between direct action and civil disobedience. Again, Arrowsmith recalls that 'when the Committee of 100 was launched ... the question arose: were direct action and civil disobedience the same thing? If not, were they of equal value?'[34]

The variety of activities undertaken by the CND and DAC in the late 1950s was not remarkably different. Both marched, leafleted and wrote to Members of Parliament. But CND focussed their energy on educational activities. In the summer of 1959 they organised a 'Nuclear Disarmament Week' whose suggested activities included 'stalls of stands in market places or shopping centres ... chain letters to three friends asking them to write to the Prime Minister and three other friends; speakers at Schools; [and] lunch time factory gate meetings.'[35] This emphasis on educational activities was in part a reaction to demands from regional groups. One such group, Sevenoaks, argued that an educational programme should take precedence 'until the movement attracts a greater measure of public support.'[36] They thought that small marches provided 'a hostile press with an excellent opportunity to ridicule the Campaign, and reassures our M.P.'s in their conviction that they can afford to disregard our lobbying and our letters of protest.'[37] There was a strong argument within the CND that effort was being wasted. 'Instead of spending time at local meetings' argued Richard Acland in 1958 'our National Names should give an equivalent number of evenings to long quiet conversations with four or five carefully chosen and carefully invited key people.'[38]

The activities of the DAC did not focus on education. They continued to do things like lobby the House of Commons during debates on Defence Motions in 1959, but this was not their main form of action.[39] In December 1958 the DAC planned an intensive campaign at the rocket base at North Pickenham which marked the beginning of their most intense year of campaigning.[40] Throughout the summer of 1959 the 'DAC staged poster parades, open-air gatherings, picketings at defense sites .... Everywhere they urged defense workers to quit their jobs or strike.'[41] This relentless activity had an effect on the authorities and in December 1959 seven leaders of the Committee, Arrowsmith, Hugh Brock, April Carter, Frances Edwards, Inez Randall, Allen Skimmes and Will Warren, were arrested and jailed. They refused the offer of release in return for giving sureties to keep the peace for one year and were held for two months.[42] For Arrowsmith, it was an example of the Government persecuting the DAC, finding obscure laws, like the 1361 Justices of the Peace Act under which they were charged, to punish them.[43] It also showed others within the movement that they could be arrested and imprisoned for seemingly innocuous activity.

One of the most contested issues in this period was participation in electoral activities. Many members of the DAC worked extensively on the 1959 campaign of Lawrence Daly in Scotland. Will Warren was Daly's election manager. Several members went to Scotland to give assistance and the group sent a van, printed pamphlets and offered to stage a press conference.[44] Some members even sent cash donations to the campaign.[45] They also supported the London Universities and Schools CND proposal to create a 'Voter's Veto' group. The CND Executive was entirely opposed to participating in the election in any way and were particularly critical of the 'Voter's Veto'. At a Co-ordinating Council meeting in January 1959 Collins 'stated that if the Direct Action Committee went ahead with their plans [for a Voter's Veto] it would be necessary for the Campaign publicly to dissociate themselves from their actions.'[46]

At its inception the objectives of the Committee of 100 were not entirely clear. For Russell the objective was simple publicity.[47] His focus on the propaganda effect of the Committees activities required highly visible, but not necessarily high risk, action. Schoenman agreed that civil disobedience could educate people by showing them the inhumanity and illegality of nuclear weapons. But it could do more. He hoped to unite the activities of the Direct Action Committee with the mass support of CND. By holding very large illegal demonstrations Schoenman thought he could force the government to its knees by 'filling the jails and thus paralysing the system to the point of collapse.'[48] This objective required an exaltation of going to prison which was visible in the rank and file of the Committee. As one member recalled of an early Committee of 100 'sit down' 'Bertrand Russell sat on the Air Ministry steps and we all sat down on the pavement. But I didn't actually get arrested. They just sort of picked me up and told me to go home. It was very disappointing.'[49]

These different attitudes permeated the group and informed the location and types of action undertaken. Pat Arrowsmith recalled that:

> certain Committee of 100 members argued that it was pointless, even possibly counterproductive, to block innocuous streets; the action should be at the bases. Others (at first the majority) said that to get thousands breaking the law conspicuously in city centres would achieve more publicity, hence be more useful, than getting (inevitably) fewer people to take action at remote bases.[50]

The Committee was launched in the autumn of 1960, and held its first demonstration in 1961.

The activity which most characterised the anti-nuclear movement in the early period was the Aldermaston march. It was particularly identified with CND even though the idea, and the organisation, of the first march in 1958 were those of the DAC. Initially sceptical, the CND supported the first march both financially and by announcing it at its inaugural meeting. The first march, following the ethos of direct action, started with a rally in Trafalgar square and ended at the Atomic Weapons Research Establishment in Aldermaston. It was highly successful attracting many times the expected number of marchers.[51]

Despite the success of the 1958 march, there was controversy within the movement about whether or not to hold another in 1959. The Executive of the CND were divided on the matter. Collins was very much for it 'believing that it would be a cohesive force in the Campaign, as well as an active means of expressing our purpose.'[52] Others within the CND, supported by the DAC, thought that the point had been made by the first march and feared that with repetition the march would lose its impact becoming almost an institution.[53] Collins' argument prevailed 'after considerable discussion' within the Co-ordinating committee.[54] Two important changes were made to the march that year. The organisation was taken over by the CND and the direction of the march was reversed so that it started in Aldermaston and ended in London symbolically bringing the protest to the seat of power.[55]

Despite their differences of opinion the CND was able to work alongside the DAC throughout its first two years. The leadership of the two organisations may not have always seen eye to eye, but they appreciated that each other's work was valid and useful. For the rank and file of both organisations, the activities of the two groups complemented each other and many people participated in both.

Relations between the groups

The primacy of the discussion of tactics tends to obscure the large spheres of agreement between all three groups. As Michael Randle, member of the DAC Executive, put it they all 'shared a rejection on moral grounds of nuclear weapons.'[56] All were in agreement that the goal was to 'Ban the Bomb', that nuclear weapons were immoral and that it was necessary to mobilise the public if they were going to be successful. The 1961 CND Annual General Meeting passed a resolution that 'CND, Direct Action and the Committee of 100 are three techniques in a united attack on preparations for nuclear war.'[57] Yet the tension that existed between those advocating different methodologies did not disappear.[58]

The attitude of the CND toward direct action was never simple. Its leadership was largely uncomfortable with such tactics, yet many of its earliest supporters were committed to direct action. Just months after its foundation the Executive committee made it quite clear that it 'felt it was very important that Direct Action should be a part of the Campaign in conjunction with other propaganda such as meetings, literature etc.'[59] Direct Action was legitimised, but not privileged, as a form of action. Peggy Duff, secretary of CND, was generally positive of the DAC saying that 'they brought to the campaign a commitment to and an understanding of non-violent techniques which was supremely important at that time and which set a tone and produced a quality for demonstration which lasted for many years.'[60] From the summer of 1958

> a division of labor was established whereby the CND would have complete charge of mass demonstrations, while DAC would be free to 'concentrate on more specialized types of action suited to a small and flexible body, including demonstrations which have to be mounted at speed, and the more radical types of direct action projects.'[61]

Both organisations seemed relatively comfortable with this breakdown of responsibility.

The formal relationship between the groups can be vividly seen in the discussions of both the CND Executive and Co-ordinating committee. The Executive of the CND wanted close contact with the DAC, to know what they were doing and to co-ordinate activity. Within the Co-ordinating committee there was also a desire to include the DAC. Some members expressed anxiety about the possible inefficiency of a division in labour while others pointed to the success that had already accrued because of CND support of DAC activity. It was clear that many members of the Co-ordinating committee wished the DAC was more actively involved in their work. At their October 1958 meeting the committee agreed 'that a special effort be made' to persuade the DAC to take up the delegate space that had been offered them.[62]

This effort paid off initially as Michael Randle was the DAC representative at their January 1959 meeting. At that meeting he asked if he was there as a delegate or an observer. The response of the Committee acknowledged that there had been some confusion on the issue, but they agreed that 'they were welcome as delegates.'[63] But this did not last. In May 1959 it was reported back to the Co-ordinating committee that two representatives of the CND, Ritchie Calder and Benn Levy, had met representatives of the DAC to discuss the relationship between the two groups. The Chairman proposed that 'after very friendly talks it had been agreed to recommend that the Direct Action Committee should no longer be represented on the Co-ordinating Committee, but that a separate Liaison Committee be set up in order to avoid confusion or difficulties on strategy and tactics.'[64] After some discussion the proposal was agreed upon. The general attitude of the CND towards the DAC was seen by members of the DAC as benign. It was described as 'one of slight distancing but general support.'[65] The executive of the CND clearly did not want their organisation accused of direct action, but saw that it had a place in the movement as a whole.

There was also a division within the DAC about what sort of relationship they should have with the CND. They did send representatives to CND Co-ordinating committee meetings and corresponded with the CND President, Bertrand Russell relying on his financial and strategic backing. Immediately after the formation of the CND the DAC sent them a letter 'asking for further co-operation.'[66] Their 1959 Policy Statement said that 'although they do not always agree on the methods to be used, both the Campaign [for Nuclear Disarmament] and the Direct Action Committee agree on the basic principle of unilateral nuclear disarmament ... and there is a formal liaison between the Direct Action Committee and the Executive Committee of the

Campaign.' DAC Executive member Hugh Brock stressed the need for the closest possible liaison between the two organisations. He criticised the actions of his colleagues for 'rocking the boat too much' saying that they would not have been so successful 'without the backing of the Campaign.'[67] On the other hand, the 1959 policy statement also asserted that 'the Direct Action Committee is a completely separate body from the Executive Committee of the Campaign for Nuclear Disarmament.'[68] This attitude was taken up by Michael Randle who was keen to illustrate the DAC's independence to the CND Executive defying the larger organisation on issues like the Voter's Veto.

Perhaps the most fundamental aspect of the relationship between the two organisations in this period was the fact that their membership largely overlapped. The DAC acknowledged that 'most participants in direct action [were also] members of local Campaign [for Nuclear Disarmament] groups.'[69] No matter how much the executives of the two groups wanted to distance themselves from one another their overlapping membership made this difficult. Collins was keenly aware of this. He thought that 'the vast majority' of the rank and file 'were loyal to executive decisions' but acknowledged that they 'also admired those who engaged in direct action.' He neatly summarised the difficult position of the leadership of both groups saying that 'the rank and file never seemed fully to realize that in their desire for the kind of campaign envisaged by the executive and their understandable, though often sentimental, feelings about direct action, there was, implicit, a contradiction.'[70]

The relationship between the CND and the Committee of 100 was characterised by much more antipathy than that of either group with the DAC. This is as much a result of the personal relationship between Cannon Collins and Bertrand Russell as any tactical difference between the two organisations. Collins clearly felt betrayed by the way in which the new Committee had been announced. Russell claimed he consulted Collins about the creation of the new group, but Collins insisted that the first he heard of it was through Victor Gollancz.[71] The timing of the launch of the new organisation was a particular bone of contention. Its creation was leaked to the media mere weeks before the Labour Party conference at which they were expected to vote for unilateralism. Collins thought that the creation of this militant group, and CND's association with it, would jeopardise their chances of getting the policy passed. The creation of the Committee of 100 resulted in the acknowledgement by Russell that he was unable to work with Collins and his resignation as President of the CND.[72] The new Committee was not just seen as competition for the CND,[73] but according to Collins it brought 'bickerings, misunderstandings, irreconcilable attitudes and strained loyalties which inevitably reduced the effectiveness of the Campaign, hindered its progress, and created such tensions between those who favoured the technique of civil disobedience and those who did not that the unity of the movement was destroyed.'[74]

These feelings went both ways. The Committee of 100 were united in their antipathy to the leadership of the CND. There was a widespread belief that their moderate tactics, particularly the reliance on the Labour Party, was not only too slow but ultimately ineffective. One member of the Committee said she 'felt CND was holding back the anti-nuclear movement because they were trying to be respectable and establishment all the time.'[75] For Schoenman, the actions of the CND did not match the danger that was posed by nuclear weapons. He called the leaders of CND, 'the cultivators of popular-unpopular causes, those indulgent phrase-makers who plague every dissident movement with their reformist illusions and irrelevant ambition.' He said their activities, were in effect saying to their supporters 'we are in imminent danger of mass annihilation; join our annual march' which, he said 'seemed pathetic.'[76]

The relationship between the Committee of 100 and the DAC was much more sympathetic. The Committee of 100's activities 'rapidly overshadowed' the DAC, and by the end of 1961 they had agreed to dissolve themselves and joined the Committee of 100 *en masse.*[77]

Youth were an important presence throughout the three organisations. The Executive of the CND encouraged the growth of youth groups requesting that all groups and regions 'foster the growth of Youth Groups wherever possible, and ... allow them representation on adult Committees and on Regional Councils.'[78] Direct action was as controversial within the Youth CND as in its older counterpart, but they took a different stance on the issue approving 'the idea of direct action and shock tactics within the law'[79] at their quarterly meeting in November 1959. In general young people tended to support the more radical activities of the DAC and later the Committee of 100.

Conclusions

The debate about tactics and methodology within the anti-nuclear movement mirrored that occurring throughout the left in the 1960s and within social movements through the rest of the century. The ability of disparate groups to unite around a common goal was undermined by their inability to agree on how best to achieve them. These differing ideas on methodology led to personal antipathies which may have been even more damaging than the tactical disputes themselves. With the creation of the Committee of 100 the extent of overlapping group membership throughout the anti-nuclear movement decreased. The divergence between the CND and the Committee of 100 required that people choose between organisations, effectively weakening the whole movement. The creation of the Committee of 100 did disrupt the functioning of the CND, even if not quite as catastrophically as Collins suggested. Without pressure to reform coming from DAC members within CND, the organisation drifted farther and farther away from the vanguard of the radical left.

Despite the importance of these issues within the movement, to those outside these divergent groups were often seen as one large amalgam. Most often the CND was used as shorthand when referring to the entire anti-nuclear movement in all its guises. This was true right from the beginning with a DAC protest in 1958 being 'one of the first occasions when the press showed itself quite incapable of distinguishing between the various wings of the movement.'[80] This was frustrating for both the CND and the other groups. Each fought hard to define their own boundaries and resented the blurring of the lines.[81]

Looking at the relationship between the CND, DAC and the Committee of 100, we can begin to unpack the assumption that a split over tactics meant that the movement itself would inevitably divide. The CND and the DAC were able to work together, sometimes even at the same demonstration, while holding radically different ideas about the best way to accomplish their mutual goals. The circumstances surrounding the launching of the Committee of 100, and the personal antagonisms between its leaders, played as much a part in splitting the anti-nuclear movement as ideological differences. Proponents of unilateral British nuclear disarmament were divided by their age, class, gender, and political beliefs. Yet they were united in their abhorrence of nuclear warfare and belief that Britain should take the moral high ground in renouncing the weapons and stepping out of the nuclear game. It was through this unity that they created the first mass movement to 'Ban the Bomb'.

Notes

1 Adam Lent, *British Social Movements since 1945: Sex, Colour, Peace and Power* (Basingstoke: Palgrave, 2001), p. 43.

2   Russell J. Dalton, *Citizen Politics in Western Democracies: Public Opinion and Political Parties in the United States, Great Britain, West Germany, and France* (Chatham, N.J.: Chatham House Publishers, 1988), p. 65.

3   Donatella della Porter and Mario Diani, *Social Movements: An Introduction* (Oxford: Blackwell, 1999), p. 182.

4   On the debate within the suffrage movement see Jill Liddington and Jill Norris, *One Hand Tied Behind Us: The Rise of the Women's Suffrage Movement* (London: Rivers Oram Press, 2000).

5   For discussion of tactics within the Indian independence movement see for example Anshu Singh, *National Movement and Communal Strife in India from 1937 to 1947 (a Study in Strategy and Interactions)* (Delhi: Kalpaz Publications, 2004).

6   See Gregory Maddox, ed., *Colonialism and Nationalism in Africa: A Four Volume Anthology of Scholarly Articles*, 4 vols. (London: Garland Publishing Inc., 1993). Particularly volumes 3 and 4 for discussions of other paths to independence.

7   For discussions of civil rights in the United States see Simon Hall, *Peace and Freedom: The Civil Rights and Antiwar Movements in the 1960s* (Philadelphia: University of Pennsylvania Press, 2005). These issues were also discussed in the Northern Irish civil rights movement. For a discussion of this see Bob Purdie, *Politics in the Streets: The Origins of the Civil Rights Movement in Northern Ireland* (Belfast: Blackstaff, 1990), pp. 137ff., 239ff.

8   This legacy is discussed in Holger Nehring, 'The British and West German Protests against Nuclear Weapons and the Cultures of the Cold War, 1957–64', *Contemporary British History* 19, no. 2 (2005), p. 231.

9   Frank E. Myers, 'British Peace Politics: The Campaign for Nuclear Disarmament and the Committee of 100, 1957–1962' (PhD, Columbia University: 1965), pp. 7, 38–9.

10   Adam Lent, *British Social Movements since 1945: Sex, Colour, Peace and Power* (Basingstoke: Palgrave, 2001), p. 40. See Jones, Sheila, *Peace News* 7 March 1958 obituary of Gertrude Fishwick quoted in Frank E. Myers, 'British Peace Politics: The Campaign for Nuclear Disarmament and the Committee of 100, 1957–1962' (PhD, Columbia University: 1965), p. 82.

11   Wayland Young, *Strategy for Survival: First Steps in Nuclear Disarmament* (Harmondsworth: Penguin, 1959), p. 40.

12   Canon L. John Collins, *Faith under Fire* (London: Leslie Frewin Publishers Ltd., 1966), p. 318.

13   Frank E. Myers, 'British Peace Politics: The Campaign for Nuclear Disarmament and the Committee of 100, 1957–1962' (PhD, Columbia University: 1965), p. 105.

14   Frank Parkin, *Middle Class Radicalism: The Social Bases of the British Campaign for Nuclear Disarmament* (Manchester: University Press, 1968), p. 3.

15   CND, 'Minutes of the National Co-Ordinating Committee, 15 May 1958', (LSE, CND/1).

16   Canon L. John Collins, *Faith under Fire* (London: Leslie Frewin Publishers Ltd., 1966), p. 315.

17   *Ibid*, p. 315.

18   *Ibid*, pp. 315–16.

19 Kate Hudson, *CND – Now More Than Ever: The Story of a Peace Movement* (London: Vision Paperbacks, 2005), p. 41. Also see Frank E. Myers, 'British Peace Politics: The Campaign for Nuclear Disarmament and the Committee of 100, 1957–1962' (PhD, Columbia University: 1965), pp. 45, 46.

20 DAC, 'Policy Statement of the Direct Action Committee against Nuclear War, 26 May 1959' (Lawrence Daly Papers, MRC MSS 302/3/15, 26 May 1959).

21 *Ibid.*

22 *Ibid.*

23 *Ibid.*

24 *Ibid.*

25 R.K.S. Taylor and Colin Pritchard, *The Protest Makers: The British Nuclear Disarmament Movement of 1958–1965, Twenty Years On* (Oxford: Pergamon, 1980), p. 42.

26 Frank E. Myers, 'British Peace Politics: The Campaign for Nuclear Disarmament and the Committee of 100, 1957–1962' (PhD, Columbia University: 1965), p. 153.

27 Bertrand Russell, 'Letter to Ralph Schoenman – 21 July 1960', in *The Selected Letters of Bertrand Russell*, ed. Nicholas Griffin (London: Routledge, 2001), p. 528.

28 Sam Carroll, '"I Was Arrested at Greenham in 1962": Investigating the Oral Narratives of Women in the Committee of 100', *Oral History* 32, no. Spring 2004 (2004), pp. 11, 13.

29 Pat Arrowsmith, 'The Direct-Action Debate', in *The CND Story: The First 25 Years of CND in the Words of the People Involved*, ed. John Minnion and Philip Bolsover (London: Allison & Busby, 1983), p. 139.

30 *Ibid*, p. 140.

31 DAC, 'Policy Statement of the Direct Action Committee against Nuclear War, 26 May 1959' (Lawrence Daly Papers, MRC MSS 302/3/15, 26 May 1959).

32 *Ibid.*

33 Pat Arrowsmith, 'The Direct-Action Debate', in *The CND Story: The First 25 Years of CND in the Words of the People Involved*, ed. John Minnion and Philip Bolsover (London: Allison & Busby, 1983), p. 139.

34 *Ibid*, p. 140.

35 CND, 'Minutes of the National Co-Ordinating Committee, 13 May 1959' (LSE, CND/1).

36 Sevenoaks CND, 'Memo from Sevenoaks CND, July 1958' (LSE, CND/1).

37 *Ibid.*

38 Richard Acland, 'Memorandum on Techniques for Nuclear Disarmament Campaign' (LSE, CND/1, 26 September 1958).

39 CND, 'Minutes of the National Co-Ordinating Committee, 11 February 1959' (LSE, CND/1).

40 CND, 'Minutes of the National Co-Ordinating Committee, 28 November 1958' (LSE, CND/1).

41 Frank E. Myers, 'British Peace Politics: The Campaign for Nuclear Disarmament and the Committee of 100, 1957–1962' (PhD, Columbia University: 1965), p. 147.

42 *Ibid*, p. 148.
43 Pat Arrowsmith, 'The Direct-Action Debate', in *The CND Story: The First 25 Years of CND in the Words of the People Involved*, ed. John Minnion and Philip Bolsover (London: Allison & Busby, 1983), p. 141.
44 Papers of Lawrence Daly, MRC, MSS 302/3/13.
45 April Carter, 'Letter to Will Warren, 14 September 1959' (Modern Records Centre (MSS/302/3/13)).
46 CND, 'Minutes of the National Co-Ordinating Committee, 3 January 1959' (LSE, CND/1).
47 Bertrand Russell, 'Letter to Ralph Schoenman – 16 August 1960', in *The Selected Letters of Bertrand Russell*, ed. Nicholas Griffin (London: Routledge, 2001), p. 533.
48 J. Minnion and P. Bolsover, ed., *The CND Story: The First 25 Years of CND in the Words of the People Involved* (Allison and Busby, 1983), pp. 10, 140. R.K.S. Taylor and Colin Pritchard, *The Protest Makers: The British Nuclear Disarmament Movement of 1958–1965, Twenty Years On* (Oxford: Pergamon, 1980), pp. 80–1.
49 Quoted in Sam Carroll, '"I Was Arrested at Greenham in 1962": Investigating the Oral Narratives of Women in the Committee of 100', *Oral History* 32, no. Spring 2004 (2004), pp. 21–2.
50 Pat Arrowsmith, 'The Direct-Action Debate', in *The CND Story: The First 25 Years of CND in the Words of the People Involved*, ed. John Minnion and Philip Bolsover (London: Allison & Busby, 1983), p. 140.
51 Peggy Duff, *Left, Left, Left. A Personal Account of Six Protest Campaigns, 1945–65* (London: Allison & Busby, 1971), p. 165.
52 Canon L. John Collins, *Faith under Fire* (London: Leslie Frewin Publishers Ltd., 1966), p. 312.
53 Chingford Nuclear Disarmament Committee, 'Letter to Peggy Duff, 8 November 1959' (LSE CND/1/3).
54 CND, 'Minutes of the National Co-Ordinating Committee, 3 January 1959' (LSE, CND/1).
55 Peggy Duff, 'Letter to Mrs Margaret Bowles, 23 November 1959' (LSE (CND/1/3)). See also Canon L. John Collins, *Faith under Fire* (London: Leslie Frewin Publishers Ltd., 1966), p. 312.
56 Michael Randle, 'Non-Violent Direct Action in the 1950s and 1960s', in *Campaigns for Peace: British Peace Movements in the Twentieth Century*, ed. Richard Taylor and Nigel Young (Manchester: Manchester University Press, 1987), p. 146.
57 Quoted in Diana Collins, *Partners in Protest: Life with Canon Collins* (London: Victor Gollancz Ltd., 1992), p. 250.
58 Paul Byrne, *The Campaign for Nuclear Disarmament* (London: Croom Helm, 1988), p. 45
59 CND, 'Minutes of the National Co-Ordinating Committee, 15 May 1958' (LSE, CND/1).
60 Peggy Duff, *Left, Left, Left. A Personal Account of Six Protest Campaigns, 1945–65* (London: Allison & Busby, 1971), p. 128.
61 DAC letter to supporters June 1958 quoted in Frank E. Myers, 'British Peace Politics: The Campaign for Nuclear Disarmament and the Committee of 100, 1957–1962' (PhD, Columbia University: 1965), pp. 145–6.

62 CND, 'Minutes of the National Co-Ordinating Committee, 7 October 1958' (LSE, CND/1).
63 CND, 'Minutes of the National Co-Ordinating Committee, 11 February 1959' (LSE, CND/1).
64 CND, 'Minutes of the National Co-Ordinating Committee, 13 May 1959' (LSE, CND/1).
65 Paul Mercer, *'Peace' of the Dead: The Truth Behind the Nuclear Disarmers* (London: Policy Research Publications, 1986), p. 58.
66 CND, 'Minutes of the Executive Committee, 18 March 1958' (LSE, CND/1).
67 CND, 'Minutes of the National Co-Ordinating Committee, 13 May 1959' (LSE, CND/1).
68 DAC, 'Policy Statement of the Direct Action Committee against Nuclear War, 26 May 1959' (Lawrence Daly Papers, MRC MSS 302/3/15, 26 May 1959).
69 *Ibid.*
70 Canon L. John Collins, *Faith under Fire* (London: Leslie Frewin Publishers Ltd., 1966), p. 329.
71 Bertrand Russell, *The Autobiography of Bertrand Russell. Volume III 1945–1967* (London: Allen & Unwin, 1969), p. 110. Cannon John Collins, 'Chairman's Report to CND Executive, 1960' (LSE CND/1/60).
72 Bertrand Russell, *The Autobiography of Bertrand Russell. Volume III 1945–1967* (London: Allen & Unwin, 1969).
73 Peggy Duff, *Left, Left, Left. A Personal Account of Six Protest Campaigns, 1945–65* (London: Allison & Busby, 1971), p. 171.
74 Canon L. John Collins, *Faith under Fire* (London: Leslie Frewin Publishers Ltd., 1966), p. 318.
75 Sam Carroll, '"I Was Arrested at Greenham in 1962": Investigating the Oral Narratives of Women in the Committee of 100', *Oral History* 32, no. Spring 2004 (2004), p. 20.
76 Ralph Schoenman, ed., *Bertrand Russell: Philosopher of the Century* (London: George Allen & Unwin Ltd., 1967), p. 4.
77 April Carter, 'Direct Action against Nuclear War', in *CND Story: The First 25 Years of CND in the Words of the People Involved.*, ed. J. and P. Bolsover Minnion (London: Allison & Busby, 1983), p. 52.
78 CND, 'Minutes of the National Co-Ordinating Committee, 13 May 1959' (LSE, CND/1).
79 *Youth Against the Bomb* (London) December 1959 quoted in Frank E. Myers, 'British Peace Politics: The Campaign for Nuclear Disarmament and the Committee of 100, 1957–1962' (PhD, Columbia University: 1965), p. 151.
80 Peggy Duff, *Left, Left, Left. A Personal Account of Six Protest Campaigns, 1945–65* (London: Allison & Busby, 1971), p. 167.
81 Kate Hudson, *CND – Now More Than Ever: The Story of a Peace Movement* (London: Vision Paperbacks, 2005), p. 67.

2
British Humanitarian, Aid and Development NGOs, 1949–Present[1]

Clare Saunders

Introduction

No historical analysis of post-1945 NGOs would be complete without a discussion of NGOs active in the field of international development and humanitarianism. Although this chapter refers to international development and humanitarian NGOs as 'humanitarian, aid and development organisations' (HADOs), it does not dispute their status as NGOs. Indeed, they are probably the single category of organisations least problematically assigned the label of NGO – they are deliberate socio-political actors (even if historically constrained by charity law), they are non-violent, and, although the largest and most respected HADOs may accept some funding from state departments, they are not wholly dependent on it. Their status as NGOs is often taken for granted to the extent that much scholarly work on NGOs has focussed almost exclusively on HADOs.[2]

Yet, as I illustrate in this chapter, they are not *just* NGOs; they have increasingly become part of the global justice movement – a network of individuals and organisations that engages in collective action to address injustices resulting from the neo-liberal agenda.[3] This chapter demonstrates how HADOs have become part of the global justice movement, an observation manifest by their campaigning against perceived negative effects of neo-liberalism, and increasing use of overtly political coalitional forms. Strangely enough, they have not lost their voice, influence or reputation by engaging in public protest, but rather, they have used the strategy of public protest alongside their more conventional repertoires to increase their organisational influence, broadening and deepening their critiques and mobilisation strategies simultaneously.

Despite this, leaders and analysts of HADOs have generally regarded them to be engaged in 'advocacy'[4] rather than to be a part of a social or political movement. This is because they are mostly bureaucratised formal organisations, and were historically tactically moderate – engaging mostly in the three pronged approach of fundraising, public awareness and humanitarian relief. In the past they were involved in overt political campaigning only to a limited extent[5] because of the constraints of charity law, their willingness to accept government funding, their tendency to be distracted by emergency appeals, and because the complex issues they raise are difficult to relay to a public audience.[6] In the course of the last decade or so, however, HADOs have increasingly supplemented these tactics with overt political campaigning which is considerably more visible in the relatively recent HADO coalitional networks of Jubilee 2000, the Trade Justice Movement (TJM) and Make Poverty History (MPH) than it was in earlier HADO 'campaigns'.

Although it contradicts the conventional wisdom of political sociology – that social movements begin radical and become institutionalised[7] – this 'back-to-front' trajectory is not unique to the HADO sector. Mold (this volume), for example, shows how the voluntary drugs sector evolved from church philanthropists with high powers of social persuasion, to defining drug abuse as a social and political problem, and culminating in the emergence of new overtly political campaign networks. Similarly, Rootes (this volume) discusses how the environmental movement grew from the conservation efforts of social elites, whose networks endowed them with political influence, into a broad-based movement. This trajectory should not be viewed as regression from status and influence; but instead as a means of increasing public support that can, in turn, actually enhance influence, if not status. It also demonstrates to us there is no clear-cut distinction between the terms NGO and social movement organisation (SMO): organisations with voice and influence that are networked and which make use of public protest can be both NGOs and SMOs simultaneously, even though the two terms are not completely synonymous.[8]

The development of British humanitarian, aid and development organisations

Despite having differing styles and issues, British HADOs, tend to have followed similar trajectories that can be best explained as general phases of development. I shall identify five main phases in the development of British HADOs, each of which is significantly more politicised than its forerunner. It should be remembered that these are generalised phases, and do some violence to the nuanced differences between NGOs. To some extent, this is because, as Halpin (this volume) explains, different NGOs follow openings and closures in the democratic system, which vary depending on their strategies and status at particular points in time. It is also the case that many HADOs continue to work on themes and issues arising from previous phases. Nevertheless, each phase represents a qualitative shift in their general nature – a departure from their normal ways of doing things, usually in both their ideological focus and action base.

It will be shown that most British HADOs began their lives providing famine relief for victims of war, which I shall call *phase one*. In *phase two*, they broadened their focus to concentrate on general relief for people in distress, whether their suffering was caused by natural disasters or human intervention, with increasing focus on developing countries and the promotion of 'development'. *Phase 3* saw the emerging strategy of political campaigning, and the development of the 'teach a man to fish' rhetoric, as the limit of aid's ability to reduce poverty in the long term was increasingly recognised. By *phase 4*, the political nature of poverty had not only been recognised, but was being targeted through intense lobbying as the ropes that had tied HADOs' hands under charity law were loosened. The most recent *phase 5* has witnessed the development of high profile campaigns and coalitions with the capacity to mobilise hundreds of thousands of demonstrators.

Phase 1: Humanitarian relief in war-torn countries (19th century–1950s)

Although Britain has a long history of establishing charitable and philanthropic agencies, many of which were established prior to the twentieth century, specific HADOs of significance did not emerge until 1919. The chief exception is the humanitarian and aid efforts of the Quakers, who deserve mention because of the instrumental role they have played in the establishment and running of many HADOs, including, most prominently, Oxfam.[9] Although Oxfam was not formally connected to the Quakers its ethos was, at least until the 1980s, heavily influenced by prominent members who were Quakers.

The British Quakers formed in 1647 by John Fox and his supporters who were seeking a form of spirituality that Christianity could not meet. They were always motivated by the themes of justice and peace, and as early as 1660 they announced their allegiance to pacifism to Charles II. The most well known statement from this Peace Testimony is: 'All bloody principles and practices we do utterly deny, with all outward wars, and strife, and fighting with outward weapons, for any end, or under any pretence whatsoever, and this is our testimony to the whole world'.[10] Their overriding concern with peace and justice meant that the rights of the disadvantaged, including refugees, asylum seekers, slaves and the poor were always priority. However, it was nearly 200 years after their original establishment in Britain that this concern was translated into the practice of overseas humanitarian action. This is because the Quakers were initially hostile to the idea of having a centrally organised ministry, and because their belief in the guidance of the spirit tended to rule out highly organised missionary or humanitarian ventures.[11]

Thus, it was not until 1868 that the Friends Foreign Missionary Association was established, with the remit of improving schools and hospitals in countries such as West China, Ceylon, Mid-India and Madagascar. Although British Quaker groups engaged in direct relief work throughout the nineteenth century – during the Irish famine, and in post-Crimean war Finland – the official vehicle for relief work, the Friends War Victims Relief Committee (FWVRC), was not established until 1870. FWVRC's first mission was to provide relief for the towns and villages that had been destroyed as a result of the Franco-Prussian war (1870), later working in eastern Europe (1879), South African Boer Camps (after 1900), the Balkans (1920s), and in France, The Netherlands, Russia, Germany, Austria and Poland during and after the First World War (1914–1923). From its outset, the Committee was committed to providing relief work 'without discrimination' on the grounds of nationality, creed, or class. Relief work continued up to, during, and after the Second World War, the most notable of which was the work of the Germany Emergency Committee (later called the Friends Committee for Refugees and Aliens), which was engaged in emergency feeding programmes in Germany. During the Second World War, the Friends Ambulance Committee, which had been active during the First World War was reactivated, mostly working in bomb shelters and evacuation hostels.[12]

Aside from the Quakers, Fight the Famine, later to become Save the Children, was probably the first significant HADO to develop, initially in response to the post-First World War humanitarian crisis in countries affected by the Allies' continued blockade of its former enemies. Indeed, war-time and post-war humanitarian crises provided the stimulus for the emergence of several humanitarian NGOs in Britain. Oxfam developed from a local initiative called Oxford Council for Famine Relief, formed in 1942 in response to the famine that followed the German occupation and Allied blockade of Greece.[13] After providing relief in Germany, it moved on to provide food and clothing relief in Eastern Europe. Similarly, Christian Aid, initially established as the Christian Reconstruction in Europe (1945) and soon changing its name to Inter-Church Aid and Refugee Service (1949), began its work in the provision of aid to refugees in the aftermath of the Second World War. A couple of years later, War on Want emerged as a response to famine caused by the Korean War.

Whilst the work of Christian Aid (see Anderson's contribution to this volume) and the Quakers, who had exerted some influence over Oxfam, was overtly religiously inspired, the work of Save the Children was markedly less so, with evidence, even in these early days, of political undertones. Indeed, Save the Children was motivated more by a sense of political injustice than by spirituality or altruistic humanitarianism. Whilst the Quakers were engaged in emergency feeding programmes in Germany and the Red Cross were focussing on medical relief, Fight the Famine (the initial name of Save the Children) was distributing highly controversial leaflets, featuring a picture of a starving infant, which were critical of the Allied Powers' blockades on Germany and its allies in Britain. And its founder members had previously been engaged in translating excerpts from the European Press in an attempt to counter what they viewed as inaccurate propaganda in the British press.

Phase 2: Relief from humanitarian crises in developing countries (1950s–1960s)

Although many British HADOs began their lives with relief work for refugees and support for others adversely affected by war, they had, by the mid–late 1950s, in an economically booming post-war developed world, become increasingly focussed upon poverty and disaster relief in 'third world' nations. By 1949, Oxford Council for Famine Relief had changed from being a war charity to an organisation concerned with 'the relief of suffering arising as a result of wars *or of other causes* in any part of the world'.[14] Christian Aid similarly expanded its remit from a focus on refugee resettlement to disaster relief and long-term development. Christian Aid's first director announced in 1952, for example, that:

> the phenomenon of acute need was being revealed as extending beyond refugees. For the servant church and its ecumenical agency, compassion could not be selective.[15]

Although Save the Children had also been heavily involved in refugee relief programmes in Europe, by the end of the 1950s it was spending the majority of its income on work in Asia. War on Want also expanded from refugee support to disaster relief in poorer countries, focussing its efforts in the 1960s on the erection of emergency buildings in localities devastated by earthquakes in places such as Skopje and Agadir, and by bombing in Vietnam.[16]

Phase 3: 'Teaching men to fish' and emerging politicisation (1960s)

By the 1960s, HADOs had begun to realise that Western development models were inappropriate in the very different social, cultural and physical environments of developing countries, and began supporting local self-help movements. In 1960, the Catholic Agency for Overseas Development (CAFOD) was established, beginning with assistance to poor families in Dominica, but by 1970, it was funding 245 self-help projects in 40 countries. One important impetus for the development of CAFOD was the need for a humanitarian outlet for members of the Catholic faith because Catholic churches were initially excluded from the British Council of Churches, which had supported Christian Aid.[17] Yet what is interesting about CAFOD is that its initial work was not confined to European post-war projects, but to the relief of suffering more generally. During this period, Christian Aid also began to support local development projects in poor countries by providing funding to local agencies, and Oxford Council for Famine Relief increasingly gave grants for projects that aimed to improve poor peoples' self-sufficiency. The 1960s also marked a significant change in Oxford Council for Famine Relief's publication imagery – from images of starving children, to pictures of progressive farmers whom it claimed had benefited from its assistance.

Alongside this development work, which increasingly emphasised the 'teach a man to fish' rhetoric and supported projects designed to enhance poor peoples' self-sufficiency, the 1960s heralded the first large-scale public awareness campaigns on the plight of those suffering from poverty and famine. The most significant was the Freedom from Hunger Campaign, which defined itself as 'a campaign attempting not to sell itself, but a crusade'.[18] It was a coalition of 76 organisations, mostly HADOs, but also including the Labour Party, the National Farmers' Union, the Quakers and a handful of women's organisations. The most active organisations were Christian Aid, Oxford Council for Famine Relief, Save the Children, War on Want, the Friends Service Council, the UK Committee for UNICEF and the UN Association. Working under the motto of 'Helping the Hungry to Help Themselves', the campaign had several strands: public awareness/education and fundraising was the remit of the 1,000 local Freedom From Hunger committees, whilst an expert group assessed requests for overseas help, developed a project list, and produced educational material for schools at home and abroad. In less than two years, Freedom from Hunger had raised over £7 million for the poor and hungry by organising thousands of fetes, opening 'bring and buy' shops, and organising sponsored walks (London to Brighton), door-to-door collections and some imaginative stunts. By 1964, Freedom from Hunger had begun work on 247 projects in 61 countries, worth £6 million. These included the provision of water supplies to rural areas, seeds and tools, veterinary training and the establishment of food cooperatives.[19]

Although Freedom from Hunger called itself a 'campaign' and significantly raised the profile of humanitarian aid and development issues, it was mostly focussed upon fundraising and practical projects, and as such did not involve the overt political campaigning that has since increasingly become part of HADOs' repertoire. It is also distinct from some of the later coalition work of HADOs in that it did not attract such a broad-range of organisational affiliates. In particular, environmental organisations were notably absent, largely because the 'new' politically minded environmental organisations – such as Friends of the Earth and Greenpeace – had not yet been formed, and the sustainable development agenda that strongly linked environmental and development issues, was, at that point, embryonic at best.

However, by the mid-1960s, many HADOs were beginning to take a political stance. One causal factor was the establishment of the Disasters Emergency Committee, which coordinated fundraising appeals for disasters, leaving HADOs with more time to consider longer-term policy and strategic issues. As early as 1965, for example, Oxfam was expressing concern about patterns of world trade, and Christian Aid and War on Want were demanding that at least 1 per cent of British GNP be spent on overseas aid. Another causal factor was the zeitgeist of the 1960s, which was marked by a widespread political awakening. The result was a change of norms and greater public awareness of political issues, including development issues, but also the environment (see Rootes, this volume), and respect for deviant families (see Brooke, this volume) and homosexuality (see Waites, this volume).

Phase 4: Poverty is political (1970s–1980s)

By the 1970s, HADOs came to realise the limits of self-help development projects. Poverty, they discovered, was rooted in the vested interests of the elite: in other words, it was political. Although Oxford Council for Famine Relief had begun to raise awareness of the politics of poverty through its briefings on the GATT (General Agreement on Tariffs and Trade) and its analysis of third world debt, it had been relatively quiet on this throughout the 1960s. This is because, in 1963, it had offended the Charity Commission with its promotion of self-help overseas development projects. Though not especially overtly political, these were described in the Charity Commission's report of that year as going beyond the declared charitable aim of 'famine relief'. As a result, in 1965 Oxford Council for Famine Relief altered its objectives in its Memorandum and Articles of Association, adopted the shorter name 'Oxfam', and was forced to change some wording on posters that advertised its overseas development work.

Nevertheless, British HADOs were increasingly realising that poverty could not be addressed exclusively through disaster relief and self-help projects. This realisation kick-started political campaigning, which was, unfortunately, initially stifled by charity law that prevented all registered charities from engaging in overt political campaigning. Despite these constraints the reality of which was demonstrated by the action taken against Oxfam, in the 1970s, War on Want, itself a registered charity, unabashedly embarked upon its successful campaigning strategy of vigorous research, lively presentation of results and aggressive lobbying. It exposed the unethical practices of several multinational companies, raised awareness of the implications of aggressive marketing of baby milk products in disadvantaged countries, and highlighted the social and ethical problems associated with the arms trade.[20]

As part of their bid to raise the political stakes of aid, trade, debt and development issues, the founders of Oxfam and Christian Aid established and funded the highly political *New Internationalist* magazine, and also set up a new student network called Third World First (later to become People and Planet). Even Christian Aid stepped up the pressure, brandishing highly controversial 'Poverty is Pollution' posters. But probably the most significant, enduring and daring political venture that HADOs embarked upon during that decade was the World Development Movement (WDM).

WDM began to develop in the summer of 1969, when a number of aid agencies including Oxfam, Christian Aid, and War on Want, teamed up with the Overseas Development Institute, the Catholic Institute for International Development and the Voluntary Committee on Overseas Aid and Development (VCOAD) to launch a new politically motivated coalition called Action for World Development. It was intended that the coalition would work to achieve what had been set out in a *Manifesto for Aid and Development*, which demanded an increase in national aid budgets and political action on aid and trade.[21] In part, it was motivated by a number of local politically-oriented 'World Poverty Action' groups, of which there were over 100 by 1972, and which wanted a national office for support and coordination.[22]

The *Manifesto* stated the need to take political action on the causes of poverty, and began with the 'offensive' locution: 'we demand ...'. However, the Charity Commission was quick to point out that Action for World Development was infringing charity laws, and stated quite categorically in its annual report that year that if charities engaged in political activity, 'their action will be in breach of trust' and that 'those responsible could be called upon to recoup to the charity any of its funds which have been spent outside of its purposes'.[23] Hence, the founder members rapidly agreed that a separate political organisation should be established to carry out the political work that they deemed so important.[24] Thus, although the World Development 'Movement' was born, the constraints of the Charity Commission prevented other organisations from working openly in partnership with it, thus precluding its development as a fully-fledged social movement. It was, however, not only Charity Commission constraints that prevented this development, but also the general lack of public enthusiasm. According to Black:

> The launch of the Manifesto was something of an anticlimax. There was no echoing roar as there had been for Hunger £Million, for Biafra, and for other emergencies. A hundred or so committed development action groups ... beavered away, trying to disentangle growth rates from commodity agreements, unearth the mysteries of ODAs and GATTs, unhook multilaterals from intergovernmentals, and work out where the poor fitted in ... But for all the achievements of the emerging development lobby, no-one could pretend that '1 per cent of GNP' and 'fair trade' evoked in the public mind the passionate concern that a Biafran child could conjure.[25]

Even though it failed to become a 'movement' in social scientists' sense of the word, because it was a single organisation rather than an informal network of organisations, it was able, on occasions, to act as a coordinating body for other HADOs. One such coordination resulted in the 1983 general election *Guide to Where the Parties Stand*, and an accompanying questionnaire to be addressed to candidates, both of which were widely used by local campaigners associated with a variety of HADOs.

Whereas other NGO sectors (e.g. women's rights, see Beaumont, this volume, and drugs use, see Mold, this volume) became moderate in the 1980s due to the rolling back of the welfare state and a subsequent immersion in service provision, it appears that, like trade unions in that decade, the HADO sector was moderated by Margaret Thatcher's apparent enthusiasm for quietening any organisation that might criticise her government's policies. It is certainly the case that during the 1980s, the Charity Commission appeared to have 'an incipient desire to contain' charities,[26] pulling War on Want into the affray. War on Want resolved its own disputes with the Charity Commission by selling its overtly political print unit to its workers, who ran it as a workers' cooperative, and by establishing War on Want Campaigns Ltd, a limited company funded by donations but not registered as a charity.[27] Oxfam seemed unfazed by Charity Commission warnings, and although it was unwilling to join in War on Want's campaign for a relaxation of charity law,[28] it continued, into the 1980s, to involve itself in politically oriented coalitions, namely the Campaign for Real Aid, and the Disarm for Development coalition. Oxfam did this despite the Charity Commissioners' findings in 1981, after a prolonged inquiry into its work, which concluded that, by law, charities could publish material based on research and direct experience, but that they were not permitted to advocate a specific line of policy, or recommend legislative changes, unless these were directly subsidiary to the achievement of their charitable purposes.[29]

Nonetheless, the Independent Group on British Aid, whose most prominent members were Oxfam, the WDM, Christian Aid and the Overseas Development Institute launched the Campaign for Real Aid in January 1982. It sought to shift the emphasis of aid campaigns away from quantity, to quality, and in the process to expose its finding that 'British aid is becoming heavily weighted towards helping British firms win ... contracts in poor countries'.[30] Its other demand was that levels of British aid be based on need, rather than the economic interests of its former colonies.[31] It sought to mobilise the public, encouraging people to write to their MPs and to their local newspapers, form local Real Aid campaigning groups, stage demonstrations and give talks at local group or society meetings. However, it appears that the Campaign for Real Aid was unable to secure as much public sympathy and support as the Freedom From Hunger Campaign had, and it was local supporters and local groups of previously existing HADOs, rather than autonomous Campaign for Real Aid groups, that spearheaded most of its work.[32]

The Disarm for Development Coalition, also launched in 1982, consisted, amongst others, of Oxfam, War on Want, Volunteers Action, WDM, and the Campaign Against the Arms Trade. It mostly involved the production of a report that challenged the West's selling of arms to poor countries and contrasted the low aid budgets with the considerably higher arms budgets. However, unlike the Campaign for Real Aid, the coalition failed to develop much before being silenced by the Charity Commission.

So, by the early 1980s, links were being made between the issues of aid/trade and peace and war. But links were also beginning to develop with other social movement sectors. Oxfam in particular, through its work with the Amazonian rubber tappers, had noticed that poverty was often directly related to environmental degradation, and thus began to make conceptual links with the concerns of the environmental movement. War on Want also began broadening out, by developing linkages with the peace movement and trade unionists, establishing a Trade Union Committee, and controversially providing a £150 grant to needy immigrant families affected by the Grunwick strike.[33]

As well as a broadening political agenda, the 1980s also saw the first ever large-scale mobilisation on aid and development issues. In 1982, WDM organised a 10,000-strong mass lobby of parliament, followed by an extensive letter writing campaign seeking to influence the Prime Minister in the run-up to the first summit of world leaders on development at Cancún, Mexico. Using the report of the Independent Group on British Aid, WDM pushed the aid agenda by writing concise briefings, and asking local campaigners to write to their MPs expressing concern over the inadequate quantity and quality of British official aid.

By the mid-1980s, British HADOs began to campaign against rules of the emergent international economic order that they believed were disadvantageous to the world's poor. In 1989, the first national campaign on debt, coordinated by War on Want, Third World First and Friends of the Earth had begun.[34] At the start of the 1990s, even the religious-inspired, and previously non-radical, Christian Aid began to overtly challenge the World Bank and International Monetary Fund (IMF), and sought to pressurise high street banks to cancel the unpayable debts of poor countries. In an expression of their newly politicised nature, Christian Aid, Oxfam, Action Aid, the Catholic Institute for International Relations and WDM were all active in the international campaign against the 1986–94 Uruguay Round of multi-lateral trade negotiations.[35]

Unsurprisingly, this flurry of political activity again attracted the attention of the Charity Commission, which focussed its attention upon Oxfam. On 25 April 1990 the Charity Commissioners decided 'to hold an inquiry into whether, in advocating and campaigning for political change whether in this country or abroad, the trustees [of Oxfam] are acting in accordance with their trusts and the restrictions of charity law in England and Wales'. Needless to say, Oxfam's trustees took the matter seriously, for if they were found guilty of breaching charity law, they might have been required to refund money spent on activities deemed non-charitable, and to pay to the Inland Revenue any related tax from which they were previously exempt.[36]

The Commissioners' 1991 report claimed that Oxfam's trustees had exceeded the limits placed upon them by charity law. According to the report, the trustees did not differentiate 'between stating a possible solution to a problem in reasoned fashion and campaigning to have that solution adopted'.[37] As a result, the Charity Commission declared that 'unacceptable political activities of the charity must cease', and certain materials destined for public circulation were ordered to be withdrawn. Fortunately, the trustees were not declared financially liable, but they were warned that future breaches of charity law would be taken much more seriously. Therefore, at least for the first half of the 1990s, Oxfam, and other charities that had learned from Oxfam's experience, began to show greater respect for charity laws, and so became rather more moderate. Commins, for example, goes so far as to suggest that for the period 1981–1995 'NGO policy work has ... taken on a more low key approach' as a result of Charity Commission constraints.[38]

Phase 5: High profile mass mobilising coalitions (mid-1990s to date)

The most recent phase in the development of the HADO NGO sector has been coterminous with, and perhaps instrumental in, the rise of the global justice movement (GJM) in Britain at the end of the 1990s.[39] It has seen an increase in high profile campaign coalitions, whose work would not have been possible had charity law constraints not been relaxed in 1995 as a result of a prolonged campaign by War on Want.[40] Indeed, had War on Want not succeeded in pressing for change in charity law, the GJM as we know it today might not have materialised. Whereas in the 1970s, the Charity Commission sent a clear message that charities should stick to '"bandaging the wounds of society" rather than try to prevent them from being inflicted in the first place',[41] it had, by 1995, reported that charities could advocate or oppose changes in law and policy if this helped them to achieve their charitable objectives.[42] This paved the way for significant and overtly political campaigns such as the campaign against the Multilateral Agreement on Investment (MAI), the Debt Crisis Network, Jubilee 2000, the Trade Justice Movement, Make Poverty History and, more recently, Your Voice Against Poverty.

In 1997, British NGOs became concerned that the MAI – which aimed to create uniform rules on market access and legal security, remove barriers to investment flows, and allow corporations the right to sue states that 'unreasonably' limited investments or capital flows – would give disproportionate power to transnational corporations.[43] The shared concern that protection of local markets, health, and environments would not be considered sufficient reasons to restrict trade[44] brought together a broad range of religious, environmental, trade union and aid organisations, including WDM, Oxfam, WWF, Northeast England Greens, Friends of the Earth, Corporate Watch, UNISON (the major public sector trade union) and Christian Aid. This campaign, which anticipated the range of interests that have become characteristic of the GJM, was the springboard from which wider and deeper critiques of the workings of the global economy were launched. Tactics included conventional lobbying and extensive letter writing, through to direct action, as when Corporate Watch occupied the London offices of the International Chamber of Commerce in 1997. As part of a growing transnational network of NGOs, the organisations involved moved on to critique the World Trade Organisation and the General Agreement in Trade and Services.

Jubilee 2000, the British forerunner and founder of the popular international Jubilee anti-debt 'movement', grew out of the British Debt Crisis Network. Led by the New Economics Foundation (NEF), Christian Aid and WDM, members of the Network lobbied to secure improvements in World Bank and IMF debt policies through Heavily Indebted Poor Country Initiatives (1996). However, the trickles of aid that resulted did little to reduce the debt burdens of the poorest countries, and resistance by creditor countries made debt reduction initiatives difficult to implement. This lack of progress persuaded NGOs concerned with trade that the issues needed a higher public profile. In 1996, the Trade Crisis Network was formed, with tentative support from CAFOD and Tearfund.[45] In 1997, a formal campaign coalition was launched, with over 70 supporting organisations including trade unions, international aid and women's organisations, and the Green Party, with Christian Aid, CAFOD, the Methodist Church Division of Social Responsibility, the United Society for the Propagation of the Gospel, the Church Missionary Society, Oxfam, WDM, Save the Children, the International Labour Organisation and NEF especially prominent among them.[46]

The initial priority of Jubilee 2000 was to ensure that unpayable debts were written off by 31 December 1999 and that all other debts were reduced to levels that would permit sustainable human, environmental, and economic development.[47] This was, however, not a straight-forward, neither a reformist task. Jubilee 2000's critique of the G8, IMF and World Bank assimilated the anti-debt movement to a broader, emergent movement critical of international financial institutions and their lack of international democracy, and, more broadly of the neo-liberal agenda. One of its most prominent moments came when in 1998 it succeeded in mobilising 70,000 people to form a human chain around the city of Birmingham in an action called to raise the profile of the issue of debt in the G8 discussions that were then taking place in the city. Although Jubilee 2000 ceased activity at the turn of the millennium, the Jubilee Debt Campaign – a smaller, less well-resourced, reconstituted version of Jubilee 2000 – has continued to work on the issue of debt.[48]

The Trade Justice Movement (TJM) was established in 2001 by a small steering group drawn from approximately 40 British HADOs. It consciously emulated the form of the Jubilee 2000 campaign, but, to the dismay of anti-debt campaigners, attempted to shift the developing HAD movement's focus away from debt and towards trade, seeking 'fundamental change to unjust rules and institutions governing international trade, so that can trade can work for all'.[49] It arose as a result of interorganisational discussions about how to best influence the UK government's input and response to the Doha round of trade negotiations, and sought to persuade the government not to sign the free trade agreement on foreign investment at the WTO meeting in Cancún. It achieved greatest prominence when it mounted a 25,000-person strong vigil outside Parliament on 15 April 2005, in the lead up to World Poverty Action Day. Its ability to organise complex and innovative campaign actions was proven yet again on 19 April 2007, when it mobilised approximately 1,000 protesters in a simultaneous lobby of every European embassy, asking ambassadors to do what they could to prevent the European Commission from imposing Economic

Partnership Agreements (EPAs), which it claimed would 'Lock Africa into Poverty'. Describing itself as a 'fast growing coalition', it consisted, in May 2007, of 80 organisations including HAD, environmental and religious organisations.

In 2004–5, Make Poverty History (MPH) emerged as a one-year campaign coalition for trade justice, cancellation of the debts of poor countries, and 'more and better aid'. It included more than 500 groups and organisations including the Jubilee Debt Campaign, the Trade Justice Movement, other HADOs, trade unions, faith groups, student unions, environmental organisations, local campaign groups and churches. Its organisers believed that 2005 provided an unprecedented opportunity to influence the UK government on issues of third world poverty because the UK was then hosting the G8 summit and holding the chair of the EU presidency. The pinnacle of its mobilisation was the 225,000-strong 'Make Poverty History' rally and march through the streets of Edinburgh on 2 July 2005. MPH, although short-lived, demonstrated social movement dynamics: organisational networking, shared concerns about the neo-liberal agenda, and employment of protest.[50]

Although the coalition formally folded in 2006, campaigns to 'make poverty history' have by no means ended. In 2007, the steering committee of MPH launched a new campaigning coalition, 'Your Voice Against Poverty', which claims that:

> the world can't wait for debt cancellation and more and better aid, trade justice, healthcare, education, water and sanitation for all and firm plans to prevent catastrophic climate change and to address its impacts.[51]

To coincide with the G8 summit in Heiligendamm, near Rostock, Germany, it organised a rally on 2 June 2007 on the banks of the Thames to encourage the Prime Minister to represent the views of campaigners in the European and G8 summits. In May 2007, 94 British organisations, from a range of backgrounds, including most of the key HADOs, Friends of the Earth and the churches, supported the campaign.

Although the GJM itself is not overtly religious, it is certainly true that the HADOS which partake in it have not been party to the trend towards secularisation witnessed in many other NGO sectors. Although the religious are not so prevalent as Paul Cloke *et al* found in their survey of fair trade supporters in Bristol (70–80 per cent of those promoting fair trade there),[52] the religious *do* widely participate in GJM mobilisations organised by HADOs. A survey of participants in the

Make Poverty History demonstration in London in July 2005 for example, found that nearly half of the participants claimed to be involved in a religious organisation (36.1 per cent actively involved and 12.6 per cent passively involved).[53]

Conclusion: Explaining the trajectory of the HADO sector

The transition from *phase one* to *phase two* – expanding relief beyond European war refugees to sufferers from multiple causes across the globe – was, in part, a response to the success of the HADO sector's campaigns during World Refugee Year (1960) for the closure of all European refugee camps by 1960. Success on that issue meant that their issue frontier needed to be extended, much as the abortion lobby's was once the 1967 Abortion Act had been passed (Brooke, this volume). The new focus was upon humanitarian relief from the consequences of earthquake and famine disasters, which HADOs and their supporters had begun to find impossible to ignore. By *phase 3*, HADOs were helping poor people to become more self-sufficient. The shift towards promotion of self-help development projects was made possible by the formation of the Disasters Emergency Committee (DEC), an initiative of the Red Cross, Christian Aid, Oxfam, Save the Children Fund and War on Want. DEC, which continues to coordinate emergency appeals, prevented duplication of effort, fostered cooperation, and reduced competition among HADOs, and thus gave them more time to focus on the structural causes of poverty.

Thus, despite the restrictions of charity laws, HADOs became increasingly politicised in their outlook and strategies throughout the 1960s and 1970s. Although most charitable HADOs avoided the political arena, or did little more than tiptoe carefully into it, Oxfam and War on Want bravely trod where others may not have dared to venture – at least until the Charity Commissioners warned them off. Their intrepid ventures into the political realm resulted, in *phase 4*, in the formation of local action groups calling for 'Action for World Development' and asking for the formation of a national coordinating body. To avoid the restrictions imposed by the Charity Commissioners, new HADOs were formed as limited companies and did not seek charity status. The *New Internationalist*, WDM and Third World First (now People and Planet) were amongst the key political ventures of those years. Other HADOs had other ways of avoiding trouble with the Charity Commission. The 1981 Charity Commissioners' report declared that charities should not promote solutions that fell outside of their charitable aims. In response to this, both Oxfam and War on Want simply modified their charitable aims as stated in their Memoranda and Articles of Association. The 1991 Charity Commission report, however, came down upon charities much more stringently and its prescriptions were harder to evade. Its declaration that charities might *propose* solutions to help them reach their charitable aims, but not *campaign* for the realisation of those proposals, imposed moderation upon the HADO sector in the early 1990s, but it was short-lived. Since 1995, charities have been permitted to engage in campaigning provided it helps them to reach their charitable aims, and this has paved the way for an era of the most politicised campaigning by British HADOs that we have seen to date.

The 1990s witnessed fairly moderate action from HADOs, but this was not only because the Charity Commission had restricted their scope. Another factor was 'donor fatigue'. The Charity Household Survey (July 1989–June 1990) revealed that in the immediate post-Cold War period the majority of British people were giving less money to third world charities than they had previously, and that over a quarter were not donating at all. As Burnell[54] explains, this was not only a matter of donor fatigue, but also a reflection of increased competition from other charities, especially health, education and environmental charities, which, as demonstrated by most of the histories presented in this volume, exploded in number from the 1970s onwards.

Despite this, Jubilee 2000 managed to become a highly successful mobilising and fundraising coalition. The fact that it was a campaign *coalition* seeking cooperation from other charities must have gone some way to help, but probably more significant was Jubilee's ability to unravel complex issues to a public audience. Thanks to Jubilee 2000, the debt issue was brought within the intellectual grasp of the average layperson, and involvement with HADOs escaped the confines of a 'cheque-book membership' restricted to making financial donations; it now involved writing letters, holding local meetings and engaging in innovative protest actions.

The backdrop to the emergence of Jubilee 2000 was a steady increase in the likelihood of the British public to participate in less conventional forms of political action, and this undoubtedly helped Jubilee 2000 to skirt the problem of 'donor fatigue'. Britain certainly had a much more participatory political culture at the turn of the twenty-first century than it did in the 1960s. The proportion of British people claiming willingness to demonstrate against an unjust law, for example, rose from 8 per cent in 1983 to 20.5 per cent in 1998.[55] This rising tide of unconventional political participation, visible in widely supported protests throughout the nineties, including direct action anti-roads campaigns,[56] allowed British HADOs to wash their hands of their previously held fear that their supporters would be offended by political action.[57]

In summary, it can be said that the humanitarian, aid and development NGO sector to which we now bear witness, with its high-profile campaigning and awareness-raising, as illustrated by Jubilee 2000, the Trade Justice Movement, Make Poverty History and Your Voice Against Poverty, has emerged as a result of successful emergency appeals, the relaxation of Charity Commission constraints, the expansion of the public's repertoire of political participation, and HADOs' highly successful experimentation with coalitional organisational forms. These factors have allowed once conventional humanitarian, aid and development NGOs to be active in both the global justice movement *and* the more staid arena of conventional NGO politics simultaneously.

Notes

1 This chapter is based upon work undertaken as part of the DEMOS project, funded by the European Commission Directorate General for Research, 6th Framework Programme contract no. CIT2-CT2004-506026. I would like to thank Chris Rootes for employing me on this project, and for his valued contribution to earlier versions of this chapter. I would also like to thank the DANGO team for organising the conference upon which this volume is based.

2 See, for example: P. Aaal, D.T. Mitenberger and T.G. Weiss, *Guide to IGOs, NGOs and the Military in Peace and Relief Opportunities* (Washington: USIP Press, 2000); M. Edwards, *NGOs, State and Donors: Too Close for Comfort* (Basingstoke: Palgrave, 1997); A. Duben, *Human Rights and Democratisation: The Role of Local Governments and NGOs* (Istanbul: Wald, 1994); D. Mitlin, S. Kickey and A. Bebbington, 'Reclaiming Development? NGOs and the Challenge of Alternatives', *World Development*, 35(10) (2007) pp. 1699–720.

3 See C. Saunders 'Using Social Networks to Explore Social Movements: A Relational Approach', *Social Movement Studies*, 6(3) 2007, pp. 227–43, for a definition of a social movement

4 Edwards, *NGOs, State and Donors*.

5 J. Clark, *Democratising Development: The Role of Voluntary Organizations* (London: Earthscan, 1991).

6 C. Bryant and M. Lindenberg, 'Responding to Globalization' in M. Lindenburg and C. Bryant (eds) *Going Global: Transforming Relief and Development NGO* (Bloomfield: Kumarian Press, 2001).

7 See D. Minkoff 'Social Movement Politics and Organization' in J.R. Blau (ed.), *Blackwell Companion to Social Movements* (Oxford: Blackwell, 2001)

and/or H. van der Heijden, 'Political Opportunity Structure and the Institutionalisation of the Environmental Movement', *Environmental Politics*, 6(4) (1997), pp. 25–50.

8   On the other hand, in keeping with the DANGO definition of NGOs, organisations without voice and influence might remain best classified as SMOs rather than NGOs.

9   Although the British Red Cross dates from 1870, it is excluded because, unlike the other organisations considered here, it did not become a development or campaigning organisation.

10   A. Heron, *The British Quakers 1647–1997: Highlights of their History* (Kelso, Scotland: Curlew Productions, 1997).

11   Nobel Prise.org. 2005, http://nobelprise.org/peace/laureates/1947/friends-council-history.html, Friends Service Council – History of Organisation, accessed 24/10/05.

12   Heron, *The British Quakers*, p. 26; R.C. Wilson, *Quaker Relief: An Account of the Relief Work of the Society of Friends, 1940–1948* (London: Allen & Unwin: 1952).

13   M. Black, *A Cause for Our Times: Oxfam the First 50 Years* (Oxford: Oxford University Press, 1991), p. 1.

14   M. Black, *A Cause for Our Times*, p. 37, emphasis added.

15   Christian Aid website, at http://www.christianaid.org.uk/, accessed 15/9/08.

16   M. Leutchford and P. Burns, *Waging the War on Want: 50 years of Campaigning Against World Poverty: An Authorised History*, London: War on Want, 2003), pp. 44, 49, 51–2.

17   The successor to the British Council of Churches is called Churches Together, and since 1980 has included Catholic churches.

18   Freedom from Hunger, 'Freedom from Hunger' (campaign leaflet, Freedom From Hunger: London), p. 1.

19   Freedom From Hunger, campaign leaflet.

20   M. Leutchford and P. Burns, *Waging the War on Want*.

21   This a belief that the World Development Movement continues to hold: 'WDM believes that the fundamental causes of world poverty cannot be overcome without changes to the policies and practices of governments and business interests in wealthy industrialised countries like Britain. So, free from charity law, WDM undertakes campaigns that change the policies of governments and companies which keep the poor marginalised' (www.real-world.org.uk/wdm.html accessed 23/09/2005).

22   World Development Movement, *A Brief History of WDM* (London: World Development Movement, 1987).

23   M. Black, *A Cause for Our Times*, p. 154.

24   S. Macdonald, *Action for World Development: The World Development Movement in the 1970s* (London: A World Development Movement Publication, 1972).

25   M. Black, *A Cause for Our Times*, p. 159.

26   M. Black, *A Cause for Our Times*, p. 269.

27   M. Leutchford and P. Burns, *Waging the War on Want*.

28   Like the World Development Movement, War on Want always firmly believed that poverty and politics were inseparable.

29   M. Black, *A Cause for Our Times*, p. 269.

30 J. Clark, 'Real Aid Making it Happen', *New Internationalist*, 126, August 1983.
31 J. Clark (1983) 'Real Aid Making it Happen', p. 4.
32 J. Clark (1983) 'Real Aid Making it Happen', p. 4
33 J. Dromey and G. Taylor, *Grunwick, The Workers' Story* (London: Lawrence and Wishart, 1978).
34 M. Leutchford and P. Burns, *Waging the War on Want*, p. 150.
35 M. Wilkinson 'Lobbying for Fair Trade: Northern NGDOs, the European Community and the GATT Uruguay Round', *Third World Quarterly*, 17(2) (1996), pp. 251–67.
36 Black, *A Cause for Our Times*, pp. 278–9.
37 Black, *A Cause for Our Times*, p. 283.
38 S. Commins, 'World Vision International and Donors: Too Close for Comfort?', in D. Hulme and M. Edwards (eds), *NGOs, State and Donors: Too Close for Comfort?* (Basingstoke: Macmillan, 1997).
39 C. Rootes and C. Saunders, 'The Global Justice Movement in Britain', in D. della Porta (ed.), *The Global Justice Movement: Cross National and Transnational Perspectives* (Boulder, CO: Paradigm Press, 2007).
40 M. Leutchford and P. Burns, *Waging the War on Want*.
41 M. Leutchford and P. Burns, *Waging the War on Want*, p. 107.
42 M. Leutchford and P. Burns, *Waging the War on Want*, p. 109.
43 J. Bray 'Web Wars: NGO, Companies and Governments in an Internet Connected World', *Green Management International*, 24 (1998), pp. 115–29.
44 K. Farnsworth, 'Anti-globalisation, Anti-capitalism, and the Democratic State' in Malcolm Todd and Gary Taylor (eds) *Democracy and Participation: Popular Protest and New Social Movements* (London: Merlin, 2004).
45 CAFOD is the Catholic Agency for Overseas Development, and Tearfund is its evangelical counterpart.
46 B. Peters, 'Jubilee 2000', *Journal Modern African Studies*, 32(4) (2000) pp. 699–700.
47 A. Petifor, 'The Economic Bondage of Debt and the Birth of a New Movement', *New Left Review*, 230 (July/August 1998), pp. 115–22; A. Petifor, 'Debt' in Emma Bircham and John Charlton (eds), *Anti-Capitalism, A Guide to the Movement* (London: Bookmarks, 2001).
48 Interview with Ann Pettifor, ex-Director of Jubilee 2000, by Clare Saunders and Tasos Papadimitriou May 2007.
49 www.tjm.org.uk, accessed 28/08/05.
50 See C. Saunders, 'The Configuration of the Global Justice Movement in Britain: Exploring Networks of Concern, Collective Action and Overlapping Memberships of Make Poverty History March Participants, Edinburgh, July 2, 2005. Paper presented to the ACI conference on 'Genealogies of the Global Justice Movement', Paris, September 30–October 1; and C. Rootes and C. Saunders, 'The Global Justice Movement in Britain'.
51 YVAP campaign leaflet, 'The World Can't Wait' (2007).
52 See Anderson, this volume.
53 C. Saunders, 'The Configuration of the Global Justice Movement in Britain'.
54 P. Burnell, 'Debate: Third World Charities in Britain Towards 2000', *Community Development Journal*, 28(1) (1993), pp. 66–81.

55   Jowell, Richard, Alison Park, Lindsay Brook, Katrina Thompson and Roger Jowell (eds) (1997) *British Social Attitudes: The 14th Report* (Aldershot: Ashgate, 1997) p. 320.
56   C. Rootes, 'The Resurgence of Protest and the Revitalisation of British Democracy', in P. Ibarra (ed.), *Social Movements and Democracy* (New York: Palgrave Macmillan, 2003).
57   C. Rootes and C. Saunders, 'The Global Justice Movement in Britain'.

3
Housewives, Workers and Citizens: Voluntary Women's Organisations and the Campaign for Women's Rights in England and Wales during the Post-War Period

Caitriona Beaumont

> For many housewives women's organizations provide the best access to cultural or educational pursuits ... resolutions are frequently passed by the branches to the national headquarters urging government intervention in matters where their particular knowledge and experience has shown that reform is both necessary and possible, and they exercise an undoubted influence upon the trend of domestic affairs. *Women in Britain* (HMSO, 1964).[1]

This 1964 description of voluntary women's organisations in a government publication signifies official acknowledgment on the part of the state of the role of women's organisations active in Britain in the 1960s. The pamphlet, which documented the position of women in Britain, reported the existence of over 100 national women's organisations made up of feminist and political groups, professional associations, religious bodies and 'social and philanthropic' organisations. It would appear therefore that voluntary women's organisations remained an important part of the social and political fabric of British life in the post-war period, just as they had done throughout the first half of the twentieth century.[2] These organisations offered, as the extract above suggests, not just an outlet for the social, cultural and educational interests of members but an opportunity for women as equal citizens to influence and shape the future of British society. This was an important consideration at a time when women were significantly underrepresented in politics, business and the professions, thereby limiting their ability to affect issues of national and economic importance.[3]

Perhaps even more significantly this reference to the role of women's organisations in the 1960s signals a challenge to the existing historical orthodoxy with regard to the progress of the campaign for women's rights in Britain. This orthodox interpretation, reinforced by the Women's Liberation Movement, argued that the women's movement was rendered ineffectual by post-war developments such as the reinforcement of traditional gender roles in the 1950s, the introduction of the welfare state and free health care, higher standards of living with more and more women going out to work and the easing of women's domestic labour as a result of the availability of new consumer goods. As a result the women's movement of the late 1940s, 1950s and 1960s was thought to have reached its lowest point only to be revitalised by the sudden emergence of a radical new Women's Liberation Movement in the late 1960s.[4] This viewpoint has now been challenged by a number of historians who have argued, albeit rather tentatively, that feminism and the women's movement survived during the 1940s, 1950s and 1960s but that the 'gulf between the mass of British women and the organised movement working on their behalf did yawn wide in this period'.[5]

More recent research on the activities of women's organisations in the post-war period has demonstrated that many women's organisations continued to campaign for women's equality during the 1940s, 1950s and 1960s and were effective in enhancing the lives of many women at this time.[6] This chapter, which focusses on the activities of three voluntary women's organisations, will argue that the achievement of the women's movement during the post-war period was not just to remain in existence but to also make a significant contribution to social, cultural and political developments during the post-war years. This contribution has not only been overlooked by historians of the twentieth century women's movement and the Women's Liberation Movement[7] but also in major studies of post-war British history and the history of social movements and non-governmental organisations.[8]

The chapter will provide an overview of the aims and activities of three of the largest voluntary women's organisations in England and Wales, the Mothers' Union (1885), the Women's Institutes (1915) and the Townswomen's Guilds (1929), throughout the late 1940s, 1950s and 1960s. These three groups can be identified as conservative, middle-class and mainstream. The use of the term mainstream refers here to the fact that the three organisations discussed appealed to large numbers of women on a national and local level and in order to ensure their widespread appeal, all three maintained a strict non-party political stance as well as distancing themselves from overtly feminist pressure groups. Such allegiances, it was believed, would alienate significant numbers of potential and existing members. It must be stressed however that this non-party political and non-feminist position did not prevent each organisation from engaging in political debates, co-operating with feminist societies to further particular causes and in campaigning for reforms which would enhance the lives and status of women. The voluntary and independent nature of each of the three groups and their ability to influence public and political debates regarding the role and status of women as citizens clearly demonstrates that each group fits into the definition of non-governmental organisations as socio-political actors even though the term NGO was not used widely used by these groups during the 1950s and 1960s.

In keeping with the wider themes of this study of post-war NGOs, the intention here is to demonstrate that the wide-ranging and diverse work of these three women's organisations directly challenges presumptions that the voluntary sector is or always has been the preserve of the radically progressive. Focussing on the national activities of the three groups the chapter will consider the role of each organisation in political campaigns and begin to assess their continued success as pressure groups in influencing public debate or achieving legislative reform in the post-war period.

Women's organisations had to face many new challenges during these years. Increasing numbers of women began to enter the workforce and women were able to limit their families in ever more effective ways. These significant social changes had major implications for mainstream women's societies whose traditional membership was made up of full time housewives and mothers. In addition the nature of traditional political campaigning and lobbying, as practised by many voluntary groups, including women's organisations, was changing as a result of the 'speeding up' of politics and public debate in a new age of television and the mass media. It will be argued that the three voluntary women's groups discussed here worked hard during the post-war years to keep in touch with the interests and needs of their members and to safeguard the effectiveness of their campaign tactics.

There is no doubt that the Mothers' Union was one of the most conservative women's organisations in Britain throughout the twentieth century. Established in 1885 and affiliated to the Church of England to support women in their role as wives and mothers, the Union campaigned against the liberalisation of divorce legislation throughout the inter-war years and divorced and unmarried mothers were not allowed to join the Union.[9] In line with Church of England teaching, the Union reluctantly accepted that the use of artificial birth control was a private matter for married couples but condemned any attempt to legalise abortion, which was considered a mortal sin. Although the Union adhered to strict moral codes and viewed home and family as the most important priorities for women, members were not expected to limit their interests to domestic concerns. The September 1934 edition of *The Mothers' Union Journal* reflected this view when it was stated that 'a mother's first place is in the home – not the only place but the first. The mother is now a citizen of her country: she has a vote and with it a great responsibility.'[10] This responsibility was one of the reasons why the Mothers' Union felt it appropriate for the organisation to speak out and campaign on issues which it regarded as important to women and Christians alike.

The National Federation of Women's Institutes, whose first branch opened in 1915, gave hundreds of thousands of women living in isolated rural communities the chance to further their education, develop their skills, meet other women and spend time away from the responsibilities of their homes, families and farming activities. Moreover, as Margaret Andrews has suggested, Institute classes, complete with graded examinations, exhibitions and competitions, acknowledged women's domestic work as a worthwhile occupation and did much to raise the status of housework throughout the 1920s and 1930s.[11] Women also had a public role to play away from home and family. The enactment of the 1928 Equal Franchise Act was celebrated by the organisation as a victory for women and an opportunity for members to 'show that they have sufficient political zeal and intelligence' to justify their new right to political citizenship.[12] Like the Mothers' Union, the Women's Institutes believed that as a voluntary organisation for women it had a duty to campaign to ensure that the rights of all women, and rural women in particular, were not overlooked.

The success of the Women's Institutes influenced the decision of the well known feminist society, the National Union of Societies for Equal Citizenship, to set up a new organisation in 1929 which would appeal to a wider membership. As a result the programme of the new Townswomen's Guilds went beyond campaigning on social and political issues to include civics, arts, handicrafts and home-craft.[13] Like the Mothers' Union and the Women's Institutes, the Townswomen's Guilds realised that to appeal to a wide range of women and to attract a mass membership, voluntary women's organisations had to provide members with a mixture of education, advice, leisure and social activities in order to be successful and influential on a local and national level.

I have written elsewhere of the contribution made by mainstream women's organisations to the history of the women's movement in England throughout the period 1928 to 1950.[14] This work has demonstrated that large voluntary women's organisations used the rhetoric of equal political and social citizenship rights granted to women in 1928 to campaign on a wide range of issues which they believed would enhance the lives of wives and mothers. These groups accepted traditional gender roles but they also demanded that the unpaid work performed by women in the home be acknowledged as an important and skilled occupation. In return for their services to society and in light of their hard-won status as equal citizens, it was argued that women were entitled to a range of social and economic rights including family allowances paid to mothers, free health care, good housing, the provision of local services, equitable state pensions, adequate maternity services and equal pay for women workers. In addition to their campaigning work, mainstream women's organisations, as demonstrated by the work of the Mothers' Union, Women's Institutes and Towns-women's Guilds, gave women the opportunity to meet other women, share their experiences and interests and engage in educational, domestic and recreational pursuits. Equally significant, membership of a voluntary women's organisation with its rules, processes and procedures, gave large numbers of women the opportunity to learn about the democratic process whilst providing them with the vocabulary necessary to discuss concepts such as political participation and social rights.

By the end of the Second World War the Mothers' Union, the Women's Institutes and the Townswomen's Guilds had firmly secured their status as national organisations representing the interests of hundreds of thousands of women and, as this chapter will assert, their involvement in a range of political campaigns secures their place in the history of NGOs in post-war Britain. Each group had supported the war effort and had made a significant contribution to assisting the state in implementing wartime initiatives such as knitting for the troops, supporting evacuated women and children and promoting home-grown food production and preservation. At the national level all three organisations became members of the Women's Group on Public Welfare, set up in 1939,[15] and gave evidence to key enquiries on post-war reconstruction, most notably the 1941 Inter-departmental

Committee on Social Insurance and Allied Services and the 1942 Ministry of Health's Design of Dwellings Sub-Committee. In both cases the aim was to ensure that the interests and needs of housewives and mothers were made known and taken into account in post-war planning and future legislative reforms.

So what became of these influential and well respected women's organisations in the post-war years? Despite losing members as a result of wartime disruption, all three groups remained large successful national organisations for women in the post-war period. Two years after the end of hostilities, 876 Townswomen's Guilds had been established in England and Wales demonstrating a swift recovery following the wartime decline. Similarly the membership of the Women's Institutes Movement had recovered by 1947 to reach a figure of 379,000. By 1950 the Mothers' Union had a worldwide membership of 500,000 although it never recovered its pre-war popularity in England and Wales. The Union demonstrated its awareness of the competition it faced from Women's Institutes and Townswomen's Guilds when it decided in 1950 to broaden local branch activity to include 'drama, book clubs and talks on national and international affairs as well as religious education in an effort to appeal to the wives of professional men.'[16]

A number of common aims and concerns can be identified when assessing the work of voluntary women's organisations in the decades following the Second World War. It can be argued that there were three overriding concerns influencing the work of the Mothers' Union, the Women's Institutes and the Townswomen's Guilds during these years. The first was the desire to re-build traditional family life after the upheaval of war and to support women in their role as housewives and mothers. The second was to protect and consolidate the rights of housewives and mothers and to monitor the impact of the increasing numbers of married women going out to work. The third concern was to continue to promote the concept of responsible and active citizenship for women. This final aim encouraged women to add their voice to a range of social and political issues which affected their lives and the lives of their families after the war.

In their attempts to promote and support family life, mainstream women's organisations were eager to highlight the needs of families in the immediate post-war years. Evidence presented to the 1944 Royal Commission on Population focussed on the factors which would encourage couples to marry and have children. Greater housing provision, modern, spacious and labour saving designs for new homes, amenities such as shops and playgrounds, were all identified as practical ways to restore and enhance traditional family life.[17] The payment of family allowances to mothers was another way to support the role of women in the family and encourage women to have children. In evidence to the Commission women's organisations insisted that any such payment must be made to mothers as the primary carers of children.[18] When in 1944 the government announced its intention to pay the new allowance to fathers the decision was denounced by many mainstream women's groups. The Mothers' Union and the Women's Institutes joined Eleanor Rathbone and the Family Endowment Society, in lobbying the government to reverse this decision. Alarmed by such a strong reaction from respected and influential women's organisations the decision was reversed and the allowance paid to mothers.[19] This important victory demonstrated that voluntary women's groups did have the ability to influence, and in this case, alter public policy in favour of women.

Along with supporting the role of women as wives and mothers, regarded as a crucial element in maintaining stable family life, one of the major issues that mainstream women's organisations had to contend with in the late 1940s and throughout the 1950s and 1960s was the growing number of married women going out to work.[20] As early as March 1944, the Mothers' Union had acknowledged that there may be 'a growing reluctance on the part of women to lose the economic independence they enjoyed before marriage or through war work.'[21] Rosamond Fisher, Central President of the Mothers' Union, went even further in her evidence to the Royal Commission on Population when she remarked that 'speaking as a feminist I say yes [to mothers working] but speaking as a mother I would say let her have a career provided it does not stand in the way of having babies ... but it almost always does.' She added that women of her generation who did voluntary work were never criticised for leaving their babies but if 'a young woman takes up a career and leaves her baby she is severely criticised. I think it is a little hard to argue that a woman should not continue her career if she has a baby, but the baby must come first.'[22]

The Mothers' Union's endorsement of the right of older married women to work outside the home is significant as it demonstrates that voluntary women's organisations were grappling with the issue of combining paid work with family life a decade before the publication of the groundbreaking text on married women's employment, Alva Myrdal and Viola Klein's *Women's Two Roles: Home and*

Work (1956). Like the Mothers' Union, Myrdal and Klein supported the concept of married women working as long as the welfare of the family was not compromised. The easiest way to achieve this balance was for wives and mothers to return to the workforce once their children were of school age and for them to engage in part-time work. The growing popularity of part-time work for women in the 1950s and 1960s reflected the reality that married women did want to work outside the home but that it was the mother who would continue to be primarily responsible for the running of the household.

The difficulty of managing this 'dual role' and the impact it may have on family life was raised in an article published in *Home and Country*, the journal of the Women's Institutes Movement, in September 1957. The article entitled 'Mothers at Work', acknowledged that many married women now went out to work and that modern women had the right to 'find fulfilment in work profitable both to herself, her family and to the community.'[23] It was argued, however, that the difficulties of married women working had to be acknowledged, for example what to do when children were ill, required after-school care or care during school holidays. The article suggested that organisations such as the Women's Institutes should bring pressure to bear on parliament, local authorities and business to create 'married women' jobs which would allow mothers to fit their work around school hours.[24] Like Myrdal and Klein, this view demonstrates that it was the woman who needed to adjust, adapt and compromise her working life to ensure the welfare of the family and the happiness of her children. Such presumptions must be viewed in the context of the 1950s when there was much public concern about the rise of juvenile delinquency amongst 'neglected children' and the importance of the mother's relationship with her young child was being emphasised in influential and popular texts, for example John Bowlby's *Maternal Care and Mental Health* (1951).

The Townswomen's Guilds were also concerned about working mothers and the difficulties encountered when trying to cope with the 'double burden' of paid work and family life. The organisation supported the introduction of reforms and services which would support working mothers. For example day nurseries, summer camps, staggered school holidays and refresher courses facilitating the re-entry of older married women into the professions were all proposed as solutions to this problem.[25] As an organisation representing mainly middle-class women the Guild expressed its concerns about well-educated women dropping out of the labour market to devote themselves to home and family. In 1962 Townswomen were asked to consider

> how little encouragement there is for the married woman who wants to go and do a job of work ... the wastage of brain and talent must be considerable when they take on work far below their capacity, as they usually do.[26]

The fact that mainstream women's organisations supported and even encouraged the decision of married women to work outside the home, as long as their children were of school age and those children were cared for by their mothers after school, was a radical stance to take in the 1950s and early 1960s. This was a time when popular women's magazines, such as *Woman* and *Woman's Own,* bombarded readers with the message that their place was in the home and that the best career for women was marriage and motherhood. Nevertheless organisations like the Mothers' Union, the Townswomen's Guilds and the Women's Institutes accepted the reality that increasing numbers of married women would go out to work. Rather than condemning these women as 'bad mothers' all three groups became increasingly concerned about the difficulties such women would encounter when trying to balance paid work with motherhood. As a result they offered practical support to their members struggling with this new role and campaigned to improve the working conditions of women both in paid work and in the home.

This cautious endorsement of women's paid work and the belief that married women workers had a contribution to make to the work-force sets the context for the support that a number of mainstream women's organisations gave to the equal pay campaign in the late 1940s and 1950s. The history of the equal pay campaign has been well-documented.[27] It is important however to acknowledge the role of mainstream women's organisations in the campaign as this demon-strates that conservative women's groups were willing to participate in campaigns which in the past have been more commonly associated with overtly feminist groups.

Following the revival of demands for equal pay for women during wartime, with increasing numbers of women entering the labour force, the Equal Pay Campaign Committee (EPCC) was set up in 1944 to co-ordinate the campaign. Over 70 women's groups affiliated to this new body including the Women's Institutes and the National Council of Women, whose affiliated membership included the Mothers' Union. The Townswomen's Guilds did not publicly support the campaign as it was deemed too political and too divisive an issue. It did report however that its members were split fifty-fifty on the question of equal pay. Some considered it 'indefensible that women's employment should play second fiddle to men's' while others believed that 'women should not be paid at the same rate as men for the same work.'[28]

The EPCC focussed on the common grades of the civil service where men and women performed the same work but received differential pay rates. In 1944 the Women's Institutes, along with the EPCC and the National Council of Women, gave evidence to the Royal Commission on Equal Pay and all three groups defended the right of women and men doing similar work to earn the same wage. When the Commission reported in 1946 it stated that no logical reason could be given why equal pay for equal work should not be introduced in the civil service but advised that immediate implementation would be unwise in view of the post-war economic crisis.[29]

The EPCC, supported by the Women's Institutes and other mainstream and feminist women's groups, continued its campaign for equal pay in the civil service into the 1950s. Traditional tactics such as writing to MPs, organising mass meetings, marches and demonstrations contributed to the decision by the Conservative Party to adopt the issue of equal pay and to finally legislate for the gradual implementation of equal pay in the civil service from 1955. Following this victory the EPCC quickly disbanded and it was not until 1970 that the Equal Pay Act outlawed discrimination in pay between men and women in the private sector. Mainstream women's organisations welcomed the passing of this Act but it does not appear that the Women's Institutes, Mothers' Union or Townswomen's Guilds were actively involved in any ongoing campaign for equal pay throughout the 1960s. This may have been due to the fact that the post-1955 equal pay campaign focussed much more on the discrimination experienced by working-class women in the industrial and service sectors. This disengagement from the campaign may reflect a class bias within mainstream women's organisations as in this case they were more willing to be outspoken on issues which affected their predominantly middle-class members. This fact however should not be used to imply that these groups had no interest in equal pay for all women. It was the Townswomen's Guilds, who had not joined the EPCC, that published this statement on equal pay legislation in the March 1967 issue of *The Townswoman*

[equal pay] may not seem of vital concern to the homebody assured of her situation as a cherished wife and adored mother, but we need to remember that the struggle for equality, whether engaged in by a few women in Parliament, or the national women's organisations, is part of a campaign for the rights of every woman everywhere.[30]

Throughout the post-war period mainstream women's organisations became increasingly interested in the new challenges faced by married women going out to work and the effect this development would have on family life. Their primary concern, however, remained with providing support and advice to full-time wives and mothers. As part of this work voluntary women's groups campaigned to improve the welfare of married women both in terms of their economic security and access to health services. The welfare state greatly improved the position of women within the social welfare system and the National Health Service provided married women with free medical care for the first time. Yet in spite of these reforms housewives continued to be economically dependent on their husbands both in terms of a housekeeping allowance and also with regard to social welfare benefits and pensions.

The records of the Mothers' Union, Women's Institutes and Townswomen's Guilds demonstrate that all three organisations devoted considerable time and energy in their efforts to monitor the position of women within the social welfare system and to campaign for reforms which would lead to more equitable treatment for women citizens. In 1945 the Women's Institutes' AGM passed a resolution calling on the government to 'include in their National Insurance Scheme some sickness benefit for all non-gainfully employed married women and non-gainfully employed widows.'[31] Members lobbied the Ministry of National Insurance requesting that housewives be classified as self-employed workers entitled to sickness benefit under the proposed National Insurance Act. All such demands were rejected and the assumption that married women should be dependent on their husbands within the new social insurance system was further entrenched.

Pension rights, income tax allowances, the financial entitlements of divorced women, widows' pensions, maintenance and inheritance law were all issues which prompted reaction by voluntary women's organisations during the post-war years. Using traditional campaign tactics, including lobbying and letter writing, mainstream women's groups challenged any attempt to discriminate against married women within the legal system which would leave them vulnerable to poverty. Growing awareness about the very real threat of poverty for separated and divorced women and their children was linked to the 're-discovery of poverty' in the 1960s and the increasing numbers of marriages ending in divorce.[32]

All three groups monitored any changes in the law in relation to the rights of women within marriage and following the break-up of a marriage and supported reforms which enhanced the rights of women in family law including the 1964 Married Women's Property Act and the 1967 Matrimonial Homes Act. In addition mainstream women's organisations closely followed proposals for legislative reform of divorce legislation throughout the 1950s and 1960s and campaigned to ensure that the right of the wife to adequate financial support following a divorce was protected in the 1969 Divorce Reform Act.[33]

Concern about the vulnerability of married and divorced women to poverty prompted the Women's Institutes to act when in 1972 the government announced plans to reform the method of payment of family allowances. A resolution passed in June 1973 stated that the movement viewed with great concern

the effect of the financial position of many mothers if Family Allowances are discontinued under the proposed new Tax-Credit System and urges Her Majesty's Government to continue with the present policy of payment to mothers.[34]

The concern expressed by the Women's Institutes that mothers were to lose their right to withdraw the family allowance at their local post office was further emphasised in *Home and Country*. In September 1972 it was stated that 'in marriages where the husband is "tight" with money, or where he has deserted or is unreliable, the fact that the woman cannot put her hands on the allowance *will* make a difference.' Readers were reminded that a mother's right to receive the allowance was hard fought for and that payment to mothers was 'one small official recognition of the job mothers do: we cannot stand by and see this small privilege taken away from us.'[35] Following representations from a wide range of women's organisations, including the Mothers' Union and Townswomen's Guilds, the government confirmed in July 1973 that any reform of the family allowance scheme would retain the guarantee that payments would be made in cash to mothers.[36]

Women's health and access to birth control information were also issues of great importance to women's organisations in the post-war years. Having welcomed the introduction of the NHS, women's groups now began to campaign for the extension of services specifically relating to women's health such as screening for cervical cancer and the right to free birth control. In 1964 the Townswomen's Guilds' AGM, which now represented 2,456 local guilds and approximately 200,000 women, passed a resolution calling for the urgent provision of 'comprehensive facilities for routine smear tests for cervical cancer and especially training of technicians to interpret the tests and the service to be made more widely known.'[37] The same year the Women's Institutes, speaking on behalf of over 400,000 women, passed its own resolution on this matter calling on the government and hospital boards to 'treat as a matter of urgency the provision of comprehensive facilities for routine smear tests for cervical cancer.'[38] As with all resolutions, letters were sent to the relevant authorities and members of both organisations were encouraged to make use of this screening service when it was available in their localities.

The extension of family planning services was another demand that mainstream women's groups lobbied for during the 1960s and early 1970s. The use of birth control and family planning had become an accepted part of family life during the inter-war years. The introduction of the contraceptive pill from 1961 and its availability on the NHS from 1963 was one of the most significant social changes to occur in the post-war years. The 1969 Family Planning Act gave local authorities the right to provide women with advice on birth control and contraceptive supplies but did not compel the authorities to do so.[39]

Believing that this was a service which should be widely available, the Women's Institutes passed a resolution in 1972 calling on the government to 'make it mandatory rather than permissive, as at present, for all Local Authorities to provide a full free Family Planning Service.'[40] The justification given for this demand was that every child should be a wanted child and that 'women should have the opportunity to plan their family in the way they feel is best for its health, welfare and quality of life.'[41] It is very significant that the reason cited for the extension of family planning services to women is couched in terms of the welfare of the unborn child and the family rather than the right of the individual woman to decide whether or when to have children. This sentiment reflects continuity in the campaigning strategy of mainstream women's organisations to always situate their demands in the context of the family rather than to focus solely on the rights of women as individuals.

Another reason why the Women's Institutes called for the greater availability of birth control information was to reduce the number of women seeking abortions. Abortion had long been a controversial issue not just for mainstream organisations but for all women's societies due to the moral implications it raised. The Mothers' Union continued to be firmly opposed to abortion on religious grounds and campaigned against any reform of the law in this area. Interestingly it was the Townswomen's Guilds, in the past so often reluctant to take a public stance on controversial or political issues, who came out in support of legalised abortion two years before the passing of the 1967 Abortion Act.

The Guilds' 1965 resolution on abortion called on the government to introduce legal abortion for women 'where it is necessary to preserve her physical or mental health; where there is a serious risk of a defective child being born; where the pregnancy results from a sexual offence.'[42] It is significant that this resolution, on what had always been a difficult moral issue, was passed without major controversy by an overwhelming majority. The Townswomen's Guilds continued to support calls for the introduction of legalised abortion and supported the work of the Abortion Law Reform Association in its campaign for legalised abortion in circumstances similar to those approved of by the Townswomen's Guilds.[43]

The aim of this chapter has been to demonstrate that mainstream women's organisations continued to highlight the interests and needs of women in the post-war period and were effective in making their demands and concerns known to the relevant authorities. Representing hundreds of thousands of women throughout the 1940s, 1950s and 1960s the three organisations discussed here continued to encourage their members to be active and responsible citizens and to make a contribution to their local communities and to public life. In 1964 the Mothers' Union reminded its members, especially those with young children, that they must keep in touch with the world outside their homes, take up voluntary work and attend evening classes, all to ensure that they are not regarded primarily as housewives but also as valued members of society.[44] Members of mainstream women's organisations were also encouraged to put themselves forward for local government as there remained 'numerous questions of deep concern to us as citizens and on which we should prompt action by the authorities.'[45]

It does appear, however, that by the late 1960s and early 1970s ageing memberships and the difficulties in recruiting young women were becoming of major concern to the three organisations discussed here. In 1970 the Townswomen's Guilds commissioned a study by the Tavistock Institute to investigate ways in which the organisation could be modernised and made more appealing to younger women. As a result the Guild focussed more on engaging its grassroots members in its campaigning work and encouraging more debate on contemporary issues at local level. The content of *The Townswoman* was revised to include greater coverage of topical issues, for example nuclear power and the importance of women's political participation.[46]

In 1969 the Mothers' Union set up a Commission to review the objects of the Union and its relations with its overseas federations. The Commission's report, entitled *New Dimensions*, was published in 1972. As a result the Union revised its objectives to allow divorced women to join the Union. This decision represented a difficult but pragmatic solution based on the social reality that divorce was now much more common and that the Mothers' Union needed to appeal to the majority of Anglican women rather than just the more devout. The desire to modernise was also evident in a statement published in *The Mothers' Union News* which urged that 'we must change our public image from the present one of the "anti-divorce" lot who meet once a month for tea and a nice innocuous talk, to an image of Christian women in action.'[47] In 1972 the Women's Institutes also expressed frustration about its ability to engage in effective action and called on members to consider how the organisation could alter its procedures to allow a quicker response to social and political questions.[48]

It is interesting that concerns about falling membership and the effectiveness of their campaign tactics came to prominence in the late 1960s when new pressure groups and NGOs such as CND and the Child Poverty Action Group were attracting much more public attention for their causes than voluntary women's organisations. This challenge was even more pronounced with the emergence of the Women's Liberation Movement. This new social movement rejected formal organisational structures, debated class difference and attracted significant media attention with its new, radical style of political campaigning. Moreover the WLM for the first time challenged traditional gender roles within society and in doing so appeared to be more relevant to the lives of young women in the 1970s than traditional women's groups.

Despite the failure of older women's organisations to attract significant numbers of new and younger members in the early 1970s and their continued association with middle-class values, the Mothers' Union, the Women's Institutes and the Townswomen's Guilds continued to support and campaign on behalf of women and today represent hundreds of thousands of women in England and Wales.[49] It seems strange therefore that these groups are so often omitted from the history of post-war British society. This chapter has argued that conservative voluntary women's organisations were effective in campaigning on behalf of women, and married women in particular, throughout the late 1940s, 1950s and 1960s. Such representations were often made in the context of the role of women as wives and mothers but it must be remembered that the majority of women were wives and mothers at this time. Equally significant is the fact that each group recognised and fought for the rights of women as housewives, as paid workers and as equal citizens and gave women the opportunity to make their voices heard in a society where women were and continue to be under-represented in public life. It can be argued therefore that the Women's Institutes, Townswomen's Guilds and Mothers' Union were effective NGOs, engaged in progressive and at times radical socio-political action, influenced political agendas, and perhaps most importantly of all improved women's lives in post-war Britain.

Notes

1   *Women in Britain* Central Office of Information, Reference Pamphlet 67, (London: HMSO, 1964), p. 25.

2   See for example: M. Andrews, *The Acceptable Face of Feminism: the Women's Institute as a Social Movement* (London: Lawrence & Wishart, 1997), C. Beaumont, 'Citizens not Feminists: The Boundary Negotiated between Citizenship and Feminism by Mainstream Women's Organisations in England, 1928–1939', *Women's History Review*, 9(2) (2000) and C. Merz, *After the Vote: The Story of the National Union of Townswomen's Guilds in the Year of its Diamond Jubilee 1929–1989* (Norwich: National Union of Townswomen's Guilds, 1988).

3   'By 1961 there were still only 8,340 female medical practitioners (15 per cent of the profession); 1,031 women in the whole legal profession (3.5 per cent); 1,580 female surveyors and architects (2.3 per cent) and 25 women MPs.' P. Thane, 'Women since 1945', in P. Johnson (ed), *20th Century Britain: economic, social and cultural change* (London: Longman, 1994), p. 395.

4   B. Caine, *English Feminism 1780–1980* (Oxford: Oxford University Press, 1997), p. 222.

5   M. Pugh, *Women and the Women's Movement in Britain, 1914–1999*, 2nd edn (London: Macmillan, 2000), p. 284.

6   J. Freeguard, 'It's Time for Women of the 1950s To Stand Up and Be Counted', unpublished Ph.D. thesis, University of Sussex, 2004 and C. Blackford, 'Ideas, Structures and Practices of Feminism 1939–1964', unpublished Ph.D thesis, University of East London (1996).

7   E. Wilson, *Only Halfway to Paradise: Women in Post-war Britain 1945–1969* (London: Tavistock, 1977) and D. Bouchier, *The Feminist Challenge* (London: Macmillan, 1983).

8   A. Marwick, *British Society since 1945*, 4th edn (London: Penguin, 2003) and A. Lent, *British Social Movements Since 1945: Sex, Colour, Peace and Power* (Basingstoke: Palgrave, 2001).

9 C. Beaumont, 'Moral Dilemmas and Women's Rights: The Attitude of the Mothers' Union and Catholic Women's League to Divorce, Birth Control and Abortion in England, 1928–1939', *Women's History Review*, 16(4) (September 2007).

10 *The Mothers' Union Journal* (September 1934).

11 Andrews, *The Acceptable Face of Feminism*.

12 *Home and Country* (May 1928), p. 67.

13 *The National Union of Townswomen's Guilds Handbook 1938* (1938), p. 25.

14 See C. Beaumont, 'The Women's Movement, Politics and Citizenship, 1918–1959', in I. Zweiniger-Bargielowska (ed), *Women in 20th Century Britain: Economic, Social and Cultural Change* (Harlow: Longman, 2001) and Beaumont, 'Citizens not Feminists'.

15 This body was set up in 1939 to act 'as a two way channel of information between statutory authority and the ordinary citizen (particularly the housewife), ... to meet a very real present day need' *Women's Group on Public Welfare: Report 1939–1945* (London: WGPW, 1945), p. 4.

16 *The Mothers' Union Workers' Paper* (July 1950), p. 68.

17 The Mothers' Union written evidence to the Royal Commission on Population, March 1944 (Evidence No. 11, The Royal Commission on Population, 1944–1949). The British Library.

18 *The Royal Commission on Population, Oral Evidence 1944–1949* (Evidence No. 5, The Mothers' Union, 13 October 1944). (London: HMSO, 1949).

19 Beaumont, 'Citizens not feminists', p. 423.

20 In 1931 women only 10 per cent of married women worked outside the home, 22 per cent did so by 1951, 30 per cent by 1961 and 47 per cent by 1981. See Pugh, *Women and the Women's Movement*, p. 288.

21 The Mothers' Union Oral Evidence to the Royal Commission on Population, March 1944. *The Royal Commission on Population 1944–1949* (London: HMSO, 1949).

22 *Ibid*, October 1944.

23 *Ibid*.

24 *Home and Country*, 39(9) (September 1957), p. 269.

25 *The Townswoman* (September 1963).

26 Merz, *After the Vote*, p. 46.

27 H. Smith, 'The Politics of Conservative Reform: The Equal Pay for Equal Work Issue, 1945–1955', *Historical Journal*, 35 (1992), pp. 401–15.

28 *The Townswoman* (October 1943).

29 See P. Thane, 'Towards Equal Opportunities? Women in Britain since 1945', in T. Gourvish and A. O'Day (eds), *Britain Since 1945* (Basingstoke: Macmillan, 1991), p. 191.

30 *The Townswoman* (March 1967).

31 *Ibid*.

32 The number of marriages ending in divorce in England and Wales increased from 137,400 (1956–60) to 284,400 (1966–70). Pugh, *Women and the Women's Movement*, p. 325.

33 See for example an article on 'Divorce Reform', *Mothers' Union News* (March 1969).

34 *Keeping Ourselves Informed: Our Concerns, Our Resolutions, Our Actions* (London: NFWI, 1981), F.6.

35   *Home and Country*, 54(9) (September 1972).
36   *Keeping Ourselves Informed*, F.6.
37   Merz, *After the Vote*, p. 47.
38   *Keeping Ourselves Informed*, G.8.
39   Pugh, *Women and the Women's Movement*, p. 326.
40   *Keeping Ourselves Informed*, G.7.
41   *Ibid*, G.8.
42   Merz, *After the Vote*, p. 47.
43   C. Francome, *Abortion Freedom: A Worldwide Movement* (London: Allen & Unwin, 1984), pp. 86–8.
44   *Mothers' Union News* (January 1964).
45   *The Townwoman* (November 1966).
46   Merz, *After the Vote*, p. 52.
47   *Mothers' Union News* (February 1964).
48   *Home and Country* 54(9) (September 1972).
49   In 2007 the Townswomen's Guilds had 41,000 members, the Women's Institutes 211,000 members and the Mothers' Union had a world-wide membership of 3.6 million women.

4
The Sphere of Sexual Politics: The Abortion Law Reform Association, 1930s to 1960s

Stephen Brooke

This chapter argues that the work of non-governmental organisations (NGOs) produces meaning about categories of identity and experience, such as gender and sexuality. Abortion is the issue at the centre of this examination. The ongoing efforts of NGOs like the Abortion Law Reform Association [hereafter ALRA] to widen access to legal abortion between the 1930s and the 1960s constructed particular ideas of femininity and heterosexuality in the public sphere.

This should not be an especially surprising argument. By the 1970s, it was clear that abortion carried considerable weight as a signifier of empowered femininity and liberated sexuality. The inaugural women's liberation conference held at Oxford in 1970 took up abortion as one of the four basic demands of feminism because it was a mark of women's freedom and autonomy: 'We want to be free to choose when and how many kids to have, if any. We have to fight for control over our own bodies, for even the magic pill [sic] or (in the case of mistakes) abortion on demand only gives us the freedom to get into a real mess without any visible consequences.'[1] By the 1980s, socialist-feminists maintained that '[i]n the fight for equality for women the ability to control fertility is fundamental .... Contraception and abortion are the twin methods by which women can gain control of their reproductive abilities'.[2] If abortion signalled the emergence of a particular kind of new femininity, it also said something about sexuality. It was shorthand for women's ability to enjoy sexual expression and fulfilment, indeed, to enjoy sex, as was suggested in 1978: 'The fight for abortion is primarily a fight for sexual freedom', a means of guaranteeing 'our right to express our sexuality freely'.[3] Abortion was thus a prism that refracted new visions of femininity and sexuality. The National Labour Women's Advisory Committee told a conference of

Socialist International Women in 1977 that 'the right to control our powers of reproduction is fundamental to the whole basis of women's rights. Women will never be able to enjoy full sexual life, education, a career or work in a society where we are at the mercy of unplanned pregnancy and the subsequent years of child-rearing'; abortion on demand was fundamental to realising that aim.[4]

The last example is somewhat misleading because it emerged from within a formal political party. For most of the century, no political party in Britain seriously discussed, let alone adopted the right to abortion as party policy. It was only in the 1970s, as a result of feminist pressure, that the Labour Party made that commitment. For this reason, the discussion of abortion in the public sphere, even in the 1970s, was left to NGOs like the National Abortion Campaign. Between the 1930s and the 1960s, the main pro-abortion organisation was ALRA. One of the roles that such NGOs play, therefore, is in establishing meaning in the public sphere about issues that are eschewed by political parties on grounds of controversy or indifference.

This chapter examines how the meaning of sexuality and gender in the public sphere was constructed between the 1930s and the 1970s by an NGO such as ALRA.[5] The abortion rights campaign between the 1930s and the 1970s offered not one, but a succession of sexual and gendered protagonists: the overburdened working-class mother; the respectable and young middle-class woman whose health and prospects might be threatened by an unwanted child or by being forced to resort to an illegal abortion; and, finally, in the 1970s, the liberated woman. In each of these cases, the issue was legal abortion, but arguments for law reform were inevitably inflected by historically contingent overtones of class, sexuality and gender. This chapter will largely be discussing the period between 1936 and 1967, thus about the first two examples.

Two points shape this picture. The first is the persistent link between class and abortion. Speaking about sexuality through the abortion issue inevitably meant talking about working-class sexuality. If abortion was a public sexual problem, it was largely perceived as a working-class problem. The second point concerns the dominant framework of femininity in this period. The abortion debate revolved around women as mothers, not individuals. As Catriona Beaumont suggests in her chapter on women's organisations, the family remained a powerful touchstone for women's activism.

The sixties formed a critical period of change with regard to both points. The focus of the abortion campaign shifted from often class-specific concerns about femininity and sexuality to more gender-specific concerns. This point should not be exaggerated, as class concerns persisted in the 1970s. But the principal protagonist at the heart of abortion advocacy changed from an overburdened working-class mother to a woman whose identity was more diffuse in terms of class and increasingly less clear in terms of marital status. In the 1930s and 1940s, abortion activists talked about illegal abortion as the problem of a class society, linking sexuality to class. In the 1960s, abortion activists seemed to talk of abortion more as the problem of a modern, liberal society. There was also a change in the link between femininity and abortion. After the abortion act, women's position in abortion advocacy was not as the lynchpin of the family, but as an individual. Motherhood became less important as a factor shaping gender in the abortion debate.

Adam Lent has argued that 'moderate campaign groups' like ALRA were not particularly good at promoting or achieving radical and feminist ends through their work.[6] ALRA was certainly moderate and its aims and strategy could not be mistaken for radical sex reform or feminism. Nonetheless, in other ways, Lent's argument is historically anachronistic and analytically reductive. It overlooks how difficult it was to talk about abortion and sexuality in the public sphere up to the 1970s. A critical point in this regard concerns the space of discourse. Mass public campaigns on the abortion issue were both unlikely and financially impractical before the 1970s. What was left to abortion advocates was a fairly narrow public sphere: the medical and legal profession; the 'official' sphere of Whitehall; the network of women's organisations (in particular the Labour party's women's sections); and, finally, Parliament. But it was only in the 1960s that wider social developments and better funding widened this public sphere to include Parliament and the press. In the 1970s, the defence of the 1967 Act and the burgeoning women's liberation movement prompted a mass movement for abortion on demand, played out in the streets as much as official spaces. Clare Saunders writes, in her chapter, about the evolution between pressure groups, NGOs and social movements. At least in the case of NGO work on abortion, we have to think about how the shape and size of the public sphere in which NGOs operated influenced their work and development.

Lent's argument also overlooks what strains of feminism and radicalism did exist in the work of ALRA activists. ALRA activists were not second wave feminists. But even in a climate that effectively shut down most discussion of sexuality and with a consciously moderate strategy, ALRA still managed to offer innovative visions of women's roles and sexuality. Even if, for example, the advocacy of abortion was largely situated in ideas of motherhood until the 1960s, ALRA activists managed to inscribe modern and often radical sexual ideas within a traditional category. Not least, abortion advocacy attempted to reconcile and normalise women's sexual and familial lives. Indeed, though the 1967 Abortion Act might be the most obvious result of ALRA's activism, the disruption of traditional ideas of motherhood, the family and domesticity was as enduring a legacy as legislative change. This chapter argues that we should note the discursive as well as legislative influence of NGO work.

Before 1967, two acts governed the practice of abortion in twentieth-century Britain, the 1861 Offences Against the Person Act, which made it an offence to procure an abortion in any circumstances, and the 1929 Infant Life Preservation Act, which stipulated that there were certain conditions that might justify a therapeutic abortion performed by a medical practitioner, such as nephritis, tuberculosis, cardiac disease, cancer, insanity and epilepsy, in order to save the life of the mother.[7] The day-to-day practice of abortion remained both unclear and inequitable for women. Middle-class women could usually buy a therapeutic, legal abortion from sympathetic doctors, albeit for a considerable sum and after much effort. Working-class women were left to unreliable and unsafe backstreet abortions. Both the legal and medical profession felt frustrated with the state of the law. In 1938, a distinguished gynaecologist, Aleck Bourne, challenged the law, performing a therapeutic abortion outside the usual criteria and then inviting prosecution; he was found not guilty.[8]

In the 1920s, sex-reformers and birth control groups had publicly pressed for greater access to birth control, often towards the end of helping working-class families in conditions of poverty and distress. But abortion remained an issue too far for most birth control activists, with notable exceptions such as Stella Browne and Alice Jenkins. Early in the 1930s, there were some indications of a thaw in this regard, with the Women's Cooperative Guild supporting a reform of the law. But, as abortion reformers such as Jenkins found, some mainstream feminist organisations like the National Citizens' Association literally met questions about abortion with silence.[9]

In 1936, Jenkins and other like-minded women, such as Dora Russell, Stella Browne, Janet Chance and Joan Malleson, founded the ALRA. At ALRA's first conference, speakers separated abortion from any natalist or Malthusian concerns; it was an issue that had to be considered 'quite apart from the subject of the decline of population'. Maternity was nevertheless a touchstone. Russell talked of 'creative motherhood' and Jenkins of 'voluntary parenthood', of women whose principal concern was not their own welfare, but the welfare of their families. Only one speaker, Stella Browne, saw abortion as a means towards sexual liberation. For her, the ban on abortion was 'a sexual taboo, it is the terror that women should experiment and enjoy freely, without punishment'. Whether constructing women as individuals or mothers, there was, nevertheless, a consistent, if tentative rhetoric of rights. Russell spoke of abortion as a 'right of woman'. Joan Malleson insisted that the choice for motherhood or for abortion 'must rest with the woman herself'.[10] ALRA's aims were, first of all, to foster discussion of abortion, and, with a reform of the law in mind, to encourage the introduction of 'social and economic reasons' as well as factors of mental or physical health, as justification for a therapeutic, legal abortion. An abortion would be legal in consultation with a medical practitioner, but, ultimately, it would be the decision of the woman herself.[11]

ALRA was not a mass organisation. Between the 1930s and the 1950s, it was largely run on a voluntary basis by Jenkins and funded by Chance. Though ALRA was connected to the women's sections of the Labour Party and the Women's Cooperative Guild, it was led by middle-class women. Some were professionals, like Malleson, a doctor. Others were married women who dedicated considerable time to voluntary activities (Jenkins was, for example, also a stalwart of Ealing's Anti-Litter League). Its board of honorary vice-presidents and its Medico-Legal Council were filled with members of the establishment, from the Conservative MPs Robert Boothby and Arnold Wilson to writers such as H.G. Wells and Julian Huxley to academics like Glanville Williams, reader in English Law at Cambridge.

In many ways, ALRA ably fits the description of an NGO offered in this volume. It was certainly an actor in the social and political sphere, an organisation independent from the state that sought out 'voice, consultation and influence'.[12] Ultimately, it pursued its aims in Parliament with a specific aim of legislative change. In that process, it became a different kind of organisation from the one that began in 1936, one with a small, but paid staff, with close connections to particular politicians at Westminster, a sensitive ear to the developing tool of public opinion polling, and, in 1966 and 1967, with a highly effective lobby organiser. But until the 1950s, ALRA's desires were more diffuse: to shape opinion among politicians and the Labour Party, to be sure, but also to influence the medical and legal professions, to attract the favourable attention of the media for its cause, and, at the ground-level, to provide information for ordinary people. The early efforts of ALRA were less about visiting Westminster, for example, than trekking to small halls and meeting rooms to talk with local women's organisations. Thus, the 'voice, consultation and influence' ALRA sought was at a number of different levels, and its understanding of the political or the social was not monochromatic. It was not, at the same time, a mass movement. In part, the numbers tell the story here: it remained a small organisation. But as will be further discussed below, before the 1970s, ALRA existed in a social and sexual context in which talking about abortion was restricted. That tens of thousands of women would take to the streets in the 1970s to protect the 1967 Act would have been unimaginable to the founders of ALRA, even if it was their efforts that laid the foundations for that Act and those demonstrations.

Discussing sex in the interwar period may not have been outré, but, as already suggested, abortion was not regarded as an easy issue for public discussion. A group like ALRA had, therefore, to be concerned about gaining legitimacy and respectability. It did so in two ways. The first was by girding itself in the armour of the reputations of the great and good. With the exception of the aging lothario H.G. Wells, none of its vice-presidents, council members or advisers, could be termed sex radicals. The legitimacy of ALRA was thus secured in its association with a respectable establishment. ALRA also achieved respectability by the kind of working-class women it reached. As members of Labour women's sections and Women's Cooperative Guilds, such women were, for the most part, older, married and respectable women. They too were anchors of respectability for ALRA.

The spaces that ALRA chose to pursue its aim of legal abortion were consciously circumscribed in the 1930s. There was no attempt to convert the general public, even if newspapers like the *Daily Mirror*, *News Chronicle* and *Reynolds News* were sympathetic. Instead, the work of conversion was focussed upon two areas. The first comprised the legal and medical profession. By doing so, ALRA hoped to influence legal and medical practice, including case law. In 1938, ALRA was in the background of the Bourne trial: Joan Malleson had been a critical connection between Bourne and the family of the girl in question. The work of education also focussed on Co-operative and Labour women. Though winning the Labour party to the cause of abortion was probably as likely as converting it to compulsory vegetarianism, ALRA assiduously went from women's section to women's section, trying to get Labour women to affiliate to ALRA, usually with considerable success.

In terms of spaces of advocacy, an unmissable chance to influence élite opinion came in 1937, when the government established an Interdepartmental Committee on Abortion, following disturbing statistics on maternal deaths from suspected illegal abortions. The Interdepartmental Committee chaired by Sir Norman Birkett was an opportunity to persuade influential opinion- and policy-makers within Whitehall. Dorothy Thurtle, the daughter of George Lansbury and a local London politician in her own right, was a member of the Committee. She was an ALRA sympathiser and later an ALRA vice-president.

Several points need to be stressed about ALRA's testimony to the Birkett Committee.[13] The most important is that the main protagonist in arguments made for abortion law reform in the late 1930s was the working-class mother. She was being driven to dangerous and illegal abortions by the economy and by the law. Unable to sustain a large family in a period of high male unemployment and unable to control her fertility because of poor access to legal contraception and no access to therapeutic, legal abortion, the working-class mother was faced with a disastrous prospect for her own health and the health of her family. ALRA's arguments thus put forward a particular kind of women – married, maternal and working-class – as the main object of sexual reform. This also projected a particular kind of sexuality, situated within the bounds of marriage and certainly unassociated with any ideas of sexual freedom. This was not an entirely constrictive framework. But, in terms of femininity, it is clear that abortion discourse represented women less as individuals than as mothers and wives. Motherhood was particularly important. ALRA's witnesses to the committee stressed that abortion was almost always about the economic context of family, rather than individual life: '[t]he reasons most often given for desiring abortion is the maintenance of an adequate standard of life for the family as a whole; whether this be judged financially, or in terms of health, house room, ambition in education, or general well-being'.[14] Abortion was not the choice of individuals, but 'parents who loyally serve the best interests of the family, as they see them'.[15] Stella Browne was forced, or chose to give evidence as an individual so that she could promote her quite different vision of abortion, as the handmaiden to sexual fulfilment for women as individuals. But, in general, the work of ALRA within the confines of the Interdepartmental Committee was to promote a particular kind of femininity, one that was within a longstanding context of marriage and the family, secured in motherhood.

Abortion was, in the hands of ALRA, less a means of facilitating free sexual expression than of guaranteeing sexual control. Sexuality was normalised by the work of ALRA not as central to personal fulfilment but to marital and even familial fulfilment. This is not to say that sexual pleasure was effaced, but rather than it was placed in a particular context. But to dismiss this as conservatism is a mistake. In its testimony to the committee, ALRA was also determined that there should be no differentiation of treatment between unmarried and married women, for example, and that women should not be subject to revealing their sex lives to a panel in order to get an abortion.[16]

The Majority Report of the Interdepartmental Committee came out in 1939, advocating no major extension of the right to abortion, though it did recommend reform of the existing law along the lines of the Bourne judgement, which stressed the assessment of the threat to a woman's physical or psychological health. Dorothy Thurtle's minority report supported the ALRA case for reform. She thought abortion should be justified in cases of rape and for women with more than four children, thus in terms of social or economic context. In 1940, Thurtle expanded her arguments into a small book, *Abortion: Right or Wrong?* In this, abortion was seen first and foremost as a question of class difference:

> There is no doubt at all that for many years operations have been performed on wealthy women for reasons of slight ill-health, and even for quite frivolous reasons. No working woman would have been able to secure the same treatment for similar reasons.

In the circumstances of 'such glaring inequalities in treatment between those women who can afford to pay for an illegal abortion ... the average woman', 'social justice' demanded 'equal facilities and treatment'.[17] But Thurtle also tried to normalise sexual activity and pleasure (albeit within marriage). This was placed in the context of a liberal modernity that excluded working-class people:

> Modern women are learning that their sex life is as important to them as to their husbands, and is not something about which to be furtive or ashamed. They know, further, that it need not be synonymous with child-bearing, and in consequence many married lives are enriched, and are fuller than those of earlier generations. Knowledge of modern scientific methods of birth control has made a significant contribution to marital happiness and mutual understanding. There are still too many women, however, who are unable

to protect themselves against unwanted pregnancies, and who consequently feel bitterly at times towards their husbands. These are the women, frequently ill-nourished, exhausted and sick, who carry the burden that their wealthier sisters refuse to carry.[18]

Without equal access to contraception and safe abortion, working-class women were, therefore, consigned to a dark age of sexual danger and anxiety.

The exclusion of working-class women from an increasingly liberal age of sexual modernity was restated in the 1947 ALRA pamphlet *Back-Street Surgery*. Janet Chance emphasised that the abortion question was about unequal access between women of different classes. In this, family life was paramount. Working-class women were not thinking of themselves, but their existing children, when they sought out abortions. They were being good mothers and responsible citizens in refusing motherhood: '... no responsible woman will wait for any golden future to find the life she wants for her children to-day. No; she would take steps to limit her family and show herself in so doing no criminal but a responsible mother and a praiseworthy citizen, if the law allowed her.'[19] In this, there was a clear argument for greater female power with respect to the law, even if it was in relationship to both the medical profession and marriage:

Who is best fitted to decide whether the pay-packet can stand another mouth to feed? The men who wrote down this law in 1861? The lawyers at the Old Bailey who wouldn't know the family if they met it in the street? The doctor who gives a few hours of his whole life to the consideration of the household? What nonsense! The father and mother in serious consultation with a doctor should have a say in managing their own pay-packet and the size of the family it will best support.[20]

The Second World War disrupted ALRA's work. In 1944, it resumed activity, attempting to rebuild its links to the women's sections of the Labour party. ALRA also looked for particular opportunities, such as the Royal Commission on Population, as means of promoting the cause of abortion law reform. In 1944, for example, ALRA wrote to the East Ham Women's Section of the Labour Party encouraging them to discuss the Royal Commission on Population and, further, to nominate possible delegates 'to represent working class mothers on the Committee'.[21] Once again, the abortion issue was identified with a particular figure, the working-class mother, and a particular sexual context, the working-class family. For a time, the organisation also remained committed to influencing case law.[22]

Early in the 1950s, ALRA began to change its thinking about strategy. The catalyst in the matter was Douglas Houghton, a Labour MP and the husband of Vera Houghton, who was the Secretary of the International Committee on Planned Parenthood and had become involved with ALRA in the late 1940s. In November 1952, he told Alice Jenkins that 'the Labour Party have asked for subjects for Private Member's Bills and that he intended to suggest Abortion Law Reform'.[23] ALRA quickly organised a meeting with Labour MPs early in 1953 and presented the case for a bill to make therapeutic, legal abortion possible 'for the "physical or mental health" of the women, or when "it appears medically or socially desirable either in her own interest or in that of the community that she shall not give birth to a child"'.[24] Ultimately, it was left to another Labour MP, Joseph Reeves, to present a bill. There was little support for the bill in the House and little interest shown in the meeting of Labour MPs with ALRA.[25] It was talked out on 27 February 1953, with only five minutes given to it. Nonetheless, Janet Chance felt that the commitment to a parliamentary strategy had reinvigorated the cause, noting to Alice Jenkins, 'I feel we have made a very definite move forward.'[26] Chance was not to see the further progress of the cause, dying in 1953.

The Reeves bill was perhaps not the most auspicious beginning to a parliamentary campaign that culminated in the 1967 Act, but it was a beginning. After that, there was a bill put to the House of Lords in 1954 by the Labour peer, Lord Amulree.[27] In 1955, ALRA tried to assess its support in parliament, and particularly within the Labour party. The sympathetic MP Kenneth Robinson warned that there were many difficulties 'chief being the obscurantist attitudes of many MPs which was very strong. Prejudice, ignorance, and fear were formidable obstacles.' A particular point of interest for ALRA was the attitude of female MPs. But both Robinson and Houghton were discouraging about relying upon female MPs to support abortion reform; the former said 'only a few' were interested, the latter counseled that it was 'not wise to concentrate on women MPs'.[28] Indeed, of the twenty-seven female Labour MPs sitting in the House between 1945 and 1964, only a handful ever expressed support or interest in the question. The lack of political support for abortion was abundantly clear in the 1950s.

What also might be suggested about the fifties is that the staple protagonist of abortion advocacy – the overburdened working-class mother – was beginning to have less purchase. The perceived position of working class women had changed. From the image of the afflicted working class mother of the 1920s and 1930s, there was instead the image of a 'modernised' working class housewife, able to control her body through contraception, limit the number of births and even take on part-time work.[29] At the same time, the welfare state and full employment had addressed the crisis of the male breadwinner so obvious in 1930s discussions of birth control and abortion. This did not diminish arguments for abortion within the circles of ALRA, but it did shift the focus to other bases for argument, such as women's health or women's rights. But what was lacking was a mobilising issue or development: as the overburdened working-class mother lost her emotive power, the class aspect of the issue also began to become more diffuse.

Ironically, the major publication by a member of ALRA, Alice Jenkins' *Law for the Rich* (1960), was very much a restatement of an older message. As her title suggested, Jenkins played up the class aspects of the problem. As a sexual issue, abortion revealed the class-divide in British society. She also stressed that abortion reform was most important in terms of women's maternal roles: it strengthen the position of the 'respectable mother'. Sexual freedom outside of marriage was not considered: '[c]onscientious mothers are disturbed by the possibility that reformed law may lead to immorality ... in recognising and assessing a risk of immorality one must remember that the principal beneficiary under new law would be the decent mother of a family who has as many children as she can cope with'.[30] Though advocates like Jenkins eschewed strict sexual codes and proscription, they did not depart, in public writing about abortion, from promoting an ethos of sexual restraint, especially for a younger generation.[31] There was no advocate such as Stella Browne (who died in 1957) to connect abortion with female emancipation or a more radical sexual politics of the body. Instead, work such as that of Jenkins made it a centerpiece of respectable sexual practice – perhaps this was not radical, but it did at least connect sexual practice with respectability.

In the early 1960s, ALRA underwent a significant metamorphosis. The organisation saw the passing of one generation and the accession of another. In 1963, Douglas Houghton became chair and Diane Munday, Vice-Chair. Munday was joined in the day-to-day running of ALRA by Madeline Simms, who worked with the Fabian Society. Munday and Simms were a Jenkins and Chance for a more modern age – very much the models of a new generation of NGO activists – representative, according to Simms' account, of the new blood in the organisation: 'in their thirties and either had young children or were newly married'.[32] It is also important to acknowledge that it was personal experience that had inspired Munday's involvement with the abortion issue. She had had an abortion herself, not as a working-class woman, but as a middle-class woman. This had been a horrific and humiliating experience:

> Diane Munday was then thirty-two, married with three sons. Each pregnancy had been a nightmare, and in each case child-birth had been followed by increasingly depressive illness. When birth-control failed and she became pregnant for the fourth time, she became desperate. Both physically and emotionally she felt she had reached her limit. Her doctor was sympathetic and referred her to a supposedly liberal London hospital, where the psychiatrist firmly rejected her request for an abortion. She considered he had treated her like a subnormal child who could not be expected to make any decisions for herself. After making panic-stricken inquiries she found her way to Harley Street, where her abortion was carried out privately and satisfactorily.[33]

In this way, Munday's experience was one of the perils of middle-class sexuality, of a middle-class woman at the mercy of the medical profession. In the early 1960s, the message about abortion became less connected with working-class sexuality and associated with the more general problems of female sexuality and women's status.

What we know of the membership of ALRA in the 1960s suggests that its middle-class composition may have increased. A membership survey in the mid-1960s showed that doctors, family planning workers and teachers formed a substantial minority of ALRA supporters. Much less evident in the ALRA of the 1960s were the longstanding connections to working-class organisations. Organisationally, ALRA also enjoyed a new infusion of funds. It was in receipt of substantial funding from the American Hopkins Funds Board, to the tune of about $US2000 a year, leaving ALRA with an annual budget of about £7000 by the time of the Abortion Act of 1967. Much of this money was spent on opinion polling.

What also spurred on the momentum of the abortion reform campaign was the sense that it had become a 'fashionable' issue, 'the next big sociological reform to be tackled by Parliament', the '"home affairs" topic of the year'.[34] Such confidence was fed by (unsuccessful) private members' bills in the Commons and Lords by Renée Short and Lord Silkin and by increased public attention to the question by the media, including a series on abortion in the *Observer* by Paul Ferris, a special television investigation by ATV, and even an abortion episode on 'Dr Finley's Casebook'.

In terms of the general climate surrounding abortion in Britain in the early 1960s, it is important to note several developments. First of all, the issue was much less coloured by concerns about working-class sexuality and reproduction. This is not to say that this question had disappeared, but the way that the issue tended to be portrayed was as an anomalous dark corner of an increasingly bright and glossy modern, liberal society. In the brave new wave of British film, including *Saturday Night and Sunday Morning* and *Alfie*, abortion was identified with sordid, back-street operations, a kind of Dickensian afterlife in modern Britain. Paul Ferris' series of articles, which became a book, *The Nameless*, turned on the hypocrisy, untruths, greed and despera-tion that underpinned the practice of abortion in Britain, whether in the backstreets or Harley Street: '[e]veryday the phones ring, the curtains are drawn, the lies are told, the money changes hands, the women breathe again'.[35] There were forces undoing this situation: the growing acceptance of abortion among doctors and, not least, the ubiquity of the experience wrought by the actions of women them-selves. The choice, it seemed for Ferris, was between accepting a modern world, in which abortion might be an affordable service, divorced from lies and hypocrisy, and staying in a 'barbaric' state.[36]

There were also immediate health issues which made abortion law reform an urgent concern. Health concerns for both mother and foetus were the most important. Reports into Maternal Deaths in England and Wales between 1952 and 1966 showed that by the mid-1960s unsafe abortion was the leading cause of avoidable maternal death. Highlighted by media reports of the horror of backstreet abortions, these long-term statistics undoubtedly did much to advance the cause of legal and safe abortion. A more immediately shocking health controversy in the early 1960s also did much to encourage public support for legal abortion. In the spring of 1961, there surfaced reports of badly deformed children born to mothers who had taken the sedative Thalidomide. By 1964, 349 children had been born in Britain with serious deformities. International cases such as those of Sherry Finkbine in the United States and Suzanne Vandeput in Belgium underlined the heartrending moral choices facing women with such deformed children. In July 1962, a National Opinion Poll showed that 72 per cent in Britain agreed with legal abortion if there was good reason to suspect a deformity in the foetus. The threat of foetal abnormality became one of the touchstones of the abortion debate in the mid-1960s; indeed, *Abortion Law Reformed*, the 'official' ALRA account of the Abortion Act, came with the dedication, 'to the thalidomide mothers for whom reform came too late'.[37]

Between the late 1930s and the early 1960s, the spaces of abortion activism had been limited largely to the backrooms of Whitehall and the meeting-rooms of local Labour parties. In the 1950s, this space had widened somewhat to the Commons. In the mid-1960s, it widened even further. The Commons and the Lords were the main fora for ALRA's work, but the revamped organisation also did a lot of work to court the press and public, using opinion polls. It also established a network of local groups in Birmingham, North West and South East London, Manchester and Bristol to link up with local newspapers.

What did ALRA say about abortion and sexuality in the 1960s? In the 1930s, as already discussed, the main focus had been the working-class mother, a focus that highlighted the differential access to legal abortion between classes. In the 1960s, at least in the work of ALRA, the link between class, sexuality and gender became less obvious, even if such arguments had not disappeared. In 1966, for example, ALRA published *In Desperation: Letters Sent to the Abortion Law Association*; four of the ten letters were from working-class mothers with too many children.[38] The so-called 'social clause' of the organisation's aims, added in 1966, to make abortion legal 'when the pregnant woman's capacity as a mother will be severely overstrained' also echoed arguments about working-class sexuality from the 1930s.[39]

Class persisted in the representation of abortion, but there is no question that this was becoming gradually more muted. We can also see other strains being worked into the argument for the reform of the law. First of all, there was a sense that the difficult access to abortion not only revealed differences between the classes, but also exploited women and forced them either into humiliation (as had been the case with Diane Munday) or into criminal behaviour. The latter was a point made, for example, by Lena Jeger, ALRA's vice-president, in her column for the *Guardian*.[40] Abortion was increasingly a question of women's rights generally, rather than working-class women's rights. Those rights were not always placed outside the traditional context of sexual life – marriage and the family – but it was still a question of rights. This emphasis upon rights was also increasingly reflected within the membership. There were a number of comments made about the distance between elements of the membership who believed abortion to be 'the inalienable right of a woman and her husband and her doctor to make this kind of decision for themselves, asserting that this is an area of private life in which, in a democratic society, the aim of the law has no right to reach' and a leadership willing to make compromises.[41] In other words, abortion law reform was moving from the rights of working-class women to the rights of women generally, and from an argument about class society and the family to one about privacy and individual rights.

In 1966, ALRA took up, for the first time, a commitment to a 'social clause', meaning that a woman could justify an abortion on for 'social' reasons, rather than as a threat to physical or mental health.[42] Obviously, this might be seen as bringing together both an older rhetoric about class and a newer rhetoric about women's rights, albeit within the context of family life. In other words, two different kinds of protagonists – the working-class mother and the middle-class professional woman or mother could be brought together in the same frame. This is why ALRA felt so strongly about the exclusion of the 'social clause' from David Steel's bill in 1966–7.[43]

There is no time in this chapter to discuss ALRA's considerable involvement with David Steel in drafting his abortion bill in 1966 and the crucial role it played in mobilising both parliamentary, medical and public opinion.[44] Briefly reviewing the debate on second reading of Steel's bill in July 1966 nonetheless does reflect some of the arguments that ALRA had put into the public sphere. This featured both older arguments for abortion and newer ones centring upon the question of the 'modern' against the 'outmoded' and how this affected women. At this point, it should be noted that the bill included a social clause. Introducing his bill, Steel remarked that in addition to the other confusions and inequities surrounding the bill, the issue of class difference stood out: '[a]ny law which means one law for the rich and another for the poor is in itself unsatisfactory'.[45] The social clause of the bill also gathered round it arguments for abortion law reform that were echoes of the interwar campaigns. John Dunwoody, a doctor and Labour member for Falmouth and Camborne in Cornwall, evoked the maternalist arguments for abortion when he stated that access to legal therapeutic abortion would help 'mothers with large families ... with low incomes ... broken down physically and emotionally' to play a fuller maternal role in 'building and maintaining the family unit'.[46] Others, like David Owen, then member for Plymouth, saw the question as the consequence of the modernisation of society and science: 'a progressive and inevitable outcome of modern medicine'.[47] There was also considerable talk of the problem of 'defective' births. Perhaps the most moving speech was by Edward Lyons, a Labour MP for Bradford East, who spoke from the experience of his wife. Told the foetus she was carrying was likely afflicted by the rubella virus, she had great difficulty in finding a legal abortion. Eventually she and her husband did succeed.[48] The Home Secretary, Roy Jenkins, made an important contribution to the debate. While emphasising that the Government's position was one of 'neutrality', he also made clear that he saw the State of the current abortion law as 'a major social problem'. In particular, he acknowledged the need to help those 'many women who are far from anxious to escape the responsibilities of motherhood, but rather wish to discharge their existing ones more effectively'. Jenkins avoided going into the social, economic or feminist aspects of the question, but did paint the existing law as 'harsh and archaic', one that forced 'law abiding citizens' to become criminals.[49] It is notable that no voice was raised in a feminist argument for abortion law reform. Indeed, Steel made it clear that he and other supporters of the bill had no intention of opening the way for abortion on demand.[50] When the vote was taken, Steel's bill was passed 223 to 49.

The passing of the Abortion Act in 1967 created a different space for the discussion of abortion, in which the question was about the extension or contraction of an existing law. It also created a different kind of NGO politics, in which anti-abortion groups were much better organised than they had been before the Act. Lent is right to suggest the Abortion Act was the culmination of decades of a particular kind of pressure group advocacy even if he is overly reductive about that advocacy. In this case, sexual reform grew out of concerns about working-class sexuality, about the normalisation of sexuality within marriage, and, not least, about shoring up women's rights as mothers. ALRA's role was not simply to pursue an unpopular cause, but to help produce particular ideas about gender and sexuality in the public sphere. Even if we do not see this as radical or feminist, in the absence of any other public rhetoric about sexuality, the organisation did highlight a particular sexual problem (of working-class sexuality) and redefined motherhood as a site of sexuality. It was another generation, and, indeed other NGOs like the National Abortion Campaign, that widened the abortion debate to emphasise a different framework, in which abortion signalled the rights of women as individuals, not simply mothers or wives, and opened up the possibility of a much more radical agenda of sexual freedom.

Notes

1 Quoted in Anne Phillips, *Divided Loyalties* (London: Virago, 1987), p. 110.
2 Labour Party, *Women, Sexism and Socialism* (London: Labour Party, 1981), p. 11.
3 Angela Phillips, Dorothy Jones and Pat Kahn, 'Abortion, Feminism and Sexuality', *Socialist Woman*, 6 (1978), p. 3.
4 Memo presented to the ICSDW Bureau Meeting, Madrid, October 1977: National Labour Women's Advisory Committee, 'Contraception and Abortion', International Institute of Social History, Amsterdam [hereafter IISH], Socialist International Women Papers [hereafter SIWP], p. 95.
5 Recent work by Matt Houlbrook has argued that the campaign for the decriminalisation of homosexuality produced a particular kind of identity for same sex sexuality. Matt Houlbrook, *Queer London* (Chicago: University of Chicago Press, 2004).
6 Adam Lent, *British Social Movements Since 1945* (London: Palgrave, 2001), pp. 8, 56.
7 On abortion in twentieth-century Britain, see Barbara Brookes, *Abortion in England 1900–1967* (London: Croom Helm, 1988); Keith Hindell and Madeleine Simms, *Abortion Law Reformed* (London: Peter Owen, 1971); Kate Fisher, *Birth Control, Sex, and Marriage in Britain 1918–1960* (Oxford: Oxford University Press, 2006).
8 See Stephen Brooke, '"A New World For Women?" Abortion Law Reform in Britain during the 1930s', *American Historical Review*, 106 (2001), pp. 450–1.
9 See Alice Jenkins, *Law for the Rich* (London: Gollancz, 1960), p. 23.
10 *ALRA Conference 1936*, 15 May 1936, pp. 9, 20, 28, IISH, Dora Russell Papers [hereafter DRP], 344.
11 See Jenkins, Appendix 3, p. 92.
12 See Introduction to this volume.
13 For a longer discussion of this, see Brooke 'A New World for Women'?.
14 Interdepartmental Committee on Abortion, Abortion Law Reform Association, Memorandum, AC Paper, No. 13, 1937, National Archives Kew [hereafter NA], Ministry of Health [hereafter MH] 71/21.
15 Abortion Law Reform Association, Memorandum, AC Paper, No. 13.
16 See Jenkins, Appendix 3, pp. 92–3.
17 Dorothy Thurtle, *Abortion: Right or Wrong?* (London: T. Werner Laurie, 1940), pp. 20, 22, 27.
18 Thurtle, p. 32.
19 Janet Chance, 'Back-Street Surgery', in Maud Ryan, Margot Edgecombe and Janet Chance, *Back-Street Surgery* (Freefolk, Hale, Fordingbridge, Hants: Abortion Law Reform Association, 1947), p. 14.
20 Chance, p. 17.
21 East Ham South Women's Section, Minute Books, 25 January 1944, 29 February 1944, London Metropolitan Archives, Islington, London [hereafter LMA], ACC 2417/H/35.
22 ALRA Private Conference, 23 March 1949, Contemporary Medical Archives [hereafter CMA], Abortion Law Reform Association Papers [hereafter ALRA], SA/ALR/A.3/1/8.

23   Alice Jenkins to Janet Chance, 7 November 1952, CMA, Janet Chance Papers, SA/ALR/A.17/6/5.
24   Statement [MPs meeting], 1952, CMA, ALRA, SA/ALR/A.17/12/3.
25   See Abortion Bill meeting, 24 February 1953, CMA, ALRA, SA/ALR/A.3/2/18.
26   Janet Chance to Alice Jenkins, no date [1953], CMA, ALRA, SA/ALR/A.3/2/3.
27   See *Parliamentary Debates* (Lords), 26 January 1954, c. 411.
28   Public meeting after Annual Meeting of ALRA, 26 November 1955, CMA, ALRA, SA/ALR/A.3/4/77.
29   See Stephen Brooke, 'Bodies, Sexuality and the "Modernization" of the British Working Classes', *International Labour and Working Class History* 69 (June 2006), pp. 118–38 and Stephen Brooke, 'Gender and Working Class Identity in Britain during the 1950s', *Journal of Social History* 34 (2001), pp. 773–95.
30   Jenkins, pp. 40, 41.
31   Jenkins, pp. 41–2.
32   Hindell and Simms, p. 112.
33   Hindell and Simms, p. 113.
34   ALRA, *Newsletter*, 14 (Spring 1966), CMA, ALRA, SA/ALR/A.11/3/12; Annual report, 1964–5, p. 19, CMA, ALRA, SA/ALR/A /1/3/21; Annual Report 1965–6, p. 8, CMA, ALRA, SA/ALR/A1/3/22.
35   Paul Ferris, *The Nameless: Abortion in Britain Today* (London: Hutchinson, 1966), p. 169.
36   Ferris, p. 169.
37   See Hindell and Simms.
38   ALRA (1966), *In Desperation: Letters Sent to the Abortion Law Reform Association* (London: ALRA), CMA, ALRA, SA/ALR/A.11/3/15.
39   ALRA, *Newsletter*, 17 (Winter 1966), CMA, ALRA, SA/ALR/A.11/3/15.
40   Lena Jeger, 'Law That Fails', *Guardian*, 24 November 1964.
41   Judith Cook, 'Interest to Procure', *New Statesman*, 13 November 1964.
42   Hindell and Simms, p. 174.
43   See Vera Houghton to David Steel, 30 January 1967 CMA, David Steel Papers, SA/ALR/A.15/5; Vera Houghton to Silkin, 22 December 1966, CMA, Lord Silkin Papers, SA/ALR/A.16/4.
44   See Hindell and Simms, *Abortion Law Reformed*; Michael Kandiah and Gillian Staerck (editors), *The Abortion Act 1967: ICBH Witness Seminar* (London: Institute of Historical Research/Institute of Contemporary British History, 2002).
45   *Parliamentary Debates* (Commons), 732, 22 July 1966, c. 1071.
46   *Parliamentary Debates* (Commons), 732, 22 July 1966, c. 1098.
47   *Parliamentary Debates* (Commons), 732, 22 July 1966, c. 1114.
48   *Parliamentary Debates* (Commons), 732, 22 July 1966, c. 1090.
49   *Parliamentary Debates* (Commons), 732, 22 July 1966, cs. 1140–2, 1144.
50   *Parliamentary Debates* (Commons), 732, 22 July 1966, c. 1075.

5
Lesbian, Gay and Bisexual NGOs in Britain: Past, Present and Future

Matthew Waites

Non-governmental organisations (NGOs) have been crucial in the lesbian, gay, and bisexual (LGB) politics of sexuality and gender which has achieved profound political, social and cultural transformations in recent decades. Because lesbian, gay and bisexual issues have so often been regarded as beyond the appropriate scope of party politics, 'issues of conscience' without a left/right alignment, national LGB NGOs have filled gaps left by political parties. The study of NGOs should therefore address LGB organisations because research on these reveals the distinctive importance of NGOs in particular contexts, such as the field of sexuality and gender politics. Analysis of the very wide spectrum of forms of LGB NGOs which have existed, from the moderate and elitist to the radical and participatory, can also illuminate broader debates over the nature and form of NGOs. This chapter will demonstrate that such analysis can help us examine the issues of how and to what extent NGOs should be 'democratic'.

Research in gender and sexuality studies, especially on lesbian, gay bisexual and transgender politics, particularly needs to focus on NGOs. Typically scholars concentrate on analysing and conceptualising Lesbian, Gay, Bisexual and Transgender (LGBT) 'social movements' in relation to social movement or citizenship theories, rarely making NGOs their central object of study.[1] Social analysis of underlying dynamics generating social movements, or the structures of citizenship, is illuminating, but alongside such work, analysis of LGB NGOs is also needed.

This chapter provides a brief history of key LGB NGOs in the United Kingdom since the 1950s, intended to compliment broader accounts of LGB post-war history and movements.[2] From a perspective critical of the privileging of heterosexuality, the chapter chronologically

discusses those LGB organisations which have had a political campaigning focus covering England, Scotland, Wales, Northern Ireland, or
the entire UK – or had a profound national impact (service provision
and social dimensions of NGOs are less discussed). The account makes
clear where possible whether organisations have been 'homosexual',
'lesbian', 'gay' and/or 'bisexual'. Transgender organisations have usually
been distinct; a history of these and their relation to LGB organisations
is beyond the scope of the chapter. The chapter proceeds through discussion of differences between organisations, with reference to debates
over radical democracy as a response to diversity in political theory, and
the 'sexual citizenship' debate.[3] A new era for LGBT politics has dawned
with the achievement of most legal equalities and the formation of the
Commission for Equality and Human Rights in 2007; and I suggest that
in this light, leading LGB NGOs need to engage in further dialogue and
change to respond.

The emergence of homosexual organisations

The *Wolfenden Report* published in 1957 advocated the partial decriminalisation of male homosexuality in England and Wales for men over 21,
and was the catalyst for the formation of the first national organisation
seeking to improve the political situation of homosexuals.[4] The Homosexual Law Reform Society (HLRS) was formed in England in 1958
to campaign for implementation of the *Wolfenden Report*'s recommendations, conceived as management of a social problem; hence
the Society was not openly 'for' or led by homosexuals. The situation contrasted with the USA, where various homophile organisations
with social functions existed from earlier in the 1950s (the Matta-
chine Society, ONE and the Daughters of Bilitis);[5] with the existence
of the Arcadie social organisation in France from 1947;[6] and with
emergent social organisations in Norway and Sweden from the late
1940s.[7]

   The development of the Homosexual Law Reform Society has been
documented by Antony Grey, secretary from 1962.[8] Grey's account
conveys the profoundly constrained circumstances in which the organisation operated, yet that it nevertheless became a resource for hope.
From London offices the HLRS played a crucial role in the ten year
post-Wolfenden struggle for the partial decriminalisation which eventually occurred in England and Wales via the Sexual Offences Act 1967.
It became, according to Weeks, 'a secretariat to the parliamentary
reformers', while also advancing a utilitarian pragmatist case for reform

in public debates, without arguing for the morality of homosexuality or 'equality'.[9]

Central to the ethos of the Homosexual Law Reform Society was a quest for respectability to legitimise decriminalisation. The Society's strategy focussed on lobbying political elites and organising public meetings to shift opinion; it was led by figures with establishment status or professional credibility such as the first chairman, surgeon and sexologist Kenneth Walker. There was no attempt to create a mass membership organisation, and the HLRS even opposed moves after decriminalisation to create male homosexual social clubs, which it feared would jeopardise public support. Hence the Homosexual Law Reform Society soon ceased to exist; it evolved into the Albany Trust, providing psychological support, and the Sexual Law Reform Society, lobbying on various sex laws.

According to Grey 'the first openly homophile group to be started in Britain was for women'.[10] From a monthly lesbian magazine *Arena Three*, launched in March 1964, quickly emerged the lesbian Minorities Research Group, to encourage research; and also a social group *A3*. Esmé Langley led these developments. Other lesbian social groups such as Kenric and Sappho, which became larger and longer lasting, soon followed. These were also facilitated by the legal status of lesbianism which contrasted with that of male homosexuality. Only after 1967 did public social and political organisations explicitly *for* male homosexuals begin to form.

The first organisation to campaign for homosexuals in Scotland was the Scottish Minorities Group (SMG), formed in 1969. This was created and led by Ian Dunn, influenced by knowing Antony Grey and the HLRS.[11] The first aim of the group was 'to promote the complete legal and social equality of homosexuals and heterosexuals'.[12] Despite the exclusion of Scotland from the Sexual Offences Act 1967, by 1971 the SMG had groups in various cities and over 200 members. From 1978 it became the Scottish Homosexual Rights Group, and focussed on achieving the partial decriminalisation of male homosexuality, achieved in 1980.[13] On political strategy Dunn commented in 1988:

> SMG tried to rework the best of Scottish radicalism and deliberately did not push ahead with an all-out attack on capitalism and society, in the way that the Gay Liberation Front tried to do. [...] The reformist outlook was characteristic of SMG. [...] We were by far and away the most radical thing happening on the personal-is-political

front in Scotland at that juncture and what we were saying and doing was astonishing in the eyes of the Scottish establishment.[14]

Grey has commented on 'the canny leadership of Ian Dunn and others who made the group ... an effective force, at once radical and level-headed, with constructive links to many facets of the Scottish establishment'.[15] The organisation subsequently became known as Outright Scotland, and from the mid-1990s worked to influence devolution and the new Scottish Parliament and Scottish Executive.[16] However since the 1990s other organisations, particularly the Equality Network, Stonewall Scotland and LGBT Youth Scotland, have come to the fore. Other organisations in Scotland have included Scottish Lesbian Feminists, created in 1975.

In England, developing from the HLRS, the North-Western Homosexual Law Reform Committee was formed in 1964, with Allan Horsfall prominent. This developed into the Committee for Homosexual Equality (later Campaign for Homosexual Equality, CHE), which emerged as a key organisation for England and Wales with Horsfall first as secretary, later chair and then president.[17] CHE differed from the HLRS in seeking, after decriminalisation, to establish gay social clubs – 'Esquire Clubs Ltd' – which Antony Grey and others feared likely to antagonise opponents. In this respect CHE drew on the example of the Dutch homosexual organisation COC. The HLRS, and its associated counselling charity the Albany Trust, disassociated themselves from such moves. In light of this and financial tensions over competition for members, relations with CHE 'slipped from the tepid to the frigid, and afterwards remained at arms length'.[18] By supporting social clubs CHE became 'the cutting edge of gay rights in England in 1970', with active groups in many cities.[19] But despite CHE being the first mass membership LGB NGO, sending a newsletter and focussing lobbying, forms of participation remained limited.

Gay liberationism and its impact

The situation was transformed by the emergence of Gay Liberation Front (GLF) from 1970, practising a dramatically different form of politics. To describe GLF as an 'organisation' might be misleading, given the way it drew on the sixties counterculture and radical movements of 1968 by developing consciousness-raising groups and spontaneous activism. Emerging in the international context of the Stonewall riots in New York during 1969, marking the emergence of gay liberationism in the United States,[20] Gay Liberation Front was the first UK organisation to publicly assert claims for both equality and liberation – notably in the GLF Manifesto of 1971.[21] The definitive history has been written by Lisa Power, using oral histories; drawing on GLF archives I have also elsewhere discussed GLF's objectives and strategies.[22]

UK GLF began meeting from October 1970 at the London School of Economics, involving students and academics among others. However it survived only until 1973 due to various splits in relation to Marxism, Maoism, feminism, and gender identities. Importantly the 'radical faeries' and practices of radical drag placed a politics of gender identity at the heart of GLF, whereas subsequent mainstream 'lesbian and gay' organisations tended to distinguish themselves from transvestite, transsexual and (later) transgender concerns.

GLF was distinctive for its loose organisational structure, with a strong ethos of participatory democracy, much debate and dispute. At the first GLF 'think-in', 'there was a very clear decision by the mass of people present to reject the rigid membership structures and organisation favoured by those traditional gay activists present'.[23] Controversy emerged, for example, over leading figures on the Steering Committee and the relationship of thematic working groups to GLF as a whole. The general picture which emerges from archives and existing histories is of an explosion of energy associated with the repudiation of institutional forms, leaving mixed verdicts among former participants about the desirability of 'organisations' for political change.

More mainstream homosexual organisations were influenced by GLF to reorganise and become more assertive and active. The National Federation of Homophile Organisations was formed at a conference in 1971, with 'the objects of providing a forum for the discussion of the problems of homophile men and women in Great Britain and Northern Ireland ...'.[24] However it was short-lived, and CHE became more prominent as a national body. CHE became less politically restrained, but only from 1974 did it campaign for an equal age of consent at 16, as GLF had. The organisation lobbied MPs on this during the 1974 general election campaign. However CHE's draft Sexual Offences Bill proposing equality, published in 1975 jointly with the SMG and the Union for Sexual Freedoms in Ireland, failed to win support from the new Labour government.[25] In terms of institutional character, CHE had a reputation for being 'too rigidly structured', in stark contrast to GLF.[26] Membership declined from 5,000 to 3,000–4,000 in the late 1970s, partly attributable to other gay rights groups emerging. There were resignations from the executive and bankruptcy loomed, leading the organisation to become a 'slimmed-down campaigning group'.[27] This set a pattern to be followed later by Stonewall.

In Northern Ireland the first gay rights campaigning organisation was the Campaign for Homosexual Law Reform, created in 1974, replaced by the Northern Ireland Gay Rights Association (NIGRA) in 1975. These organisations focussed heavily upon achieving extension of the partial decriminalisation of male homosexuality, eventually achieved in 1982.[28] NIGRA continues to exist, but currently a key organisation is the Coalition on Sexual Orientation (COSO), which emerged to represent LGBT groups after the Belfast Agreement and Northern Ireland Act 1998.

Stonewall, Outrage! and the Equality Alliance Experiment

After the election of a Conservative government led by Margaret Thatcher in 1979, organisations seeking sexual equality struggled to make an impact. From the mid-1980s AIDS led to a growth of anger and political consciousness in LGB communities. The radical AIDS organisation ACT UP (AIDS Coalition to Unleash Power) emerged in the United States in 1987, and a 'chapter' appeared in London from 1989.[29] However, what most focussed resistance was 'Section 28' of the Local Government Act 1988, legislation passed by the Thatcher government which prohibited local authorities funding activities which would 'intentionally promote homosexuality' or 'teaching ... the acceptability of homosexuality as a pretended family relationship'.[30] After CHE's decline, attempts to reinvigorate campaigning initially led to the founding of the Organisation for Lesbian and Gay Action (OLGA).[31] From the brief disorganisation of OLGA emerged two very different organisations: the lobby group Stonewall and the radical activist group Outrage!

Stonewall, named after the Stonewall riots, was formed in 1989 by a group including several public figures from the arts, such as actors Ian McKellan and Michael Cashman, not previously at the heart of radical LGBT activist networks (although some were, notably Lisa Power of Lesbian and Gay Switchboard and the International Lesbian and Gay Association). According to Angela Mason, not initially involved but Executive Director of Stonewall 1992–2002, Stonewall 'was set up in 1989 as a professional lobby group, trying to construct a civil rights agenda'.[32] Mason's appointment was interesting, since she had previously been a radical figure in GLF, as Angie Weir;[33] her later OBE and move to become Director of the New Labour government's Women and Equality Unit 2002–2007, overseeing same-sex civil partnerships and a discrimination law review, was indicative of Stonewall's success and influence.

From small beginnings the London-based organisation has grown and can claim considerable credit for focussing lobbying and winning equality reforms,[34] including the inclusion of 'sexual orientation' in the Equality Act 2006, forming the basis of the new Commission for Equality and Human Rights from October 2007.

Initially a 'lesbian and gay' organisation in the 1990s, Stonewall eventually shifted into line with broader trends to include bisexuals; I have argued elsewhere that the initial omission of bisexuality influenced endorsement of medical knowledge-claims emphasising the fixity of sexual identities.[35] Stonewall has also shifted from being a primarily English organisation, by developing Stonewall Scotland from 2000, and Stonewall Cymru in Wales from 2002, echoing devolution. LGB Forum Cymru was established in Wales in 2002 through joint funding from the National Assembly of Wales and Stonewall; it changed its name to Stonewall Cymru to obtain greater resources from Stonewall.[36]

Stonewall has become increasingly involved in conducting research, including that commissioned and funded by government.[37] This suggests Stonewall has become regarded as a crucial arbiter of expertise, fulfiling some functions similar to the Disability Rights Commission, Equal Opportunities Commission and Commission for Racial Equality, prior to their recent merger. However, despite some research highlighting Stonewall's central role in mainstream debates, especially over the age of consent,[38] there has been limited recent research on Stonewall, especially from within the discipline of politics.

Lisa Power has commented that, after OLGA, Stonewall 'was set up as a defensive structure, to stop it from being taken over by the straight left, which was what kept happening'.[39] Yet as Lucas notes, reflecting views from Outrage!, 'there was suspicion from other sectors of the gay community who believed that the group was giving itself airs and graces, and that it was being run by political hacks and media-hungry celebrities. There was also resentment that Stonewall was completely unaccountable, yet could claim to speak for lesbians and gay men'.[40] In the aftermath of apparent failures of pure participatory democracy in GLF and OLGA, Stonewall emerged in a climate of pragmatism, adopting other NGOs rather than political parties as models to justify a lack of a membership structure and formal democratic procedures.

Stonewall took its form as a lobbying organisation as a strategy to engage with the inhospitable context of the Conservative government. In its public statements it was scrupulously non-aligned in relation to political parties, and it sought to work with LGB groupings in all parties including the Tory Campaign for Homosexual Equality (TORCHE). This political neutrality, preserved in the face of readily apparent discrepancies in party policies on LGB issues, was sometimes subject to criticism during the years of Conservative government, particularly when Ian McKellan visited Prime Minister John Major for tea in 10 Downing Street.[41] As Tony Blair led Labour calls for equalisation of the age of consent as Shadow Home Secretary in 1994,[42] and New Labour hegemony emerged, some noted similarities of style and presentation between the suited and respectable leaders of Stonewall and the New Labour modernisers. A shared political vocabulary concerned with 'citizenship', 'community' and circumscribed forms of 'equality' became apparent. But in public Stonewall ensured it presented itself scrupulously as politically neutral.

Yet the passage of time and recent publications have increasingly revealed links between Stonewall and the New Labour project. Details emerge in the autobiography of leading political journalist Matthew Parris, a gay man and formerly a Conservative MP (1979–1986), who after resigning became a founder and board member of Stonewall.[43] Parris was invited by Nicholas de Jongh, Guardian theatre critic, together with Ian McKellan and others to meet and organise a group opposing Section 28 – in a bar of the gay club Heaven in London, provided free by the owner Richard Branson. Parris' vivid description conveys the flavour of the new form of gay politics associated with Stonewall, and both its interpersonal links and ideological affinities to the New Labour project:

> Peter Mandelson, who was by now thought a well-informed and influential link with the Kinnockite Labour Party, agreed to come along to as many of our meetings as he could, to help us in our plans. [...] Peter Mandelson, conspiratorial at the best of times, seemed especially so in the black-walled and windowless upstairs bar of Heaven, where we sat on big leather sofas trying not to be distracted by the gorgeous and minimally clad barmen who would flit in with refreshments for the gang. Before Peter Mandelson joined us, Nick de Jongh did explain something about the exact status of Peter's attendance according to Peter's explicit instructions – his presence not secret but not official: not to be hidden but not advertised; not representing the Labour Party but there *from* the Labour Party to guide us as himself, as it were, yet not *as* himself – not as a public name himself .... Or something. It was all too complicated

for me. I just thought it was good of him to come. Obviously he was gay. [...] That self-recruited, self-appointed group in Heaven, with no rules, no constitution, no name, no agenda, no minutes, no agreed procedure and no institutional form at all, was really the core upon which the Stonewall Group for Homosexual Equality was afterwards founded.[44]

This passage can be read as a condensed expression of many of the wider tensions with which Stonewall was struggling: between public respectability and private pleasures; between the securities of knowing your team, and the exclusionary dangers of relying on existing networks. It is suggestive of an insufficient focus on democracy, representation, formalisation and accountability which might partially account, for example, for the limited ethnic diversity and religious representation in early Stonewall, and its inadequate focus on Scotland and Wales, as it initially developed.

Relations between New Labour and Stonewall can be interpreted in a broader context. New Labour's project of 'modernisation', exemplified in its 1997 general election manifesto, has been criticised for its neglect of equality strands including gender and 'race'/ethnicity.[45] Similarly there was no mention of 'sexual orientation' or 'lesbian and gay', the age of consent or Section 28 in the 1997 manifesto, which proposed only to end 'unjustifiable discrimination'. Yet it can be argued that multiculturalism of a problematically circumscribed kind,[46] and a progressive approach to same-sex relationships, have actually been key elements in the political ideologies of 'modernisation' espoused by the New Labour leadership, perhaps especially the 'Blairites'. This can be seen in developments such as equalisation of the age of consent and civil partnerships being cited by party leaders such as Blair, when asked to clarify and substantiate the meaning of progressive politics and modernisation, and the value of a Labour government.[47]

This must be understood as the inheritance of earlier generations of progressive Labour thinking. Even for the originators of Labour modernisation, gay sexuality was an issue articulated to define a new progressive politics. Tony Crosland addressed the issue in the concluding chapter of *The Future of Socialism*, published in 1956. In a section titled 'Liberty and Gaiety in Private Life: the Need for a Reaction against the Fabian Tradition', Crosland commented:

... it is not only dark Satanic things and people that now bar the road to the new Jerusalem, but also, if not mainly, hygienic, respectable, virtuous things and people, lacking only in grace and gaiety. This becomes manifest when we turn to the more serious question of socially-imposed restrictions on the individual's private life and liberty. There come to mind at once the divorce laws, licensing laws, prehistoric (and flagrantly unfair) abortion laws, obsolete penalties for sexual abnormality, the illiterate censorship of books and plays, and remaining restrictions on the equal rights of women.[48]

Another key Labour moderniser, Roy Jenkins, enacted this manifesto as Home Secretary, facilitating partial decriminalisation of male homosexuality in 1967, and later reviewing sexual offences in the 1970s.[49]

The crucial role of Stonewall in LGB politics over the past two decades needs to be interpreted in light of this progressive politics of 'modernisation', particularly in the Labour Party. Stonewall's ascendance and eventual success in achieving civil rights and legal equalities has achieved the liberal equal rights objectives of modernisers such as Crosland. It is certainly the case that many on the Labour left have also been at the forefront of campaigning for anti-discriminatory law reforms. This has not been the exclusive preserve of either right or left in the party and some figures in Stonewall such as former GLF activist Angela Mason, have certainly come from the radical left (see above). Nevertheless it can be argued that Stonewall's emergence dovetailed in key respects with Labour modernisation from 1983, and that Stonewall's legal equality agenda was already a part – albeit a largely concealed part – of the modernisation agenda pursued by New Labour from the 1990s. As New Labour hegemony now diffuses and changes character under Gordon Brown, and with the legal equality agenda largely fulfilled by the recent Sexual Orientation Regulations 2007 outlawing discrimination in provision of goods and services (including by Catholic adoption agencies), this throws into relief the contemporary politics of Stonewall as an NGO. If Stonewall won reforms as a vehicle for aspects of progressive modernisation sought by the social democratic left, pursuing a liberal equal rights agenda, can it still have the same future role? Further progress will require challenges to the social structures and cultural discourses which sustain the status of gendered heterosexuality above that of same-sex relationships, as suggested in both materialist and post-structuralist feminist analyses.[50] LGB NGOs seeking to advance a more transformative politics must therefore now seek alignment with a multi-dimensional centre-left politics capable of conceptualising and countering the socially and culturally entrenched nature of multiple inequalities. This means seeking association with various forces within a renewing Labour party, other left and centre parties, various progressive and radical NGOS and social movements. It cannot mean more of the same. Comparisons to more participatory, activist and/or radical organisations have been a constant source of debate since Stonewall's inception. However, according to Mason: 'When the Stonewall Group was set up much was made of its differences from more "radical" groups like Outrage. Clearly differences in tactics are important, but discussions about reform and revolution often obscure the deeper historical process'.[51] Nevertheless comparison of Stonewall to Outrage!, and also to the short-lived Equality Alliance of the 1990s, serves to further illuminate contemporary dilemmas about the future of LGB NGOs.

Outrage! was formed in 1990 as a radical activist organisation which, like GLF, utilised direct action as one strategy. Its origins and development are chronicled by Ian Lucas in *Outrage! An Oral History*.[52] Influenced by ACT UP, it emerged as a focus for angry resistance to queerbashings, AIDS and Section 28, with a focus on generating publicity in the media through high profile protests and 'zaps'. The most prominent member has been Peter Tatchell, whose website contains extensive resources on Outrage! campaigns and activities (www.petertatchell.net), though he is not appointed to a position of leadership. Recent Outrage! work includes protests against human rights abuses worldwide and work to defend LGB asylum seekers.

While contrasts of style between Stonewall and Outrage! have been readily apparent, these have generally disguised more profoundly important agreement on many substantive objectives including a comprehensive agenda for equality in law and policy. Outrage! has typically criticised the pace of change while Stonewall has engaged political party leaders in conversation, but as the quote from Mason above suggests, these roles can be seen in a broader perspective as largely complimentary in achieving shared goals.

Lucas' account documents splits over the politics of racism, gender and other issues, revealing the deeply problematic nature of direct participatory democracy as practised by Outrage! (anyone could attend and speak at meetings), and the difficulties of reconciling this with a pluralistic politics addressing multiple inequalities. For example, a group called Lesbian Avengers split from Outrage! in the mid-1990s, but dissipated in 1997. The predominance of the highly skilled, charismatic and vocal Peter Tatchell as an individual within Outrage!, particularly in its media representation, illustrates that participatory structures are no guarantee of genuine democratic dialogue or equality between individuals within organisations.

The Equality Alliance is another organisation which is illuminating to consider in relation to debates over participatory democracy. This was formed in 1998 as an alliance of LGBT campaigning groups, intended to coordinate campaigning. However the Alliance was short-lived as a large organisation with sizeable participation, although it continued to function for several years via an email list, executive committee and annual conference – particularly through the impressive commitment of Andrew van Doorn.

The Equality Alliance was formed from London as a loose umbrella organisation to which, it was intended, a wide variety of lesbian, gay, bisexual and/or transgender groups could affiliate. It was thus distinctive for being 'LGBT'. The initial conception of the organisation's substantive agenda was largely focussed upon 'equality', seeking legal equalities and non-discrimination, seen as a shared focus for a variety of LGBT groups. This was despite such groups being otherwise divided on a variety of issues: for example, differences between lesbian feminists and transgender groups over the cultural desirability of transvestism. Thus in its substantive equality agenda, the Equality Alliance replicated the central agendas of lesbian and gay groups such as Stonewall, and the leading UK transgender group Press for Change. The central purpose of the Equality Alliance was not to innovate in demands, but rather to fulfil a practical function by publicising and coordinating LGBT campaigns in which the multiplying variety of local and national LGBT groups could be involved.

At the first Equality Alliance conference a wide variety of LGBT organisations were represented; there were approximately 100 individuals present. I attended in an individual capacity, conscious of the potential to use the experiences and data from notes and participant observation at a later date. What was strikingly memorable, though not surprising, was the cacophony of disputing voices speaking as soon as the agenda turned to defining key campaign issues. The first issues proposed were those already most publicly prominent: the age of consent for sex between men, and Section 28, for example. But then various groups sought to counterbalance, for example, the focus on gay male issues inherent in addressing equalisation of the age of consent. A transgender group advocated a focus on transgender rights, and a lesbian proposed a focus on lesbian parental custody. Requests from the male chair to restrict a list of issues to a workable 5 or 6, fell on deaf ears, and the list grew to 12–14; a committee was elected to somehow operationalise these. The creation of the Equality Alliance thus unleashed a flurry of competition for attention, but hopes were dashed when the organisation rapidly disappeared. The objective of central founding members was to achieve a unity of focus, but in practice this risked focussing the diverse strands of LGBT campaigning organisations on specific agendas, particularly gay male agendas, which were already the most publicly visible and well-resourced. LGBT organisations in their diversity were unwilling to subscribe to this programme.

This can be interpreted in light of debates over democracy and diversity in political theory. Theorists such as David Held note the tension between representative democracy and direct or participatory forms of democracy, and have explored the relationships of these to various understandings of liberalism.[53] More specifically, Ernesto Laclau and Chantal Mouffe's *Hegemony and Socialist Strategy* has proposed 'radical democratic politics', a multi-dimensional politics addressing multiple inequalities.[54] This involves building 'chains of equivalence' between various democratic struggles, and a politics of 'articulation' involving the creation of discourses to link these struggles. Laclau and Mouffe[55] have turned from Marxism and feminism to wrestle again with liberalism as a resource for addressing diversity; yet have sought to distinguish their radical democratic politics from a conventional liberal politics of diversity, particularly through a post-structuralist emphasis that identities and subjectivities are socially and discursively constituted, rather than pre-political.

At the heart of Laclau and Mouffe's radical democratic politics lies a hope of, and belief in, the capacity of diverse groups to form alliances and work together. This approach repudiated alternative conservative and Hobbesian notions, for example, that unrestrained, unchecked diversity must allow selfish interests to predominate, leading to disorder and damaging consequences. While liberal democrats argue the need for restrained representative democracy to ensure sufficient dialogue within the political realm for effective government, radical democrats influenced by participatory socialist traditions have tended to put more emphasis on the possibility of participation improving politics.

In this light the Equality Alliance can be interpreted as somewhat akin to an experiment with radical democracy in LGBT politics. The foregrounded concept of 'equality', particularly understood in terms of formal (legal and policy) equalities, can be interpreted as an attempt to articulate 'chains of equivalence' between struggles of diverse LGBT groups. Forms of organisation such as the initial conference and large committee sought a purity of participatory representation. The loose-knit network structure of the organisation (as an 'alliance') sought to institutionalise recognition of diversity. But what is suggested by the subsequent decline and demise of the Equality Alliance within a few years, however, is that the initial agreed framework and discourse were insufficient to sustain the project in the context of limited resources, lack of an effective core group, and limited support for a core purpose of focussing lobbying on specific issues.

Stonewall has sometimes been criticised in LGBT circles, to some extent fairly, for being undemocratic, elitist, English and London-centric, middle class and excessively white. Yet Stonewall has survived and functioned effectively in relation to its goals. The contrast with the Equality Alliance suggests that issues of funding, stability, long-term strategy, purpose and sustainability are crucial. The now widely-forgotten Equality Alliance should be remembered and studied by those concerned with the future of LGBT politics, since it illustrates the limitations of ideals without resources and strategy. It suggests that a politics of radical participatory democracy, in the context of diversity, is even more difficult to operationalise in practice than it appears in theory. If it was difficult to operationalise an alliance to pursue an 'equality' agenda primarily concerned with formal equalities in law and policy, how much more difficult would it be to sustain organisations seeking full social equality (or 'liberation')?

This can all be considered in the context of the 'Sexual Citizenship debate'. Initiated by David Evans,[56] the debate has revealed divisions between those such as Jeffrey Weeks who have a tendency to argue that claims for inclusion in citizenship can be socially transformative,[57] and others like Evans, and Bell and Binnie, who have focussed more on how such claims can be problematically assimilationist and de-radicalising.[58] As I have commented elsewhere,[59] Bell and Binnie's conception of a radical vanguardist queer politics lacks engagement with political theory, particularly the engagements of feminist theorists of multiculturalism and radical democracy (such as Chantal Mouffe and Judith Squires[60]) with liberalism. From the latter work emerges a tempered belief in vanguardism and greater emphasis on the deeply problematic process of achieving dialogue between the extremely diverse groups suffering inequality in contemporary societies. Hence the need for liberal democratic institutions and practices, imperfect NGOs, and recognition of the limitations of pure direct participatory democracy when addressing diversity. This suggests NGOs cannot be expected to be purely democratic if they are also to function in a sustained way, although Stonewall might nevertheless have done more (especially in its early years, and through resources on its website) to foster grassroots activism and mobilisation. But both radical democratic theory and the sexual citizenship debate suggest we do need to pose again the questions of participation and representation within sustainable, established LGBT NGOs, particularly to engage with pervasive and urgent debates over Islam and multiculturalism via achieving appropriate representation of Moslems and other religious groups; and also to counter tendencies towards assimilationism and bureaucratisation in relation to government.

The future of LGB NGOs in the UK

LGBT politics in the UK has arrived at a new juncture. The Equality Act 2006 has created a new Commission for Equality and Human Rights from 2007, and hence a new set of institutional mechanisms to promote equality with respect to 'sexual orientation' (and change of gender). Civil partnerships, while distinct from marriage, are legally almost identical. The achievement of formal equalities in most areas of law implies the need to reconsider the role of leading LGB NGOs.

Stonewall's focus has been primarily on non-discrimination in law, rather than broader dimensions of social policy, citizenship and rights related to the specific needs of LGB people. In the context of growing debates over non-legal aspects of social and cultural citizenship, it is apparent that there are many future agendas to pursue. It takes more than formal equalities in law and policy to combat the inequality between heterosexuality and lesbian, gay and bisexual sexualities.

LGB NGOs therefore need to shift focus to more varied campaigns, and are doing so. But some are more advanced in this respect than others, and so have more to offer. LGBT Youth Scotland for example is a national organisation (with no parallel in England) which focusses on supporting and sustaining LGBT youth groups and young people, and on a variety of strategies to inform and train youth practitioners.[61] It has a strong record of conducting empirical social research compared to some other Scottish LGBT organisations, apparent in its now conducting research on same-sex domestic violence among people of all ages (not only young people). Therefore if LGBT politics needs to look beyond formal equalities, and at the specific needs of LGBT young people as I have suggested elsewhere,[62] then LGBT NGOs such as LGBT Youth Scotland deserve increasing financial support and greater recognition relative to others.

To what extent do LGB NGOs have the desire, capacity or ideology to move beyond a focus on formal equalities? For Stonewall and others, moving beyond the formal equalities agenda involves transforming into a different kind of organisation: changing focus, conducting more research of better quality, and developing more high quality resources to inform, empower and mobilise individuals and other organisations. But the question now facing mainstream LGB NGOs is whether it is possible to combine working with government with continuing challenges to government.

Acknowledgements

Thanks to Jeff Meek, PhD student in the Department of Economic and Social History at University of Glasgow, for information and references in relation to Scotland. Thanks also to Lucy Robinson for feedback at the conference from which this book developed.

Notes

1   B. Adam, J.W. Duyvendak and A. Krouwel, *The Global Emergence of Gay and Lesbian Politics: National Imprints of a Worldwide Movement* (Philadelphia: Temple University Press, 1999). S.M. Engel, *The Unfinished Revolution: Social Movement Theory and the Gay and Lesbian Movement* (Cambridge: Cambridge University Press, 2001), D. Evans, *Sexual Citizenship: The Material Construction of Sexualities* (London: Routledge, 1993), D. Bell and J. Binnie, *The Sexual Citizen: Queer Politics and Beyond* (Cambridge: Polity Press, 2000).

2   Plummer, K. 'The Lesbian and Gay Movement in Britain: Schisms, Solidarities and Social Worlds', in B. Adam *et al*, *The Global Emergence of Gay and Lesbian Politics*, pp. 133–57.

3   Laclau, E. and Mouffe, C., *Hegemony and Socialist Strategy: Towards a Radical Democratic Politics* (London: Verso, 1985). On sexual citizenship see note 1.

4   Committee on Homosexual Offences and Prostitution, *Report of the Committee on Homosexual Offences and Prostitution* (London: HMSO, 1957). M. Waites, *The Age of Consent: Young People, Sexuality and Citizenship* (Houndmills, Basingstoke: Palgrave Macmillan, 2005); chapter 5.

5   Blasius, M. and S. Phelan, *We Are Everywhere: A Historical Sourcebook of Gay and Lesbian Politics* (London: Routledge, 1997).

6   F. Martel, *The Pink and the Black: Homosexuals in France since 1968* (Stanford: Stanford University Press, 1999), pp. 57–66.

7   B.D. Adam, *The Rise of a Gay and Lesbian Movement* (Boston: Twayne Publishers, 1987), pp. 60–1.

8   A. Grey, *Quest for Justice: Towards Homosexual Emancipation* (London: Sinclair-Stevenson, 1992); also A. Grey, *Speaking Out: Writings on Sex, Law, Politics and Society 1954–1995* (London: Cassell, 1997).

9 J. Weeks, *Coming Out: Homosexual Politics in Britain, from the Nineteenth Century to the Present* (London: Quartet Books, 1977); p. 175; pp. 168–82. S. Jeffery-Poulter, *Peers, Queers and Commons: The Struggle for Gay Law Reform from 1950 to the Present* (London: Routledge, 1991), chapters 2–4.

10 Grey, *Quest for Justice*, p. 135; pp. 135–7, 154.

11 I. Dunn 'Scotland: Against the Odds', in B. Cant and S. Hemmings (eds) *Radical Records: Thirty Years of Lesbian and Gay History* (London: Routledge, 1988), pp. 34–41.

12 B. Dempsey, *Thon Wey: Aspects of Scottish Lesbian and Gay Activism* (Edinburgh: USG, 1995).

13 Jeffery-Poulter, *Peers, Queers and Commons*, pp. 142–7; B. Dempsey (1998) 'Piecemeal to Equality: Scottish Gay Law Reform', in L. J. Moran, D. Monk and S. Beresford, *Legal Queeries* (London: Cassell, 1998), pp. 155–66.

14 Dunn, 'Scotland ...', p. 38.

15 Grey, *Quest for Justice*, p. 154; see also I. Dunn 'Making it Happen: The Making of the Gay Community in Scotland', in E. Healey and A. Mason (eds) *Stonewall 25: The Making of the Lesbian and Gay Community in Britain* (London: Virago, 1994), pp. 111–21.

16 Dempsey, 'Piecemeal to Equality ...', pp. 163–5.

17 A. Horsfall 'Battling for Wolfenden', in Cant and Hemmings, *Radical Records*, pp. 15–33.

18 A. Grey, *Quest for Justice*, pp. 154–8.

19 L. Power, *No Bath but Plenty of Bubbles: An Oral History of the Gay Liberation Front 1970–1973* (London: Cassell, 1995), p. 13, pp. 10–14.

20 See manifestos in: Blasius and Phelan, *We Are Everywhere*, part IV.

21 Reprinted as Appendix 2 in: Power, *No Bath ...* , pp. 316–30.

22 Power, *No Bath ...*; Waites, *The Age of Consent*, pp. 119–30; also L. Robinson, *Gay Men and the Left in Post-war Britain* (Manchester: Manchester University Press, 2007).

23 Power, *No Bath ...*, p. 44.

24 Grey, *Quest for Justice*, p. 173.

25 Waites, *The Age of Consent*, pp. 127, 132.

26 Horsfall, 'Battling ...', p. 27.

27 Jeffery-Poulter, *Peers, Queers and Commons*, p. 157.

28 Jeffery-Poulter, *Peers, Queers and Commons*, pp. 147–54.

29 I. Lucas, *Outrage!: An Oral History* (London: Cassell, 1998).

30 M. Waites, 'Homosexuality and the New Right: the Legacy of the 1980s for New Delineations of Homophobia', *Sociological Research Online*, 5, 1, May 2000, <http://www.socresonline.org.uk/5/1/waites.html>; M. Waites, 'The Fixity of Sexual Identities in the Public Sphere: Biomedical Knowledge, Liberalism and the Heterosexual/Homosexual Binary in Late Modernity', *Sexualities*, 8 (5) (2005), pp. 539–69.

31 Lucas, *Outrage!*, p. 5.

32 A. Mason 'Introduction', in Healey and Mason, *Stonewall 25*, p. 5.

33 Power, *No Bath ...*

34 A. Palmer, 'Lesbian and Gay Rights Campaigning: A Report from the Coalface', in A.R. Wilson (ed.) *A Simple Matter of Justice?* (London: Cassell, 1995).

35 Waites, *The Age of Consent*, pp. 158–82; Waites, 'The Fixity ...'.

36   S. Jones and N. Wooding, 'Brief Overview of Stonewall Cymru and the Former LGB Forum Cymru' (undated), http://www.stonewallcymru.org.uk/cymru/english/about_us/225.asp (accessed 25/09/2007).

37   Department for Children, Schools and Families, *Homophobic Bullying: Safe to Learn: Embedding anti-bullying work in schools* (Nottingham: DCSF Publications, 2007).

38   D. Rayside, *On the Fringe: Gays and Lesbians in Politics* (New York: Cornell University Press, 1998), Waites, *The Age of Consent*, pp. 158–82.

39   Lucas, *Outrage!*, p. 9.

40   Lucas, *Outrage!*, p. 9.

41   Evans, *Sexual Citizenship*, p. 117.

42   Waites, *The Age of Consent*, p. 168.

43   M. Parris, *Chance Witness: An Outsider's Life in Politics* (London: Penguin, 2002), pp. 356–8.

44   Parris, *Chance Witness*, pp. 357–8.

45   L. Back, M. Keith, A. Khan, K. Shukra and J. Solomos 'The Return of Assimilationism: Race, Multiculturalism and New Labour', *Sociological Research Online*, 7(2) (2002). <http://www.socresonline.org.uk/7/2/back.html>.

46   D. McGhee, *Intolerant Britain?* (Maidenhead: Open University Press, 2005).

47   T. Blair, *Speech at Stonewall Equality Dinner*, 22 March 2007, http://www.number10.gov.uk/output/Page11336.asp (accessed 1 October 2007).

48   A. Crosland, *The Future of Socialism* (London: Constable & Robinson Ltd., 2006), p. 403.

49   Waites, *The Age of Consent*, pp. 96–157.

50   S. Jackson, 'Heterosexuality, Heteronormativity and Gender Hierarchy: Some Reflections on Recent Debates', in J. Weeks, J. Holland and M. Waites (eds) *Sexualities and Society: A Reader* (Cambridge: Polity Press, 2003).

51   Mason, 'Introduction', p. 5.

52   Lucas, *Outrage!*

53   D. Held, *Models of Democracy*, third edition (Cambridge: Polity Press, 2006).

54   Laclau and Mouffe, *Hegemony and Socialist Strategy*.

55   C. Mouffe, *The Return of the Political* (London: Verso, 1993).

56   Evans, *Sexual Citizenship*.

57   J. Weeks, *Invented Moralities: Sexual Values in an Age of Uncertainty* (Cambridge: Polity Press, 1995), J. Weeks, 'The Sexual Citizen', *Theory, Culture and Society: Special Issue on Love and Eroticism*, 15(3–4) (1998), pp. 35–52; J. Weeks, *The World We Have Won* (London: Routledge, 2007).

58   Bell and Binnie, *The Sexual Citizen*; for discussion see Waites, *The Age of Consent*, esp. pp. 32–9.

59   M. Waites, 'The Sexual Citizen: Queer Politics and Beyond' – Book Review, *Gender, Place and Culture*, 9(1) (2002), pp. 84–6.

60   J. Squires, *Gender in Political Theory* (Cambridge: Polity Press, 1999).

61   http://www.lgbtyouth.org.uk/home.htm

62   Waites, 'The Fixity ...'

6
Human Rights Campaigns in Modern Britain

Tom Buchanan

Introduction

The history of human rights organisations, both in Britain and internationally, has been a surprisingly neglected field. Indeed, Stephen Hopgood has recently written that a 'void' exists where 'work on the culture of human rights ought to be found'.[1] As for much of the voluntary sector, this has typically been the preserve of the 'official' history, often written by those with a close personal involvement, and even the occasional work of hagiography. This is not to dismiss the value of this kind of source. However, while insiders have the advantage of personal knowledge and insight, they often tend to shy away from – or indeed draw a veil over – painful internal issues. They are also more likely to be affected by an institutional teleology. Therefore, with the greater availability of good archival sources it is now possible for historians not only to go beyond the ambiguities of 'official' history, but also to understand these organisations fully as historical entities, within a proper social and political context.

The focus of this chapter will be on a group of organisations that were centrally concerned with 'human rights' issues. This term is used advisedly as the phrase 'human rights' only gradually gained widespread acceptance and usage in Britain during the post-war period. As Stefanie Grant, an early Amnesty employee recalled, there was no such thing as 'human rights work' in the mid-1960s, and Amnesty was initially thought of as 'an adoption organisation [for political prisoners]'.[2] Until the 1960s the term 'civil liberties' was more commonly used. However, during the period covered in this paper all of the groups under discussion came to see themselves as 'human rights' organisations. Hence, the National Council for Civil Liberties (NCCL) was reborn in 1989 as 'Liberty', a 'human rights organisation'.[3]

The organisations that will be discussed here are highly diverse in terms of their principles, structures, and modes of action. Apart from Amnesty International (founded in 1961) they did not form part of the tremendous flowering of social movements during the 1960s and 1970s. Two of them were established before the Second World War – PEN International in 1921, and the NCCL in 1934[4] – while JUSTICE was founded in 1956–7. Moreover, both Amnesty and PEN present cases of organisations which were founded in Britain but which have subsequently become thoroughly internationalised. However, both have retained strong British branches, and in both cases the British role remains important. (Amnesty International still has its headquarters, as well as a British Section, in London). There are, of course, many other British organisations which have campaigned either against the abuse of human rights in particular countries or for the enlargement of specific rights both domestically and internationally, but these will only be referred to here when directly relevant.

How helpful is the term 'NGO' when studying these organisations? They are clearly all 'non-governmental organisations' in the broadest sense of the term. Likewise, they are all organisations that shared – or came to share – the 'quest for influence' and socio-political relevance emphasised in this volume. But are they 'NGOs'? The problem is that the term 'NGO' carries modern connotations of professionalism, a pre-determined purpose or mission, and a career structure. (For instance, it is increasingly common to make a career in the human rights 'sector', moving from one voluntary organisation to another, in a manner that was far less feasible in the 1960s). However, while these organisations might conform to such an 'NGO' model today, this does not necessarily help us to understand their history and evolution. Indeed, some of them started off as something entirely different. For instance, PEN was initially a dining club for writers which 'meddles not with politics'.[5] It only became interested in freedom of expression in response to the rise of Nazism in the 1930s. JUSTICE grew out of concern within the legal profession about state repression in Hungary and South Africa, but almost immediately concentrated its energies on miscarriages of justice within Britain itself. Amnesty started out as a one-year campaign on behalf of 'prisoners of conscience', modelled on a recent UN Year for Displaced Persons, and only became permanent in response to a remarkable public response. Hopgood has recently written that Amnesty was never a mere 'NGO', and places it instead within a tradition of 'religionless Christianity'.[6] Likewise, there is an interesting clash over precisely this question in the literature on the International

Commission of Jurists (ICJ). The historian Howard Tolley saw his book as presenting 'one NGO model for human rights practitioners', but the former ICJ staff member Lucian Weeramantry argued that such a view obscured what was unique about the organisation.[7] The same danger applies whenever 'NGO' is used as a convenient label. It is worth emphasising, therefore, that this chapter is concerned with a disparate group of constantly-evolving organisations which were driven by a broad range of political and religious motivations.

Historical overview

The campaign against the slave trade is generally regarded as the precursor and model for British human rights organisations. The Anti-Slavery Society had its origins in the eighteenth century, but was formally established in 1839. It remained an influential body into the twentieth century, and added the words 'for the Protection of Human Rights' to its title in 1957.[8] However, while the impact of the struggle against slavery was considerable – notably and most directly on the women's suffrage campaign – the practical importance of the Anti-Slavery Society in the years since 1945 was relatively small. There was still important work to be done (such as the 1956 supplementary convention on the abolition of slavery and related practices), but the focus of human rights campaigns in the immediate post-war decades lay elsewhere: above all on political imprisonment and freedom of expression.

The most significant development within Britain before the Second World War was the formation of the NCCL. This was set up by the radical journalist Ronald Kidd as a response to police harassment of the Hunger Marchers (and specifically the use of *agents provocateurs*) in 1934.[9] Its initial purpose was to send eminent writers and lawyers as observers to monitor police action on demonstrations, but it soon developed into a 'permanent watchdog body'[10] at a time when state and police powers were rapidly expanding. The NCCL was strongly identified with the Communist left, although it was always presented by its founders as a non-party organisation.[11] The NCCL was staunchly anti-fascist, but, if anything, even more suspicious of what it regarded as the threat posed by an authoritarian government and Metropolitan police force. Hence its criticism of the 1936 Public Order Act which was principally directed against Mosley's BUF marches. Other anti-fascist bodies which adopted what would now be regarded as 'human rights' issues in the 1930s included the Relief Committee for the Victims of Fascism and For Intellectual Liberty.[12] PEN also emerged as a critic of fascism during the 1930s, but it was equally critical of communist dictatorship and never had a branch in the Soviet Union.

The situation was transformed by the Second World War and the international agreements reached during its immediate aftermath. The war had created an expectation of a new 'world order' within which universal human rights would be enshrined and protected. The most significant texts were the 1945 Charter of the United Nations (UN) and the UN Declaration of Human Rights (UDHR) which was agreed by the General Assembly in December 1948.[13] Although the onset of the Cold War put a brake on the development of an institutional 'regime' for the protection of human rights, one can note Britain's participation in the 1950 European Convention for the Protection of Human Rights and Fundamental Freedoms.[14] Much of the credit for the emphasis placed on human rights in the UN Charter was claimed by the US non-governmental organisations which attended the San Francisco conference as consultants for the State Department. While many historians have endorsed this claim, it has recently been challenged by Kirsten Sellars. Interestingly, she cites the reaction of the British diplomat Gladwyn Jebb who described the non-governmental bodies as 'simple folk', deluded as to their real influence: 'I very much doubt whether 42 British groups of the same character would have come to the same conclusion'.[15] Even so, the signing of the UDHR was a remarkable achievement, the full dimensions of which – as well as their impact on the work of NGOs – would not become clear for a number of years. In effect, the UDHR created an enduring internationally-agreed bill of rights: henceforth voluntary groups could campaign for their implementation either in full or individually. Hence, the London-based organisation 'Article 19' was established as late as 1987 specifically to campaign for freedom of expression as enshrined in article 19 of the UDHR.

This call for universal human rights initially received only a limited response amongst non-governmental organisations for two principal reasons. First, the idea of universality was, in effect, a novel one. Existing human rights organisations, such as the NCCL and the French *Ligue des droits de l'homme* (established in 1898 during the Dreyfus affair) had been identified with the Left, as was the International Association of Democratic Lawyers (IADL, established in 1946). The often illiberal positions adopted by the NCCL during and after the Second World War (with regard, for instance, to the detention of British fascists) led one MP to quip in 1947 that it should be renamed the 'National Council for <u>Some</u> Civil Liberties'.[16] Indeed, during

1945–48 a Freedom Defence Committee was established by anarchists and intellectuals on the non-Communist left precisely to take up civil liberties cases that the NCCL would not handle.[17] Secondly, the political polarisation imposed by the Cold War stalled further international agreement for more than a decade, and divided the human rights organisations. For instance, the ICJ was established in 1953, with a strong base amongst anti-Communist West German lawyers, at least in part as a response to the pro-Soviet stance of the IADL. The ICJ was also in secret receipt of CIA funds, a fact that was belatedly made public – with nearly catastrophic consequences for the organisation – in 1967.[18]

Within Britain, most 'human rights' work during the fifteen years after World War Two was concerned with political imprisonment either under the right-wing dictatorships in Spain and Portugal or in the new Soviet satellite states.[19] In the late 1950s organisations with close links to the Communist Party started to campaign for an 'Amnesty' for prisoners in Spain and Portugal. This work was far from universalist: campaigns for the release of prisoners in, say, Spain formed part of a wider campaign on the Left against the Franco dictatorship, while the same applied to the right-wing and Catholic groups which adopted the cause of political prisoners in Yugoslavia and elsewhere in Eastern Europe. As Bertrand Russell wrote in 1956: 'Mankind is divided into two classes: those who object to infringements to civil liberties in Russia, but not in the US; and those who object to them in the US, but not in Russia. There seems to be hardly anybody who just objects to infringements of civil liberties …'[20] Even so, important lessons were being learnt. Peter Benenson, a barrister and Labour candidate who went on to found both JUSTICE and Amnesty International, frequently visited Spain to attend political trials in the later 1940s and 1950s, representing organisations such as the International Brigade Association and the Labour Party's Spanish Democrats Defence Fund.[21] It is, therefore, possible to see a new 'human rights' sensibility beginning to emerge in certain quarters during the 1950s. This was reinforced by a growing awareness of the rights of colonial peoples at a time of bitter rear-guard imperial actions in, for instance, French Algeria and British Kenya, as well as the intensification of the apartheid system in South Africa.

The formation of JUSTICE in 1956–7 marked an important turning point. This was an organisation of lawyers that was brought together in response to the twin stimuli of the Treason Trials in South Africa and the Soviet repression of the Hungarian uprising in November 1956. Peter Benenson seized the opportunity to create a new body that would bridge party lines and combine the different organisations of Labour, Conservative and Liberal lawyers in defence of the rule of law. JUSTICE was, in effect, founded at a crowded meeting at Niblett Hall, London, on 17 January 1957, where Gerald Gardiner (later Lord Chancellor) spoke of his recent visit to South Africa on behalf of the ICJ. With a trademark flourish, Benenson stated that JUSTICE was an acronym that stood for 'Joint Union of Societies to Insure Civil Liberties in England and Elsewhere'.[22] During the following months the new organisation took shape under the secretaryship of Tom Sargant, and became the British branch of the ICJ (which was then headed by the British lawyer and academic Norman Marsh). JUSTICE continued to take an interest in the South African trials, but from 1958 it focussed on Britain and generally left international issues to the ICJ.[23] During the 1960s its energies were channelled into questions such as criminal injuries and the creation of the office of Ombudsman.

Although Peter Benenson had been the inspiration behind JUSTICE, he soon became frustrated with what he saw as a narrow, professionally-based organisation that would never be able to mobilise a broader constituency in defence of human rights. Meanwhile, he felt that the NCCL, which might have fulfiled this role, lacked credibility as it was too close to the Communist Party.[24] The work of PEN to some extent foreshadowed that of Amnesty during this period but it was limited to supporting imprisoned writers, principally though not exclusively in the Soviet bloc.[25] During the late 1950s and early 1960s the charismatic, mercurial Benenson went through a personal and political crisis. He began to distance himself from the Labour Party, converted to Catholicism, and ceased practising as a barrister due to ill-health. He also opened himself up to a range of social and religious movements: his correspondence of the time records his admiration for Frank Buchman's Moral Rearmament movement and the work in Sicily of the social activist Danilo Dolci. Out of this heady mixture of ideas emerged in late 1960 the concept of a year-long campaign for the 'forgotten prisoners', jailed solely for their political beliefs. With characteristic energy Benenson threw himself into this new campaign and gathered the support of likeminded lawyers, journalists and religious activists. Amongst the most notable of these were the Quaker activist Eric Baker, who coined the term 'Prisoner of Conscience', the Irish statesman Sean MacBride, and the lawyer Louis Blom Cooper. The newspaper proprietor David Astor was a more peripheral, but highly influential and well-connected presence during the early years of Amnesty. Astor's involvement brought access not only to the campaigning skills of the

Observer newspaper, but also to sources of information on post-colonial Africa such as the Africa Bureau.[26]

Benenson's exact reasons for launching the Amnesty campaign remain somewhat opaque. The comment by Pierre Sané, a former Secretary General of Amnesty, in 1998 that the organisation was not established to free Prisoners of Conscience but to 'contribute to the full realisation of human rights for all'[27] makes a valid point. Certainly, Benenson's sights were set far higher than creating a mere 'Red Cross of the Cold War'[28]: instead, he hoped to dissolve the Cold War and, in the process, transform the lives of Amnesty's volunteers. However, the eventual shape of Amnesty was to a large degree moulded by the unprecedented public response to the appeal that Benenson had issued in an article in the *Observer* on 28 May 1961. Amnesty's membership developed rapidly both within Britain and in western Europe, and its branches were entrusted with a practical activity: letter-writing campaigns in support of groups of three prisoners of conscience spread across the East, West and Third worlds. Although the central direction of Amnesty remained essentially in the control of legal and professional elites, there was no question that the mould of previous human rights organisations had been broken. Amnesty was politically impartial and very much a mass membership organisation. At the same time, the name 'Amnesty' had been wrested from the existing leftist campaigns, which proceeded slowly to fade away.[29]

The strength and commitment of Amnesty's members helped to save it when Benenson was forced to step down in 1967 following a bitter and complex internal dispute.[30] Subsequently the organisation was placed on a more stable and professional basis by Martin Ennals, who had previously run the NCCL and had spent eight years with UNESCO. During the 1970s Amnesty's range of interests continued to expand to include torture and 'disappearance' (this reflected the profound impact of human rights abuses under military governments in Greece, Chile and Argentina during this period). Amnesty International was awarded the Nobel Peace Prize in 1977, and by the 1980s this British-based organisation had become something of an international phenomenon. Amnesty also fostered the emergence of new and complementary human rights organisations. For instance, Helen Bamber, who as a young woman had witnessed the Nazi concentration camps, was an Amnesty activist in the 1960s and 70s and worked closely with the Amnesty doctors group. In 1985 she established the Medical Foundation for the Care of the Victims of Torture.[31]

If the human rights abuses of assorted military juntas galvanised Amnesty's work during the 1970s, developments closer to home helped to revive the 'civil liberties' tradition that had flagged during the 1950s.[32] The NCCL, for instance, had gone into a 'slow decline', both in terms of membership and financial resources, which reached a 'nadir' in the early 1960s.[33] However, its fortunes revived in the changed climate of the later 1960s, when it proved able to respond to demands for a widening sphere of personal freedom. During the 1970s the NCCL took a pioneering interest in areas such as gay and women's rights. Its first women's officer was Patricia Hewitt, who later served as General Secretary (1974–1983) prior to her career as a Labour politician. The NCCL also took a keen interest in Northern Ireland where a Northern Ireland Civil Rights Association (NICRA) was established in 1967. In turn, the Northern Ireland conflict and the numerous miscarriages of justice associated with it (such as the case of the 'Birmingham Six') stimulated the interest of a growing number of progressive British lawyers.

A further stimulus was provided by the Thatcher government's perceived authoritarianism and centralisation of state power during the 1980s, which invigorated a broader critique of the failings of British democracy. One response was the creation of 'Charter 88' in 1988, which was named rather pretentiously after the Czech dissident group Charter 77 and demanded a written constitution for Britain. At the same time, however, Thatcherism's redefinition of 'freedom' (heralded by the activities of the anti-trade union National Association for Freedom in the 1970s) also posed difficult questions. For instance, the NCCL was bitterly divided over issues such as how to respond to the coal miners' strike of 1984–5: in particular, should the rights of miners who wanted to work be upheld alongside the rights of strikers in the face of repressive policing?

The advent of Tony Blair's 'New Labour' government in 1997 appeared to mark a new era in which human rights and civil liberties – and the concerns of their advocates – would be central to government policy. Hence, the historic 1998 Human Rights Act whereby the Labour government incorporated the 1950 European Convention into British law, the Freedom of Information Act (2000) and the repeal of the despised Section 28 of the 1988 Local Government Act (which restricted the promotion of homosexuality). However, events since the 9/11 attacks of 2001 and the Iraq War of 2003 have served as a reminder that there can never be an easy accommodation between the state and the defence of human rights. Both Liberty and Amnesty have, in different ways, found themselves in the forefront of criticism of the British and US governments' conduct during the 'War on Terror'.

Motivations

The human rights movement, in its many different forms, has clearly made a profound impact on British public life and, indeed, internationally. What have been the main factors driving it forward?

Events

All of these campaigns have been responsive to perceived abuses and injustices, be it police brutality in Britain in the 1930s or torture in Latin American dictatorships. In other words, all have started with 'real events' rather than growing out of abstract ideas. (Here, for instance, one can note the limited immediate impact of the UN Declaration of Human Rights). However, two important qualifications need to be entered.

First, such abuses of power had existed long before groups such as NCCL or Amnesty were created to confront them. Hence, we are dealing here with the ability of voluntary organisations to identify and, ultimately to 'create' an issue. In the case of Amnesty, for example, the idea that political prisoners should be assisted because they were political prisoners, rather than because of the beliefs that they held or because of the unpleasantness of the regime that had incarcerated them, was simple but revolutionary. In the social science literature the work of human rights NGOs is often referred to as a process of 'norm setting' but this does not necessarily explain why new 'norms' are defined or become accepted at specific historical moments. One might also ask why some abuses result in campaigns while others do not? For example, Margaret Keck and Kathryn Sikkink have pointed to the 'non-campaigns' in the history of international human rights networks. Hence, western activists in the later nineteenth century campaigned against foot binding in China, but not against female infanticide or concubinage.[34]

Secondly, one can also encounter a certain mythologisation of 'events' in the founding of such organisations. For instance, Benenson always claimed to have set up Amnesty as a personal response to reading a report in the *Daily Telegraph* while travelling to work on the London underground. Apparently, two Portuguese students had been jailed for seven years under the Salazar regime for making a public toast to liberty. This story remains well-known and still features on the

Amnesty International website. Perplexingly, however, I was unable to find the original news item in the *Daily Telegraph* when researching the early history of Amnesty, and it should be noted that the students involved have never been traced or identified. In this case, therefore, the 'event' itself that triggered Benenson's new approach to political imprisonment remains shrouded in mystery and has become something of a foundation myth for Amnesty.[35] This, of course, is not to deny that there was a considerable amount of repression in Salazar's Portugal at that time.

Individuals

Many voluntary organisations begin with a 'visionary' individual, and often proceed to pass through very similar stages of development. The first stage is often the frenetic development of a new idea or insight, resulting in an initial focus of activity which may lead to an organisation or campaign. Of course, the human qualities necessary for this phase – tremendous energy, charisma and inspiration – may be exactly what is <u>not</u> needed once an organisation is up and running. This certainly corresponds to the role played by Benenson in Amnesty. However, there are striking historical parallels to be drawn with the careers of similar individuals, such as Henri Dunant, founder of the Red Cross, or the Rev. Bruce Kenrick, founder of Shelter.[36] The obituary notice on Kenrick might apply in some measure to all of these men: 'an innovator, not an administrator ... [who] slipped into obscurity'. Indeed, the 'prophet outcast' is quite a familiar figure in the voluntary campaigning sector.

If dynamic individuals are of vital importance initially (transformative ideas tend not to emerge from a committee), a second tier of individuals is usually required to put their ideas into practice. Such people are likely to require more professional and administrative skills: these are the people who will turn an idea or ephemeral campaign into an enduring 'NGO' on a bureaucratic basis. Far more research remains to be done here: who were these people, what was their background and training, and what were their political assumptions? One could look with profit at Tom Sargant, who put flesh on the bare bones of JUSTICE as secretary from its inception until 1982; Martin Ennals, who uniquely administered both NCCL and Amnesty and was the brother of the Labour Cabinet minister David Ennals; Elizabeth Allen, who replaced Ronald Kidd at the NCCL and ran the organisation from 1941–60; Tony Smythe, one of Allen's successors, who was also a radical peace activist and worked for the mental health organisation

MIND;[37] or Eric Baker, who played an understated founding role in Amnesty, and was formerly involved in CND and missionary work.[38]

Professions

The most important recent contribution to understanding the trajectory of human rights work in Britain and France has been the comparative work of Mikael Rask Madsen. Madsen places the legal profession at the centre of his argument: in effect, the lawyers seized the moment in the post-war world and used the emergence of a new language of universal human rights as an opportunity to restore their autonomy, status and credibility, dented by the war and the coming of the welfare state. There is no doubt that much of the initiative was taken in Britain during the 1950s and 1960s by lawyers, notably Benenson, Norman Marsh, Louis Blom Cooper and Peter (later Lord) Archer. This applies even more compellingly to the 1970s and 1980s with the growth of specialist legal practices dealing with human rights cases. In other words, it can be argued that lawyers did not simply adopt the cause of human rights: they largely created it in its modern form.

However, some caveats need to be entered here. Benenson did not approach Amnesty primarily as a lawyer: indeed, a major part of his disgruntlement with JUSTICE was precisely that it was limited to the legal profession. His close associate Tom Sargant reflected in 1985 that Benenson 'realised [that] he was too confined by the legalities of Justice, and the fact that he had lawyers who had to act legally'.[39] Many other aspects of Benenson's background also came into play, such as his political experience and, very importantly, his religious convictions. Many other lawyers who played an important role in human rights work also straddled the world of politics – for instance, Gerald Gardiner and Frederick Elwyn Jones (respectively Lord Chancellor and Attorney General in the Wilson governments of 1964–1970), and Harriet Harman (legal officer for the NCCL between 1978 and her election as an MP in 1982). While the law was clearly the single most important profession within the emergence of the human rights voluntary organisations, the human rights sensibility in the post-war world also owed much to other social groups such as artists (especially in the visual arts) and those from a diverse range of religious backgrounds.[40]

Social constituencies

None of these ideas would have gained any traction without wider support, although only Amnesty, of the organisations that have been under discussion, could be said to be a mass membership organisation.

In the case of JUSTICE the question was primarily whether a base of support could be built within the legal profession and associated groups. The NCCL struggled to attract more than 5,000 members until the late 1960s, but its institutional support in the legal profession and the trade unions was always more important than individual membership. However, the rise of Amnesty requires more attention as there was no specific constituency in mind. The timing of its launch, in the early 1960s, was significant as Amnesty coincided with some very propitious developments. First, in political terms, it benefited from a drift away from the left (some early Amnesty members were disillusioned 'post-'56' ex-Communists) as well as a movement away from two-party politics in general. Although Amnesty's supporters came from all parties and none, it could be identified principally with the Liberals and the centre-right of the Labour Party. Secondly, Amnesty benefited from a drift away from organised religion – one might say the 'honest to God' generation.[41] In both religion and politics Amnesty seemed to offer a new belief system allied to practical action. Thirdly, the boom in higher education provided a very important constituency amongst students, whom Benenson assiduously courted. School and university students have consistently been attracted to Amnesty's brand of impartial but impassioned politics. Finally, Amnesty drew crucial support from women who provided the core of the volunteers who ran both the central office and the local groups. Such women kept the movement afloat despite Benenson's appointment of a succession of incompetent male administrators.

Conclusion

British human rights campaigns have evolved considerably during the twentieth century. The 'civil liberties' tradition best represented by the NCCL in the 1930s was principally concerned with political rights within Britain, and identified with a specifically British ideal of constitutionality and personal liberty, harking back to Magna Carta, the Tolpuddle Martyrs and the rights of the 'free-born Englishman'. Since 1945, of course, this tradition has broadened to include a far wider range of issues, including rights related to mental health, gender and sexual orientation. At the same time, with the advent of Amnesty International and other related organisations since the 1960s there has been an internationalisation of human rights campaigning that is less overtly political and which has developed a very broad basis of public support. Such organisations can be placed more in the context of the religious and philanthropic concerns of earlier centuries and reflected a belief that British influence could be used for morally beneficial purposes. Hence David Astor, reflecting in the 1980s on the success of Amnesty, observed that 'there's a strong tradition here [in Britain] of trying to rescue people'.[42] However, with the development in the late twentieth century of a more fully developed national, European and international regime for the protection of human rights, the differences between these two traditions have greatly diminished.

Notes

1 Stephen Hopgood, *Keepers of the Flame; Understanding Amnesty International* (Ithaca & London: Cornell University Press, 2006), p. vii.

2 Cited in Ann Marie Clark, *Diplomacy of Conscience: Amnesty International and Changing Human Rights Norms* (Princeton & London: Princeton University Press, 2001), p. 12.

3 In a recent interview Shami Chakrabarti, Director of Liberty, was asked about the distinction between 'human rights' and 'civil liberties': 'It's fascinating the way some people cling to one phrase and not the other. If we're talking about the civil and political rights in the Human Rights Act like free speech and protest, privacy, fair trials etc I don't see the distinction. The danger is of some people on the left and right of politics using "civil liberties" as a means of protecting just citizens or people they like, as opposed to all "human beings"' (*The Independent*, 16 October 2007).

4 An earlier National Council for Civil Liberties had been established during the First World War and was dissolved in 1919.

5 John Galsworthy's letter to *The Times*, 24 April 1923. See also Marjorie Watts, *P.E.N.: The Early Years, 1921–1926*, Archive Press, London, 1971. PEN was established by the writer Catharine Dawson Scott, 'one of those marvellous Edwardian women who went around founding things' (*The Times*, 2 August 1974).

6 Hopgood, *Keepers of the Flame*, pp. 3 and 8.

7 Lucian G. Weeramantry, *The International Commission of Jurists: The Pioneering Years* (The Hague: Kluwer Law International, 2000), p. 10; Howard B. Tolley, *The International Commission of Jurists: Global Advocate for Human Rights* (Philadelphia: University of Pennsylvania Press , 1994), p. xvii.

8 William Korey, *NGOs and the Universal Declaration of Human Rights: 'Acurious Grapevine'* (Basingstoke: Palgrave, 1998), Chapter 5.

9 There is a helpful entry on Ronald Kidd by Mark Pottle in the *New Dictionary of National Biography*. K.D. Ewing and C.A. Gearty, *The Struggle for Civil Liberties: Political Freedom and the Rule of Law in Britain, 1914–1945* (Oxford: Oxford University Press, 2000) is written from a legal perspective and contains surprisingly little analysis of the role of the NCCL.

10 Mark Lilly, *The National Council for Civil Liberties: The First Fifty Years* (Basingstoke: Macmillan, 1984), p. 4.

11 Sylvia Scaffardi, *Fire Under the Carpet; Working for Civil Liberties in the 30s* (London: Lawrence & Wishart, 1986), p. 85. Scaffardi was Ronald Kidd's

partner and worked alongside him in the running of the NCCL (see her obituary in *The Guardian*, 30 Jan. 2001). The exact nature of the NCCL's links to the Communist Party remains subject to debate. Brian Dyson has argued that 'those wishing to discover hard evidence of manipulation by, or consultation with, the CPGB over NCCL policy will not find it in the surviving NCCL archives nor, I suspect, anywhere else – apart, of course, from the deeply suspicious minds and undoubtedly biased reports of members of MI5 and Special Branch ...' (*Liberty in Britain, 1934–1994; A Diamond Jubilee History of the NCCL* (London: Civil Liberties Trust, 1994), p. 64. However, there is no doubt that some NCCL policies, as well as the presence in its ranks of the notorious fellow-travellers such as the barrister DN Pritt, tainted the organisation for many years and 'damaged credibility' (in the words of Robert Benewick, 'British pressure group politics: The National Council for Civil Liberties', *Annals of the American Academy of Political and Social Science*, vol. 413, 1974, pp. 145–57, 155). An MI5 dossier of 'Communist controlled-penetrated organisations' circulated in December 1948 concluded with regard to the NCCL that: 'There is ... a preponderant Communist element in the Executive Committee; the Chairman is L.C. White, of the C.S.C.A [Civil Servants' Clerical Association], whose Communist background and outlook are notorious' (The National Archives, Kew, HO 45/25583 865004/190).

12   On 'For Intellectual Liberty', see David Bradshaw's two-part article, 'British Writers and Anti-Fascism in the 1930s', *Woolf Studies Annual*, vol. 3 (April 1997) and vol. 4 (April 1998).

13   The literature on human rights is vast. For a brief historical summary see Tom Buchanan, 'Human Rights', in *The Palgrave Dictionary of Transnational History* (forthcoming 2008, Palgrave Macmillan). For a fuller recent account see Micheline R. Ishay, *The History of Human Rights: from Ancient Times to the Globalisation Era* (Berkeley: University of California Press, 2004). See also Jan Herman Burgers, 'The Road to San Francisco: The revival of the Human Rights Idea in the Twentieth Century', *Human Rights Quarterly*, 14(4) Nov. 1992, pp. 447–77.

14   This is discussed at considerable length, but with little reference to the role of NGOs, in Brian Simpson, *Human Rights and the End of Empire: Britain and the Genesis of the European Convention* (Oxford: Oxford University Press, 2001).

15   Kirsten Sellars, *The Rise and Rise of Human Rights* (Stroud, Gloucestershire: Sutton, 2002), p. 10. Sellars' work is somewhat polemical but provides an important counter balance to the rather sanctimonious and self-congratulatory tone of some of the literature on the role of human rights NGOs. Andrew Moravcsik also concludes that the role of the British NGOs in this sphere was marginal in 'The Origins of Human Rights Regimes: Democratic Delegation in Postwar Europe', *International Organisation*, 54(2) Spring 2000, pp. 217–52, this reference to pp. 236–7.

16   Dyson, *Liberty in Britain*, p. 31, citing William Shepherd MP.

17   The FDC is now best remembered for the high-profile role taken by George Orwell, who served as vice-chairman: see George Woodcock, *The Crystal Spirit* (Harmondsworth: Penguin, 1970), pp. 19–23.

18 See Tolley, *The ICJ*, chapter 6. Sir Hartley Shawcross, the Labour politician and former Nuremberg trial prosecutor had been the leading British participant in the formation of the ICJ.

19 However, it should be noted that during the 1950s the NCCL concentrated very largely on issues related to mental health, and played an important role in the passing of the Mental Health Act of 1959.

20 Russell to Sidney Hook, 8 June 1956, cited in Hugh Wilford, *The CIA, the British Left and the Cold War: Calling the Tune?* (London: Frank Cass, 2003), p. 216.

21 See Tom Buchanan, 'Holding the Line: The Political Strategy of the International Brigade Association', *Labour History Review*, 66(3) 2001, pp. 163–84, and 'Receding Triumph: The British Opposition to the Franco Regime, 1945–59', *Twentieth Century British History*, 12(2) 2001, pp. 163–84.

22 Brynmor Jones Library, University of Hull, JUSTICE papers, DJU 1/1, Tom Sargant to Hartley Shawcross, 15 Jan. 1957.

23 On the formation of JUSTICE see Helen Roberts, 'Witness: The Origins of Justice', *Paragon Review* [Brynmor Jones Library, University of Hull], 6, Nov. 1997, pp. 20–4.

24 In 1983 Benenson wrote that the NCCL was 'an organisation I avoided [in the 1950s] because it was then under Communist influence; for that reason it was a suspect and largely uninfluential body' (typescript in the Amnesty International archives).

25 Maurice Cranston, *Human Rights To-day* (London: Ampersand, 1962), pp. 96–100.

26 The Africa Bureau had been founded in 1952 by the Rev. Michael Scott, an anti-apartheid and peace activist and a close associate of Astor's. (See Scott's obituary in *The Times*, 16 Sept. 1983 and Anne Yates and Lewis Chester. *The Troublemaker: Michael Scott and his Lonely Struggle against Injustice* (London: Aurum Press, 2006)).

27 Hopgood, *Keepers of the Flame*, p. 208.

28 Cranston, *Human Rights To-day*, p. 104, footnote.

29 For a detailed and archive-based account of these events see Tom Buchanan, '"The Truth will Set You Free …": The Making of Amnesty International', *Journal of Contemporary History*, 37(4) 2002, pp. 575–97. See also Jonathan Power's *Amnesty International; The Human Rights Story* (London: Fontana, 1981) and *Like Water on Stone: The Story of Amnesty International* (London: Allen Lane, 2001); Egon Larsen, *A Flame in Barbed Wire; The Story of Amnesty International* (New York: W.W. Norton, 1979).

30 For a detailed account see Tom Buchanan, 'Amnesty International in Crisis, 1966–7', *Twentieth Century British History*, 15(3) 2004, pp. 267–89.

31 See the profile of Helen Bamber in *The Guardian*, 11 March 2000, and Neil Belton, *The Good Listener* (London: Phoenix, 1999).

32 This section draws in part on Mikael Rask Madsen, 'France, the UK, and the "Boomerang" of the Internationalisation of Human Rights (1945–2000)' in Simon Halliday and Patrick Schmidt, eds, *Human Rights Brought Home* (Oxford & Portland, Oregon: Hart, 2004), pp. 78–83.

33 Dyson, *Liberty in Britain*, p. 38.

34 Margaret E. Keck and Kathryn Sikkink, *Activists Beyond Borders* (Ithaca & London: Cornell University Press, 1998), pp. 39–40.

35   The full details are set out in Buchanan, 'The Truth will Set You Free', p. 576, footnote 6.

36   For Dunant, see Caroline Moorehead, *Dunant's Dream: War, Switzerland and the History of the Red Cross* (Bury St. Edmunds: HarperCollins, 1998); for Dolci see Michael Bess, *Realism, Utopia and the Mushroom Cloud: Four Activist Intellectuals and their Struggles for Peace, 1945–1989* (Chicago and London: University of Chicago Press, 1993); for Kenrick see the obituary by Michael White in *The Guardian*, 19 Jan. 2007. Ronald Kidd was similarly eclipsed within the NCCL, although this was partly due to his ill-health following a road accident.

37   Obituary in *The Guardian*, 29 March 2004.

38   Baker briefly took the helm of Amnesty in 1967 following the resignation of Peter Benenson. For his career see his obituary in *The Times*, 23 July 1976.

39   Interviewed by Andrew Blane and Priscilla Ellsworth as part of the Amnesty International Oral History Project (AIOHP), transcript, 21 June 1985, transcript, p. 32.

40   I am currently working on a research project on political imprisonment and the movement for human rights in post-war Britain.

41   A reference to the book published by John Robinson, Bishop of Woolwich and an early supporter of Amnesty, in 1963 (see Hopgood, *Keepers of the flame*, pp. 62–3).

42   Interviewed 20 June 1985 (AIOHP), transcript p. 21.

7
The Anti-Apartheid Movement: Pressure Group Politics, International Solidarity and Transnational Activism

Rob Skinner

The Anti-Apartheid Movement (AAM) is popularly acknowledged as one of the more 'successful' late-twentieth-century social movements. Yet its significance is not located in the birth of a democratic South Africa, but in the various ways it embodied the shifting nature of political activism in Britain and the relationship between domestic and global political culture. The movement provides a useful link between 'traditional' political activism and more recent social movements: at its outset an offshoot of the anti-colonial establishment, with links to the successors of nineteenth-century humanitarian networks, it also became, through its particular repertoire of action, and as part of a global institution, an example of the new forms of social and political activism that have developed since the 1960s.

Much of the scholarship on international anti-apartheid activism has been influenced by new social movement theory, including Håkan Thörn's recent excellent comparative account which suggests the movement was central to the development of global civil society.[1] Both in chronological terms – with its origins in the 1960s – and as an example of radical and confrontational politics, the AAM would appear to fit neatly into the category of new social movement, rather than NGO. However, the historical development of anti-apartheid activism cannot easily be captured within any particular theoretical terminology. The AAM could be viewed as a single issue pressure group, while at other times a diffuse movement embodying a range of attitudes from anti-colonialism, through human rights advocacy, to an element within a broader anti-Thatcherism – not to forget traditional (and neo-) Marxism. While its most obvious organisational form was the AAM itself, and the equally important

International Defence and Aid Fund (IDAF), a range of political and civil society organisations engaged in anti-apartheid activities. Moreover, attempts to promote solidarity with South African liberation movements led to one-off campaigns and direct action protests linked to, but not controlled by, the AAM. Above all, anti-apartheid was a campaign of solidarity, and as such took its lead from political actors external to national politics – it is a movement that cannot be understood purely in terms of British socio-political action.

An account of the development of the movement highlights a number of themes identified by the editors as characteristic of the history of NGOs. Consumer boycotts, sanctions and disinvestment campaigns exemplified the ways in which the political role of the citizen has expanded dramatically beyond mere participation in the democratic process, while its ideological framework underlined the growing significance of race and human rights in contemporary politics. Perhaps most importantly, close analysis of the AAM forces us to problematise the assumption that the post-war period saw a fundamental secularisation of social action. The influence of Christian activists within the movement suggests that the legacy of religious philanthropy and social service continued to play an important role in the socio-political realm, and that, at least, the moral dimension of politics remained critical to the development of new forms of movement activity.

As the editors argue, it is the function as much as the form that constitutes the significance of NGO activity, and the AAM functioned as a bridge between local, national and global realms of political activity. As this chapter will show, AAM activities introduced new agendas for the expression of internationalist ideologies, blending established modes of voicing concern for distant others (from the rhetoric of humanitarianism through to the language of solidarity) with new forms of direct action, an emerging discourse of human rights and a politics of consumption. Most significantly, this was a transnational movement; while domestic political culture played a significant role in shaping its identity, the AAM must also be understood in terms of wider processes. Having framed its campaign in global terms, the AAM demonstrates the extent to which post-war socio-political action cannot be understood in purely national terms.

The Anti-Apartheid Movement: formation and historical background

Anti-apartheid activities in Britain were centred on the AAM, its affiliated committees and local organisations. Yet, the AAM should not be viewed simply as an organised pressure group, but also as a more widespread political movement that tied the question of apartheid to broader political questions, such as anti-colonialism and human rights. It emerged as a formal organisation in the wake of the Sharpeville massacre of March 1960. The event, which prompted widespread condemnation and stimulated global interest in the issue of apartheid, coincided with a campaign to boycott South African consumer products that had been active since mid-1959, when individuals connected to the anti-colonial Committee of African organisations, came together with South African exiles to promote anti-apartheid activities along the lines of those being pursued within South Africa.[2] A boycott month, which had been launched with a rally in Trafalgar Square on 28th February, raised public awareness of the issue of apartheid, which was compounded by the Sharpeville shootings – a silent protest outside South Africa House following the event attracted 400 people, including Labour Party leader Hugh Gaitskell. Plans for a long-term Anti-Apartheid campaign had been discussed prior to the Sharpeville massacre, notably the establishment of an 'Anti-Apartheid Co-Ordinating Committee' to direct the activities of local groups.[3] Sharpeville was nevertheless the catalyst for serious discussion of a long-term campaign, including plans to lobby for official sanctions against South Africa.[4] With the banning of the liberation movements in South Africa, it seemed that the focus of resistance to apartheid would shift to international campaigns aimed at placing pressure on South Africa from outside.

The national AAM in Britain emerged with a particular aim – to persuade state and civil society institutions, as well as individuals, to exert influence on the South African government. Much of its efforts came, therefore, within the realm of formal politics, reflecting what some have seen as its limited capacity to organise a sustained and effective boycott campaign.[5] To a significant extent this meant that, at least until the 1980s, it was a largely London-based movement, focussed on campaigns led by the national executive and aimed at political institutions, both domestic and international. The influence of metropolitan political circles was enhanced by the presence in increasing numbers of South African political exiles,[6] whose links with the AAM gave the movement a transnational character, reflected in its choice of tactics and policies: it was a movement essentially driven by South African aims, yet concentrated upon British politics and society.

Sharpeville, then, gave impetus to processes that were already in place.[7] The more diffuse anti-apartheid movement had deep historical roots, drawing together strands of an older humanitarian tradition with the newer forms of activism. Before the 1959–60 boycott campaign, apartheid had already become established as a point of reference for debate surrounding Britain's changing international role. In the media, South African society had become a topic of interest well before the BBC's *Panorama* presenter Richard Dimbleby had compared Sharpeville to Guernica and Belsen in its historical significance.[8] Similarly, mainstream political lobby groups, church organisations, and trade unions had engaged with the issue of apartheid well before 1960. Support came from both Labour and Liberal MPs, including the Liberal leader Jo Grimond and future Cabinet Minister Barbara Castle, President of the AAM from 1962 to 1964. Extra-parliamentary groups, such as the Movement for Colonial Freedom and the Africa Bureau, also provided key channels of support.[9] Anti-apartheid activism thus emerged from within the strand of anti-colonial activism present in left wing politics since the late 1940s.

Prominent individual anti-apartheid campaigners played their role in developing a critique of South African policy, beginning with the maverick Anglican priest Michael Scott.[10] Scott, who had come to international prominence as a critic of the South African government at the United Nations in the late 1940s, was one of a small but significant group of Christians who forged anti-apartheid activities during the 1950s. John Collins, Canon of St. Paul's Cathedral, used his position within the church as a platform for trenchant criticism of apartheid and established a fund to support the accused in South Africa's 'Treason Trial' of the late 1950s which became, in the form of IDAF, the primary source of material assistance to the South African liberation movements.[11] But perhaps the most well known of the pioneering anti-apartheid priests was Trevor Huddleston, who had worked within Johannesburg's black communities, establishing himself as a symbol of Christian opposition to apartheid. Huddleston's book, *Naught for Your Comfort*, was in many ways the founding text of the anti-apartheid movement, notable for the moral force of its straightforward condemnation of the effects of apartheid.[12] Furthermore, Huddleston had been quick to realise the importance of international opinion in the campaign against apartheid, calling in 1954 for a cultural boycott of South Africa.[13] While Huddleston, Scott and Collins were somewhat isolated voices within the Anglican church, their efforts emphasised the continuing importance of religious values to the development of post-war social movements.

However, support from some sectors was less than wholehearted. The Trades Union Congress (TUC), for example, was markedly cautious when it came to fraternal solidarity with black workers in South Africa, and throughout the 1950s its instinctive anti-Communism kept it in closer contact with the 'mainstream' white union organisation, rather than its more radical black counterpart. Similarly, support for Collins' Defence and Aid funds and the Boycott movement was lukewarm at best, and it was not until the early 1970s, prompted by resurgent black trade union activism within South Africa, that the TUC began to take a more actively critical stance towards apartheid.[14] Thus, while it is possible to locate anti-apartheid across a long historical context, the links between the movement and older forms of international solidarity are complex and at times ambiguous. What set those isolated voices such as Huddleston and Collins apart from the more cautious official stance of church and labour institutions was their desire to align themselves closely with the developing nationalist resistance within South Africa – even at the cost of strained relationships with those institutions that had historical links with the country. Anti-apartheid therefore emerged out of new transnational relationships and networks, rather than established international links.

In mainstream politics, what was true of the TUC also held for the Labour Party. Despite the strong support for anti-apartheid within the party, and the presence of some of its leading figures on the AAM executive, the party also maintained a somewhat ambiguous stance on South Africa. Keen not to antagonise the South African government and concerned to avoid South Africa's withdrawal from the Commonwealth, the Attlee government had maintained cordial relations with South Africa following the coming to power of the National Party in 1948.[15] By 1960, however, the party was providing strong support for the Boycott campaign and the fledgling AAM, although approval for the Movement's radical stance on issues such as South African exclusion from the Commonwealth, was more muted.[16] The stance of the Party shifted again when the Wilson government came to power in 1964. Within three years, the AAM published a pamphlet outlining the numerous ways in which the Labour government had placed the economic value of cordial relations with South Africa above its anti-apartheid principles.[17] It is clear that the Labour Party, in terms of individual members and local parties, played a significant role in the development and character of the AAM through to 1994, but the ambiguities of the relationship between the Movement and the Party are illustrative of the problematic relationship between the established political system and the concerns of groups seeking to tackle issues that moved beyond the concerns of 'traditional' political actors. The initial surge of interest in anti-apartheid that followed Sharpeville and

South African withdrawal from the Commonwealth had dissipated by the mid-1960s. This was not to say that the movement was moribund – for despite financial difficulties membership had risen and a number of local groups had been established.[18] In terms of the public and the media, however, it was not until the latter part of the decade that anti-apartheid would re-emerge as an issue, in the form of direct action protest against sporting links with South Africa.[19]

Forms of action: from boycott to sanctions

The late 1950s had witnessed the growth of new forms of unconventional political activism characterised by the boycott movement itself and Campaign for Nuclear Disarmament (CND). At the outset, however, there was no counterpart to the civil disobedience of the Committee of 100 within the AAM. While we may wish to question generalised assumptions regarding the popularity of sixties radicalism, the influence of the anti-establishment ethos and innovative forms of mobilisation that characterised 1960s protest did have an effect upon the AAM. It was in the realm of cultural contact that the issue of apartheid returned to centre stage in Britain, with the abandonment of the English cricket tour to South Africa in 1968 following the inclusion of South African born Basil D'Oliveira in the English team.[20] The popular attention provided an opportunity for anti-apartheid activists to highlight sporting contacts as a way of bringing the issue of apartheid to the forefront of public debate.[21] One activist, the radical Young Liberal Peter Hain, took a leading role in establishing a group prepared to employ direct action to disrupt tours by the South African rugby and cricket teams in 1969 and 1970. The Stop the Seventy Tour (STST) campaign ensured that the South African rugby team was confronted by a series of protests, including a clash between 7,000 protestors and 2,000 police in Manchester.[22] Opposition to the planned cricket tour rapidly grew in strength, drawing in established church institutions, trades unions and political parties – Prime Minister Harold Wilson made his own public statement of opposition to the tour and eventually it was called off by the cricket authorities.[23] The success of the campaign was due to a large extent to the combination of the AAM's lobbying with the STST committee's direct action in a multi-dimensional repertoire of tactics. As Thörn argues, however, the mobilisation of direct action by anti-apartheid activists shifted public debate from one about the effectiveness of the boycott to one centred upon the legitimacy of direct action, resulting in the marginalisation of the AAM during the 1970s.[24]

While individual political actions via direct action protest and consumer boycotts, were a fundamental element of movement culture, engagement with mainstream political processes continued to play a key role. This was particularly evident in attempts to lobby government and business to impose economic and trade sanctions. In this context, the overlap between the AAM's function as a conventional political actor and that of a transformative 'space of action'[25] is most obvious; in calling for sanctions, AAM activists were concerned to promote a clear influence upon the South African government, one that would 'diminish the capacity of the state to sustain minority rule'.[26] It is here, perhaps, that attempts to measure the success of the movement are most applicable. For some observers, the South African case does indeed demonstrate the capacity of sanctions to influence political change,[27] yet this must be understood in terms of sanctions in the widest definition of the term, social and cultural in addition to economic. As with the boycott campaign, the call for sanctions originated with Congress leaders within South Africa in the late 1950s, although the earliest attempts at inter-governmental pressure came with the Government of India's withdrawal of its High Commissioner in 1946.[28] Stronger international measures, what Klotz describes as 'strategic sanctions' at the state level, came with the UN backed arms embargo, introduced in 1963. In Britain, however, the Wilson government, while halting arms deals with South Africa in 1964, confirmed that it would honour existing agreements, resulting in what was best a partial embargo.[29]

During the 1970s, the question of sanctions became linked with debates around the structural foundations of apartheid, influenced by neo-marxist theories of underdevelopment and neo-colonialism.[30] The continued trade and financial connections between South Africa and the UK (over the course of the 1960s, net direct investment in South Africa had risen from £9 million to £70 million),[31] began to be seen by some radical critics as evidence that the strength of apartheid reflected the fact that racialism was an 'essential factor' in the growth of capitalism.[32] Within South Africa, meanwhile, the psychological- and identity-based philosophy of Black Consciousness had helped to stimulate a resurgence of protest, beginning with a wave of strikes in 1973, The Soweto uprising of 1976 brought the issue of apartheid firmly back onto the international agenda. While the event sharpened the worldwide critique of apartheid, some began to argue that capitalist interests might in fact work as agents for the removal of apartheid restrictions,[33] providing a justification for continued economic, social and political contact with South Africa. By the 1980s, South Africa's two largest trade partners, Britain and the USA, firmly held to a policy of 'constructive engagement'. The sanctions debate began, therefore, to reflect wider international divisions – all the more as the South African government under P.W. Botha adopted a neo-liberal language of reform seemingly in accord with the political philosophies of Margaret Thatcher and Ronald Reagan.[34]

Under these circumstances, the AAM's campaign for sanctions was easily aligned with a broader critique of the policy and ethos of 1980s neo-liberalism. Continued attempts by AAM leaders failed to persuade the British government to alter its policy of engagement,[35] but served to establish support for sanctions – and the AAM more generally – congruent with an expression of dissatisfaction with 'Thatcherism' in a wider sense. Specific sanctions campaigns intensified over the course of the 1980s, with varying degrees of success. The international arms embargo, made mandatory by the UN in 1977, provided impetus to campaigns against specific companies that continued to supply military equipment to South Africa, as well as more general protest against South African militarism and its development of nuclear weapons.[36] Attempts to lobby the Conservative government in Britain had little success, but it was nevertheless claimed (with some justification) that the international arms embargo helped undermine the South African military efforts in Angola, having a direct impact on its defeat at Cuito Canavale in 1988.[37] Oil, of which South Africa possessed no domestic sources, was perceived to be apartheid's 'Achilles heel',[38] and attempts to cut off supplies while leaky at best, did significantly increase the costs of apartheid and probably contributed to the slowing of economic growth in the 1970s and 80s.[39]

Beyond the level of government activities, the AAM paid close attention to the involvement of British-based businesses in South Africa, disseminating information on such links and directing grassroots' action against specific companies and institutions, such as picketing of Shell petrol stations in 1986. Associated campaigns such as the church-based End Loans to South Africa, formed in 1974 to protest against loans given to the South African government by the Midland Bank, aimed to promote more general disinvestment.[40] Perhaps the most sustained – and successful – of such campaigns was that aimed at Barclays Bank, causing significant loss of retail customer business, particularly in the student sector, which played a significant role in the bank's decision to sell its South African subsidiary in 1986.[41] Over 30 years, then, a fundamental aspect of AAM activity was the attempt to increase economic pressures on South Africa, through sanctions and disinvestment campaigns, operating across a range of state, business and civil society institutions, and incorporating a variety of tactics ranging from conventional lobbying to direct action.

The 1980s: local groups and anti-Thatcherism

From the mid-1980s, when the Botha government declared a State of Emergency within South Africa, the AAM reached the height of its popular support in Britain. In part, as suggested above, this reflected the degree to which opposition to apartheid formed part of a wider resurgence of protest groups emerging in the nexus of developments at the international level (Cold War tensions, growing concerns over environmental issues) and protest against the policies and political values of Thatcherism, illustrated by the revival of interest in CND.[42] In the case of the AAM, the revival of interest began in the wake of the Soweto uprising in 1976 and the death in custody of the Black Consciousness leader Steve Biko the following year; a dramatic growth in support came, however, as a response to the explosion of township violence in the mid-1980s, and the increasingly repressive response of the Botha government. Thus, while reflecting the climate of international and domestic attitudes, it is important to remember that developments within the movement remained closely tied to developments within South Africa.

During the mid-1980s, the activities of local AAM groups became an increasingly important marker of movement identity and represented the complex interplay between transnational and domestic political activism. The importance of local groups was recognised by the national AAM from the outset, as nodes of activity through which the national campaign could be coordinated.[43] Local groups appear to have differed markedly in size and character across Britain, from the large and highly organised metropolitan and regional movements such as those based in Bristol, Birmingham and Scotland, to an array of smaller, loosely organised, and often short lived groups. By the end of the 1960s, the national AAM had been supplemented by around 40 local groups, although the numbers did not expand significantly until the 1980s, when the number of local groups rose to 189 in 1986.[44] Local groups represented the popular base of the AAM, although their relationship with the national office was at times problematic,[45] creating a sense of two interrelated, but distinct, movements.

In general terms, local groups often followed a pattern similar to that of Southampton AAM, with a small core of dedicated activists and a wider group of more passive supporters.[46] Fieldhouse suggests that the activist core often saw their involvement with the AAM in terms of a wider political engagement, while the peripheral supporters viewed anti-apartheid as a specific moral issue, distinct from politics.[47] Such generalisations may be of limited use – it is clear that individuals supported AAM in a variety of ways and for a range of reasons – yet the link between AAM membership and wider political involvement has been acknowledged.[48] To a certain extent, this reflected the anti-Thatcherism of 1980s protest movements, and the strong left wing and trade unionist character of many AAM activists. Thus, despite attempts to elicit cross party support, the AAM has invariably become associated with the political left, in which the expression of solidarity with the struggle to end apartheid became a simultaneous expression of discontent with the British government, or a reflection of conflicts between central and local government.

The AAM struggled, at both national and local levels, to avoid close identification with the 'far left'. To an extent, this derived from the propensity of the South African government to describe its opponents – both domestically and internationally – in the language of Cold War anti-communism, as well as the support provided to the liberation movements by the Soviet Union. However, during the 1980s, the struggle between the AAM and elements of the communist left did begin to pose serious difficulties, particularly in the case of the City of London Anti-Apartheid group, whose links with the Troyskyite Revolutionary Communist Group (RCG) led it into direct conflict with the national office over militant tactics and ideology. In 1982, the City Group launched a series of pickets outside the South African Embassy in Trafalgar Square, which culminated in a continuous vigil from April 1986 until 1990. The picket exemplified the City Group's advocacy of direct action tactics and it was these, together with their insistence that anti-apartheid should be explicitly linked with wider anti-imperial and anti-racist campaigns – contrary to the AAM's insistence upon a single issue campaign – that brought RCG supporters into conflict with the AAM.[49]

Even within mainstream AAM activities, direct action tactics were employed, from the disruption of events, for example the annual raising of national flags on Shakespeare's birthday at Stratford-upon-Avon, or protests aimed at performers who had worked in South Africa such as Marti Caine, to more covert attempts to publicise official links with apartheid, such as the Southampton AAM group's monitoring of arms exports.[50] Local groups were also at the forefront of national campaigns against specific companies who maintained trade and financial links with South Africa, such as Barclays Bank and Shell. These activities, together with fundraising and publicity, were a central function of local AAM groups. Some larger groups were able, however, to initiate local initiatives that complemented national campaigns. At times, this meant forming alliances with other organisations in specific campaigns, as in the case of the cooperation between Southampton AAM, the university lecturers' union, AUT, the Southampton student union, and the Southampton City Council to block the participation of South African delegates in the inaugural World Archaeological Congress.[51] Of particular – and increasing – importance in this context were links with church organisations, as the South African churches found themselves at the forefront of opposition to apartheid during the 1980s; a relationship compounded by the appointment of Trevor Huddleston as President of AAM in 1983.

Local groups also sought to forge links with organisations and institutions in their own area. In some cases this was a further reflection of contemporary circumstances, notably the heightened tensions in community relations following outbreaks of rioting in many UK cities during the early 1980s. Both Bristol and Birmingham AAM groups recognised the need to link anti-apartheid campaigns with anti-racism, in the case of Bristol through collaboration with community organisations in the St. Paul's area, in a campaign to create an 'Apartheid Free Zone'.[52] However, despite the involvement of black community leaders such as the Labour MP Bernie Grant, the relationship between the AAM and black community organisations was often uneasy, based in part on the tension between the movement's desire to maintain focus on the single issue of apartheid and the apparent link between apartheid and racism in a wider sense. Stuart Hall has characterised links between the AAM and black community organisations as the interaction between 'two contiguous and related, but not unified, dicourses about racism'.[53]

More successful, perhaps, was the collaboration between AAM groups and Local Authorities, who were both a site of political struggle during the 1980s, and a route for the integration of social movement activists into mainstream political activity.[54] This was most strongly evident in those councils controlled by the Labour Party, such as Sheffield, where the local AAM group not only worked with the council (led by future Home Secretary David Blunkett) on the establishment of an Apartheid

Free Zone in the city,[55] but also to convene a conference on 'Local Authority Action Against Apartheid' in 1983, which resulted in the creation of a steering committee to advise and coordinate Local Authority anti-apartheid policies, including purchasing policies, the inclusion of anti-apartheid in education, and the promotion of the cultural boycott.[56] However, as the decade progressed, efforts to trim the power of local authorities, such as the Local Government Act of 1986, set limits on the freedom of local authorities to impose anti-apartheid restrictions.

During the 1980s, anti-apartheid became a significant factor in British extra-parliamentary politics. Increased support gave impetus to the lobbying activities of the national executive, and resulted in tangible success, for example the Barclays boycott, and the disruption and cancellation of cultural events. Such successes illustrate the increasing level of international interest in the issue of apartheid, which reflected the heightened intensity of civil unrest within South Africa; they also mirrored the escalation of anti-apartheid pressure around the world, exemplified by the US Comprehensive Anti-Apartheid Act of 1986 as well as measures agreed by the Commonwealth.[57] But anti-apartheid activism also reflected the domestic political climate of 1980s Britain: many core activists engaged with the issue as part of a wider political effort in opposition to the Conservative government. The AAM represented a means to oppose Thatcherite policies, both in terms of direct protest against continued official support for the South African regime, but also as an expression of wider dissatisfaction.

The politics of culture and communication: the Mandela campaign

The British AAM was not simply a reflection of the national political environment, however, for it also operated as a form of transnational activism within a global anti-apartheid campaign. Key to this campaign was the communication of information and propaganda through various media. The AAM newsletter, *Anti-Apartheid News*, launched in 1964, was an important conduit for information on the political situation within South Africa, despite continued financial difficulties.[58] In addition, the AAM and other organisations produced a series of literature on South Africa, and the ANC established an Information and Publicity department in the early 1970s. The AAM paid close attention to media strategies, including the cultivation of contacts with journalists working in the established media, with varying degrees of success – while the UK media showed an interest in South African affairs, it was felt that the media exhibited a bias against anti-apartheid.[59]

Beyond the established media, the AAM began to construct what Thörn describes as an 'anti-apartheid public space' through literature, music, film and other cultural products.[60] The iconography of anti-apartheid, including its characteristic black and white badge, as well as posters and T-shirts, as well as the formation of the ANC cultural group Amandla, became part of a deliberate 'cultural turn' in anti-apartheid strategy from the late 1970s.[61] Most successful of all was the construction of a mythology around the figure of the imprisoned ANC leader, Nelson Mandela, which began with a campaign to mark his 60th birthday in 1978.[62] The plight of political prisoners had long been a key concern of anti-apartheid campaigners, and in 1964 attention was focussed on efforts to persuade the South African government not to impose the death penalty upon the defendants in the so called 'Rivonia trial' of the leaders of the ANC's armed wing, including Mandela.[63] With its focus on humanitarian assistance for those imprisoned for their part in political resistance, centre stage was taken by IDAF, but the AAM maintained its own campaign for the release of political prisoners through the 1970s and 80s.

The most well known of these efforts was the Free Mandela campaign, which became a key component of the narrative of anti-apartheid during the 1980s. In what was arguably the clearest example of transnational activity within anti-apartheid, international solidarity movements and sympathetic organisations such as the British Labour Party worked in direct support of campaigns within South Africa. By the late 1980s, the image of Mandela achieved a remarkable degree of public recognition, through public memorials such as the sculpture on London's South Bank and the renaming of numerous streets and university student union buildings. The Mandela campaign was also effective in attracting support via popular culture, including the commercially successful single 'Nelson Mandela' released by the ska group the Specials in March 1984, the 'Freedom Festival' organised by the Specials' Jerry Dammers and Dali Tambo, son of the ANC President in 1986, and the formation of 'Artists Against Apartheid' in the same year.[64] The culmination of these efforts was the 'Freedom at Seventy' campaign, timed to coincide with Mandela's birthday in 1988, an event marked by a concert in Wembley station broadcast on television and radio in over 60 countries worldwide. An opinion poll taken at the time of the concert, and the Freedom March from Glasgow to London that followed shortly afterwards, suggested that over 90 per cent of the population were familiar with Mandela's name (in contrast to that of their own local MP).[65]

The struggle over the representation of apartheid saw continued efforts on the part of the AAM to disseminate information about events within South Africa and to sustain public attention for over 30 years. That it achieved this with increasing success was, as Thörn suggests, partly due to technological developments that enabled the rapid reproduction and communication of information.[66] The 'information politics' of the AAM thus developed within the context of broader changes in media technology linked with increasing globalisation of culture.[67]

Conclusion: anti-apartheid, transnational social movements and global civil society

There were various levels of participation in anti-apartheid activities. Some leading activists engaged with anti-apartheid as a form of conventional politics, involving direct contact with official representatives of state and business institutions, or global organisations such as the UN. Others may not have engaged in the politics of anti-apartheid at this level, but nevertheless saw involvement with the movement as engagement with politics more broadly. This was particularly the case during the 1980s, when the AAM could be viewed as part of an extended front of opposition to Thatcherism. Yet, at the same time, movement activists often made it clear that anti-apartheid was a self consciously single issue campaign. The apparent singularity of purpose, should not, however, mean that the movement be defined merely as a narrowly focussed pressure group. For participation in anti-apartheid also meant participation in a movement culture (anything from the wearing of badges to attending events); engagement, therefore, with a wider collective community of activists. Perhaps most importantly, it meant participation in the boycott of South African goods, an activity which represented the intersection between individual political action and organised political campaign, between conventional politics and new forms of political culture, and between the national politics of Britain and the national politics of South Africa. Anti-apartheid thus constituted a space in which various levels of political engagement – in a variety of national contexts – coalesced into a social movement whose identity was defined in relation to transnational political dynamics.

It is this transnational dimension that makes the AAM important for the study of post-war modes of political organisation in Britain. While elements of the anti-apartheid social movement may usefully be described as NGOs (the AAM itself as an institution, or IDAF, for example), the movement as a whole cannot be viewed as an organisation in a conventional sense. Most significantly, it was a movement that operated across national borders, connecting distant and distinct political cultures in different parts of the world in a transnational network of activists. The creation of this network was facilitated by advances in communication and individual mobility which in themselves have developed in the context of economic and cultural globalisation. Anti-apartheid thus represents an emergent phenomenon of contemporary political activity: a movement operating simultaneously in both a national and global political space; this global civil society, in contrast to national civil societies, has been defined as a space in which 'a diversity of political cultures interact and intersect'.[68] Anti-apartheid thus provides a key example of the ways in which post-war political participation has stretched the definition of organised political activity – in terms of both form and the arena in which it operates. It is necessary to assess the relationship between the AAM and British political culture, but it cannot be fully understood without reference to developments in socio-political action beyond the level of the nation state.

Notes

1 Håkan Thörn, *Anti-Apartheid and the Emergence of Global Civil Society* (Basingstoke: Palgrave, 2006).
2 Christabel Gurney, '"A Great Cause": The Origins of the Anti-Apartheid Movement, June 1959–March 1960', *Journal of Southern African Studies*, 26(1) (2000), pp. 123–44.
3 *Ibid*, p. 143; Minutes of Boycott Committee Meeting, 16 March, 1960, Archive of the Anti-Apartheid Movement, Bodleian Library, Oxford, AAM archive, MSS AAM 2.
4 Minutes of Boycott Committee Meeting, 20 April, 1960, AAM Archive, MSS AAM 2.
5 Roger Fieldhouse, *Anti-Apartheid: The History of the Movement in Britain*, (London: Merlin Press, 2005), p. 30.
6 ANC representative Tennyson Makiwane played a leading role in the boycott campaign from its foundation as an offshoot of the CAO in 1959, while SA Liberal Party activist Patrick van Rensburg acted as Director of the campaign until early 1960, Gurney, 'A Great Cause', p. 137; on the issue of South African political exiles more generally, see Mark Israel, *South African Political Exile in the United Kingdom* (Basingstoke: Macmillan, 1999).
7 Gurney, 'A Great Cause', p. 144.
8 Howard Smith, 'Apartheid, Sharpeville and "Impartiality": The Reporting of South Africa on BBC Television 1948–61', *Historical Journal of Film, Radio and Television*, 13(3) (1993), pp. 251–98.

9   Stephen Howe, *Anticolonialism in British Politics: The Left and the End of Empire* (Oxford: Clarendon Press, 1993); see also David Goldsworthy, *Colonial Issues in British Politics, 1945–61* (Oxford: Clarendon Press, 1971).

10 Ann Yates and Lewis Chester, *The Troublemaker – Michael Scott and His Lonely Struggle Against Injustice* (London: Aurum Press, 2006).

11 Denis Herbstein, *White Lies – Canon Collins and the Secret War Against Apartheid* (Oxford: James Currey, 2004).

12 Trevor Huddleston, *Naught for Your Comfort* (London: Collins, 1956); see also the recent biographies of Huddleston: Robin *Denniston, Trevor Huddleston – A Life* (Basingstoke: Macmillan, 1999); Piers McGrandle, *Trevor Huddleston – Turbulent Priest* (London: Continuum, 2004).

13 *Observer*, 10th October, 1954. Privately, Huddleston had advocated international action against apartheid for some time: T. Huddleston to Collins, 20th February 1953, Lambeth Palace Library, Papers of Canon Collins, MS 3300, f. 112.

14 John Major, 'The Trades Union Congress and Apartheid, 1948–1970', *Journal of Southern African Studies* 31(3) (2005) pp. 477–93.

15 R. Hyam, 'Africa and the Labour Government, 1945–1951', *Journal of Imperial and Commonwealth History*, XVI, 3 (1988) pp. 148–72.

16 Fieldhouse, *Anti-Apartheid*, p. 26.

17 A. Darnborough, *Labour's Record on Southern Africa* (London: Anti-Apartheid Movement, 1967).

18 Fieldhouse, *Anti-Apartheid* pp. 60–3.

19 Adam Lent, *British Social Movements since 1945: Sex, Colour, Peace and Power* (Basingstoke: Palgrave, 2001), pp. 112–14.

20 Bruce Murray, 'Politics and Cricket: The D'Oliveira Affair of 1968', *Journal of Southern African Studies*, 27(4) (2001), pp. 667–84.

21 Although protest against sporting links with South Africa had begun as early as the Cardiff Empire and Commonwealth Games in 1958, see M. Keech, 'The Ties that Bind: South Africa and Sports Diplomacy, 1958–1963', *Sports Historian*, 21 (2001).

22 *Times*, 27 November 1969.

23 Fieldhouse, *Anti-Apartheid*, p. 97.

24 Thörn, *Anti-Apartheid*, pp. 156–7.

25 *Ibid*, p. 11.

26 Mark Orkin, 'Introduction: The Case for Sanctions Against Apartheid', in Orkin, M. (ed), *Sanctions Against Apartheid* (Cape Town: David Phillip, 1989), p. 2.

27 Audie Klotz, 'Making Sanctions Work: Comparative Lessons', in Crawford, N. and Klotz, A. (eds), *How Sanctions Work: Lessons from South Africa* (Basingstoke: Macmillan, 1999), pp. 264–87.

28 *Times*, 12th June 1946.

29 Arianna Lissoni, 'A History of the AAM and its Influence on the British Government's Policy towards South Africa in 1964' (MA dissertation, London School of Economics, 2000), available online via <http://www.anc.org.za/ancdocs/history/aam/dissertation.htm>; Fieldhouse, p. 79.

30 See for example, H. Wolpe, 'Capitalism and Cheap-Labour Power in South Africa: From Segregation to Apartheid', in *Economy and Society* 1:4 (1972), pp. 425–56.

31 Ruth First, Jonathan Steele, Christabel Gurney, *The South African Connection – Western Investment in Apartheid* (London: Penguin, 1973), p. 332.

32 *Ibid*, p. 291.

33 Merle Lipton, 'The Debate about South Africa: Neo-Marxists and Neo-Liberals', *African Affairs*, 78(310) (1979), pp. 57–80.

34 For an overview of these developments, see Shula Marks and Stanley Trapido, 'South Africa since 1976: An Historical Perspective', in Johnson, S. (ed.) *South Africa No Turning Back* (Basingstoke: Macmillan, 1988), pp. 1–51. On the language of reform, see Deborah Posel, 'The Language of Domination, 1978–83', in Marks, S. and Trapido, S., *The Politics of Race, Class and Nationalism in Twentieth Century South Africa* (Harlow: Longman, 1987), pp. 419–43.

35 R. Fieldhouse, *Anti-Apartheid*, pp. 180–91.

36 Anti-Apartheid Movement, *How Britain Arms Apartheid* (London: AAM, 1987).

37 Robert Davies, 'After Cuito Canavale' in Orkin, *Sanctions* , pp. 198–206.

38 First, Steele, Gurney, *South African Connection*, pp. 103–6.

39 Neta C. Crawford, 'Oil Sanctions Against Apartheid', in Crawford and Klotz, *How Sanctions Work*, pp. 103–26.

40 Fieldhouse, *Anti-Apartheid*, pp. 87–95.

41 Nerys John, 'The Campaign Against British Bank Involvement in Apartheid South Africa', *African Affairs*, 99 (2000), pp. 415–33.

42 See Paul Byrne, *Social Movements in Britain* (London: Routledge, 1997), p. 93.

43 A Boycott Committee meeting in December 1959 noted the 'urgent need for local committees', and it was subsequently reported that by the following February, over thirty such committees had been established. Minutes of Boycott Committee Meeting, 29 December 1959; 3 February 1960, AAM archives, MSS AAM 2.

44 Fieldhouse, *Anti-Apartheid*, pp. 310–29.

45 *Ibid*, pp. 319–20.

46 David Hoadley (Southampton AAM), witness seminar on Local Anti-Apartheid Groups, London, 3rd June 2006.

47 Fieldhouse, *Anti-Apartheid*, p. 311.

48 Andy Chaffer (Birmingham AAM), Judith Sawyer (Richmond AAM), Witness seminar on Local Anti-Apartheid Groups, London, 3 June 2006.

49 Fieldhouse, *Anti-Apartheid*, pp. 218–27.

50 Andy Chaffer (Birmingham AAM), Paul Blomfield (Sheffield AAM), David Hoadley (Southampton AAM), witness seminar on Local Anti-Apartheid Groups, London, 3 June 2006.

51 Peter Ucko, *Academic Freedom and Apartheid: The Story of the World Archaeological Congress* (London: Duckworth, 1987).

52 Gerard Omasta-Wilsom (Bristol AAM), witness seminar on Local Anti-Apartheid Groups, London, 3 June 2006.

53 Stuart Hall, 'The AAM and the Race-ing of Britain', paper presented at the symposium, 'The Anti-Apartheid Movement: a 40-year perspective' held at South Africa House, London, 25–26 June 1999. Also available online via <http://www.anc.org/ancdocs/history/aam/symposium.html#Hall>; see also Elizabeth Williams, 'Black British solidarity with the South African liberation movements', paper presented at the workshop on 'Liberation Struggles

in Southern Africa, International Solidarity and the Anti-Apartheid Movement: New Perspectives', held at the School of Oriental and African Studies, London, February 3, 2006.

54 Lent, *Social Movements*, pp. 173–8.
55 Paul Blomfield (Sheffield AAM), witness seminar on Local Anti-Apartheid

Critically review the social, scientific + historical literature on what motivates individuals to volunteer and or be

philanthropic.

Seeking to promote welfare of others esp by donating money to good causes, generous + benevolent.

66 Thörn, *Anti-Apartheid*, pp. 122–3.
67 *Ibid*, pp. 196–9.
68 *Ibid*, p. 205.

8
Stopping the Poor Getting Poorer: The Establishment and Professionalisation of Poverty NGOs, 1945–95[1]

Tanya Evans

After the Second World War it was widely believed that the welfare state had eradicated poverty. Within this context, voluntary organisations that represented the needs of the poor did not fare well in terms of funding or government influence. This situation was to change however in response to a number of high profile social surveys written and published in the 1960s. These built on Titmuss' arguments and challenged the orthodoxy that the Attlee government had abolished want in Britain.[2] In the process poverty was re-defined and people were stunned to discover that certain groups within British society, particularly the elderly and large families, had fallen through the gaps in the welfare state and become poorer.[3] The account of the establishment and professionalisation of poverty NGOs from 1945 to 1995 that follows is based predominately on my research of the archives and oral histories with members of the staff of the National Council for the Unmarried Mother and her Child (NCUMC) which became One Parent Families (OPF) in 1973.[4]

Brian Abel-Smith and Peter Townsend's *The Poor and the Poorest*[5] published shortly before Christmas in 1965, in order to make maximum impact, and in the wake of Townsend's, 'The Meaning of Poverty'[6] and *The Family Life of Old People*,[7] Margaret Wynn's, *Fatherless Families*,[8] Peter Marris's, *Widows and their Families*,[9] Harriet Wilson's *Delinquency and Child Neglect*[10] and Virginia Wimperis', *The Unmarried Mother and her Child*[11] undermined the belief that the welfare state was an unqualified success. Collectively, these publications and their campaigning authors heavily influenced the voluntary sector and, in turn, mainstream politics. Like-minded academics, social workers, administrators of the social services and sociologists with the London School of Economics at its heart grouped together from the mid-50s to widen the awareness that universal benefits were inadequate to tackle poverty, that some people within British society were more likely to be poor than others particularly the elderly, children and the disabled, and to change the way the government dealt with the needs of these groups. This 'rediscovery of poverty' amongst social researchers as well as others in the 1960s had an enormous political, social and cultural impact on the voluntary sector from the 1970s. Many entirely new pressure groups were formed during this period including the Child Poverty Action Group (CPAG) in 1965, Shelter on behalf of the home-less in 1966, and the Disablement Income Group in 1965 which was initiated by two housewives suffering from multiple sclerosis writing a letter to *The Guardian* describing the poverty of disabled people.[12]

Some commentators have suggested that from the mid-60s, some individuals' disillusionment with the incapacity of the Labour govern-ment to adequately tackle poverty, illustrated by the absence of any mention of legislative provision for poor families in the Queen's speech of 1964, encouraged many to desert the Labour Party and to turn to the voluntary sector to ameliorate the lives of society's poorest. Many socialists sought professional work in voluntary organ-isations determined to stop the poor getting poorer. The poverty lobby was formed partly as a result of this flight from the Labour Party. Others argued that the Labour government at the time was seri-ously constrained by a number of financial crises.[13] A more significant development in the creation of the lobby was the expansion of socio-logy and social administration as academic subjects and social work as a profession which created a class of people who found graduate jobs within these NGOs.[14] Some were important to their origins. The CPAG was formed by individuals, including Townsend, a number of mem-bers of the Quaker's Social and Economic Affairs Committee of which Harriet Wilson was one, and others who had been stunned by the poverty they had researched, investigated and learned more about from the work of their colleagues. They demanded that the Labour government adopt a coherent policy with regard to family poverty.[15] Increasing numbers of graduates with professional qualifications were employed as *paid* staff in a number of these voluntary organisations over the course of the 1970s and as a result they became staffed pre-dominately by professionals. Nonetheless, volunteers remained crucial to their management and administration. OPF as an organisation that had existed since 1918 as the NCUMC was enlivened by an influx of these young graduates in the 1970s who brought new skills, a coherent political identity, often formed in higher education institutions in the late 60s, and a change in emphasis to the workings of the organisation.[16] Help the Aged was another organisation that was repackaged as a result of these reforms. It was created in 1961 by middle-class volunteers who had long been involved with the Voluntary Christian Service Group. Professionalisation resulted in the social work, fundraising and policy work departments of many organisations becoming much more effective.[17]

The poverty lobby represented a number of groups which worked to influence the income maintenance policies of government in the interest of the poor.[18] The tactics and strategies of these new political groups differed in emphasis and style from those of the immediate post-war years although they shared some characteristics with voluntary organisations which had campaigned successfully in the 1920s and 30s including the NCUMC. Nonetheless, the high profile political lobbying undertaken particularly by the CPAG in the 60s and 70s resulted in the CPAG being regarded as the vanguard of the lobby. This organisation stood apart from the others due to its use of the media and frequent public assaults on government. The professionalisation of all of these groups occurred in a number of different areas including lobbying activity focussed on parliament and Whitehall, the utilisation of the media which was also undergoing a transformation at the time and becoming more critical of government, and in the advice given to clients as well as in fundraising.

These NGOs focussed on the poverty of poor families throughout the 70s and they did so by demanding that the government increase family allowances. The campaign for the implementation of the Finer Report also demonstrated the importance of developing allegiances and using particular tactics within the lobby. The Report helped to galvanise these NGOs in the 1970s and in many ways helps us as historians to identify the most important actors within the lobby. The Committee on One Parent Families was appointed late in 1969 under the chairmanship of Sir Morris Finer after many years of campaigning by the lobby.[19] Their Report was eventually published in 1974 and it made important recommendations addressing the poverty of lone mothers and their children. It marked the recognition, for the first time, of the poverty of poor families within mainstream political discussion. The Government, however, chose to largely ignore the report's recommendations because of their cost implications. These NGOs fought hard to maintain the increased prominence of child poverty that the Report had achieved. Although many individuals within the poverty lobby expected the government to satisfy their demands immediately, the Labour party was constrained by the economic crisis of 1974. They continued to press the Government to hold a parliamentary debate on the Report and formed the Finer Joint Action Committee. This Committee first met in July 1974 and included a number of familiar allies including OPF, the CPAG, Gingerbread, Mothers in Action and many others.[20] The Committee lobbied individual MPs, made contact with the political parties and used the media to publicise their concerns. They concentrated their efforts on urging the Government to hold a proper debate on the Report.[21] Although they failed to have Finer's major recommendations implemented OPF was successful in campaigning for the introduction of Child Interim (later to become One Parent Family) benefit which was the first nod the government made towards the special needs of one parent families.

The Finer Report was formulated at the same time that OPF changed its function and name to provide for all unsupported mothers. The NCUMC became the National Council for OPF from 1973. This development had a long trajectory but it symbolised the changing perception of unmarried mothers as abnormal to normal with a new focus on their shared poverty and material circumstances with other unsupported mothers.

From the 1970s poverty NGOs relied particularly on the use of the media and academic research to fuel the fire of their campaigns. Shelter, headed by the media-savvy journalist Des Wilson who championed the significance of an organisation's image, used the shocking film *Cathy Come Home* as well as adverts in the press to successfully raise funds.[22] A 1966 advertisement describing one family's 'Home Sweet Hell' in *The Times* encouraged the public to donate £50,000 (around £400,000 in today's money) in only one month of campaigning.[23] By the late-60s Shelter was extremely well funded with a turnover of several million in contrast to other NGOs that tended to operate on a shoestring budget. Nonetheless others also used the press to add to their funds. Tony Lynes has talked about how dependent CPAG was upon the media for money:

> I can remember one occasion when it looked as if the coffers were getting a bit low, and I reported the fact to the *Guardian* and it ran an article one day saying 'CPAG threatened with extinction through lack of money', and the following day somebody rang and offered us a very generous donation.[24]

All organisations used the broadsheet press, particularly *The Times* and the *Guardian* to advertise their work. Frank Field has suggested that he used the letters page of *The Times* in order to influence civil servants and MPs and if he wanted to make an impression on left-liberal intellectuals outside as well as inside government he wrote letters to, and articles for, the *Guardian*.[25] The media was used both to influence individual MPs and civil servants as well as to raise the profile of organisations more generally. Over the years NGOs created a lengthy contact list of people in the media sympathetic to their aims.[26] The support of individual journalists was crucial particularly for organisations like OPF because of the unpopularity of their client group. Magazine articles, television or radio programmes and letters to agony aunts in women's magazines resulted in a flurry of requests for help from the NCUMC/OPF.[27] During the 1950s and 60s a mention on Evelyn Home's page in *Woman* and in the 1970s and early 80s, on Marje Proops' advice page in the *Daily Mirror,* would bring forth a flood of women knocking on the office doors of OPF on Kentish Town Road.[28] Richard Todd, also at the *Mirror,* was particularly interested in the work of the CPAG.[29] Journalists were invited to become members of the management committees of these organisations. Frances Cairncross was working as economics editor on the *Guardian* when she was asked to become Honorary Treasurer of OPF in 1979.[30] Andreas Whittam Smith, who went on to found the *Independent*, and Mary Ann Sieghart were also financial journalists who became involved with OPF as Honorary Treasurers.[31] Celia Brayfield was a member of the Committee of Management who worked as a freelance journalist and author and was also a lone parent. She shared her many media contacts with the Council.[32] Anne Spackman who worked as Vice Chair for the Council was Deputy Editor of the 'Weekend' Section of the Independent and specialised in social affairs and European family policy.[33] Celia Weston was another active member of the Management and Policy Committees. She wrote for a number of daily papers and specialised in education as well as campaigning in the Women's and Trade Union movement.[34] Pat Healey at *The Times* was another important ally for the lobby as a whole and highlighted the needs of poor families in carefully written and well-informed articles throughout the 1970s. During the 1970s and 80s the broadsheet media was much more susceptible to stories created by pressure groups than they are now.[35] Paul Lewis worked hard to maintain an increased media profile on behalf of OPF in the 1970s.[36] Articles supporting the Council's work were aimed at attracting the attention of Britain's political elite and resulted in the increased profile of the organisation as well as the clients it represented. A carefully maintained relationship with the media was crucial to the popularity of poverty NGOs in terms of campaigning as well as fundraising.

The use of empirical evidence by the poverty lobby was another tactic used with renewed vigour to support their case for people's needs and to influence policy. Some academic studies had an enormous impact on particular individuals within the civil service and parliament and were fed into the policy-making process in a variety of ways. Some NGOs existed as a quasi-civil service informing opposition MPs. This Fabian oriented approach was used by most organisations within these NGOs.[37] Tony Lynes had many contacts within the civil service through which he filtered CPAG material.[38] The Supplementary Benefits Commission (SBC) kept a file on the CPAG but not on any other of the organisations within the poverty lobby. Officers within the Commission often discussed material brought to their attention by the group, no doubt due to Titmuss' relationship with Lynes.[39] These empirical studies were also crucial to changing conceptions of the poor that resulted in their increased 'normalisation' during this period. The move from understandings of the 'problem family' and the pathologisation of unmarried mothers as psychologically deviant that were pervasive throughout the 1950s changed after the 60s. During the 1970s most people who worked with, for, and on behalf of the poor came to believe that structural rather than personal factors resulted in their poverty. These beliefs filtered their way through to the civil service and as a result to ministerial level albeit not without a degree of scepticism.[40] It has been suggested by Stephen Brooke that the discursive legacy of organisations was as, if not more, important than victories regarding legislative change.[41] The work of poverty NGOs was crucial to this changing perception and empathy of the poor during this period. However, this was to change again in the 1980s as beliefs about the underclass became prevalent amongst the political elite once more and in the 1990s as structural explanations came to the fore again.[42]

OPF became increasingly dependent on the opinions, research and activities of academics working within their field to provide evidence to inform their campaigns. They had also long relied on the information they gathered from individual case studies of poor women and their children in their attempts to influence the government. The research of Virginia Wimperis and particularly that of Margaret Wynn, nonetheless, helped inform others campaigning on behalf of the lobby in the 1970s. Dennis Marsden, Joseph Rowntree Fellow and Lecturer at Essex University in the 1960s, and author of *Mothers Alone*[43] written as part of Townsend's *Poverty in the UK project*, presented a paper at

OPF's annual conference in 1968, chaired a working party for the organisation on a single parent family allowance and became a member of OPF in 1973. At the conference he outlined the results of his research.[44] His work was also considered by civil servants, though mostly dismissively, working on behalf of the Finer Committee.[45] Jenny Levin who chaired the Legal and Social Policy Committee in the 70s following Professor Schapiro's resignation, was a senior lecturer in law at the University of London and was heavily involved in the campaign for the transformation of family law in the 1980s.[46] Schapiro had been a professor of political science at LSE and a barrister for many years.[47] Carol Smart was to become Director of OPF in 1984 but prior to that was a Research officer at the Institute of Psychiatry and returned to academia in the mid-80s.[48] Betsy Dworkin was a member of the Committee of Management and Policy Sub-Committee and Honorary Secretary in the late 80s and early 90s. She was a Harvard and LSE graduate who specialised in social administration and education priorities.[49] Jane Lewis was Professor of Social Policy at the LSE when she became a member of the Committee of Management late in 1991.[50] All of these individuals were important to the formulation of policy and many continue to research and work in the interests of lone mothers. Della Nevitt at the LSE used her relationship with Titmuss and McGregor to write the Council's plans for a one parent family benefit in the recommendations they made to the Finer Committee. OPF produced numerous reports, publications, and research challenging myths about unmarried mothers and using empirical evidence to state their case to Government and to question existing policies. Over the years they campaigned for the positive representation of lone parents in the media and challenged reports that depicted them as responsible for the breakdown of society.[51] The Council also acted as a conduit between the media and lone parents who could be asked directly about many of the issues that concerned them.[52] In the early 1990s to some extent OPF used an informal 'family alliance' amongst NGOs formed of groups like Barnardos, Relate and the Family Policy Studies Centre in order to challenge the belief in the new 'Victorian values' and that the 'nuclear family' was the only type of family that could be promoted in social policy and politics.[53]

From the 1960s the poverty lobby put together deputations that were used to inform and bring pressure on government to address the problems of the poor. They were helped by the restructuring of the social security system. The poverty lobby exploited the creation of the DHSS in 1968 that resulted in the increased prominence of social security issues in the Cabinet. The lobby relied on the press to publicise their efforts to influence civil servants and MPs. They sent letters to MPs, Party Whips, and representatives of all voluntary national organisations in order to further their cause.[54] If a pressure group was to be successful during this period, as in any other, it had to negotiate carefully with parliament and consult frequently with those who held office regardless of their political allegiances. These activities resulted in family poverty coming to the fore during the 1970s.[55]

From this time many organisations recognised that emphasis had to shift from providing 'charity' for poor clients to making them aware of their rights.[56] This development had its roots within an American welfare context.[57] In the early 70s much of OPF's activity was focussed on what many have described as an 'old-fashioned' form of voluntary work doling out advice to unmarried mothers who wrote to them on an individual basis. The increase in state funding for some voluntary groups from the 1970s influenced their increased professionalisation.[58] From the mid-1970s social work departments, created in 1971 as a result of the Seebohm Report of 1968, increasingly took over the care of unmarried mothers and their children from charity workers.[59] From 1976 the Council stopped handing out grants to unmarried mothers and the department changed its role from that of traditional social work to one of welfare rights. In 1979 the Social Work department was renamed the Advice and Rights Department. The Family Law and Legal Advice Centre was established in 1976 to help mothers deal with their legal problems. This service was directly related to the increase in the numbers of mothers who became lone parents on divorce or after separation. The organisation's first lawyer, Frances Logan, was appointed in 1979.[60] In line with these trends, most organisations were encouraged to become more in touch with the clients that they represented.

A number of factors led to OPF, together with other NGOs, becoming more responsive to the needs of its members. The development of welfare rights was just one of these. Gingerbread, one of many representative groups established at this time, was formed in 1970 claiming to more accurately represent lone mothers in Britain because it was run by lone mothers themselves.[61] As a consequence, lone mothers were actively sought as members of the Committee of Management of OPF from this time. Most of the management committees of other NGOs became increasingly aware that their clients needed to be a part of the management process of the organisation. Most groups had a metropolitan base and as the years passed their London-centric nature was criticised together with the elitist, predominately middle-class, characteristics of their leaderships. These elitist organisations were well-positioned to access the corridors of power within Whitehall, parliament, and the media but it was hard to conceptualise them as representative of their clients.[62] Some organisations opened up regional offices in order to deal with some of these problems of representation and democracy. The CPAG had branches in Manchester, Liverpool, Oxford, Birmingham, and Bristol and OPF had ones in Manchester and South London. However, OPF's offices were quick to fold in the 1980s due to lack of funds. In the process, however, some groups within the lobby became more adept at incorporating the demands of their grass-roots members.

Members of the CPAG have also discussed the tension between radical activists within the organisation and those who hoped to exert Fabian academic influence on government.[63] There also existed tensions between those individuals involved with the organisation who went on to work within the establishment and those who remained resolutely outside of it. Especial ire was focussed on Brian Abel-Smith by others who had been involved with the CPAG when he became senior policy advisor to Richard Crossman at the DHSS from 1968–1970 and then senior policy adviser to David Ennals (1976–8). Titmuss was also a focus for criticism when he became Chairman and Deputy-Chairman of the SBC. Both advised Crossman when he was Secretary of State for Social Services.[64] Field challenged the establishment tactics of his former colleagues within the CPAG and Crossman and Abel-Smith were threatened and angered by Field's aggressive campaign. Nicholas Timmins labelled this a 'public assault' against the Labour Party in the 1970s.[65] Field encouraged the separation of the poverty lobby from the Labour Party when he declared that the poor had got poorer under Labour.[66] Field refused to accept the financial constraints on the Labour Party at the time which meant the government found it hard to meet their demands. Those who worked with government thought that many of the lobbyists were politically naïve. Abel-Smith shared many of the same concerns as the CPAG regarding the government's proposals for means-tested benefits for families in the early 70s. He was also more conscious than others who worked outside of government of the financial limits the government worked within.[67] Field, himself, was to become an MP in 1979. Broadly speaking, the beginning of the 80s brought an end to in-fighting within organisations on the subject of elitism and representation as organisations changed to reflect their base and in the struggle against the common enemy of Thatcherism.[68] The non-partisan nature of the campaigning strategies of these organisations, although most possessed an obvious leftist slant and tensions between the politics of staff members were to remain, was to become a significant feature of their success by the end of the 70s. Certain individuals deliberately fostered this culture, including Field and Ruth Lister within the CPAG and Paul Lewis within OPF.[69]

In the late 70s and early 80s Lewis, Deputy Director of OPF, worked hard to cultivate a number of sympathetic contacts in both Houses in order to promote the concerns of unmarried mothers in parliament. The Council was always careful to make sure that it was represented at political party conferences each year and would often hold fringe meetings on issues relating to the needs of one-parent groups.[70] During the 80s in the campaign against Social Security Reform, they relied heavily on Lord McGregor, as President, to put forward the Council's case in the House of Lords.[71] Tessa Jowell was a member of the Committee of Management from the late 70s to the late 80s and a vital conduit between OPF and the Labour Party.[72] OPF corresponded frequently with MPs especially the members of the all-party group on widows and one parent family group.[73] They were quick to identify important allies and targeted young MPs and backbenchers also keen to further their own careers.[74] Many members relied upon personal contacts in order to persuade politicians to support their cause. Volunteer Catherine Porteous, recruited as a Friend from 1962 who later became Chairman of the Committee of Management for many years, was enormously well-connected and wrote many letters and initiated meetings with numerous politicians in order to garner their support.[75] The need for cross-party support was recognised by most people who worked within the lobby by the late 70s to early 80s particularly in the face of the social security cuts threatened and instituted by the Thatcher Governments. This development was not popular amongst all the staff employed within these NGOs and many left-wing activists found it hard to 'sleep with the enemy' in the interests of their clients. Jane Streather, who had worked for the CPAG (in disagreement much of the time with Frank Field) before becoming Director of OPF in 1978 opposed many of Paul Lewis' tactics to try to woo the Tory party after their election in 1979 and preferred to focus instead on Whitehall. Lewis also experienced much opposition from left-wing colleagues in his attempt at non-partisan campaigning.[76] The organisation continued to attend fringe meetings at party conferences in the attempt to provoke debate on issues close to their heart.[77] One-to-one meetings with MPs remained a vital aspect of

OPF's work and were a key to their success in the late 80s and early 90s.[78]

Networking with organisations that shared some of their policy goals as well as key individuals was crucial to the success and longevity of many organisations. Strong alliances had been formed in the campaign for the implementation of the Finer Report. In response to Government cuts OPF joined the Anti-Social Security Cuts Group organised by the CPAG and used their contacts with Lord McGregor and Jane Ewart Biggs to fight for their cause in the Lords.[79] They campaigned with the Disability Alliance and the Spastics Society against government plans to make Child Benefit means-tested in 1983. After protracted pressure Norman Fowler eventually promised in July 1983 that Child Benefit would not be changed.[80] They also worked closely with the Maternity Alliance which was formed from OPF, the CPAG and the Spastics Society. With the London Voluntary Service Council they were involved with talks with the London Boroughs Association and the GLC about the funding of voluntary organisations within the capital.[81] They also joined forces with a number of organisations to protest against rate-capping and the abolition of the GLC which led to a severe financial crisis at the Council in 1985/6 due to the loss of £90,000 of their yearly budget.[82] They produced briefing papers, lobbied MPs and included the staff and members of the Committee of Management in their struggle.[83]

The tactics of pressure groups did not change markedly over the course of the twentieth century although emphasis on particular strategies may have altered according to the priorities and expertise of particular individuals involved with the group at any one time.[84] Indeed the cult of individual personalities had an enormous impact on most of the organisations involved with these NGOs.[85] Frank Field and then later Ruth Lister within the CPAG, Des Wilson within Shelter and Sue Slipman within OPF all transformed their organisations in ways associated with their own particular personality traits.[86] In response to Sue Slipman's direction in the mid-1980s, in the words of some, OPF started to act less reactively and more proactively. Re-structuring occurred as the result of a major funding and staffing crisis and as Slipman introduced a business model into the management of the organisation. Most voluntary organisations had dialogues with management consultants from the mid-80s. With modernisation came a realisation that the Conservative Government had to be seduced into passing legislation and initiating change that worked to the benefit of lone parents. In a sense the same tactics that were used in the 1970s continued to be used but OPF learned how to frame their campaigns in more politically sophisticated ways. Many other voluntary organisations and staff within OPF were vehemently opposed to Slipman's methods and declared the organisation and her to be traitors.[87] In effect, the Government was persuaded to implement changes that the organisation hoped would improve the lives of unmarried mothers. In the late 1980s and early 1990s the Council's profile was to grow enormously and they were to achieve a number of objectives that they had been working towards throughout their history. It was only then, as well as in the 1920s, that the Council appeared to influence the very highest levels of government in Cabinet.

What is clear is that academics, government and key media players took poverty NGOs seriously from the early 1970s. Organisations managed to achieve what they did because of the loyalty and enthusiasm of key members of staff, and the possession of powerful allies in Parliament, local government, other voluntary organisations, and the Press. The lobby was crucial in bringing the issue of social security to the fore in political discussion.[88] It put pressure on the Labour governments of the 70s to respond to the poverty of families even if they ultimately failed to change the 'strategic development of income maintenance policy'.[89]

The lobby campaigned with varying degrees of success during the 80s and early 90s. It may be true that the impact of the lobby was felt more widely during the 1970s when the political climate was more favourable to their demands. During the 1970s the media profile of the lobby within the broadsheet press was much higher than it was in the 1980s because people were beginning to learn about the causes and consequences of poverty. As organisations became more media savvy and more conscious of the significance of forging power relations with government, the civil service and the media they learned to flourish once again in the more favourable political climate of the 1990s as they had in the interwar period. Moreover by the early 1990s, many of the individuals involved with the poverty lobby in the 1970s, had to some extent become part of the establishment after long and illustrious careers in the voluntary sector.[90]

All of the groups discussed continue today and most have undergone similar developments regarding their management and structure although at different stages in their history.[91] From the late 1970s most organisations restructured in response to the demands of members who argued that they should become less elitist and metropolitan. All of the organisations represented the individual cases of many thousands of people who came to them asking for help from across the country and they utilised these cases on a personal and political level while gathering information for wider social and political change.[92] Most of the organisations now have regional offices and use telephone help lines, websites offering information and advice services, printed publications, and work with other agencies that offer advice and help as well as providing training courses in order to learn about and foster the independence of the clients that they represent. Most have also concentrated on the business-side of their activities and employed management consultants and professional fundraisers to enable them to increase their profits from the mid-1980s.[93]

The poverty lobby was certainly successful in changing the opinions of academics and officials that worked with and on behalf of the poor during the 1970s. Whether it sustained that power it is harder to gauge and whether it impacted on the wider political culture is even more complicated to ascertain.[94] Many would also argue using the concept of relative poverty first suggested by Peter Townsend that the gap between rich and poor has widened since the establishment of the lobby. Others have suggested that a concentration on the tax and benefit system to the exclusion of other aspects of poverty in the 1970s led to the poverty of poor families being exacerbated from the 1980s.[95] Nonetheless, many would also agree that these NGOs remain respected, resourceful and imaginative in their attempts to stop the poor getting poorer.

Notes

1 The research behind this chapter was funded by ESRC grant number RES-000-23-0545 and was carried out by the author as Research Fellow and Professor Pat Thane as Principal Investigator.

2 R. Titmuss, *The Problems of Social Policy* (London: H.M.S.O., 1950) and *Essays on the Welfare State* (London: Allen and Unwin, 1958).

3 R. Lowe, *The Welfare State in Britain Since 1945* (Houndmills: Palgrave Macmillan, 2005), p. 148.

4 The archive is held at The Women's Library (hereafter TWL) 5/OPF.

5 B. Abel-Smith and P. Townsend, *The Poor and the Poorest* (London: G. Bell and Sons, 1965).

6 P. Townsend, 'The Meaning of Poverty', *British Journal of Sociology*, 18, no. 3, September 1962, pp. 210–27.

7 P. Townsend, *The Family Life of Old People* (London: Routledge, 1957).

8 M. Wynn, *Fatherless Families* (London: Michael Joseph, 1964).

9 P. Marris, *Widows and their Families* (London: Routledge, 1958).

10 H. Wilson, *Delinquency and Child Neglect* (London: Allen and Unwin, 1959).

11 V. Wimperis, *The Unmarried Mother and her Child* (London: Allen and Unwin, 1960).

12 The letters page of *The Guardian* was also where the National Housewives Register and the playgroup movement were initiated in the 1960s. Gingerbread was founded by a woman who placed an ad in *Time Out*. See H. Curtis and M. Sanderson, *The Unsung Sixties, Memoirs of Social Innovation* (London: Whiting and Birch, 2004), pp. vii, 264, 298 and 381–2. P. Whiteley and S. Winyard suggest that between 1965 and 1985 17 new groups were established and by the end of the 1970s there existed 42 groups that could be defined as part of the poverty lobby, *Pressure for the Poor: The Poverty Lobby and Policy Making* (London: Methuen, 1987), pp. 3, 11, 47.

13 M. McCarthy, *Campaigning for the Poor, CPAG and the Politics of Welfare* (London: Croom Helm, 1986); Whiteley and Winyard, *Pressure for the Poor*, p. 1. These writers' frustration with the Labour Party has heavily influenced these accounts of the history of the poverty lobby. See also P. Alcock, *Understanding Poverty* (Houndmills: Palgrave, 1993, 1997), chapter 13 and D. Donnison, *The Politics of Poverty* (Oxford: Martin Robertson, 1982), pp. 126–7.

14 See also, M. Meyer-Kelly, 'The Child Poverty Action Group 1965–1974: The Origins and Effectiveness of a Single Issue Pressure Group' (University of Bristol PhD. thesis, 2001), D. Bull in Curtis and Sanderson, *The Unsung Sixties*, pp. 116–24 and J. Lewis, *The Voluntary Sector, the State and Social Work in Britain, The Charity Organisation Society/Family Welfare Association since 1869* (Aldershot: Edward Elgar, 1995), p. 104.

15 McCarthy, *Campaigning for the Poor*, p. 1; Alcock, *Understanding*, p. 200 and R. Lowe, 'The Rediscovery of Poverty and the Creation of the Child Poverty Action Group' and 'The Formation of the Child Poverty Action Group', *Contemporary Record*, vol. 9, no. 3 (Winter 1995), pp. 602–37. This is the published account of the Witness Seminar recorded at the Institute of Historical Research 17 November 1993 where those involved with the group discussed its origins.

16 Interview with A. Richardson, former Head of Finance and Fundraising at OPF between 1979 and 1987 and now a freelance fundraiser (3rd March 2006). See also, Whiteley and Winyard, *Pressure for the Poor*, pp. 53–4.

17 For a broad account of the process of professionalisation in British social movements see A. Lent, *British Social Movements since 1945, Sex, Colour, Peace and* Power (Houndmills: Palgrave, 2001). Regarding OPF: on social work see the Interviews with H. Fletcher, Senior Social Worker for OPF between 1975 and 1983 now Assistant General Secretary of NAPO (10th March 2006) and P. Letts, Advice Worker for OPF between 1978 and 1986 (20th April 2006). On policy see Interview with P. Lewis, Information Officer and then Deputy Director of OPF between 1976 and 1983 now a freelance financial journalist (7th February 2006). On Fundraising see the Interview with A. Richardson.

18 Whiteley and Winyard, *Pressure for the Poor*, p. 16.

19 OPF Committee of Management Minutes, 4th December 1969, TWL/5/OPF/02/01/1/1k.

20 Finer Joint Action Committee Papers 1975 (hereafter FJACP), 15th April 1975, TWL/5/OPF/2/7.

21 TWL/OPF FJACP 5/OPF/2/7 and Policy and Social Sub-Committee Papers, 22nd September 1975, 5/OPF/2/1/4/1/b.

22 *Cathy Come Home* was broadcast nationally just before and shortly after the establishment of Shelter. The organisation was given the rights of the film for its first two years and it utilised repeated screenings to raise their funds and profile. See E. Ware in Curtis and Sanderson, *The Unsung Sixties*, pp. 19–28.

23 *Forty Years of Shelter*, (2006), p. 12, www.shelter.org.uk.

24 'The Formation of the Child Poverty Action Group', p. 634.

25 I. Bradley, *The Times*, April 1980. See also M. Meyer Kelly, 'The Rise of Pressure Groups in Britain 1965–1974: Single Issue Causes and their Effects', in M. Meyer-Kelly and M. Kandiah (eds), '*The Poor Get Poorer Under Labour*': *The Validity and Effects of CPAG's Campaigns in 1970* (London: Institute of Contemporary British History, 2003), p. 19.

26 OPF Annual Report (hereafter AR), 1964–5, TWL/5/OPF/10/1/a, p. 32.

27 OPF AR, TWL/5/OPF/10/1/a, 1963–4, p. 20.

28 OPF AR, TWL/5/OPF/10/1/a, 1984, p. 13. Committee of Management Minutes (hereafter CMM), November 1961, TWL/5/OPF/2/1/1/1h.

29 Meyer-Kelly, 'The CPAG', p. 190.

30 OPF CMM, 15th February 1979; 20th June 1979, TWL/5/OPF/2/1/1/10; 17.3.82;20.10.86, TWL/5/OPF/02/01/1/1q.

31 TWL/5/OPF/2/1/1/2c/23 and AGM p. 2.

32 TWL/5/OPF/2/1/2c/23.

33 TWL/5/OPF/2/1/1/3/e.

34 TWL/5/OPF/2/1/2c/23.

35 Interview with H. Fletcher.

36 Interview with P. Lewis.

37 Alcock, *Understanding Poverty*, chapter 13.

38 Tony Lynes (the first full-time employee of CPAG and prior to that a research assistant to Titmuss who was the Vice-Chair of the SBC) 'The Formation', p. 624. Meyer-Kelly, *The CPAG*, p. 136.

39 Meyer-Kelly, *The CPAG*, p. 159.

40 G. Beltram, Assistant Secretary in the Research, Statistics and Information Branch of the DHSS in 1970 and J. Stacpoole, Assistant Secretary in charge of the Family Allowances Branch in 1970, speaking at the Witness Seminar, 'The Poor Get Poorer Under Labour': The Validity and Effects of CPAG's Campaign in 1970' held 18 February 2000 (London: ICBH, 2003), p. 28. On the normalisation of unmarried mothers see K. Kiernan, H. Land and J. Lewis, *Lone Motherhood in Twentieth-Century Britain* (Oxford: Clarendon Press, 1998), pp. 110–12.

41 See Stephen Brooke's contribution to this volume.

42 Lowe, *The Welfare State*, p. 149 and J. McNicol, 'From 'Problem Family' to 'Underclass', 1945–95, in H. Fawcett and R. Lowe (eds), *Welfare Policy in Britain: The Road from 1945* (London: ICBH, Macmillan, 1999).

43 D. Marsden, *Mothers Alone: Poverty and the Fatherless Family* (Harmondsworth: Penguin (1969) 1973).

44 OPF Conference Proceedings 1968, Session 2, *The Human Rights of Those Born Out of Wedlock: A Consideration of the Needs and How They Might be Met.* Correspondence with MPs, Frank Field, TWL/5/OPF/7/1/1 and Committee of Management 4th October 1973, TWL/5/OPF/02/01/1i.

45 The National Archives (hereafter TNA) BN 89/47, 10th March 1970 and BN/89/16, 24th June 1970–31st December 1970.

46 OPF CMM 4th July 1974, TWL/5/OPF/2/1/1/1h.

47 List of officers, TWL/5/OPF/2/1/1/3e.

48 10th January 1984, TWL/5/OPF/2/13/b/4. She is now Professor of Sociology at Manchester University.

49 Memo of Committee of Management 1989, TWL/5/OPF/2/1/1/2c.

50 List of officers 1991–2, TWL/5/OPF/2/1/1/3e.

51 OPF AR, TWL/5/OPF/10/1/a, 1983, p. 8; 1985, p. 11; 1986, p. 14; 1988, p. 16.

52 OPF AR, TWL/5/OPF/10/1/a, 1989, p. 16.

53 OPF CMM, 27th April 1991, 5/OPF/02/01/1/1q.

54 OPF CMM, 5th December 1918 and 28th February 1919, 5/OPF/02/01/1/1a.

55 Meyer-Kelly, *The CPAG*, p. 134.

56 See also Alex Mold's chapter.

57 'The Formation of the Child Poverty Action Group', pp. 23–5.

58 Lewis, 'The Voluntary Sector', p. 64.

59 Lewis, *The Voluntary Sector*, p. 124 and H. Macaskill, *From the Workhouse to the Workplace: 75 years of One Parent Family Life* (London: National Council for One Parent Families, 1993), pp. 31–7.

60 OPF AR, TWL/5/OPF/10/1/a, 1976–7, pp. 18–20 and AR 1979, p. 4.

61 Whiteley and Winyard divide the groups they label as part of the poverty lobby into 'promotional' groups who campaign on behalf of their clients and 'representational' groups who represent the poor themselves. Whiteley and Winyard, *Pressure for the Poor*, p. 26. Gingerbread and One Parent Families announced their merger in March 2007. The records of Gingerbread are also held at The Women's Library but are uncatalogued and unavailable for research see TWL/5/GNB.

62 David Donnison, Tony Lynes, Brian Abel-Smith and John Veit-Wilson speaking on 'The Formation of the Child Poverty Action Group', pp. 630–2. See also Halpin's chapter in this volume.

63 'The Formation of the Child Poverty Action Group', pp. 630–4.

64 Hilary Land 'The Formation', p. 631 and Abel-Smith speaking on the same, pp. 632–3.

65 McCarthy, *Campaigning for the Poor*, pp. 120–33. '*The Poor Get Poorer Under Labour*', p. 29.

66 McCarthy, *Campaigning for the Poor*, p. 116.

67 Meyer-Kelly, *The CPAG*, p. 146.

68 Veit-Wilson, 'The Formation' pp. 631–2.

69 On CPAG see Meyer-Kelly, *The CPAG*, p. 183. See also Interview with P. Lewis.

70 OPF Management Team Papers 1977–1981, TWL/5/OPF/2/13/a/1 and see also the correspondence with MPs listed above n. 74.

71 OPF CMM, 2nd March 1987, TWL/5/OPF/02/01/1/1q.

72 *Ibid*, 20th September 1988.

73 Correspondence with MPs 1974–1985, TWL/5/OPF/7/1–3; 5/OPF/7/2/1–6; 5/OPF/7/3/1–6.

74 Interview with P. Lewis. On CPAG tactics see Meyer-Kelly, *The CPAG*, pp. 183–6.

75 Interview with Catherine Porteous former Chair of the Friends of OPF and then of the Committee of Management. Involved with OPF between 1962–1993 (12th July 2005).
76 Interview with J. Streather, former Deputy Director of CPAG between 1972–1975 and then Director of OPF between 1978–1984 (23rd March 2006) and with P. Lewis.
77 OPF CMM, 29th June 1982, TWL/OPF/2/1/1/1q.
78 Director's Department, 1991, 5/OPF/2/4.
79 OPF AR, TWL/5/OPF/10/1/a, 1980, p. 13 and CMM 2nd June 1986; CMM 19th January 1987; 2nd March 1987, TWL/5/OPF/2/1/1/1q.
80 OPF AR, TWL/5/OPF/10/1/a, 1983, p. 5.
81 OPF AR, TWL/5/OPF/10/1/a, 1983, p. 7.
82 OPF AR, TWL/5/OPF/10/1/a, 1984, p. 9.
83 OPF AR, TWL/5/OPF/10/1/a, 1985, p. 16.
84 Whiteley and Winyard, *Pressure for the Poor*, p. 57.
85 See also Lawrence Black's discussion of Mary Whitehouse and Buchanan's of Peter Benenson.
86 On Field see McCarthy, *Campaigning for the Poor*, pp. 105–16 and on Wilson see E. Ware in Curtis and Sanderson, *The Unsung Sixties*, pp. 19–28.
87 Interview with C. Porteous and S. Slipman, former Director of OPF between 1985–1995 (14th July 2005).
88 R. Wendt, Principal Private Secretary to the Secretary of State for Social Services Richard Crossman, 1968–1970, 'The Poor Get Poorer', p. 30.
89 Whiteley and Winyard, *Pressure for the Poor*, pp. 136 and 155.
90 R. Wendt 'The Poor Get Poorer', p. 42. Field has been MP for Birkinhead since 1979, Ruth Lister left the CPAG in 1987 and is now Professor of Social Policy at Loughborough and has contributed to numerous government committees, Sue Slipman left OPF in 1995 to work for the Training and Enterprise Council, then Camelot and the Financial Ombudsman Service and is now Chief Executive of the Foundation Trust Network. Chris Pond was Director of the Low Pay Unit 1980–97, set up by Field as an offshoot of the CPAG during the mid-70s, was a Labour MP between 1997 and 2005 and after losing his seat in 2005 became been Chief Executive of OPF. He left in 2006 to work for the Financial Services Authority. See also Lent, *British Social Movements*, pp. 167–70, 192–6.
91 Alcock, *Understanding Poverty*, p. 205.
92 Donnison, *The Politics of* Poverty, p. 129.
93 Lewis, *The Voluntary Sector*, p. 150.
94 'The Formation of the Child Poverty Action Group', p. 5.
95 Donnison, 'The Poor Get Poorer', p. 38.

9
The Changing Role of NGOs in Britain: Voluntary Action and Illegal Drugs[1]

Alex Mold

In February 1967 Mollie Craven published an article in the *Guardian* newspaper entitled 'My son takes heroin.' Craven stated that 'we parents of addicts are a neglected and ignored group. We want to be able to help our pathetic children, even while they cause us suffering which tears us apart. We can help each other.'[2] Craven's appeal for help resulted in the establishment of the Association of Parents of Addicts (APA) an organisation that provided advice to the families of addicts and established a day centre to care for 'young people with serious drug problems.'[3] APA later became the Association for the Prevention of Addiction, and more recently still, Addaction. As Addaction it now claims to be Britain's largest specialist drug and alcohol treatment charity, providing services to over 25,000 people in 70 different services throughout the country.[4] In another article in the *Guardian* published in 2007 to mark the 40 year anniversary of the founding of APA, journalist Alison Benjamin commented that 'This evolution from a small, self-help and pressure group called the Association of Parents of Addicts (APA) to Addaction, a charity with a £25 million budget that helps more than 25,000 people a year, is a striking illustration of society's changing relationship with drugs.'[5]

This is an accurate assessment, but the experience of organisations like APA is, in some ways, representative not just of changes in the way we deal with drugs, but of the fate of the voluntary sector as a whole. Organisations like Addaction now operate as 'social businesses', offering services to individuals such as drugs users, often in place of statutory facilities but largely funded by the government. Such groups act as 'service providers' to government 'commissioners.' This is a marked difference to the early experiences of APA, which was run by volunteers, funded through charitable donations, and received a limited amount of *ad hoc* support from the London Boroughs Association and the Ministry of Health.[6] Clearly, it is not just the size of these groups that has altered; the very relationship between voluntary organisations and the state appears to be radically different.

To explore this relationship in more detail this article will take as a case-study the voluntary activity that surrounded illegal drug use from the 1960s to the present. Focussing on individual case studies allows us to explore important issues surrounding socio-political activity in the twentieth and twenty-first century in greater depth. Analysing what Jeremy Kendall and Martin Knapp have called the 'loose and baggy monster' of the third or voluntary sector is potentially overwhelming as this encompasses a huge range of organisations and types of activity.[7] Looking at one area of action is not only a more manageable enterprise but also generates some bigger questions which can, in turn, be applied to other case studies and the sector as a whole.

A close examination of the voluntary activity around illegal drugs highlights the importance of three chronological phases. The first phase was the period from the 1960s to the 1970s, when a significant number of drug voluntary groups first began to appear. The emergence of these groups can be related not just to rising drug use but also to a changing perception of need. Drug users were just one of a number of what Beveridge described as 'distressed minorities', catered for by a string of new organisations.[8] In the second phase, during the 1980s, the drug voluntary sector expanded still further as drug use became seen as a major social and political problem. Expansion was also facilitated by a significant injection of funds from central government in the form of the Central Funding Initiative (CFI). In some ways this could be seen as indicative of the 'rolling back' of the state, as the state sought to move responsibility for groups like drug users onto voluntary and private organisations. Yet, as will be seen, the state retained a crucial role in coordinating and directing activity. This can also be observed in the final phase, from the 1990s to the present. Since the 1990s, drug users have increasingly come together to form their own groups to agitate for change in the legal framework that regulates drugs as well as to demand improvements in service provision. Whilst some of these groups remain very much outside the state, others appear to have become incorporated within it. This would suggest that despite much interest in the notion of voluntary organisations as key repositories of social capital in civil society, the state remains crucial to any analysis of their wider role.

What the case study of the drugs voluntary sector also reveals is an astonishing diversity of action. Groups were established throughout this period to campaign for drug users; to provide information; to offer legal advice; to provide treatment; to give advice; to coordinate the sector; to advise on service provision and to organise self-help efforts. Considering the nature and impact of these different organisations raises questions about how to describe and interpret this activity. The 'terminological tangle' which surrounds any analysis of the activity that takes place away from the state and the market is a familiar problem, but has particular relevance here.[9] The term 'NGO' is not one that organisations working in the drugs field have used until very recently, and even then, mainly by groups that operate in an international context. Throughout the period from the 1960s to the present most groups referred to themselves as 'voluntary organisations'. By using the term NGO, are we in danger of applying a 'new' concept retrospectively? Moreover, does seeing NGOs not simply as 'non-violent organisations that are neither dependent upon government nor serving an immediate economic interest' but as socio-political 'players' result in a tendency to focus on only the more overtly 'political' organisations?[10]

Despite these problems there is no need to discard the label NGO entirely, as it draws attention to the wider role that such organisations play. Indeed, socio-political action assumes many forms. Some groups, such as Narcotics Anonymous (NA), reject the notion that they are political 'players' altogether, although they clearly have a socio-political function. Other organisations, through their complete dependence on the state for financial support, are questionably 'non-governmental'. At the opposite end of the spectrum, there are groups such as Addaction that operate more like businesses. There is clearly a diversity of activity that in a sense defies all simple labels such as 'voluntary organisation', 'NGO' or 'non-profit'. Only by considering a case study in detail can we make sense of this. Focussing on one particular issue can help us to reach a more nuanced understanding of socio-political activism and the various forms that this takes. In this way a 'special interest' becomes of more general concern.

New politics, new problems and new organisations: 1960–1970s

Drug use and some of the problems surrounding this has been a focal point for voluntary action since at least the nineteenth century, when Christian organisations such as Spelthorne St Mary and the Sisters of the Community of St Mary the Virgin treated female alcoholics.[11] Voluntary provision of drug addiction treatment existed alongside private and statutory institutions, but during the 1960s a significant number of new voluntary groups appeared. One reason for this growth was the increasing prevalence of drug use. Until the sixties, the use of illegal drugs was comparatively rare in Britain. In 1959 there were 454 known drug addicts, by 1969 there were 1,462: small numbers in comparison to today, but a significant increase none the less.[12] Moreover, drug use appeared to be becoming a wider social and cultural phenomenon. Newly reported cases of drug addiction tended to be found in young people, and in those who had started taking drugs for recreational, rather than therapeutic purposes.[13] Drug use and the smoking of cannabis in particular, became a celebrated part of the counter-culture and underground 'scene.'[14] This increase in drug taking brought with it a rise in the medical, social and legal problems associated with drug use, problems which were largely un-catered for by the statutory sector. Indeed, the statutory response to drug use was almost exclusively confined to treatment within NHS Drug Dependence Units and law enforcement by the police. Voluntary groups began to emerge to fill this gap.

At the same time, the expansion of voluntary action in the drugs field was matched by a more general growth in voluntarism in a range of other areas. This can be explained by two key factors. Firstly, by the 1960s confidence in the totality of statutory welfare services was beginning to crumble.[15] A series of dramatic exposures highlighted significant deficiencies in welfare provision in a number of areas, prompting the establishment of organisations to campaign for, and provide, improvements.[16] Poverty, for example, was 'rediscovered' and a number of organisations such as the Child Poverty Action Group and Shelter came into being in order to agitate for more resources and better services.[17] Secondly, an apparently 'new' form of politics and political activity began to develop and take on the interests of Beveridge's 'distressed minorities.' The appearance of new social movements, such as those concerned with civil rights, women's rights and the environment, drew attention to previously marginalised groups and interests.[18] Many new voluntary organisations were established around these issues. Some of these organisations were orientated towards service provision, others took on a more campaigning role, and many combined both.

This pattern of overlapping origins and functions could also be found in the drugs field. The charity Release, for example, which was established in 1967 to provide legal assistance to people arrested for drug offences, also undertook campaigning work in a number of areas.[19] Release saw their defence of the legal rights of the drug user as a way of providing individual aid, but also as a way of critiquing government policy on drugs. They argued that the drug problem could not be solved by the 'conventional means of criminal reprimand'; they felt that 'medical or social solutions [were] more likely to be successful.'[20] To this end Release agitated for reform of the drug laws, and in particular the legalisation of cannabis. They also campaigned for improvements in treatment facilities for drug addicts, especially those using barbiturates and drugs other than heroin. Release lobbied government directly and indirectly, through informal contacts with people like the chief inspector of the Home Office drugs branch, Bing Spear, and by giving evidence to government committees like the Wootton Committee on amphetamines and LSD and the Deedes Committee on police powers of search and arrest in 1969.[21]

It could be argued that despite these efforts, Release's achievements were modest. On key issues, like the legalisation of cannabis, Release appeared to have little success. But, assessing the impact of an organisation like Release on its campaigning activities alone is perhaps unfair. By providing a service – legal aid – Release was fulfiling an important role, and one that was just as 'political' as campaign work. The presence of organisations like Release presented a covert critique of existing statutory services for drug users and of the notion that the welfare state could provide comprehensively for the needs of all its citizens. At the same time, ensuring that the legal rights of drug users were respected was not simply the giving of aid to vulnerable individuals, but was rooted in a 'new' form of politics interested in different political issues. Caroline Coon, one of the founders of the organisations stated that 'For me, Release was not about drugs per se ... For me Release was essentially about civil liberties, legal rights and what we now call human rights.'[22] This wider conception of rights was crucial for dealing with the problems of 'quality of life, equality, individual self-realisation, participation and human rights', representative, for Habermas, of a 'new' form politics.[23] In a sense, therefore, the very existence of projects like Release is perhaps more important than their specific achievements, as it can be seen as evidence for the presence of a different kind of politics and political action. This suggests that there is a need to look at what organisations did more broadly and not just at achievements in the narrow sense of success or failure in bringing about legislative change. By providing services organisations like

Release were engaging in a different kind of politics in a different kind of way.

Yet, they could not entirely escape the 'old' politics that surrounded them. As I have argued elsewhere, 'old' political issues revolving around class and gender played a role in shaping Release's activities.[24] Furthermore, in order to survive financially the organisation accepted a grant from the Voluntary Services Unit (VSU) of the Home Office in 1974. Although there is little evidence to suggest that taking money from the state made Release any less inclined to take on controversial issues or activities, it was an important moment in line with a more general shift. The funding of voluntary organisations by the state had been discussed since at least the turn of the century, but from the 1970s onwards statutory funding of voluntary activity became more common. The establishment of the VSU in 1973 and the publication of a series of reports pointing to the value of voluntary action were indicative of a greater degree of interest by the state in the role played by voluntary groups in welfare service provision. 'Old' politics clearly continued to exist alongside the 'newer' variety.

Rolling back the state: the 1980s

Indeed, the dynamism around 'new' politics in the 1960s and 1970s, and the emergence of organisations concerned with new problems working in new ways, did not go unnoticed by more conventional political players. By the 1980s the idea the voluntary organisations could contribute something distinctive and of value was taken on by the New Right. The Conservative government, led by Margaret Thatcher, regarded the state as an inefficient and ineffective provider of welfare, and considered its monopoly on the provision of services to have resulted in a culture of passivity and dependence amongst welfare recipients.[25] The suggested solution to this problem was to 'roll back the state'; to reduce the role of central government in the provision of welfare. The 'rolling back of the state' was to be achieved in two closely related ways. Firstly, by placing greater emphasis on the involvement of voluntary organisations in the delivery of health and social services; and secondly by creating a 'market' in welfare, allowing statutory and non-statutory bodies to bid for contracts to provide specific services.[26] In both these developments the role of the voluntary sector was crucial. Not only was the voluntary sector regarded as being more responsive, more innovative and more cost-effective than the statutory sector, it was also thought to be able to reduce reliance on the state through the 'invigorating' experience of self-help and community care.[27]

The drugs field was a crucial test area for such a policy. During the 1980s illegal drug use in Britain appeared to be increasing at an alarming rate and spreading across the country on an unprecedented scale. An apparent growth in the use of heroin caused particular concern: the number of known heroin addicts rose from just over 2,000 in 1977 to more than 10,000 by 1987.[28] Moreover, heroin use was being reported in urban areas throughout the country.[29] This was in contrast to previous decades, when it was thought that drug use was largely confined to London.[30] To combat this seemingly worsening problem, the government introduced the CFI for drug services in 1982. Initially, the CFI was designed to provide £6 million over three years to organisations providing services to drug users throughout the country, but the programme was extended in January 1986, partly in response to the discovery of HIV/AIDS amongst injecting drug users. Under the initiative a total of £17.5 million pounds was awarded between 1983 and 1989.[31]

What was significant about the CFI was that it was open to service providers in both the statutory and voluntary sector. In and of itself statutory funding of voluntary groups in the drugs field was nothing new. Various voluntary groups involved in caring for drug users had received funding from the Home Office (like Release) and the Department of Health and Social Security (DHSS) as well as local authorities. Most of this funding, in line with more general support for non-statutory groups in the health field, was provided under Section 64 of the Public Health Services and Public Health Act, 1968 and largely confined to headquarters administrative expenses for voluntary bodies working on a national basis.[32] Both the coordinating body the Standing Conference On Drug Abuse (SCODA) and the Institute for the Study of Drug Dependence, a drugs information service and specialist library, received funding in this manner.[33] Smaller, local groups tended to receive funds on an *ad hoc* basis or from local authorities, such as the London Boroughs Association.[34] Most agencies, however, were chronically under-funded. The government's expert group on drug issues, the Advisory Council on the Misuse of Drugs, noted in 1982 that 'The non-statutory agencies involved in treatment and rehabilitation rely on an insecure combination of local and central government funding and exist under the constant threat of financial collapse.'[35]

Yet, providing central funds for voluntary organisations in order to prevent them from disappearing was not the sole reason for opening up the CFI to non-statutory groups. A DHSS circular informing regional authorities of the introduction of the CFI stated that its purpose was:

> not to remove from statutory authorities the responsibility for providing services and training but, by making additional funds available to them and to voluntary organisations, to remedy more rapidly than would otherwise have been possible, the inadequacy of the network of services for people with drug related problems.[36]

Fostering the participation of voluntary organisations was vital because, as Under-secretary of State for Health and Social Security, John Patten, told MPs, there was a realisation that 'the problem is not necessarily going to be ameliorated and controlled ... by action within the National Health Service alone.' Moreover, 'A very great deal of expertise, in terms of prevention and counselling, is in the voluntary sector, not in the National Health Service.'[37] Yet, non-statutory groups did not just provide expertise: there was a feeling amongst DHSS officials that voluntary organisations offered something statutory authorities could not. A senior civil servant in charge of the CFI asserted that voluntary groups 'could be more flexible in what they did' that as they 'were not tied to a specific service approach ... they were more willing to initiate different types of services.'[38] The CFI, by offering substantial funding to voluntary organisations, was designed to make use of this. Even so, a senior civil servant remarked that 'we were quite surprised that we got so many applications from the voluntary sector'; clearly developments on the ground had been somewhat invisible at the central policy level.[39] However, once the DHSS were aware of the extent of voluntary sector involvement in the field a clear commitment was made to enhancing its role in drug service provision. This can be seen in the grants made under the CFI: of the 188 grants issued, 58 per cent went to statutory organisations and 42 per cent to non-statutory groups.[40] Such significant support for voluntary organisations cannot be explained by necessity alone: this must be related to a much broader strategy for involving the non-statutory sector in health and social service provision.

Indeed, in many ways, the CFI for drug services represents a microcosm of key aspects of Conservative welfare policy in this period. The term 'initiative' was a particular favourite of the Thatcher administration. Numerous 'initiatives' were launched to tackle a range of social issues particularly in the inner-cities. Urban development grants, for example, were designed to foster regeneration by using public funds to pump-prime development in areas such as the London Docklands and Merseyside. Central to these policies was the notion of 'partnership' with private companies and voluntary organisations which would be expected to support projects in the long-term.[41] In the health field, 'initiative' had a particular meaning. From 1982 onwards a number of central funding initiatives were launched in areas where the government wanted to raise standards.[42] A DHSS official noted that 'The funding of schemes is deliberately limited in duration to preserve their development and catalyst role. They are not intended as a prolonged substitute for local funding'. Health and local authorities were expected to find the money for continuing schemes from within their regular sources of funding and voluntary bodies were required to carry on raising their own funds.[43]

Such a scheme cast central government in the role of initiator of new services rather than their long-term funder. The central funding initiatives thus encapsulated a key aspect of the Thatcherite policy of 'rolling back the state': reducing direct statutory involvement in welfare provision by changing the function of the state from that of provider, to manager, but through a command and control model. This transition was later confirmed through the NHS Care and Community Act in 1990. The act created an internal market within health and social care by establishing a divide between the 'purchasers' of services and the 'providers' of these. Local authorities, for example, were able to 'purchase' a particular service, such as a needle exchange for injecting drug users, from a local 'provider'. The 'provider' could be a statutory, voluntary or private organisation; these were expected to 'compete' within the internal market for the custom of the 'purchaser'. Competition, it was argued, would make services more cost-effective and responsive to consumer demand.[44]

The creation of the internal market, it has been suggested, helped to replace 'welfare statism' with 'welfare pluralism' as a range of organisations took on functions previously performed by the state.[45] Within this 'mixed economy of care' particular significance was placed on the part played by voluntary organisations.[46] The voluntary sector was regarded as being more flexible than the statutory sector and, crucially, more able to enhance citizen participation.[47] Reliance upon the state could be further reduced as individuals were encouraged to help themselves and their communities.[48] Of course there is a paradox here – as statutory support for voluntary organisations increased elements of what was distinctive about the voluntary, as opposed to the statutory sector could be seen to have diminished.[49] Susanne MacGregor and

Ben Pimlott asserted that some organisations were transformed into *'de facto* agencies of the state, which financed them and indirectly determined their policy'.[50] Such a situation clearly raises questions about how non-governmental many supposedly non-governmental agencies really were.

Non-governmental or newly governmental? NGOs and drugs 1990s–present

Issues surrounding the independence of voluntary organisations reliant upon statutory funding persisted into the 1990s and beyond. Indeed, the more marketised approach to public services resulted in the proliferation of different groups, but many of these were often tied (to a greater or lesser extent) to the state. The introduction of service agreements, or contracts, between a local authority purchaser and voluntary or private sector providers in the 1990s had a significant effect on the way voluntary organisations operated. Contracts imposed professional standards of assessment, management and evaluation on voluntary agencies. For many volunteers, this appeared to threaten the very nature of voluntarism. Some organisations were also concerned that contracting could compromise their campaigning roles and diminish their autonomy. Still others were worried that contracting would make their organisations more bureaucratic and formalised.[51]

Evidence from the drugs field suggests that at least some of these fears have been realised. Statutory support for voluntary organisations in the drugs field continued apace in the 1990s. This was initially spurred on by the need to combat HIV/AIDS, but more recently has tended to focus on treatment provision and on breaking the supposed link between drug use and crime. One expert observer of the drugs field who had worked in the drug voluntary sector for more than 25 years noted that 'there's been a lot more money coming into the field, and some voluntary agencies have done quite well out of this'.[52] Key organisations, like Addaction, have become very big service providers. Other groups have diversified. Turning Point, which as Helping Hand worked with drug and alcohol users in the 1960s and 1970s, brands itself as a 'social care' organisation, annually offering services to approximately 130,000 people with 'complex needs'.[53] Such organisations are 'social businesses' providing services on behalf of the state and as a result, a veteran voluntary sector worker observed, have 'become more tied into central government'. This, he contended, raised questions about the 'degree to which you can be an independent critique of government ... while at the same time being drawn closer and closer together, tied closer and closer in because of funding schemes'.[54]

However, the social business model is by no means the only form that voluntarism around illegal drugs has taken in recent years. The creation of a quasi-market in public service provision has also resulted in greater attention being paid to the views of users of services themselves. Since the 1990s there have been a string of schemes aimed at involving the patient or service user in decisions about their own care and wider service provision. The introduction of the Children Act in 1989 and the National Health Service and Community Care Act in 1990 required local and health authorities to consult with voluntary organisations and users in planning and decision-making.[55] The Citizen's Charter, established in 1991, gave users of public services a series of rights and expectations to be drawn on when dealing with service providers.[56] These were built on by the Labour government in the NHS Plan of 2000, and its desire to create a 'patient-centred' NHS.[57] In 2001, the Health and Social Care Act made it a statutory obligation for health and social services to involve service users in the planning and delivery of services. Greater attention was being paid to the recipient of public services in all areas.

The impact of these developments on the drugs field can be seen at the national and local level. In 2001 the National Treatment Agency (NTA) was established. This special health authority was tasked with improving the availability and effectiveness of, and access to, treatment services. Involving drug users was seen as being central to their work. As well as funding research to find out what drug users views of treatment were, the NTA supported attempts to establish a national users' organisation and provided financial assistance to groups such as the Methadone Alliance (now known just as the 'Alliance') who provide advocacy and support for drug users in treatment across the country. Drug users were also represented on the NTA's board. This level of user representation was carried forward to the regional level too. Local drug services, commissioned by Drug Action Teams or DATs, were also required to involve drug users in decisions about services. Most DATs now support a user group for their region, who comment on service delivery and future planning.

Yet, alongside this state-sponsored user involvement there are other kinds of user groups that exist largely outside the state. Not only do we see the involvement of active users, but also of user activists. The groups and individuals behind drug user produced publications like *Black Poppy* and the *Users' Voice,* and organisations such as the John Mordaunt Trust, the UK Harm Reduction Alliance and Transform, often took a more challenging stance. Like the early gay AIDS organisations these groups have their own agendas which do not necessarily fit with those of the government.[58] In interviews with user activists three issues have emerged as central concerns. The first issue was the potentially empowering effect of user involvement. One user activist described empowerment in the following terms:

> user involvement can be so empowering, because it empowers you not just if your working in your clinic ... [to] get better conditions for the clients of the service and for the staff that work in it, and solutions to issues. But also in your life: the knock on effect that having a voice can have is enormous ... it's about, I think, we feel, taking your control back.[59]

With empowerment has come increased attention to the second issue: drug users' rights. These rights are increasingly being conceptualised not just in the sense of a right to certain kinds of treatment or even input into treatment, but in a broader, human rights sense. Another long-standing user activist commented that: 'the main thing that I really felt that [is] different from the early days is that everybody suddenly started talking about their right to use drugs'.[60] From this, almost inevitably, have come calls for changes in the drug laws, the third issue to emerge strongly from interviews with user activists. Many user activists believe that drugs should be legalised, even if some do not think this is a realistic goal. A male user activist commented that 'I see the anti-prohibition and treatment side as being absolutely inextricably linked.' He went on to say that 'I think the users' movement has to challenge prohibition. If it doesn't, it's incomplete. It's just a service lobby.'[61]

   The interest of drug users in issues such as these surrounding rights, representation and empowerment, hint at the emergence of a social movement. The appearance of similar groups in other countries, particularly in the Nordic states, has led some commentators to posit the existence of an international drug users' movement.[62] Moreover, as the quotations from drug user activists in Britain demonstrate, the state and users do not always agree on the meaning and purpose of user involvement. For some drug users, user involvement is not just about improving service provision, but about broader social and political goals. Yet for the state, user involvement is seen as a way of making services more responsive to the needs of the consumer, as a vital tool within the increasingly marketised welfare state. These different objectives may well bring users into conflict with the state. Yet, there are significant limitations to user power. Working closely with local or national government might enable some users to gain access to policy-making circles and effect change, but the charge sometimes levelled at user involvement is that it can be tokenistic. User activists in the drugs field, and in other areas, have often described user involvement in services as being a box-ticking exercise, as another task for bureaucrats.[63]

At the same time, drug users are clearly not a homogenous mass who all want the same thing. This has led some critics to question how far it is possible for user groups to be representative. A former senior worker in the drugs voluntary sector commented that 'the user groups we hear about tend to be about those user groups who are currently using. We don't hear very much about, from the other perspectives, for instance from the NA.'[64] He contended that 'the biggest user groups are NA', an argument that would seem to be born out by NA's claim that there are at least 500 separate weekly NA meetings held across the UK today.[65] Yet, NA is an organisation that outwardly rejects any notion of political engagement by refusing to 'express opinions on any civil, social, medical, legal or religious issues'. NA describe themselves as a 'non-profit fellowship of men and women for whom drugs had become a major problem – recovering addicts who meet regularly to help each other stay clean'. Membership is, by its very nature, anonymous and directed inwards at 'working with each other to achieve recovery'.[66]

Despite this, NA clearly has a socio-political presence. The recent growth in abstinence-orientated self-help groups for drug users like NA (the number of weekly NA meetings has more than doubled since 1991) is having an impact, especially on treatment provision.[67] Within drug addiction treatment there seems to be a move away from the long-term prescription of methadone to addicted patients and towards a greater emphasis on abstinence orientated programmes, similar to those run by NA.[68] This would suggest that NA do have a degree of socio-political influence. Yet, their outward denial of a political function would appear to be significant. NA's apparent refusal to engage makes them difficult to situate: they do not seem to be like other political 'players' in the drugs field, but are evidently more than 'just' a self-help group. Here is an organisation that is obviously 'political', despite their rejection of such a role.

Conclusion

The problem of how to describe and explain NA is, to an extent, indicative of wider difficulties with describing and explaining the sector as a whole. Much of the activity around illegal drugs in this period was directed towards service provision. Groups that had a campaigning aspect to their work, like Release, usually combined this with other more service orientated activity. But, this does not mean that their activity was necessarily less 'political' than the more vocal organisations found in other fields. Indeed, by providing services not only were these groups criticising statutory provision (or the lack of) they were attempting to find a solution to a problem that they had themselves identified. Taking a case-study approach, therefore, highlights the importance of the seemingly more 'quiet' and apparently less radical groups and organisations. This would suggest that judgements about the impact of NGOs should not be seen simply in terms of the success or failure of specific campaigns, but about new ways of dealing with new problems. Indeed, the diversity of action pointed to by this article, especially when coupled with change over time, might lead us to conclude that it is impossible to say anything definitive about the role of voluntary organisations (or NGOs) across one sector, let alone as a whole. But, if we are dealing with a 'new' form of socio-political engagement then perhaps we need to look to new ways of describing and assessing this activity.

Indeed, when developing new modes of analysis understanding the context in which these groups formed and operated must remain crucial. The case study examined in this article points to the relevance not only of the micro-politics of one sector, but also to the macro-politics of changing ideas about voluntarism, the state and socio-political action. Voluntary groups that sprang up to cater for the 'distressed minorities' of the 1960s and 1970s were seen largely as plugs to fill the gaps in a leaky welfare state; in the 1980s they were to be 'rolled in' to a welfare state that was never fully 'rolled back'; in the 1990s they were drawn into still closer relationships with the state through contracts, and since 2000 have provided consumer or user input into services. Yet, at the same time, voluntary groups appeared independently of the state and were often critical of its actions. This can be seen most recently in the emergence of a drug user movement that seeks to challenge government policy on drugs in a number of crucial areas. If, as Frank Prochaska has observed, some charities are 'swimming into the mouth of Leviathan' others seem to be succeeding in giving it in indigestion.[69]

Notes

1 This article is based on research undertaken for an Economic and Social Research Council funded project (grant reference number ESRC RES-000-23-0265) held by Professor Virginia Berridge. For a more detailed exploration of this work see A. Mold and V. Berridge, *Voluntarism, Health and Society*

Since the 1960s: Voluntary Action and Illegal Drugs (Palgrave, forthcoming).
Sections of this article are reproduced with permission from A. Mold and
V. Berridge, 'Crisis and opportunity in drug policy: changing the direction
of British drug services in the 1980s', *Journal of Policy History*, 19(1) (2007),
pp. 29–48; and A. Mold and V. Berridge, 'The Rise of the User? Voluntary
Organisations, the State and Illegal Drugs', *Drugs: Education, Prevention and
Policy*, 15(5) (2008), pp. 457–61, reprinted by permission of the publisher,
Taylor & Francis Ltd.

2   M. Craven, 'My son takes heroin', *The Guardian* 24 February 1967.

3   Association for the Prevention of Addiction (APA) Newsletter, November 1970,
Modern Records Centre, University of Warwick, (MRC) MSS.171/3/18/2.

4   See http://www.addaction.org.uk/.

5   A. Benjamin, 'We can help each other' *The Guardian G2*, 22 February 2007,
10–13.

6   Grants under Section 64 of the Health Services and Public Health Act, 1968
– Drug Addiction; Position in October 1972; London Boroughs Association,
Report of General Purposes Committee, 22 November 1972, The National
Archives, London (TNA), MH 154/430.

7   J. Kendall and M. Knapp, 'A loose and baggy monster: boundaries, definitions and typologies' in J. Davis Smith, C. Rochester and R. Hedley, *An
Introduction to the Voluntary Sector* (London: Routledge, 1995).

8   Beveridge quoted in G. Finlayson, *Citizen, State and Social Welfare in Britain
1830–1990* (Oxford: Oxford University Press, 1994) p. 328.

9   Phrase 'terminological tangle', quoted in N. Deakin, *In Search of Civil Society*
(Basingstoke: Palgrave, 2001) p. 9.

10 Discussion Points for the DANGO Conference, 5–6 July 2007.

11 H.B. Spear, *Heroin Addiction Care and Control: The British System 1916–1984*
(London: DrugScope, 2002) p. 52.

12 Figures from H.B. Spear, 'The Growth of Heroin Addiction in the United
Kingdom', *British Journal of Addiction*, 64, (1969), pp. 245–55, p. 247;
G. Stimson and E. Oppenheimer, *Heroin Addiction: Treatment and Control in
Britain* (London: Tavistock, 1982), pp. 208–9.

13 See Ministry of Health, *Drug Addiction: Report of the Second Interdepartmental
Committee* (London: HMSO, 1965) p. 5.

14 J. Green, *All Dressed Up: The Sixties and the Counterculture* (London: Pimlico,
1999) pp. 173–201.

15 Finlayson, *Citizen and State*, p. 329.

16 N. Deakin, 'The perils of partnership: the voluntary sector and the state
1945–1992', in Davis Smith, Rochester and Hedley, *An Introduction to the
Voluntary Sector*, pp. 49–50.

17 See article by Evans in this volume.

18 J. Habermas, 'New social movements', *Telos*, 49 (1981) pp. 33–7; P. Byrne,
Social Movements in Britain (London, 1997); N. Crossely, *Making Sense of
Social Movements* (Buckingham, 2002).

19 A. Mold, '"The Welfare Branch of the Alternative Society?" The Work of
Drug Voluntary Organisation Release, 1967–1978', *Twentieth Century British
History*, 17(1) (2006) pp. 50–73.

20 C. Coon and R. Harris, *The Release Report On Drug Offenders and the Law*
(London, 1969) pp. 36–7.

21 Written statement for the ACDD Search and Arrest Committee, 1969, MRC MSS.171/3/12/13; d'Agapeyeff, *Release*, Section XII; C, MRC MSS.171/5/1/2. Coon, 'We were the Welfare Branch of the Alternative Society', in H. Curtis and M. Sanderson, *The Unsung Sixties: Memoirs of Social Innovation* (London: Whiting & Birch, 2004), p. 190.

22 Coon, 'We were the Welfare Branch of the Alternative Society', p. 185.

23 Habermas, 'New Social Movements'.

24 Mold, 'The Welfare Branch of the Alternative Society?', pp. 50–73.

25 Finlayson, *Citizen, State and Social Welfare in Britain*, pp. 357–60.

26 Deakin, 'The perils of partnership': pp. 54–62; J. Kendall and M. Knapp, *The Voluntary Sector in the United Kingdom* (Manchester: Manchester University Press, 1996) pp. 201–5; J. Lewis, 'Developing the Mixed Economy of Care: Emerging Issues for Voluntary Organisations', *Journal of Social Policy*, 22(2) (1993) pp. 173–92.

27 For an overview of welfare policy under Thatcher see R. Lowe, *The Welfare State in Britain Since 1945* (3rd edition, Basingstoke: Palgrave, 2005), pp. 317–27, pp. 350–7.

28 Home Office, *Statistics of Drug Addicts Notified to the Home Office, 1988* (London: HMSO, 1989).

29 Advisory Council on the Misuse of Drugs, *Treatment and Rehabilitation* (London: HMSO, 1982), p. 25.

30 Ministry of Health, *Drug Addiction: Report of the Second Interdepartmental Committee*, p. 8.

31 S. MacGregor *et al.*, *Drug Services in England and the Impact of the Central Funding Initiative* (London: ISDD, 1991), p. 1.

32 Letter from Mr JC Eversfield, DHSS to Mr Platten, Town Clerk London Borough of Enfield, 20 December 1971; TNA MH 154/433.

33 For SCODA see TNA MH 154/1192, and SCODA annual reports in Drug-Scope Library; for ISDD see TNA FD 23/1949 and ISDD annual reports in DrugScope Library.

34 Heroin addiction: London Boroughs Association; working party reports on rehabilitation, 1968–1974, TNA MH 154/430.

35 ACMD, *Treatment and Rehabilitation* (London: HMSO, 1982), p. 77.

36 Letter from DHSS to all Regional Health Authorities regarding Treatment and Rehabilitation report of the ACMD; Central Funding Initiative, (HN (83)13 LASSAL (83)1), 25 April 1983, Department of Health Archive, Nelson, Lancashire (DOHA) OCG/1/1/3.

37 House of Commons, *Fourth Report from the Social Services Committee, Session 1984–1985: Misuse of Drugs* (London: HMSO, 1984–1985) DHSS evidence, p. 170.

38 Interview conducted by Mold and Berridge with senior civil servant, 2/05/06.

39 *Ibid.*

40 MacGregor *et al.*, *Drug Services in England and the Impact of the Central Funding Initiative*, pp. 71–4.

41 On urban initiatives see S. MacGregor and B. Pimlott, 'Action and Inaction in the Cities', in S. MacGregor and B. Pimlott (eds) *Tackling the Inner Cities: The 1980s Reviewed, Prospects for the 1990s* (Oxford: Clarendon Press, 1990).

42   Note on Central Initiatives by John H. James, 30 April 1986, DOHA, DAC/ 0007/V0004; Memorandum from DC Nye to Mr Alderman, Miss Davies, Mr Hillier, Mr Lutterloch, Mr Pagan and Mr Woolley, regarding new initiatives, 14 December 1983, DOHA, DAC/0026/V001.
43   Note on Central Initiatives by John H. James, 30 April 1986; DOHA, DAC/0007/V0004.
44   On changes in the welfare state in this period see Lowe, *The Welfare State*, pp. 317–27.
45   M. Harris, C. Rochester and P. Halfpenny, 'Voluntary Organisations and Social Policy: Twenty Years of Change', in M. Harris and C. Rochester (eds) *Voluntary Organisations and Social Policy in Britain: Perspectives on Change and Choice* (Basingstoke: Palgrave, 2001), p. 3.
46   Lewis, 'Developing the Mixed Economy', pp. 173–92.
47   Kendall and Knapp, *The Voluntary Sector in the UK*, p. 138; Deakin, 'The Perils of Partnership', p. 54.
48   Lowe, *The Welfare State in Britain*, p. 320.
49   Lewis, 'Developing the Mixed Economy', pp. 183–91.
50   MacGregor and Pimlott, 'Action and Inaction', p. 9.
51   Lewis, 'Developing the Mixed Economy', pp. 183–91.
52   Interview conducted by Mold and Berridge with drug voluntary sector worker, 14/01/05.
53   See http://www.turning-point.co.uk/About+Us/
54   Interview with drug voluntary sector worker.
55   M. Locke, P. Robson and S. Howlett, 'Users: At the Centre or on the Sidelines?', in Harris and Rochester, *Voluntary Organisations and Social Policy In Britain*, pp. 199–212.
56   Cm 1599, *The Citizen's Charter* (London: HMSO, 1991).
57   Cm 4818, *NHS Plan: A Plan for Investment, A Plan for Reform* (London: The Stationery Office, 2000).
58   On AIDS groups see V. Berridge, 'AIDS and the Rise of the Patient? Activist Organisation and HIV/AIDS in the UK in the 1980s and 1990s', *Medizin Gesellschaft und Geshichte*, 21 (2002) pp. 109–23.
59   Interview conducted by Mold with a user activist, 19/07/05.
60   Interview conducted by Mold with a long-standing user activist, 13/12/05.
61   Interview conducted by Mold with a male user activist, 30/05/06.
62   J. Anker *et al.*, 'Introduction', in *Drug Users and Spaces for Legitimate Action* (Nordic Council for Alcohol and Drug Research: Finland, 2006), p. 7.
63   See, for example, J. Birchall and R. Simmons, *User Power: The Participation of Users in Public Services* (London: National Consumer Council, 2004) and F. Branfield and P. Beresford, *Making User Involvement Work: Supporting Service User Networking and Knowledge* (York: Joseph Rowntree Foundation, 2006).
64   Interview between Mold and a former senior drug voluntary sector worker, 25/02/05.
65   See http://www.ukna.org/.
66   *Ibid.*
67   B. Wells, 'Narcotics Anonymous in Britain: The Stepping Up of a Phenomenon', in *Heroin Addiction and the British System, Vol. 2*, ed. by J. Strang and M. Gossop (London: Routledge, 2005), p. 168.

68 T. Carnwarth and C. Ford, 'Methadone Challenged on its Home Turf: Is There a Worrying Methadone Backlash About?', *Drink and Drug News* (8 May 2006), p. 9.

69 F. Prochaska, 'Voluntary Action – Renaissance or Decline?', downloaded from http://www.historyandpolicy.org/Voluntary%20action.pdf.

10
There Was Something About Mary: The National Viewers' and Listeners' Association and Social Movement History

Lawrence Black

Launched in 1964 by Mary Whitehouse and Norah Buckland, the 'Clean-up TV' campaign entered the public spotlight at a large, rowdy meeting at Birmingham Town Hall that May. The campaign's manifesto, with 366,355 signatures, was delivered to Parliament in June 1965, the year in which the campaign became the National Viewers' and Listeners' Association (NVALA), purporting to be the unofficial voice of viewer opinion, feeding this back to influence broadcasters. It combined its case for a viewers' council with a stream of invective directed at political leaders, programmes (the 'disbelief, doubt and dirt that the BBC projects into millions of homes through the television screen', as the manifesto put it) and Director-General Hugh Carleton Greene.[1] With broadcasting axial to its worldview, it fired diatribes on issues from abortion to satire and pornography, the whole gamut of liberal permissiveness *or* profanity. What started as a single-issue campaign, rapidly developed aspirations to be a broadcasting pressure group or NGO, voicing viewer opinion and held forth on a host of broader issues to take on the fac[,]ade of a social movement.

NVALA can then be understood in terms of the history of NGOs and social movements. Quite contrary to its portrayal in narratives of the period, it seems emblematic of the 1960s. A non-party, extra-parliamentary, anti-establishment, grassroots campaign utilising the media, led by a woman and employing a participatory rhetoric of viewers' rights, seemed modern in form, if not content. But NVALA rarely features in recent surveys of social movements, which have taken environmental, peace and feminist movements as their model; echoing New Left assumptions about their liberal-radical politics.[2]

NVALA was avowedly traditionalist and critical of progress and modernity, more readily comparable to the US Christian right, although not achieving anything like its influence or media access. Historians can learn from NVALA's failures *or* marginalisation and ought to explain not reflect its marginality.

NVALA's campaign was not to repeal legislation, nor in favour of new laws, but for enforcement of the BBC's professed values (the manifesto quoted the dedication to 'almighty God' and 'peace and purity' at Broadcasting House) and the 1964 Television Act that prohibited broadcasting material that 'offends against good taste or decency or is likely to encourage or incite ... crime ... disorder or to be offensive to public feelings.' It claimed to influence the 1982 Indecent Displays Act and the Broadcasting Standards Commission established in 1988.[3] Affinities between Thatcher and Whitehouse (made a CBE in 1980) were grounded in moral notions of 'Victorian values'. Whitehouse became one of the 'populist heroines of the right' – reactionary she was, but she was a portent of the future.[4]

NVALA was critical of, yet contingent upon, popular affluence. Affluence seemed to afford a more expressive politics, concerned with moral and cultural issues of taste and choice more than instrumental economic interests. Parkin's seminal study *Middle Class Radicalism* focussed on the Campaign for Nuclear Disarmament (CND) and shifts away from mass, class, party politics. Since it was preoccupied with values and the quality of life, NVALA also makes demands upon concepts such as Inglehart's postmaterialism.[5]

Suggestive parallels can be drawn with the New Left, which like NVALA defined culture as the key political terrain and the power of the media as paramount.[6] As the New Left and CND were products of discontent with the politics of the left, so NVALA grew from what it perceived as a loss of values in the Church and amongst Conservatives. Like CND, its Christian core of activists hinted religion was more of a factor than political historians (who have assumed a process of secularisation other than when addressing multiculturalism) have allowed in modern British history.[7]

In other ways, NVALA fits familiar themes. It deployed (exploited, critics argued) the rhetoric of participation that was rife in 1960s Britain – opening up the BBC to viewer power, as women, workers, students, consumers and nationalists tackled other institutions.[8] For Nash, Whitehouse personified not only moral retrenchment against permissiveness, but the fear and isolationism that coincided with de-colonisation and European integration.[9] Their vision of Britain was firmly declinist, bemoaning the demise of standards. Here Mary's perversity was apparent. Whilst most commentators targeted amateurism, NVALA criticised professional control of broadcasting, a case it advanced in emotive terms at odds with the increasing professionalism of formal politics.

NVALA made the personal viewing experience political; albeit as a necessity, born of TV's domestic intrusion, rather than any more self-conscious identity politics. The TV can 'talk *at* us!', supporters complained, 'we can never talk back!' As Whitehouse saw it 'atheist liberals' were ignoring the 'responsibility of television – that it comes into the home'. If TV had to invade the home, she asked at Birmingham Town Hall, 'why concentrate on the kitchen sink when there are so many pleasant living rooms?'[10]

A viewers' council

Clean-Up TV's morphing into NVALA aimed to forge a more constructive role, moving from protest to participation. When Lord Normanbrook died in June 1967, NVALA saw an opportunity in the appointment of a new BBC Chairman to press for a viewers' council. Whitehouse won from Postmaster General (PMG) Ted Short an admission that 'a consensus of opinion' decides what is broadcast. 'We submit', she replied, 'it is only through ... an independent representative council that this consensus can be obtained'.[11]

The new Chairman, Lord Hill, raised hopes sufficiently for NVALA chair, Conservative MP Major James Dance, to convene a meeting of prospective council members at the Commons in 1968. Present besides NVALA and Moral Re-Armament (MRA) supporters, were Conservative broadcasting spokesman Paul Bryan MP and bodies with NVALA affinities – the Headmistresses Association (Mrs. Manners), Baptist Union, Young Wives groups and Rotary Clubs. The meeting heard how a viewers' council could respond to those MPs who 'indicated how very valuable reports on programmes of the kind produced by *Which?* on consumer goods, would be'.[12]

Whitehouse increasingly conceived NVALA's 'role as a middle-class value-for-money, help-for-the-consumer organisation'. But this model was vitiated by NVALA's values that made it more prone to police culture than feedback a range of views. To take the Consumers' Association as an example, NVALA was suspicious of its assessments of the use-value of goods alone. When a report on impotence alluded to aphrodisiac literature and featured on BBC radio, Whitehouse's ire was aroused.[13]

From 1969, in response to domestic setbacks, international efforts increased. There were dealings with the National Audience Board and Nixon's Commission on Obscenity and Pornography in America; in Europe with groups opposed to liberal regimes on pornography, like the European Union of Women. In the 1970s NVALA helped spawn the Festival of Light, a Christian revivalist initiative against moral pollution. But a viewers' council remained central to its thinking. Premised upon a faith that Britons 'believe in a Christian way of life', a council would revive a Christian BBC ethos – a Reithian purpose, but less broadcaster-dominated, more interactive. Announcing his conversion to NVALA in 1970, Neil Hamilton argued 'viewers and producers should not be seen as two opposing sides', but that a council would increase broadcasters' 'responsiveness to our views' and fight 'silent censorship ... wherein opposing viewpoints are suppressed by editors or ... by a subtle ridicule.' It reiterated its case to the Annan Committee on Broadcasting (1977). Even critics recognised its aspiration to be a third sector force of viewer opinion by inviting it to the 1981 National Consumer Congress.[14]

Another reason for shifting to the viewer representation model was to negotiate the charge that NVALA were censors. Its case was that the liberal elite used 'any weapons to silence any opposition to their 'progressive' ideas' and that the BBC had imposed 'blanket censorship' on covering the NVALA. But it was easy to see where these fears originated when Whitehouse wrote that: 'if it were the only way of preventing the gradual erosion of our Christian values ... we would not hesitate to call for control over certain influences which confuse liberty with licence'. And when programmes like *Pinky and Perky* were censured for fostering juvenile delinquency by mocking parents, this seemed signally sinister. 'We believe in self-control ... exercised by responsible citizens', a 1967 discussion concluded, but this was 'an ideal'. What was needed, was public control via a body with the 'duty of relating the output of both BBC and Independent Television Authority (ITA) to the accepted standards of public taste and morality'.[15]

In 1968, PMG John Stonehouse outlined objections to a broadcasting version of the Press Council in Whitehouse's presence. If at 'arms length', the BBC governors and ITA remained ultimately accountable to parliament. To 'superimpose another statutory body' would 'lead to bureaucracy' and 'curb the creative genius which we want from broadcasters'. NVALA's 1966 letter to MPs highlighted what it considered the PMG's and parliament's impotence *vis-à-vis* the BBC. NVALA asserted its 'campaign is a grassroots, spontaneous movement' to 'establish the right of those who pay £67 million a year in licence fees to have their views taken into account'. To NVALA the licence fee presently amounted to 'taxation without representation'.[16]

Strategy: The Mary Whitehouse experience

NVALA's flexibility belied its doctrinal rigidity, but denoted its strategic setbacks. It was litigious – Whitehouse personally and for prosecutions under obscene publications and blasphemy laws. It monitored programme content and instituted a TV award. Its repertoire (like most campaigning NGOs) was of recruiting, public meetings, media coverage and lobbying, protesting and heckling authority. Petitioning parliament evinced its critique was of liberal conspiracy – the structures of governance were sound, but the personnel and culture at the BBC and in politics were wrongly manned.

The BBC's response was nervous, but minimised NVALA's impact by starving it of publicity. Such a response worked (in that Whitehouse was marginalised), but bolstered NVALA's case that the BBC was immune to criticism. Observers were sent to NVALA conventions. *Woman's Hour*, on which Whitehouse had first appeared in 1953, feared having her on when *Cleaning-up TV* was published in 1967, because editor Monica Sims felt 'if Mrs. Whitehouse did give her views, I'm afraid a majority of our listeners might write to support her'. From 1965 it was decided that 'all letters from avowed members' of NVALA 'should be referred unanswered to the secretariat'.[17]

In litigation over Johnny Speight's aside that Whitehouse was worse than a fascist since she cloaked her beliefs, the BBC's counsel grasped the resistance to any 'capitulation so far as this lady is concerned'. He advised the BBC against 'giving Mrs. Whitehouse the opportunity to appear in the role of a martyr'. A similar approach was adopted to the NVALA awards. BBC management opted to be 'cool and non-committal'. For *Dixon of Dock Green* (which won the first award for its portrayal of the police, although criticised for showing how crime was undertaken) to accept might give NVALA valuable publicity, but to refuse since 'Mrs. Whitehouse had consistently attacked fellow actors and used violent language about the BBC' was likely to generate even more. It was decided not to boycott the awards, but to avoid comment on them.[18]

Whitehouse tailored arguments to suit multiple scenarios. She wrote to Wilson when he became Prime Minister arguing economic growth depended 'upon the character of the British people' which was being 'devitalised by the constant portrayal of sex, violence and destructive satire, from stage [and] TV screen'. The PMG's 'self-imposed impotence' over intervening in programme content, she held, discouraged viewers from complaining. When the licence fee was raised from £5 to £6 in 1968, the NVALA campaigned for a pensioners' (a core constituency) exemption. It suggested the increase be referred to the Prices and Incomes Board since at 20 per cent it exceeded government policy.[19] In 1968 it made a case for including broadcasting in the Race Relations Act. Whitehouse's targets included *Til Death us do Part* and airtime with Tariq Ali, Ruth First or Stokely Carmichael. For Whitehouse such broadcasts demonstrated the 'lack of understanding amongst television professionals, of the power of television to accentuate problems'. But broadcasters argued they were reporting attitudes not inciting them.[20]

Direct action was mooted, including a women's march on London in 1964. Another leading supporter, John Barnett, Chief Constable of Lincolnshire, proposed civil disobedience against a licence fee increase in 1965. The Archbishop of Westminster's representative preferred to 'proceed with great prudence'.[21] But NVALA rejected turning off or switching channels – 'Silence means assent', 'Don't moan, Phone!' were its slogans. It encouraged (short, polite) letter writing, an activity that reinforced middle-class biases in the membership, besides giving housewives the 'gumph' (as one put it) to express themselves.[22]

Suggestive of Whitehouse's awareness of the limitations to other strategies or weight the movement could wield through membership alone, was correspondence with high profile BBC or political figures. This aimed to convert private discussions into the public domain via open letters. Petition support was brought to the signature of such missives – '366000 supporters' was the sign-off on Whitehouse's June 1965 letter to the PM. The etiquette of whether replies could be cited in NVALA literature was raised. A reply from Wilson that got lost in the mail in 1965 generated questions in the Commons. No. 10 concluded: 'Mrs. Whitehouse is clearly a most tiresome woman, out for all the publicity she can get.'[23]

Whitehouse was image and media conscious, serving a spell as *Daily Sketch* TV critic in 1967. The *Daily Mail* reckoned by 1970 'the sophistication of the television personalities and other public people she now meets' had 'rubbed off on this former schoolteacher'. She visited the hairdresser every 10 days. However excluded NVALA were, they made good copy *because* they transgressed the prevailing norms of public discourse.[24]

Whitehouse's charisma was a resource, if her singular personality rendered NVALA a virtual mass movement. What also made it newsworthy was rooting arguments in specific programmes – Britons' common cultural diet. This could verge on the post-modern when she launched tirades against TV characters, dismissing Alf Garnett as a 'silly and vulgar old man' in 1967. Whitehouse herself rapidly became caricatured in popular culture – endorsed (to her chagrin) by Garnett in an episode of *Til Death* in 1967. The new liberal elite 'subconsciously welcomed' Whitehouse (rather as they had created Garnett) as a godsend, affirming their progressive credentials.[25] *Humanist News* could not help but compliment Whitehouse's 'moral seriousness' and that she was 'not rich ... not educated ... single-minded and energetic.' Opponents struggled to define NVALA – drawing analogies with French Poujadism (for its crypto-fascism and opposition to taxes) and McCarthyism (for its conspiracies of communists ensconced in the BBC hierarchy).[26]

Before NVALA there were 'clean-up' branches in South Wales, Birmingham, Nottingham, Manchester, Mansfield and London. But the extent to which this was a sham behind the accoutrements of a mass movement was revealed by Dance in 1967, agreeing the council and executive roles could simply be swapped. By most accounts behind the annual convention the executive was self-perpetuating and criticism of Whitehouse was sacrilege – all credence to critics who thought it an MRA front.[27]

Its claim to represent the viewing public was hard pressed. Membership was 7,000 by 1968 and peaked in the mid-1970s. But Whitehouse told the 1968 Convention that with Church support, plus manifesto signatories, some 'one million people have, in some practical way, expressed their support of our work'.[28] In correspondence to the BBC Whitehouse claimed to speak for 3/4 million viewers and was amazed it considered them a 'fringe movement' rather than 'representative'. But BBC Secretary, Kenneth Lamb, disputed NVALA's claims, since it was reluctant to say which organisations affiliated *en bloc*. Normanbrook exploited the lack of any provably close link between the petition's signatories and the outpourings of the NVALA leaders, to refuse to meet with them.[29]

Whilst it targeted the young in the press (Cliff Richard won its 1970 award), NVALA was a movement of the older generation and the provinces. Whitehouse was 53 when the campaign started and many activists were retired or housewives. Its manner as much as anything distinguished it from its liberal quarry. A Warwickshire councillor's wife complained at Birmingham Town Hall that the BBC was 'behaving like an adolescent'. Yet as the meeting chair, Councillor Pepper, put it, it dismissed complaints in a 'smooth, urbane' way. Pepper warned of danger 'if we allow ourselves to become over-emotional', yet concluded, 'if we stand by and say nothing while the decline is going on we can't complain when the ultimate fall takes place'.[30]

Wilson was informed it represented the 'repugnance which exists in the provinces for much of what has come to be known as "swinging London"'. By 1970 NVALA imagined itself 'the voice of the silent millions', not 'a noisy pressure group representing a tiny minority, but a manifestation of an awakening democracy'. Whilst open to all, 'as our national institutions are founded on ... Christian concepts, so VALA reflects ... the values inherent in our national heritage'. It saw itself not as a 'man-made movement concerned simply with raising the standard of broadcasting', but as uniting those with 'a passionate desire to enrich the quality of life'. With 'groups all over the country' it envisioned reaching out to 'every sphere of the nation's life – education, politics, social and moral issues'. If broadcasting 'was the launching pad of the permissive society', then 'in the 1970s it could become the pacemaker of the responsible society'.[31] There was no coincidence that NVALA was pronounced 'national valour' and no lack of certainty in its mission: 'in the last century it was inevitable that Trade Unions should become an essential part of industrial life, so today it is natural that a viewers and listeners association should arise'.[32]

Supporters

Prominent NVALA patrons came from the military and religious elite: an Air Chief Marshall, Lord Bishops, plus personalities like Catholic-convert, Malcolm Muggeridge. Dowager Lady Birdwood lead NVALA in London.[33] In attempting to assemble support with cognate groups in civil society, NVALA, like many NGOs, faced difficulties once speaking beyond its immediate campaign and membership. There were achievements – the Scottish Housewives Association, whose Secretary Mrs. E. Pattulo was a Whitehouse supporter, shifted its support from Cyril Black's Public Morality Council in 1964, something he regretted, whilst supporting Clean-up TV.[34] Black was Tory MP for Wimbledon, a temperance campaigner and President of the London Baptist Association.

Churches were NVALA's best recruiting ground. Of the mass of letters in its archives, most were from non-conformists – Presbyterian and

Evangelical Free Churches, Baptist Chapels – and from outside of England, where Protestantism remained stronger. The Catholic Church's opposition to permissiveness was resolute, so disgruntled Anglicans were more apparent. Amongst non-religious groups, typical was Rotary International that explained its 'strictly non-party approach to political matters' precluded institutional support, although individuals might help. Replies in this vein were received from the National anti-Vivisection Society, Girl Guides and British Legion Scotland.[35]

The Catholic Teachers' Federation (CTF) backed NVALA, requesting parents, staff and pupils sign the manifesto in 1965. This was countered by Charles Curran (Carleton Greene's successor and like him a Catholic), with adult educationalist and future Arts Council Secretary-General Roy Shaw and Tony Higgins (Nottingham CTF President). They questioned the propriety of NVALA's methods, highlighted other Catholic media initiatives and a Papal encyclical ('Miranda Prorusus') that emphasised parental and educators' responsibilities. By 1966 the CTF was inched away from supporting Whitehouse. Higgins concluded of campaigning against NVALA that 'their attitude is based on emotion not reason, they are not open to argument'.[36]

The Mothers Union (MU) briefly embraced the campaign at its inception. But the manifesto only won the support of two of the 13 area dioceses it was dispatched to. 'Though sharing a common concern for declining moral standards', most were unwilling to hold solely the BBC accountable and felt 'the writers of the manifesto had invalidated it as a responsible or constructive document by their use of intemperate language'. The Norfolk Group wanted to persuade broadcasters 'in the normal way by discussion, preferably not of the heated, over-emotional type reflected in the manifesto'. Such conclusions were relished by Doreen Stephens, head of BBC TV family programmes. She nursed the MU as a barrier against 'this other "monstrous regiment of women"… the Birmingham Women "Vigilante" group'.[37]

Another characteristic was that NVALA feared 'being dominated by the broadcasting professional unless viewer's representatives' made their voice heard. It saw as 'one of the most ominous developments' that the BBC appeared 'more concerned with the rights of young playwrights than with the community.' Whitehouse's case was that related experts – police, doctors – had as legitimate a claim to control output. This bore on NVALA's model for participation. David Frost, speaking at NVALA's 1970 Convention, argued pre-broadcast vetting by a Viewers' Council would kill new besides bad ideas, since 'an amateur cannot be expected to make a judgment'. His belief that viewers were too intelligent to be brainwashed was (revealingly) met with cries of 'no'.[38]

NVALA reveled in its oppositional status, its everyday DIY activism, appealing for funds for Whitehouse's 'spartan' office to tackle the might of the BBC. In this vein Whitehouse celebrated the 'I'm Backing Britain' movement of Surbiton typists – who after devaluation in 1967 promised to work through their tea breaks – in a letter to Wilson penned, in a sure sign of commitment, on New Years Day.[39] NVALA tactics were also a reaction to the professionalisation of politics, that party now seemed managerial, remote from popular concerns and utilised the machinery of public relations.

It also defiantly valued housewifery and parenting. The femininity deployed by the group, first formed as 'Women of Britain', was conservative. Whitehouse was formally listed as Mrs. E.R (Ernest) Whitehouse, her husband's moniker. As Buckland told NVALA's founding audience 'many women feel that the training they are trying to give their children is being undermined by the television' and this was why Whitehouse resigned her teaching job in December 1964 to devote herself to campaigning.[40]

Contexts

A key context for NVALA was the waning of Christianity, as relative economic and social security after 1945 undermined the security sought in religion or rigid cultural norms. Besides declining church numbers, it was secular morality – the self-liberation fostered by affluence and permissiveness, trends that culminated in 1963: Profumo, the pill, *TW3*, relaxing of BBC codes – that prompted NVALA. Brown argues these secularising trends were borne by women – and three quarters of NVALA members were women. As Fryer presciently declared in 1963, 'Mrs. Grundy is with us still'.[41]

NVALA blamed the Church response as much as secularisation – itself questioning established authority. John Robinson (the Bishop of Woolwich)'s *Honest to God* (1963) seemed to swim with permissive tides. NVALA supporter Arnold Lunn's *Cult of Softness* (softness was a NVALA keyword, denoting, like Thatcherism's 'wet', fatal irresolution) wanted less indulgence of individual weakness and more moral guidance.[42]

Whitehouse's involvement in MRA from the 1930s discouraged church and political support. MRA's tactics, clandestine air, moral purity and anti-communism infused NVALA. In 1963 MRA's leader Peter Howard lambasted the 'dirt' peddled by the BBC and the Edinburgh festival.

Howard endorsed Whitehouse's campaign.[43] MRA links were not denied (and much discussed via Labour MP Tom Driberg's expose), but its controlling hand and finances were. NVALA asserted its authenticity as a 'spontaneous' (recurrent in its lexicon) 'expression of the determination of ordinary people ... to preserve their homes and families from the seeping immorality ... portrayed on television'. Buckland found 5 per cent of members were MRA active. But there was a conspiratorial aspect to NVALA. TV writer (and Labour Lord) Ted Willis accused it of scare tactics and by the 1970s it frequented right-wing para-politics.[44]

Also unable to offer much guidance or support was a Conservative Party, hamstrung by a modernity it had introduced in legislation on divorce, gambling and obscene publications. Women's sections and MPs like Dance voiced anxiety about the break-up of traditional values and youth crime. Party leaders concurred that material well-being had bred rather than assuaged social and moral problems, but were keener to advocate family and individual responsibility than more rigorous state policing. They were not minded to tamper with popular tastes they had introduced via ITV in 1955. The notion of the Anglican church as 'the Tory party at prayer', was fragmenting.[45]

The chances of the party acting on Whitehouse's strictures were then limited. From 1965 the new leader Edward 'Heath's cool corporatism', Campbell argues, 'distanced him ... from the keepers of the party's moral conscience – women'. NVALA articulated and liberated visceral elements in popular conservatism.[46] Like CND for Labour, NVALA pricked Conservatism's moral instincts. It signalled the discontent with party and willingness to engage in extra-parliamentary protest that Marsh detailed. Whilst part of the boom in pressure groups, Whitehouse was herself wary of them. Vocal minorities on abortion and homosexuality, she felt, were behind the permissive legislation passed under the Wilson government, to which she might have added the evidence in H.H. Wilson's seminal *Pressure Group*, on the commercial lobby behind ITV.[47]

'The campaign', MP Jasper More warned Prime Minister Douglas-Home in June 1964, 'is assuming the dimensions of a mass movement.' Since its 'leaders are conservative supporters', More worried this might damage party support. A month later Bill Deedes (who in 1966 addressed NVALA's first convention) proposed a 'consumers council' for broadcasting. But the Cabinet chose to await the research initiated by Rab Butler.[48]

Labour had little truck with NVALA. Tony Benn, a non-conformist, interested in more participatory democracy and critic of the BBC establishment, disagreed with NVALA views on programmes, but acknow-ledged their efforts.[49] Six Conservative MPs were present at the 1965 meeting that set up NVALA: Cyril Osborne and five from the party's broadcasting committee, including Dance. Whitehouse addressed the Committee, but there was little discussion of NVALA's agenda, until Julian Critchley (a speaker at NVALA's 1972 convention) revived some notion of a Broadcasting Council in 1970.[50]

Much as NVALA's campaign was intolerant of the shift to a more self-expressive, less deferential culture, its own lack of restraint put it at odds with that strain of Conservatism that eschewed ideology and pre-ferred to appear low-key. This was its un-doing, since in other ways it articulated widespread concerns about TV. Leading conservatives were key to marginalising Whitehouse – locating her as beyond the pale. Most support was tacit. The National Women's Advisory Committee chair suggested meeting, but only once she had appraised levels of local support. Paul Bryan turned down an offer to speak at the 1969 Convention, assuring Whitehouse of his support, but that they ought not appear to be in league. John Selwyn Gummer's foray into *The Permissive Society* mentioned Whitehouse only once, despite dealing with her precise canon – professional liberals, drugs, sex, abortion, legal pornography in Denmark, the 'lilac establishment', Church and TV. And the sorts of MP that did openly associate with Whitehouse – Dance, Gerald Nabarro and future MP Neil Hamilton (NVALA chair in 1972) – were outsiders.[51]

Besides secularisation and Conservatism, TV mobilised NVALA. It was Britons' most common culture in this period – by 1970 more than 90 per cent had a TV and they were Europe's most avid viewers. If a church habit declined, some of its power had switched over to TV. TV has been central to debates about social capital in modern demo-cracies. Most have concluded it was corrosive, but all have tended to regard TV as one-step removed from politics, rather than having a history as an issue in its own right.[52]

TV pressure groups and debates

TV was a political issue from ITV's advent. COSMO (founded in Bloomsbury's Cosmo Place) and TRACK (Television and Radio Com-mittee, chaired by Roy Shaw, with leading liberal media commentator Richard Hoggart and a membership of TV writers) countered NVALA from 1965. COSMO, whose leading light was Avril Fox, Labour coun-cilor in Harlow, whose beliefs meshed Sufi and feminism, rebutted

Whitehouse' claim to speak for women.[53] The Standing Conference on Television (Television Viewers' Council (TVC) from 1963), pre-dated NVALA's interest in viewer-programmer dialogue. It convened educational, children's, consumer and advertising bodies, with the BBC and ITA. Participants included Higgins, Hoggart and TV researchers like Halloran and Himmelweit (who sat on its Committee). NVALA dismissed these as BBC fronts, but COSMO persisted to campaign for abolition of the Obscene Publications Act, as did TVC's influence in Groombridge's work.[54]

Mary Adams, assistant BBC TV controller 1954–58, appointed to the ITA by Benn in 1965 and closely involved in the Consumers' Association, chaired TVC. Its purpose, she explained, was 'to express viewers' viewpoints ... to communicate with the providers'. Adams drew parallels with the consumer movement: 'the viewer, like the ... consumer of goods and services, needs information and advice ... and protection ... an organisation to represent him'. The key was that 'the professionalism of the providers calls for reciprocal expertise ... by viewers'. But there were differences with NVALA. TVC had no ambition to be 'an unofficial television ombudsmen' and aimed to creatively engage broadcasting professionals. It recognised 'pleasure is part of the serious business of television' and conceived viewer's role as more than 'a thousand letters or telephone calls to programme providers', which meant 'little in an audience of millions'.[55]

TVC co-sponsored research at Birmingham University's Centre for Contemporary Cultural Studies (CCCS). Hoggart chaired CCCS from 1963, with Stuart Hall as research fellow. In 1966 Hoggart made a brief conciliatory approach, inviting Whitehouse to CCCS after a confrontation with Hall.[56] For Whitehouse, Hoggart was the '*eminence grise*' behind Carleton Greene, but like her, was represented as a puritan moralist after the Pilkington report (1962) criticised ITV. His review of *Cleaning-Up TV* thought it posed legitimate questions about TV, if the wrong answers.[57] Another parallel between conservative and radical cultural critics highlighted in Hoggart's review, was TV drama's 'firesiding' effects. As Pilkington was occupied by the triviality of ITV output, so NVALA saw TV 'trivialise and cheapen human relationships and undermine marriage and family'. Sex and violence desensitised viewers by reducing social issues to spectacle. Here Whitehouse sounded like Marcuse, who saw popular culture diffusing such issues (although *Cathy Come Home*'s contribution to Shelter would seem to confound this).[58]

Hall's concerns, as a teacher after editing *New Left Review* and writing *The Popular Arts*, were not dissimilar to Whitehouse's. These were partly driven by debates in the National Union of Teachers about TV's impact and 'debasement of standards'. These too readily ascribed blame to cultural producers and were 'too eager to think in terms of censorship and control'. In 1960 Hall wrote of how sensual appeals figured in the 'montage of 'success', seducing our consciousness, undermining and corrupting moral standards, encouraging a weak, flaccid, self-indulgence at odds with adult critical standards'; of how, 'sex has become the ... salesman of prosperity, on the television screen' and 'capitalism which emerged with the Methodist Sunday School and the gospel of work, now offers ... the gospel of promiscuity'.[59] This is a telling extract, suggesting that so far as cultural politics were post-materialist, they shared certain qualities and terms of debate, far apart as their politics were.

Research into television was ineluctably drawn into this debate. Social psychologist Hilde Himmelweit, concluded TV 'aroused aggression as often as ... discharged it' in children. The NVALA preferred William Belson's work, who Himmelweit steered the TVC away from, but even he distinguished effects *'caused* by, from those ... *correlated* with, the possession of a television set'.[60] The Television Research Committee at Leicester University, appointed by the government in 1963, took the bulk of Whitehouse's flak – for the duration of its research (its first report took six years) and the interim conclusions of its secretary, sociologist James Halloran. Working papers stressed the complexity of relationships between the viewer and medium and of suitable research methods. Halloran accepted the NVALA and the 'efficiency of that Association's public relations' fed a popular sense that TV was a factor in behaviour and attitude formation. But definitive conclusions or policy implications were harder to reach – 'the picture is not clear'.[61]

These equivocal results were not unwelcome for politicians. But NVALA, mistrusting professional experts, pilloried the '"precious" sociological research into the effects of TV violence ... at Leicester'. 'Research of this kind asks the wrong questions and inevitably comes up with the wrong answers – if any answers at all!' It was a 'basic fact of human psychology – that people, and especially children are deeply affected by their environment, of which TV is an all-pervading part'. As the NVALA-supporting Stoke Rotary Club president put it, all that 'was needed was good sense'.[62] NVALA undertook its own research, revealing predictable insights into its mindset.

Conclusions

Sociologists in the 1970s were much concerned with middle-class protest and pressure group influence on government. Wallis analysed the NVALA as a less-educated fraction of the middle-class at odds with a younger upwardly-mobile generation of more secular values. But class alone was explanatorily insufficient and concepts of status and cultural defence emerged. More than a differential erosion of material security, their traditional values of self-discipline (the protestant work ethic, in short) were threatened. Wallis termed the NVALA's ideology 'cultural fundamentalism', drawing out its opposition to pluralism, a society reluctant to make value judgements about what to NVALA, more than anyone in the sixties, seemed uncontrolled social change. NVALA craved stability, respect for the order of things as they were in its vividly imagined recent past.[63]

These studies pointed towards conceiving the NVALA as a social movement. NVALA's exclusion from such literature would not have surprised Whitehouse, whose critique of liberalism as in practice intolerant, echoed New Right thinking. But by accepted definitions of social movements – 'a collective, organised, sustained and non-institutional challenge to authorities, powerholders or cultural beliefs and practices' – NVALA fits. It exhibited key concepts in the taxonomy of social movements: affective ties; cognitive liberation; charisma; (paradoxical) media savvy; tactical innovation and, however rhetorically, participatory democracy.[64]

NVALA's stress on values was less anti-materialist – business and ITV were spared its harshest criticism – than post-materialist. As most NVALA members saw it: 'what we've got is a non-materialistic problem' for which the answer lay in Christian values. Whitehouse told Heath that her 'experience ... speaking around the country' and the lesson of his 1970 election victory was 'that concern over the libertarianism of the "permissive" society ran even deeper than anxiety over the economic state'. Essex VALA argued in 1970 'however much politicians may focus attention on economic matters ... we shall continue to be in trouble until the moral issues are sorted out'. Parkin saw CND as evidence that 'groups and individuals may be as deeply concerned about the defence or propagation of secular moral values which are unrelated to material and economic interests'. Secular apart, this holds for NVALA.[65]

Sixties Britain saw debate about the efficacy of representative institutions sparked by a wealthier, better-educated electorate, by the concentration of power in Whitehall, the welfare state and industry and by a sense of powerlessness and national 'decline'. And pressure groups saw participation and accountability as watchwords. NVALA seemed at one with this, but its social profile complicates Inglehart's generational and educational patterning of post-materialism (and Parkin's portrait of CND members). NVALA might be seen less as reactive to post-materialist trends, than an agent of them. Inglehart after all posited that 'the transition to postindustrial society will entail a renewed emphasis on spiritual values', particularly amongst post-materialists afforded time for ethical matters. And these values were not necessarily, NVALA shows, bound to be progressive. NVALA then questions not post-materialism *per se*, but suggests a more contested – less economically determinist, more culturally manifold – process than Inglehart's linear modernisation. NVALA were post-materialists, but not as Inglehart knew them; just as the NVALA is a rejoinder to many assumptions about the political nature of social movements.[66]

Notes

1 M. Whitehouse, *Cleaning-up TV: From Protest to Participation* (London: Blandford Press, 1967), p. 23.

2 A. Lent, *British Social Movements since 1945* (Basingstoke: Palgrave 2001); H. Nehring, 'The Growth of Social Movements', in H. Jones and P. Addison (eds), *Companion to Contemporary Britain, 1939–2000* (Oxford: Blackwell, 2005); P. Byrne, *Social Movements in Britain* (London: Routledge, 1997).

3 The Commission became OfCom in 2003.

4 B. Campbell, *The Iron Ladies* (London: Virago 1987), p. 4.

5 F. Parkin, *Middle Class Radicalism* (Manchester: Manchester University Press, 1968); R. Inglehart, *Culture Shift in Advanced Industrial Society* (Princeton: Princeton University Press, 1990).

6 D. Dworkin, *Cultural Marxism in Postwar Britain* (Durham, NC: Duke University Press, 1993).

7 J. Garnett *et al.* (eds.), *Redefining Christian Britain* (London: SCM Press, 2007).

8 S. Fielding, *Labour and Cultural Change 1964–70* (Manchester: Manchester University Press, 2003), pp. 18–20, ch. 8.

9 D. Nash, *Blasphemy in the Christian World* (Oxford: Oxford University Press, 2007).

10 *The Viewer* 3 (March 1968); Whitehouse to Lord Aylestone (15 April 1968), NVALA Archive, Essex University, Boc 47 (NVALA 47); K. Bird report (6 May 1964), BBC Written Archives Centre (WAC) T16/585.

11 Short to Whitehouse (3 May 1967), Whitehouse to Wilson (24 June 1967), NVALA 16 (2000 Accession).

12 Minutes meeting (26 March 1968), NVALA 44; M. Tracey, D. Morrison, *Whitehouse* (Basingstoke: Macmillan, 1979), ch. 8.

13 *Observer* (10 November 1968); Curran to Whitehouse (19 June 1966), NVALA 17 (2000).

14 NVALA 26 (2000); Tracey, *Whitehouse*, pp. 188–90; *The Viewer and Listener* (Summer 1970); Letter (30 January 1981), NVALA 123.

15 Whitehouse, *Cleaning-up TV*, pp. 148–9, 165; 'Censorship? Television and NVALA' (c.1967), NVALA 108.

16 Speech, 16 December 1968, NVALA 59; Circular Letter to MPs (14 February 1966), NVALA 54; Clean-up TV 'Draft Constitution', NVALA 1.

17 Sims memo (16 January 1967), Whitehouse speaker File II, 1963–72'; Controllers' meeting minutes (7, 14 December 1965), WAC T16/585.

18 Advice (26 April 1967); BBC management minutes (22 May, 5 June 1967), WAC R134/609/1, 2.

19 Whitehouse to Wilson (25 October 1964), National Archives (NA) HO259/719; *National VALA News* (November 1967); *Wolverhampton Express and Star* (22 July 1968).

20 Whitehouse, Hill, Callaghan correspondence (13, 28 May 1968), NVALA 108; Whitehouse's 1968 convention address, NVALA 7 (2000); Whitehouse to Callaghan (23 February 1968), NVALA 58.

21 Rev H. Goodwin (author of anti-*Honest to God* tract, *The Principles of Broadcasting*) to Buckland (13 April 1964), NVALA 79; Barnett to B. Charles-Dean (14 April 1965), Monsignor P. Casey to Whitehouse (4 March 1965), NVALA 80.

22 *NVALA – What is It?* (1966), NVALA 1; *The Viewer and Listener* (Summer 1970); M. Tracey and D. Morrison, 'Opposition to the Age' (Social Science Research Council report, 1978), p. 29, NVALA 76.

23 Note (17 June 1965); Whitehouse to Wilson (10 June 1965), NA HO 259/719.

24 *Daily Mail* (20 May 1970).

25 (London) *Evening News* (2 March 1967); C. Booker, *The Neophiliacs* (London: Collins, 1969), p. 256.

26 *Humanist News* (April 1967), p.11; *Spectator* (24 February 1967).

27 Minutes (25 February 1965), NVALA 1; Dance to Whitehouse (15 June 1967), NVALA 80; R. Wallis, 'Moral indignation and the media: an analysis of the NVALA', *Sociology* 10 (1976).

28 Secretary's Report 1968 Convention, NVALA 7 (2000); D. Cliff, 'Religion, morality and the middle class' in R. King, N. Nugent (eds): *Respectable Rebels: Middle Class Campaigns in Britain in the 1970s* (London: Hodder and Stoughton, 1979).

29 Whitehouse-Lamb correspondence (1968), NVALA 37; Normanbrook to Whitehouse (21 June, 22 September 1965), NVALA 42.

30 *Melody Maker* (17 October 1970); K. Bird report (1964).

31 Whitehouse to Wilson (24 June 1967), NVALA 16 (2000); *Viewer and Listener* (Summer 1970).

32 Wallis, 'Moral', p. 278; 'Draft Constitution'.

33 Obituary, *Guardian* (30 June 2000) tells of her far right links and, like Whitehouse, 'weird taste in spectacles'.

34 Black to Pattulo (4 December 1964), NVALA 80.

35 Letters, NVALA 77–9; Rotary International and others (6 August 1968), NVALA 13 (2000).

36 *Catholic Herald* (5 November 1965); Higgins to Curran (7 January 1966), WAC R44/1, 189/1.

37 MU Central President to Whitehouse (12 February 1964), NVALA 80; 'Summary of Diocesan Mothers' Union Reports ... to the manifesto from

'the women of Britain' (n.d., 1964); Norfolk Group report (1964); Stephens memo (n.d., 1964), WAC T16/585.

38 *Viewer and Listener* (Summer 1970); *What NVALA Believes* (1966), NVALA 1; *Spectator* (16 September 1966).

39 *The Viewer and Listener* (Summer 1970); Whitehouse to Wilson (1 January 1968), NVALA 59.

40 Circular (25 October 1964); Minutes meeting (25 February 1965), NVALA 1.

41 C. Brown, *The Death of Christian Britain* (London: Routledge, 2001), pp. 1, 7, 191–3; 'Introduction' in M. Collins (ed.), *The Permissive Society and its Enemies* (London: Rivers Oram, forthcoming); P. Fryer, *Mrs Grundy: Studies in English Prudery* (Dobson Books: London, 1963).

42 J. Robinson (ed.), *The Honest to God Debate* (London: SCM Press, 1963); A. Lunn, *The Cult of Softness* (London: Blandford Press, 1965), pp. 6–8.

43 C. Brown, *Religion and Society in Twentieth-century Britain* (Harlow: Pearson, 2006), pp. 198–201, 232–51; Howard to Whitehouse (11 August 1964); NVALA 80; In 2001 NVALA became 'Mediawatch' and MRA, 'Initiatives of Change'.

44 T. Driberg, *The Mystery of Moral Re-armament* (London: Secker & Warburg, 1964); Buckland to Whitehouse (28 June 1966) NVALA 80; Clean-Up TV newsletter (30 September 1964). Willis notes (1967), WAC R134/609/1.

45 M. Jarvis, *Conservative Governments, Morality and Social Change in Affluent Britain, 1957–64* (Manchester: Manchester University Press, 2005), pp. 143–7.

46 Campbell, *Iron Ladies*, p. 99; Chair Hemel Hempstead Conservative Association to Whitehouse (n.d.c. 1969), NVALA 20.

47 B. Pym, *Pressure Groups and the Permissive Society* (Newton Abbot: David & Charles, 1974), pp. 12, 148; A. Marsh, *Protest and Political Consciousness* (London: Sage, 1977); H.H. Wilson, *Pressure Group* (London: Secker & Warburg, 1961).

48 J. More to PM's PPS (24 June 1964), NA PREM11/4646; Jarvis, *Conservative governments*, p. 146.

49 Benn to G. Thomas (22 December 1965), NVALA 16 (2000); Fielding, *Labour*, p. 196.

50 Minutes (25 February 1965), NVALA 1; Executive minutes (15 February 1967), NVALA 10 (2000); Broadcasting Committee minutes (14 June 1967, 9 December 1970), Conservative Party Archive, Bodleian Library, CRD3/20/1; J. Critchley, *Counsel for Broadcasting* (1971).

51 C. Doughty to Whitehouse (6 February 1965), NVALA 80; Bryan to Whitehouse (5 June 1969), NVALA 45; J.S. Gummer, *The Permissive Society* (London: Cassell, 1971).

52 L. Black, 'Whose Finger on the Button? British Television and the Politics of Cultural Control', *Historical Journal of Film, Radio and Television*, 25 (2005); C. Pattie, P. Seyd and P. Whiteley, *Citizenship in Britain* (Cambridge: Cambridge University Press, 2004), pp. 250–61.

53 A. Fox, *The Emerging Ethic* (Portlaw: Volturna Press, 1971); *Guardian* (2 December 1965).

54 Whitehouse, *Cleaning-up*, pp. 133–46, 192–4; B. Groombridge, *Television and the People* (Harmondsworth: Penguin, 1972).

55 M. Adams, 'Television Consumers', *Consumer News* (January 1964).

56 CCCS annual reports (1965–69), Hoggart Papers, Sheffield University, 6/4/3,4, 9; Hoggart to Whitehouse (7 February, 1 June 1966), 4/6/218–220.

57   *The Scotsman* (18 December 1965); *New Society* (16 February 1967), p. 245; Hoggart's obituary, *Guardian* (24 November 2001).
58   Review, *New Society*; *NVALA – What is It?*; Cliff, 'Religion', pp. 138–9; M. Donnelly, *Sixties Britain* (London: Longman, 2005), pp. 80–1.
59   Dworkin, *Cultural Marxism*, p. 117; S. Hall and P. Whannel, *The Popular Arts* (London: Hutchison, 1964), pp. 23–4; Hall, 'The Supply of Demand', in E.P. Thompson (ed.), *Out of Apathy* (London: Stevens, 1960), p. 82.
60   H. Himmelweit *et al.*, *Television and the Child* (Oxford: Oxford University Press: 1958), p. 20; SCTV minutes (13 February 1963), WAC S322/125/1; Cliff, 'Religion', pp. 138–9; W.A. Belson, *Television and the Family* (London: BBC, 1959), pp. xvii, 127–34.
61   J.D. Halloran *et al.*, *Television and Delinquency* (Leicester: Leicester University Press, 1970); J.D. Halloran (ed.), *The Effects of Television* (London: Panther Books, 1970), pp. 22, 63.
62   *The Viewer and Listener* (Summer 1970), *The Viewer* (March 1968).
63   Wallis, 'Moral', pp. 282–6.
64   J. Goodwin and J. Jasper (eds), *The Social Movements Reader* (Oxford: Blackwell, 2003), pp. ix, 3.
65   Tracey, 'Opposition', p. 43; Whitehouse to Heath (27 June 1970), NVALA 59; Essex VALA leaflet, WAC R78/2, 348/1; Parkin, *Middle Class Radicalism*, p. 33.
66   Inglehart, *Culture Shift*, pp. 177, 211, ch. 10.

11
Environmental NGOs and the Environmental Movement in England[1]

Christopher Rootes

Introduction

Britain, it has been said, has the oldest, strongest, best-organised and most widely supported environmental lobby in the world.[2] Although environmental movements are best conceived as networks of actors of which many are organisations of varying degrees of formality, they are complex and amorphous phenomena that cannot simply be reduced to those organisations.[3] Nevertheless, organisations are generally the most visible and most stable constituents of movements. While there is disagreement about whether, at this stage of its development, the collectivity of environmental NGOs (ENGOs) constitutes a movement or is, instead, better characterised as a 'lobby' or a 'policy advocacy community', ENGOs are, even for students of environmental movements, an appropriate object of study.[4]

The per capita density of membership of ENGOs may be greater in some other countries, but the organisational complexity and diversity of ENGOs in Britain is remarkable. A glance at the characteristics of a dozen of the most prominent and/or best-funded makes this apparent (see Table 11.1).

Some of these ENGOs (notably the National Trust (NT), the Royal Society for the Protection of Birds (RSPB), and the Wildlife, Woodland and Wildfowl and Wetlands Trusts) devote a high proportion of their resources to the acquisition and preservation of the properties and reserves they manage, and are only rarely involved in public campaigns. Some (notably WWF) raise funds and promote environmental education in Britain but conduct most of their practical work abroad. Others (such as Friends of the Earth (FoE), Greenpeace and the Campaign to Protect Rural England (CPRE)) are principally campaigning

Table 11.1 Leading British environmental NGOs (2005)

	Year Founded in UK	Members/ Donors/ Supporters	Income/ Budget	Staff size	Local groups	Manage property or reserves?	Focus
RSPB	1889	1,042,000	£63,000,000	1,500	175[1]	Yes (190)	Birds and their habitat, nature reserves
National Trust	1895	3,400,000	£315,000,000	>4,000	>60[2]	Yes	Landscapes, historic buildings
Wildlife Trusts*	1912	588,000	*	>1,500	47	Yes (>2,200)	Wildlife and habitat, nature reserves
CPRE	1926	60,000	£3,000,000	50	200	No	Countryside, land-use planning
Wildfowl & Wetland Trust	1946	139,000	£14,000,000	275	–	Yes	Birds and wetlands
BTCV	1959	365[3]	£23,000,000	588	No[4]	No[5]	Community conservation projects
WWF-UK	1961	330,000	£39,000,000	290	200[6]	Not in UK	Conservation, sustainable development overseas
FoE (E, W, NI)	1971	102,000	£9,000,000[7]	159	200	No	Environmental protection, social justice
Woodland Trust	1972	147,000	£21,000,000	223	No	Yes	Woodland (preservation and new planting)
Greenpeace UK	1977	221,000[8]	£11,000,000[9]	100	102	No	Environmental protection (esp. marine), nuclear

Table 11.1 Leading British environmental NGOs (2005) – *continued*

	Year Founded in UK	Members/ Donors/ Supporters	Income/ Budget	Staff size	Local groups	Manage property or reserves?	Focus
Sustrans	1977	N/A	£22,000,000	163	No	No	Walking, cycling
Wildlife & Countryside Link**	1980	35 organisations[10]	–	–	–	–	–

Notes:

Staff numbers include part-time staff, where separately declared as such, as 0.5 of full-time.
*umbrella organisation representing autonomous local/regional groups.
**umbrella organisation linking autonomous member organisations.

1. Plus 110 youth groups.
2. Plus >40 property-based groups of 'friends' or 'volunteers'.
3. BTCV has only 365 'members' with voting rights, but according to its website 'supports 140,000 volunteers'.
4. BTCV 'supports 2,225 local community groups' but these are not BTCV groups as such.
5. BTCV assists with management of various projects but does not manage property or reserves of its own.
6. Estimated for 2002.
7. Includes £3.8 million for FoE Trust.
8. Includes 8,000 'active supporters' who assist in delivery of Greenpeace campaigns.
9. Figure for 2004; includes £1.9 million for Greenpeace Environmental Trust.
10. Including all of the above except BTCV and Sustrans.

Sources: Annual reports, websites and information supplied by organisations themselves.

organisations. Some are affiliates of transnational ENGOs (FoE, Greenpeace and WWF), others (including CPRE) are not. Some (including FoE and CPRE) have hundreds of largely autonomous local groups, others (notably Greenpeace) have local groups but restrict their activities to those approved by the national organisation; others have no local groups at all. Some (notably FoE and CPRE) actively encourage local groups' involvement in campaigns, others (such as the NT, RSPB and the Wildlife Trusts) largely restrict them to providing volunteer labour for practical conservation activities. Some are membership organisations in which members can, in principle, hold officers to account, others (including the Woodland Trust) have members but allow them no effective role in governance, and others (British Trust for Conservation Volunteers (BTCV), Sustrans) have no formal mass membership at all. Some employ many staff and organise volunteers for practical conservation, others employ only core professional staff and intermittently mobilise their supporters in public campaigns. Some (including WWF and BTCV) depend to a significant degree upon government grants or corporate donations, others (notably Greenpeace) refuse them altogether. Some are registered charities, others have charitable status only for subsidiary activities. Wildlife and Countryside Link and the Wildlife Trusts are umbrella organisations coordinating and/or representing autonomous national, regional or local ENGOs. Thus, even within this short list, there is great diversity.

These large organisations are, however, only part of an extraordinarily rich and complex organisational field. Some idea of its range and complexity can be gained from entries in the Environment Council's database, *Who's Who in the Environment? (WWE?)*, (1999). *WWE?* listed over 1,000 organisations, many of them government departments or agencies, industry groups, groups whose interests are only peripherally or incidentally environmental, or groups operating only at local or regional levels. Excluding these, in the most comprehensive survey of ENGOs in Britain to date, during 1999–2000 144 organisations were surveyed, including almost all the national ENGOs listed in *WWE?*[5]

Among the thematic concerns listed by ENGOs in *WWE?*, wildlife habitats ranked first (41 per cent), followed by farming, fishing and forestry (30 per cent), parks, reserves and landscapes (13 per cent), the built environment (12 per cent) and flora and fauna (11 per cent). Respondents to our survey reported the main fields of activity of their ENGOs as environmental education (62 per cent) and nature conservation (55 per cent). Thus, although the public image of environmentalism may be shaped by high profile campaigns over pollution, nuclear energy, roads and airports, it is the natural environment that is of greatest concern to most ENGOs.

Early history

ENGOs began to emerge in England in the middle of the nineteenth century.[6] Among the first was the Commons Preservation Society (1865); created to guarantee protection of public access to open land, its notable achievement was the preservation of London's commons. The Society for the Prevention of Cruelty to Animals (later RSPCA), established in 1824, actively supported early campaigns to protect wildlife. Specialised societies proliferated, but the first national association concerned with all forms of wildlife was the Selborne Society for the Protection of Birds, Plants and Pleasant Places (1885).

The background to and context for the emergence of this first wave of ENGOs was increasing awareness of the impacts of industrialisation upon the natural environment and the health of the human population. At the dawn of the nineteenth century, Romantic poets, appalled by the visible ravages of coalmines and factories, celebrated natural landscapes; they were soon succeeded by reformers who tried by political means to address environmental ills. Concerns with pollution of air and water excited protests and protective legislation, civic initiatives created urban parks, and the characteristically British idealisation of the countryside became embedded as a counterpoint to the squalor of the new industrial towns.

Also around this time, scientific investigation and exploration enhanced interest in and understanding of the natural world. Nature study groups, focussed upon field studies, gradually became divorced from increasingly professionalised science, but amateurs founded influential conservation organisations. Natural history societies came and went, but by the late nineteenth century something that might be called a conservation movement existed. It was, however, an elite rather than a mass movement; its activists saw legislation as the means by which nature might be protected, and they owed their successes principally to 'the influential positions of many of those who championed the cause'.[7]

The three largest ENGOs today all date from the late nineteenth or early twentieth centuries. The Society for the Protection of Birds (later RSPB) emerged in 1889 from the campaign against the trade in feathers for ladies' fashion. The National Trust for Places of Historic Interest or Natural Beauty (NT) (1895) grew from the Lake District Defence Society and the Commons Preservation Society; the National Trust Act (1907) empowered the NT to declare its property inalienable, gave it protection from compulsory purchase, and thus encouraged landowners to donate property. The Society for the Promotion of Nature Reserves (1912), the ancestor of the present Royal Society for Wildlife Trusts compiled lists of areas deserving protection and raised money to purchase sites that might then be entrusted to the care of others. By 1930, when the RSPB acquired its first reserves, the first regional wildlife trust had been established in Norfolk; by 1941 it was managing 15 reserves.[8]

The social changes and political democratisation that followed the 1914–18 war were reflected in the changing character of ENGOs. Whereas pre-war NGOs were mainly initiatives of resourceful, socially and politically well-connected individuals who sought royal or aristocratic patronage, in the inter-war years new groups drawing upon different social bases were formed. The Council for the Preservation of Rural England (CPRE) was an enterprise of middle-class professionals, but the Ramblers' Association embraced the working class, conjoining the assertion of ancient rights to roam the countryside with radical politics. While the Ramblers supported demands of an increasingly urbanised population for access to the countryside, CPRE aimed to protect it from unplanned urbanisation resulting from unprecedented house building, extension of urban railways, and the proliferation of automobiles.

Arguably the most influential of all English ENGOs during the twentieth century, CPRE was established as an umbrella organisation bringing together 40 NGOs including the NT, the Royal Institute of British Architects, the Royal Automobile Club, the County Council Association, the Society for the Preservation of Ancient Buildings and the Central Landowners Association. Funded by architects and planners, CPRE lobbied decision-makers for the creation of areas of special protection, including national parks, and the extension of planning controls to the countryside. Because its leaders were 'pillars of society', CPRE's pressure for universal rural planning quickly resulted in the Town and Country Planning Act 1932 and the Restriction of Ribbon Development Act 1935.[9]

The second world war and its aftermath

The 1939–45 war more drastically impacted the environment than that of 1914–18. Not only were all available human resources mobilised for total war, but also immense damage was done to the natural environment as meadows and woodland were destroyed to maximise agricultural production and extraction of minerals. With scant regard for traditional husbandry, these pressures continued into the period of post-war reconstruction. Public interest in the natural environment revived only slowly.

Plans for national parks had been devised even while war raged, and post-war legislation realised many of CPRE's ambitions. The Town and Country Planning Act 1947 established the modern, comprehensive land use planning system, and 'green belts' were designated around towns and cities. The 1949 National Parks and Access to the Countryside Act empowered the Nature Conservancy (NC), established in 1948, to designate sites of special scientific interest (SSSI) and envisaged the designation of Areas of Outstanding Natural Beauty. The first National Parks – in the Peak and Lake Districts – were created in 1951. However, the Labour government's concern to maximise production of cheap food meant that such designations delivered little practical protection; the 1947 Agriculture Act encouraged an agricultural boom that accelerated degradation of the natural environment.

If achievements in policy were mixed, the early postwar years brought renewed formation of ENGOs. Specialised nature protection associations, including the Wildfowl and Wetlands Trust, the Herpetological Society, and the Mammal Society were established, as was the Conservation Corps, now the BTCV. Meanwhile, public interest in the natural environment was stimulated by developments in communications technology: film and television became more accessible, the RSPB formed a film unit, the BBC established a natural history unit, and cheap colour reproduction made available an increasing supply of attractive guide books. The pull of such developments was balanced by the push of increasing evidence of pollution: the catastrophic London smog of 1952, the deteriorating condition of many rivers, and alarms about indiscriminate use of pesticides.

The emergence of modern environmentalism

Although public interest in nature conservation slowly reawakened during the 1950s, it was during the 1960s and, especially, the 1970s that the modern mass environmental movement developed.[10] This period of organisational innovation began with the launch of the World Wildlife Fund (WWF) in 1961. A bridge between the old and the new, WWF was, like the early nature conservation organisations, an elite initiative to raise funds for wildlife conservation, enjoying royal patronage and relying on wealthy individuals for initial funding. But, in a foretaste of what was to come a decade later, it employed mass media to broadcast its message: WWF-UK was launched by an appeal through the pages of a mass-market newspaper (the *Daily Mirror*) and it was, nominally, a mass membership organisation from the outset.

Another indicator of change was the emergence of new mechanisms to promote a common approach among ENGOs. Although cooperation and division of labour have always characterised British environmentalism, increasing awareness of the need to connect the diverse concerns of the growing number of ENGOs stimulated the formation in 1969 of a Committee (later Council) for Environmental Conservation (CoEnCo).[11]

It was, however, the spread from North America of new, deliberately transnational campaigning environmental organisations that marked the decisive change. The first of these – Friends of the Earth (FoE) – was established following the 1970 visit to London of Bill Brower, the former director of the leading US nature preservation organisation, the Sierra Club. Brower split with the Sierra Club following a series of arguments over policy and financial accountability. Believing that to meet emerging environmental challenges, an environmental organisation needed to be open to a range of environmental issues extending well beyond nature protection, Brower also realised that, in order to address environmental problems that recognised no borders, the new organisation needed to be transnational.

And so, after establishing FoE in the US in 1969, Brower embarked for Europe to encourage the formation of affiliated organisations. In London, Brower was introduced to student activists who had failed in earlier attempts to interest the National Union of Students in environmental issues, and encouraged them to set up what became an autonomous FoE organisation.

FoE's earliest campaigns in England were a 'hotchpotch' that attracted little attention until in May 1971, in response to the decision by drinks manufacturer Cadbury Schweppes to switch to non-returnable bottles, FoE organised a 'bottle drop' on the pavement outside Schweppes' London headquarters.[12] This 'media stunt' provided impressive photographs for the Sunday papers and so raised the profile of FoE that it was besieged with phone calls from people wanting to know how they could become involved. As a result, local FoE groups proliferated: by 1973 there were over 70. Meanwhile, the national office became preoccupied with preparations for the 1972 Stockholm UN Conference on the Human Environment; even at this early stage, FoE became associated with concerns about global environmental justice and inequalities between the rich industrialised and poor 'Third' worlds.

Wary of the limitations that the Charity Commissioners then imposed upon registered charities (see Saunders, this volume), the founders of FoE were determined to be free to take politically controversial positions, and in 1971 they incorporated FoE in England as a limited company.[13] But in 1976, in order to take advantage of the financial benefits of charitable status, donations to charities being tax-exempt, FoE set up a parallel fund-raising and research organisation registered as a charity.

Although FoE is generally considered the vanguard of the new environmentalism, sharply distinct from the nature conservation organisations that preceded it, there were important continuities. FoE was insistent on the scientific basis of its claims, and several of its national activists were science graduates. Thematically, too, there were continuities: FoE was the first ENGO in the UK to campaign 'for whales, endangered species and tropical rainforests, and against acid rain, ozone depletion and climate change'.[14]

A large part of the novelty of FoE consisted in the *style* of its actions rather than the substance of its campaigns. Nevertheless, though its occasional forays into direct action excited – and deliberately sought to exploit – media attention, a great deal of FoE's effort was invested in assembling, printing and distributing dossiers of information. Although the conservation establishment mostly looked askance at 'improper' publicity-seeking, FoE was committed to action that was not only non-violent but legal.[15] Indeed, to the frustration of those of its members and supporters who yearned to be more directly active, FoE pressed its claims within the system. Such discontents were crystallised when FoE's long campaign against nuclear energy appeared to fail. FoE invested heavily in the inquiry into the Windscale nuclear reprocessing plant, and when the 1978 inquiry report dismissed FoE's arguments and led critics to portray its strategy as naïve, many supporters were disillusioned.[16]

Inspired by the example of Greenpeace's high profile direct activism in North America, disaffected FoE activists in 1977 set up a British branch of Greenpeace and immediately embraced a strategy of media-friendly calculated law-breaking of the kind that FoE had eschewed. Whereas FoE had patiently elaborated an evidence-based case against nuclear reprocessing, Greenpeace activists blocked the pipes through which the nuclear power station discharged wastewater into the Irish Sea.

Greenpeace's hallmarks in North America were its commitment to 'bearing witness' and to non-violent direct action (NVDA) designed to draw public attention to environmental ills and to pressure governments and corporations to act to remedy them, and its adroit exploitation of mass media attention in the pursuit of its goals. Their introduction into the UK marked a step change in the development of environmentalism that influenced many established ENGOs and, later, when Greenpeace itself had become an ENGO rather than simply an activist group, inspired a new generation into altogether more radical forms of action and organisation.

Whereas FoE was concerned with 'getting the science right', Greenpeace privileged action to the extent of being cavalier about the science and reckless in the claims it made, with the result that it was forced into embarrassing admissions of error. This, and its financial crisis, provoked intervention by the leadership of Greenpeace International. Those directors of Greenpeace UK considered responsible for past errors were forced out or sidelined and by 1987 there had been an almost complete turnover of staff. Under the new regime, campaigns were closely managed and coordinated by the leadership who themselves continued to operate informally and to make decisions among themselves.

In parallel with the organisational changes introduced from 1984, there was a shift to greater caution and attention to detail in Greenpeace's use of evidence in its campaigns and public statements. Although Greenpeace, like FoE, was incorporated as a limited company, it too later established a parallel charitable trust to support scientific research and education.

Despite the rhetoric of political participation that permeated the social movement politics of the late 1960s, it is noteworthy that the founders of neither FoE nor Greenpeace envisaged them as democratically accountable mass membership organisations. Rather, they were seen as vehicles for uninhibited campaigning and public protest by committed activists determined to advance the cause of environmental protection. Thus, at the outset, their concerns privileged campaigning effectiveness over democratic participation.[17] But whereas Greenpeace, structured to ensure the autonomy of its governing elite, was never a mass membership organisation, FoE became a relatively decentralised organisation in which grassroots activists have a constitutionally recognised role, and it soon established a national membership system.

FoE became a grassroots, mass membership organisation almost by accident. By 1980 there were 250 local groups, and they demanded greater say in management and campaign strategy. In 1981 an alliance between national office staff and local groups successfully challenged the national leadership.[18] Internal institutionalisation and centralisation of power within organisations are often seen as concomitants, but during its first 10–15 years, even as it grew in size and was organised into specialised campaign departments, FoE became more decentralised and participatory, with largely autonomous local groups and activists consulted where they possessed relevant expertise.

Despite a shaky start, Greenpeace UK became a singularly successful protest organisation, spectacularly adroit at exploiting media attention to put pressure on governments and corporations. With campaigns against whaling and sealing, and later against the off-shore activities of oil companies, Greenpeace became perhaps the foremost advocate of marine conservation, with mitigating climate change via clean energy, preserving ancient forests and opposition to nuclear energy among its campaign priorities.[19]

The story of ENGOs in the 1970s is dominated by the emergence of FoE and Greenpeace, but theirs is not the whole story. Another 1970s innovation, the Woodland Trust, was an altogether more conventional organisation; Sustrans, best known for its promotion of cycle paths, was another; interestingly, and a foretaste of things to come, neither was concerned to involve supporters in their governance.

The 1980s: growth and innovation

The 1970s introduced a period of dramatic growth in the numbers of ENGOs, their members and supporters (see Table 11.2).[20] Between 1971 and 1981, membership of the largest and longest established organisations, NT and RSPB, grew fourfold; between 1981 and 1991, it doubled again. During the 1980s, however, the most spectacular growth occurred in the newest and most activist organisations, FoE and Greenpeace. Although they remained small by comparison with older conservation organisations, from the late 1980s, when they began to use direct mailing techniques, their numbers surged.

In addition to their high profile anti-nuclear campaigns, FoE and Greenpeace launched major campaigns on nature protection issues. Despite the reservations of some traditional conservation organisations about their campaigning, FoE and Greenpeace were included in renewed efforts at coordination. Frustrated by the weakness of the Nature Conservancy, and keen to escape the straitjacket of charitable status, ENGOs as diverse as RSPB, RSNC, WWF, FoE and Greenpeace in 1980 collaborated to form Wildlife Link to coordinate their activities. With direct access to civil servants and regular meetings with ministers, Wildlife Link greatly increased the political influence of ENGOs. Even though

Table 11.2   Membership of selected environmental NGOs (1971–2006) (thousands)

	1971	1981	1991	2001	2006
National Trust (NT)	278	1,046	2,152	2,729	3,480
Royal Society for the Protection of Birds (RSPB)	98	441	852	1,020	1,062
Wildlife Trusts[1]	64	142	233	382	657
World Wide Fund for Nature (WWF)	12	60	227	287	330
Woodland Trust[2]	–	20	63	100	160
Campaign to Protect Rural England (CPRE)[3]	21	29	45	59	60
Friends of the Earth (FoE)	1	18	111	95	102
Greenpeace	–	30	312	224	221

Notes:
1. Includes The Royal Society for Nature Conservation/Royal Society for Wildlife Trusts.
2. Figure for 1981 from D. Evans, *A History of Nature Conservation in Britain*, 2nd edn. (London: Routledge, 1997), p. 197.
3. Council for the Preservation of Rural England 1926–1969; Council for the Protection of Rural England 1969–2003.

Sources: Adapted from P. Haezewindt, 'Investing in Each Other and the Community: The Role of Social Capital', in C. Summerfield and P. Babb (eds) *Social Trends 33* (London: The Stationery Office, 2003), and supplemented with information supplied by the organisations themselves or drawn from their websites.

conservation organisations were wary of alienating supporters they assumed to be socially and politically conservative, they were nevertheless influenced by the rise of the new campaigning organisations, and gradually came to see the value of high profile public campaigns as adjuncts to more traditional lobbying.

The 1980s was a decade of renewed organisational innovation. Indeed, more than one-third of the ENGOs existing at the end of the twentieth century were established in that decade alone, the newcomers including the Whale and Dolphin Conservation Society, Marine Conservation Society, Environmental Investigation Agency, Pond Conservation, Plantlife, Froglife and the Herpetological Conservation Trust.[21]

The 1990s: consolidation, challenge and cooperation

Both the growth of existing ENGOs and the rate of formation of new ENGOs slowed after 1989. But whereas FoE and Greenpeace grew little if at all, several ENGOs grew by nearly 50 percent, and the Wildlife Trusts and the Woodland Trust grew yet more strongly.

The most striking innovation of the decade was the emergence, from 1991, of a new generation of environmental 'disorganisations'. Earth First! and its urban offshoot, Reclaim the Streets, were essentially banners under which a younger generation of activists, to whom FoE and Greenpeace appeared bureaucratic and timid, might take direct action proportionate to what they perceived to be the urgency of environmental issues. No less concerned than their predecessors with protecting nature, they were more radically critical of capitalist consumerism and more committed to grassroots participation in direct action. Early actions targeting the importation of rainforest timber were soon succeeded by a focus upon protests against roadbuilding, loosely networked by an *ad hoc* campaign coalition, ALARM.

These 'disorganisations' deliberately avoided establishing themselves as formal organisations that might be vulnerable to the kinds of legal sanctions that were to force the withdrawal of FoE from direct action against the building of the M3 through Twyford Down, and Greenpeace from action against BP's oil exploration in the North Sea. But just as the popularity and campaigning successes of FoE and Greenpeace had enhanced older ENGOs' opportunities for successful lobbying, so the 'radical flank' effect created by the new radicals provided ENGOs with increased political leverage; the polite representations of 'reasonable' ENGOs were more visible and audible in the corridors of power when radical activists were in the streets loudly demanding action.[22]

The new international agenda crystallised in the Rio Earth Summit (UNCED) of 1992 encouraged collaboration among ENGOs and beyond. To remedy shortcomings of coordination among British NGOs in the UNCED process, ENGOs increased cooperation with aid, trade and humanitarian organisations such as Oxfam.[23] Collaboration was not always easy. Following UNCED, the broadly inclusive Real World Coalition sought to promote sustainable development, but its agenda was increasingly formulated as one of social justice and, even before its formal launch in 1996, RSPB, CPRE, the Wildlife Trusts and Greenpeace withdrew.[24] Thus an enduring fault line emerged between WWF and FoE, which have become increasingly concerned with social justice issues, and ENGOs such as RSPB and CPRE, which have reverted to a narrower nature protection agenda.[25]

2000 and beyond: innovation renewed?

By the end of the century, almost 20 per cent of Britons claimed membership of one or more environmental organisations, and in 2000, the combined membership of the eleven major ENGOs listed in the official statistical digest, *Social Trends*, totalled 5.5 million.[26] Of these, most – and all the largest – were conservation organisations (see Table 11.1). Despite their undoubted significance, neither FoE nor Greenpeace ranks among the top ten in terms of income, staff numbers, or grant income from private foundations and trusts.[27]

Most ENGOs experienced continued growth during the early years of the century, and new ones continued to be formed, Buglife – The Invertebrate Conservation Trust, the Association of Rivers Trusts, and the Grasslands Trust among them. The rate of organisational innovation slowed as the remaining niches were filled, as less charismatic species acquired organised champions and the importance of habitat became more widely appreciated, but it is unlikely to cease if only because differences over campaign priorities and between assertive personalities cannot always be contained within existing organisations.

The universe of ENGOs in England today is much larger and more complex than it was. ENGOs have changed: their agendas are broader; they employ a wider repertoire of methods to advance their aims; and they are better connected one with another.

Networks

The only systematic survey of British ENGOs in the 1980s concluded that organisations tended to have network links either with a few 'core' organisations, or with others in their own thematic sector.[28] That, however, was before the new campaigning organisations consolidated their influence and eroded the distinction between nature protection and other environmental organisations.

From the 2000 survey, FoE appeared most central to the network, followed by WWF, Greenpeace, Wildlife and Countryside Link, CPRE and RSPB, with secondary networks linking ENGOs specialising in 'organic' and 'transport' issues. This marks a considerable change since the 1980s. Of the six organisations that Lowe and Goyder listed as the core of the movement – CPRE, FoE, RSPB, NT, CoEnCo and the Civic Trust – only the first three appeared to be at or near the core of the network in 2000; NT appeared marginal, and the latter two did not appear at all.[29] Greenpeace, marginal in the early 1980s, and WWF, then identified as a non-core species protection organisation, have moved to positions more central to the network than RSPB and CPRE.

Nature protection is still the predominant concern of ENGOs, and most ENGOs remain niche players with specialised functions and narrow thematic concerns. Large organisations such as NT and the Wildlife Trusts may be marginal to the network, but they are influential in their own right, their size giving them opportunities of direct access to civil servants and ministers not enjoyed by smaller organisations acting individually. Wildlife and Countryside Link has grown to embrace 37 ENGOs, and informal, *ad hoc* and bilateral cooperation has increased. Collaborative campaigns are increasingly common, and increasingly extend beyond nature protection to issues of human well-being. It is significant that FoE, despite being relatively small, should appear central to the environmental network, for FoE has an exceptionally broad remit, grassroots base and strong international links, and has proceeded furthest in the embrace of social justice.[30]

Specialised networks linking diverse local campaigns, such as Airport Watch and Roadblock!, are increasingly common. None has yet been formalised as an ENGO, and among ENGOs it is generally FoE that has been most involved, rather than larger, better resourced, conservation organisations. FoE may have become institutionalised, but it has not simply switched from activism into research and lobbying. Research and lobbying were always part of FoE's repertoire, but even after it was forced by the threat of litigation to withdraw from protest at Twyford Down, FoE supported anti-roads activists' camps and provided training in non-violent direct action, seeing direct action as complementary to its own campaigns even while its contacts with direct action groups are necessarily informal.

Widening repertoires, broadening agenda

Although ENGOs have become less timid about campaigning, few have greatly changed their tactics. CPRE, considered the most 'establishment' of the major ENGOs, is an exception, its 2003 name change – from the Council for the Protection of Rural England to the Campaign to Protect Rural England – reflecting a shift from discreet lobbying to more active public campaigning that began during the 1980s.

There has, however, been no universal shift toward advocacy among conservation ENGOs. The NT, despite threatening to awaken and to take a more direct advocacy role, remains the 'sleeping giant' of the British environmental movement. Though claiming to be 'committed to influencing the management of the whole environment, through development of best practice on our own land and also through advocacy of "green" solutions', the NT's size means that it is routinely consulted on conservation matters and has the capacity to respond, and so sees little need to campaign more publicly.[31]

Principally focussed upon practical measures to preserve wild birds and their habitat, RSPB is wary of protest, but has occasionally been willing to mobilise its members: it encouraged over 300,000 objections against a proposed airport at Cliffe in Kent, and contributed 1,500 marchers to the November 2006 Climate Chaos march in London. The mix and range of RSPB's concerns have changed. In the late 1970s and early 1980s, it expanded its interests in habitat conservation and began to take a more active stance towards government. Recognising the futility of putting great effort into conservation projects in England while key habitats were destroyed along migratory routes elsewhere, RSPB was in 1992 instrumental in setting up Birdlife International, and thus evolved from a strictly national organisation into one increasingly concerned with global environmental change, albeit one with a sharp focus upon birds.

More striking changes have taken place in WWF. By the end of the 1970s, WWF had changed from a small fundraising organisation focussed on endangered species and habitat destruction into an international ENGO concerned with conservation issues generally. Since 1990, WWF has tried to strike a balance between protecting ecosystems and meeting economic needs of local communities.

Initially science-led, by the mid-1990s WWF-UK was appointing staff more for their familiarity with policy than their scientific credentials; Jonathon Porritt, former Director of FoE and Green Party candidate, was appointed a trustee.[32] Moreover, WWF assisted other, more radical groups, funding anti-road protests as well as nurturing 'hundreds of smaller conservation organizations'.[33]

Like RSPB, WWF was nervous of alienating supporters whom it presumed to be narrowly interested in conservation, but since Rio has worked to form a common agenda among development and environment NGOs, including Action Aid, Oxfam, Christian Aid, Save the Children, CAFOD and FoE.[34] Since 2000, WWF-UK has spent less than one-sixth of its budget on 'species', and an increasing proportion on 'levers for long term change' (including education and information) and on projects aimed at rejuvenating rivers, giving people better access to clean water and improving fishing. WWF highlights partnerships with aid charities and the Department for International

Development to tackle poverty, overconsumption and climate change, which it sees as the greatest threats to the environment.[35]

This has brought it close to FoE which, from the mid-1980s, became increasingly involved in campaigns to promote human rights and economic development in the global South. This reflected the views of members who were often also members of Amnesty International or Oxfam, rather than other ENGOs.[36] Central to the network of British ENGOs, FoE's interactions with other groups increasingly include aid and development charities and organised labour. These help set FoE's agenda, which is also influenced by connections through FoE International to ENGOs in over 70 countries from North and South.[37]

The increasingly transnational agenda of environmentalism affects how ENGOs see themselves and justify their positions. FoE and WWF now employ the concept of sustainable development to promote a reformist agenda in which the environment cannot be isolated from a wider range of human concerns.[38] They and other ENGOs, including RSPB and Greenpeace, signed up to Make Poverty History and/or the Trade Justice Movement and there is now consensus that environmental protection has an ineradicable human dimension.[39] There are signs of reciprocation: the 'Stop Climate Chaos' (SCC) coalition, launched in 2005, includes aid and development charities as well as most larger ENGOs.

Even campaigning ENGOs are concerned not to be painted into a corner as 'merely' protest groups, and so portray themselves as proponents of positive changes that would benefit both the environment and people. Sometimes the desire to do – and be seen to do – something positive has led ENGOs into improbable partnerships. Thus Greenpeace, the scourge of oil companies and coal-burners, offered advice even to Shell and BP on their (faltering) shift toward renewable energy, and collaborated with an electricity utility to establish the UK's first offshore wind farm. Such 'positive campaigning' does not mean Greenpeace has abandoned criticism; it remains primarily a campaigning organisation committed to non-violent direct action and to 'bearing witness'.

ENGOs generally stake their claims – and their legitimacy – on their scientific credentials, and have thus earned the respect of government and industry. But because public understanding of science is limited, the more responsive an ENGO is to its members, the more difficulty it has in remaining science-guided. Thus, while FoE national officers attempt to set campaign priorities according to expert, science-based advice, their concessions to members' local, often scientifically question-able, concerns mean that FoE's campaign agenda is a compromise.[40] Even less democratic ENGOs are anxious not to seem unresponsive to sup-porters, and so science more reliably informs ENGOs' expert advice than their public face.

Although this has irritated ministers wary of unreliable allies, it has not diminished ENGOs' influence. 'Ministers never refuse to meet CPRE', a very focussed organisation with insider status and strong channels of communication to policymakers.[41] WWF-UK was even described by Michael Meacher, UK Environment Minister (1997–2003), as 'his alternative civil service', although WWF insists that its standing with government and acceptance of corporate donations have not inhibited its ability to criticise.[42] But if CPRE and WWF have sought to be critical insiders, others have been more wary. Although FoE seeks to influence policy and engage government agencies, it does not seek ongoing partnerships with them in imple-menting policy, regarding itself instead as 'a campaigning organ-ization' whose job 'is to raise the standards' that others are charged to implement.[43]

Conclusion

The receptivity of conservation ENGOs to the agenda-setting efforts of more activist, campaigning organisations is only partly a tribute to the energy, increased professionalism and scientific credibility of the latter. It also reflects broader changes in British society. Less deferential and more demanding of opportunities to participate as they have become better educated and more affluent, the British have become more willing to participate in demonstrations and consumer boycotts. Although there has been no consistent rise in direct action, increasing numbers of people approve of those who take principled action even where it is beyond the law. Thus citizens would not condemn, and courts would not convict, activists who, in the name of environmental protection, destroyed GM crops.[44]

Conservation organisations have not leapt aboard the activist band-wagon, but they have become less nervous about being judged guilty by association. The relaxation of charity law since 1995 has helped; registered charities no longer fear that campaigning publicly for policy changes will jeopardise their charitable status. Emboldened by the results of surveys of supporters, ENGOs have become more audacious in extending their agenda beyond traditional core issues.

The history of ENGOs in England is not simply one of phases marking a linear progression from nature conservation through environmentalism to radical ecologism. In each period, new nature protection organisations and networks have formed, and in recent decades, new 'environmental' and 'ecological' organisations have embraced protection of the natural environment. New 'disorganisations' such as Rising Tide and the Camps for Climate Action have arisen even as others such as Reclaim the Streets have disappeared, but the numbers of people involved are small – no more than a few thousand at any one time. Meanwhile, ENGOs continue to flourish, and it is the service-providing, reserve-managing conservation organisations, rather than those focussed principally upon advocacy and campaigning, that represent the great majority of the more than five million 'members' of ENGOs.

Despite continuing conflicts among ENGOs over the environmental implications of renewable energy infrastructure, climate change has emerged as a unifying frame for the broad range of ENGOs and informal groups. It remains to be seen whether the urgent need for measures to mitigate climate change will lure more ENGOs into advocacy or whether, perhaps, the increasing centrality of climate change to political agendas will push advocacy groups into more specialised, practical roles.

Notes

1 This chapter draws liberally upon C. Rootes, 'Nature Protection Organizations in England' in C.S.A. van Koppen and W. Markham (eds) *Protecting Nature: Organizations and Networks in Europe and the United States* (Cheltenham and Northampton, MA: Edward Elgar, 2007), pp. 34–62. It derives from the TEA (Transformation of Environmental Activism) project (EC DG Research contract: ENV4-CT97-0514) (www.kent.ac.uk/sspssr/TEA.html). I am indebted to Debbie Adams, Sandy Miller and Ben Seel for assistance with collection and/or analysis of data, to Julie Barnett for permission to use material from interviews she conducted in 2003 as part of our Environment Agency project, 'Working with Special Interest Groups', and to Clare Saunders for comments on earlier versions.

2 J. McCormick, *British Politics and the Environment* (London: Earthscan, 1991), p. 34.

3 C. Rootes, 'Environmental movements' in D.A. Snow, S.A. Soule and H. Kriesi (eds) *The Blackwell Companion to Social Movements* (Oxford and Malden, MA: Blackwell, 2004), pp. 608–40.

4 C.J. Bosso, *Environment Inc.: from Grassroots to Beltway* (Lawrence, KS: University Press of Kansas, 2005).

5 C. Rootes and A. Miller, 'The British Environmental Movement: Organizational Field and Network of Organizations'. Paper presented at ECPR Joint Sessions, Copenhagen, April 14–19, 2000.

6   England, by far the most populous country of the UK, is juridically and politically distinct from Scotland, Northern Ireland and Wales. Because the legislative contexts and constellations of environmental organisations differ from one country to another, this chapter focusses on England, although some organisations also operate in other parts of the UK.

7   D. Evans, *A History of Nature Conservation in Britain*, 2nd edition (London: Routledge, 1997), p. 34.

8   *Ibid*, p. 52.

9   P. Lowe and J. Goyder, *Environmental Groups in British Politics* (London: Allen and Unwin, 1983), p. 37.

10 P. Rawcliffe, *Environmental Pressure Groups in Transition* (Manchester: Manchester University Press, 1998), pp. 15–16.

11 P. Lowe and J. Goyder, *Environmental Groups in British Politics* (London: Allen and Unwin, 1983).

12 R. Lamb, *Promising the Earth* (London and New York: Routledge, 1996), p. 38.

13 *Ibid*, pp. 35–6.

14 www.foe.co.uk, 25 March 2005; Lamb, *Promising the Earth,* ch.7.

15 Evans, *Nature Conservation*, p. 104.

16 Lamb, *Promising the Earth,* p. 87.

17 M. Diani and P. Donati, 'Organizational Change in Western European Environmental Groups: A Framework for Analysis', *Environmental Politics*, 8(1), pp. 13–34. Reprinted in C. Rootes (ed.) *Environmental Movements: Local, National and Global* (London: Cass, 1999).

18 Lamb, *Promising the Earth* pp. 97–9.

19 www.greenpeace.org.uk, 1 November 2006.

20 Self-reported membership numbers are only one, variably reliable, indicator of an organisation's vitality and influence. 'Member' means different things to different groups: some count all donors and volunteers as members; others restrict 'membership' to formal subscribers, or the small numbers whose positions are named in their articles of association. Because their 'members' must pay dues to receive benefits, organisations that provide services are more likely to count members accurately; advocacy organisations may be more casual because benefits are not usually confined to formal subscribers. The size of an organisation's membership generally reflects the effort and resources devoted to recruitment; advocacy groups and conservation organisations have, since the 1990s, tended to concentrate resources on their core activities rather than on recruiting new 'members'.

21 Rootes and Miller, 'The British Environmental Movement'.

22 Rawcliffe, *Environmental Pressure Groups in Transition*, pp. 24, 180.

23 Rawcliffe, *Environmental Pressure Groups in Transition*, p. 212; Rootes and Saunders, 2007).

24 Rawcliffe, *Environmental Pressure Groups in Transition*, p. 214.

25 C. Rootes, 'A Limited Transnationalization?: The British Environmental Movement', in D. della Porta and S. Tarrow (eds) *Transnational Protest and Global Activism* (Lanham, MD: Rowman and Littlefield, 2005), pp. 21–43; C. Rootes, 'Facing South? British Environmental Movement Organisations and the Challenge of Globalisation', *Environmental Politics*, 15(5), 2006, pp. 768–86.

26 M. Johnston and R. Jowell, 'Social Capital and the Social Fabric', in R. Jowell, J. Curtice, A. Park, K. Thompson, with L. Jarvis, C. Bromley, and N. Stratford (eds) *British Social Attitudes: The 16th Report* (Aldershot: Ashgate, 1999), p. 183.

27 J. Cracknell and H. Godwin, *Where the Green Grants Went 3: Patterns of UK Funding for Environmental and Conservation Work* (London: Environmental Funders Network, 2007).

28 Lowe and Goyder, *Environmental Groups in British Politics.*

29 Rootes and Miller, 'The British Environmental Movement'.

30 Rootes, 'Nature Protection Organizations in England', pp. 34–62.

31 www.nationaltrust.org.uk, 2 September 2005.

32 B. Szerszynski, 'Framing and Communicating Environmental Issues. Part 2, Entering the Stage: Strategies of Environmental Communication in the UK', Report to Commission of the European Communities, DG XII, SEER PL 210943, 1995, p. 35.

33 Rawcliffe, *Environmental Pressure Groups in Transition*, p.138; WWF-UK, 'A selection of environmental organizations in the United Kingdom', 2001, www.wwf.org.uk (accessed 11 February 2006), p. 2.

34 Rawcliffe, *Environmental Pressure Groups in Transition*, p. 217.

35 Rootes, 'Nature Protection Organizations in England', pp. 48–9.

36 FoE Senior Local Campaigns Officer interview, 2003; G. Jordan and W. Maloney, *The Protest Business? Mobilizing Campaign Groups* (Manchester: Manchester University Press, 1997).

37 B. Doherty, 'Friends of the Earth International: Negotiating a Transnational Identity', *Environmental Politics*, 15(5), 2006, pp. 860–80.

38 C. Rootes, 'Facing South? British Environmental Movement Organisations and the Challenge of Globalisation', *Environmental Politics*, 15(5), 2006, pp. 768–86.

39 C. Rootes and C. Saunders, 'The Global Justice Movement in Britain', in D. della Porta (ed.) *The Global Justice Movement* (Boulder, CO: Paradigm, 2007), pp. 128–56.

40 FoE Senior Local Campaigns Officer interview, 2003.

41 Conder interview, David Conder, CPRE, 8 June 2000.

42 White interview, Stuart White, WWF-UK, 26 July 2000.

43 FoE Senior Local Campaigns Officer interview, 2003.

44 C. Rootes, 'The Resurgence of Protest and the Revitalization of British Democracy', in P. Ibarra (ed.) *Social Movements and Democracy* (New York: Palgrave Macmillan, 2003), pp. 137–68.

12
NGOs and Fair Trade: The Social Movement Behind the Label

Matthew Anderson

In 2004, on the tenth anniversary of the FAIRTRADE Mark in the UK, Harriet Lamb, Executive Director of the Fairtrade Foundation, declared that, 'Fairtrade, backed by a vibrant social movement of people throughout the country, is now bedding into the mainstream, giving thousands of producers in developing countries the chance to build a better future and to compete in the all too cut-throat global markets.'[1] The successful mainstreaming of the FAIRTRADE Mark has been acclaimed as one of the most significant retail trends of the past decade.[2] With sales growing at an annual rate of 40 per cent and total sales reaching £493 million in 2007, Britain has become the leading European Fairtrade market. This success has prompted speculation as to why Fairtrade has taken root so firmly in Britain. Many commentators in answering this question have looked to the British consumer. Journalists have reported that 'Britons over the past decade have become a nation of ethical shoppers.'[3] Some have looked to investigate 'How consumer power sparked a Fairtrade revolution on our high streets.'[4] Fairtrade's success in mobilising consumer support has certainly been impressive, but is this the full story?

This chapter sets out to question whether consumer demand alone can really provide an adequate explanation for the growth of Fairtrade in Britain. By adopting a methodology that looks beyond the 'ethical shopping trolley', a wider fair trade social movement, grounded in the work of non-governmental organisations (NGOs) and Alternative Trade Organisations (ATOs), is revealed. It has been argued that the origins of the modern fair trade movement can be traced back to the 1960s.[5] And indeed it was during the first UN Development Decade that NGOs started to publicly make the case for the reform of international trade regulations in order to promote 'Third World' development. But instead the focus of this chapter will be on the 1970s and 1980s. It was during this period that NGOs first pioneered a business model recognisable by modern definitions as 'fair trade'.[6] The 1970s and 1980s witnessed two significant developments that marked the beginning of the fair trade movement in Britain. Firstly, in a bid to widen interest and demonstrate the relevance of their campaigns, NGOs began to relate international trade and development to the shopping choices of individual consumers in 'the North'. Secondly, NGOs also started to look more critically at their own trading ventures and questioned whether they could be used to demonstrate the viability of an alternative model of trade consistent with their development philosophy. This chapter will argue that the emergence of fair trade in late twentieth century Britain has only partly been the result of 'the market' responding to consumer demand. Of greater significance, although often overlooked, was the way in which NGOs successfully began to integrate political consumerism within their existing campaigns.[7] In particular, many Christian development agencies have persistently promoted fair trade, such that their supporters have been urged to use their role as consumers to support the policies already articulated by these NGOs.

Akira Iriye has argued that the growth of NGOs has been, 'one of the most impressive developments of twentieth-century world history'.[8] He points out that since the 1970s political scientists and international relations scholars have recognised the growth of NGOs and incorporated this within their analyses of international affairs. But he berates the fact that the standard histories of the twentieth century are, 'singularly lacking in any reference to NGOs, domestic or international'.[9] So perhaps it should not be surprising that the story of the British fair trade movement has largely been left to be catalogued by internal histories. Unfortunately, with limited resources and numerous pressing demands, documenting an organisation's history has often been low on the agenda.[10] This has resulted in frequent gaps in an organisation's 'collective memory' and, on occasions these gaps have been filled by 'founding myths'.[11] So rather than piecing together a series of internal histories, what is required is a critical reassessment of the existing historical archives in order to gain a fuller understanding of how fair trade has developed as a movement over the last 30 years.

Fair trade may not yet be a popular subject for historians of the twentieth century, but there is certainly a growing trend for business schools to incorporate fair trade within their syllabuses and research profiles. It would seem churlish not to welcome this contribution to the study of fair trade. But in approaching fair trade almost exclusively in terms of its contribution to the corporate social responsibility agenda, only limited opportunity is provided to investigate the wider social movement. For instance, recent work by Alex Nicholls and Charlotte Opal explores the business case for fair trade and looks at the issues of risk management, brand differentiation and customer loyalty. Ultimately, Nicholls and Opal characterise fair trade as 'a consumer-driven phenomenon, underpinned by the growth of "ethical" consumption more generally'.[12] They further argue that 'fair trade is entirely a consumer choice model, it operates within the larger free trade model of unregulated international commerce'.[13] So although this research provides a valuable insight into fair trade as a model of social enterprise, its narrow focus on the consumer as the main market driver largely obscures the valuable contribution made by NGOs in shaping the historical development of the fair trade movement.

Some of the most innovative contemporary work on fair trade has emanated from geography departments both in the United States and Britain. Michael Goodman, in investigating the expansion of fair trade in the United States, has highlighted the role of direct action campaigns that targeted well-known brands such as Starbucks and attempted to shame them into converting to fair trade. The success of these campaigns has led Goodman to argue that 'Activist groups are the fundamental vanguard fostering fair trade markets. In some ways, fair trade is more of a consumer-dependent movement for change rather than a consumer-led movement.'[14] By this, he means that consumers themselves have not instigated campaigns for fair trade, rather they have been an essential force to be mobilised by activist groups.

In Britain, research by Clive Barnett, Nick Clark, Paul Cloke and Alice Malpass has also attempted to develop a broadly political, rather than a narrowly economic approach to fair trade and ethical consumerism. This has led them to reassess the role of organisations involved in fair trade. They argue that 'Rather than thinking about their role in terms of providing information so that consumers can express their preferences in markets, it might be more appropriate to see them as mobilising support of people as "consumers" in order to effectively campaign to actually change the ways in which markets are structured and regulated.'[15] Ultimately they argue that NGOs have utilised fair trade to 'raise awareness of campaigns, before enrolling ordinary people in more "active" forms of political engagement, like donating, joining as a member, or volunteering'.[16] Whether donating can really be classified as a more active form of political engagement than purchasing fair trade products is debatable, but none the less this work has made a valuable contribution in highlighting the agency of those organisations involved in campaigning for fair trade.

The absence, in much of the current literature, of any historical framework has undermined attempts by academics to understand and contextualise the international growth of fair trade. This chapter sets out to provide one part of this framework by exploring the historical contribution of NGOs to the development of the fair trade movement in Britain. The main focus of this chapter is on four organisations (Oxfam, Christian Aid, Tearcraft and Traidcraft) from the mid-1960s through to the early 1990s.[17] With reference to these case studies, this chapter will show that NGO involvement extended beyond direct action campaigns and contributed to every aspect of the fair trade movement, from raising awareness of the impact of low commodity prices on producers in the 'Third World', to pioneering the concept of 'alternative trade', establishing the Fairtrade Foundation and launching the FAIRTRADE Mark. At times it seemed as if the fair trade movement was being pulled in conflicting directions (particularly when it came to engaging with commercial companies), but arguably it was these discussions about the true meaning of 'fair trade' that allow us to understand the central dynamics of the movement.

1960s UN development decade

In a recent study of the fair trade coffee sector, Gavin Fridell defines the heyday of the fair trade movement as lasting from the 1940s up until the 1970s.[18] Fridell argues that 'the development path initiated by fair traders in the late 1980s marked a significant shift from the more radical vision of the network formulated from the 1940s to the 1970s'.[19] Specifically he claims that the 1980s saw the emergence of 'a distinctly different development model for the fair trade network based on the abandonment of its statist orientation and the strengthening of its neo-Smithian market orientation to conform to the demands of neoliberal globalisation'.[20] But this chronology is the result of an idealised interpretation of the trading operations of these organisations during the early part of their history (1940s to 1970s) which then leads to an overly negative assessment of their recent history (1980s to present). Fridell's analysis is further distorted by adopting a definition of the term 'fair trade movement' that is so broad that it incorporates virtually all international trade and development programmes. Fridell states that 'this movement has no official existence but rather is a term used here to encapsulate a variety of initiatives headed by Southern governments, international organizations, and NGOs with the purpose of radically altering the international trade and development regime in the interest of poor nations in the South'.[21]

Fridell's assessment places particular focus on the 1960s and the UN's first Development Decade. It was this campaign that led governments to increase the total value of official development assistance from $5.2 billion in 1961 to $6.6 billion in 1967.[22] And it was at the second United Nations Conference on Trade and Development (UNCTAD-2) in 1968 that the phrase 'trade not aid' was first coined. But these approaches to development relied on a macro-level approach, focussing on raising official aid and restructuring international trade relations. In contrast, the fair trade movement looked to encourage a greater understanding among consumers of the conditions for individual producers, and dealt with questions of international development on a human scale.

The first UN Development Decade had raised hopes of a 'Third World' development programme on a scale comparable to that seen during European reconstruction under the Marshall Plan. But the modest target of five per cent annual growth rate in the incomes of the poor countries was only achieved by a handful of countries and even in those countries the benefits of economic growth were still not felt by the very poorest. Between 1953 and 1967, world trade as a whole increased by an average of 6.9 per cent per year, but the gains from international trade continued to be amassed disproportionately by the industrialised countries of the North. As a result low-income countries' overall share of export earnings declined from 27 per cent in 1953 to 19 per cent in 1967.[23] In this context, the emergence of the fair trade movement in the 1970s should be understood not as an extension of inter-government development campaigns championed during the 1960s, but as a new (non-governmental) initiative responding to the failings of previous development models. Rather than look to the development programmes of the United Nations, it was the philosophy of organisations such as the International Co-operative Alliance that shaped the development of the fair trade movement.[24]

I   Development and relief: Oxfam

Oxfam is a particularly interesting case study because it reveals the pioneering role NGOs played, but also illustrates the inevitable controversies that arose from having an international trading company owned by one of Britain's most well known charities. Oxfam's trading history can be traced back to 1959 when Leslie Kirkley, the then director of

Oxfam, brought back pin cushions made by Chinese refugees in Hong Kong. These pin cushions found their way into the two shops run by Oxfam at that time. In December 1964, these relatively *ad-hoc* trading arrangements were formalised with the formation of Oxfam Activities Ltd. and in 1967 Oxfam's imports from the 'Third World' were consolidated to form Helping by Selling (HbS). Given this chronology, it is perhaps understandable that many commentators have identified Oxfam's early trading ventures with producers from the 'Third World' as being the first example of fair trade in Britain. But a detailed evaluation of the terms of trade operated by Oxfam Activities and HbS during the 1960s reveals a commercial outlook incompatible with modern definitions of fair trade.

The justification for Oxfam operating an importing company throughout the 1960s seemed to be a straightforward case of responding to the desperate need for employment that existed throughout the 'Third World'. A campaign leaflet stated that 'One in every three people in need of work in the so-called developing countries of Africa, Asia and Latin-America is unable to get a regular job.'[25] These sentiments were consistent with the first UN Development Decade's focus on 'trade not aid'. But this explanation also resembled arguments used by multinational corporations (MNCs) to justify their presence in oppressive regimes including South Africa.[26] Simply buying from producers in the 'Third World' did not represent an alternative model of trade, even if it was an NGO that owned the trading company. In reality, throughout the 1960s, HbS was trading along essentially commercial lines. Products imported from the 'Third World' were to be stocked in Oxfam's growing network of shops and sold for a profit which would then contribute towards Oxfam's international development budget.[27] In 1969, HbS was already proving a commercially successful venture with profits of £10,000 on sales of £28,000 and by 1974 HbS profits had reached £90,000 on sales of £343,564.[28]

HbS was soon to prove an important source of income, representing 47 per cent of Oxfam Trading sales by 1974.[29] But this level of commercial success led some Oxfam staff to question the trading principles of HbS. In 1973, Roy Scott, an Oxfam Trading manager, began work on creating a new type of trading venture. Scott believed that HbS was only 'a very limited "fair-trade" importing programme'.[30] He argued that HbS was too close to the trading values of commercial importers and in a drive to make profits they were ignoring the development potential of international trade. Instead, he argued that Oxfam's trading operations should act as a practical demonstration of 'the kind of socially "ideal" trade system most supporters of the Third World believe is necessary'.[31] It was through this critique of Oxfam's existing trading programme and in the search for an alternative model, that the concept and principles of the modern fair trade movement emerged.

Scott's solution was to remove the middleman and form an international co-operative, 'a "bridge" linking worker-producers of very poor countries with the ordinary shopper here in Europe'.[32] The role of the consumer was not envisaged by Scott in either charitable or paternalistic terms. He argued that Bridge should, 'guarantee a fair price to producers, and the availability of their products also at a fair price to the common man in the consumer's country'.[33] What Scott envisaged was a totally independent organisation, established with an Oxfam grant but then expected to be self-financing. The management board would be made up of democratically elected representatives of producers and consumers. Scott believed this model had the potential to become a 'brave independent movement liberating producers entirely from continuing charity support'.[34]

But Oxfam was not ready to let go of its trading company and saw that through international trade it could set out its development agenda in a practical manner – beyond campaigning. Guy Stringer recognised its value as a practical demonstration: 'It will almost certainly be impossible to dramatically change western-based, capital-serving trade systems merely through critical attack.'[35] Rather than forming a new international co-operative network, Bridge was established in June 1975 as a new subsidiary company, with its own board of management, but control remained with Oxfam. Although this model was not as progressive as outlined in Scott's original vision Bridge still pioneered a model of international trade that prioritised a more equal relationship between the producer and consumer. Bridge's mission statement from November 1975 stated it was 'dedicated towards providing the best possible employment, earnings, working and social environments for producers; and fair prices, quality and service for customers'.[36]

One year on, Oxfam's Director Guy Stringer was able to announce the first distribution of the producer dividend, a moment he described as 'a very significant advance in the history of Oxfam Activities, and in my view of Oxfam'.[37] This announcement was partly tempered by the news of Roy Scott's resignation. Unhappy at the way the Bridge trading philosophy had been diluted, Scott decided to leave Oxfam and establish a new Alternative Trading Organisation called One Village.[38] With sales reaching £2.4 million by 1985 and net profits of £102,000 the Bridge model adopted by Oxfam proved that 'fair trade' could work to empower producers and be commercially viable. By 1990 Bridge's annual sales had reached £5.5 million, with net profits of £188,000. This firmly established Bridge as one of the leading European ATOs.

II   Christian agencies: Christian aid

With the Fairtrade Towns initiative gaining momentum over the last five years, researchers are now beginning to consider the role played by Christians as fair trade campaigners.[39] Research by Paul Cloke and colleagues for instance has shown that 70 to 80 per cent of people actively promoting Bristol's Fairtrade City campaign are Christians.[40] This research builds upon the work of previous studies that have looked more generally at the importance of religious motivation for those engaged with voluntary activities. David Gerard, in his analysis of the European Values Study dataset, discovered that 'over 70 per cent of all volunteers describe themselves as "a religious person" and over 50 per cent attend church at least monthly'.[41] Christian Aid, as the official agency of the British Council of Churches, provides a valuable case study of the role played by Christian NGOs in developing grassroots support for fair trade in Britain.[42]

Christian Aid first began its work in 1945, as Christian Reconstruction in Europe. Its original mission was to help refugees, and to rebuild church and family life in post-war Europe.[43] From 1949, the organisation became Inter-Church Aid and Refugee Service, marking a broadening of its stated purpose to include disaster relief more generally and longer term development. In 1957, Inter-Church Aid and Refugee Service held a door-to-door collection in 200 towns and villages across the UK. This was the first Christian Aid Week, and it raised £26,000.[44] The concept of Christian Aid Week proved a very effective way of raising not only funds but awareness. Reflecting the widespread public recognition of Christian Aid Week, in 1964 the organisation changed its name to Christian Aid.

In 1969, as the first development decade drew to a close, Christian Aid recognised that there was still much to be done in order to create 'a climate of public opinion in Britain that will accept the need for change in existing political and economic systems'.[45] They argued that governments had an obligation to promote 'responsible citizenship' in a world of inter-related nations.[46] In particular, they called on the

Commonwealth leaders to fulfil their commitment to play a 'creative role in the future strategy of development'.[47] Christian Aid believed that initiatives such as the Commonwealth Sugar Agreement demonstrated the potential of the Commonwealth to pioneer a 'new style of responsible international relationships'.[48]

From the early 1970s Christian Aid's campaign underwent a change of strategy and an important element of this was that 'responsible citizenship' was increasingly defined in terms of consumer responsibility. The effectiveness of this approach was demonstrated in April 1973 when Christian Aid petitioned the European Community (EC) Commissioners. Christian Aid implicated the EC in the 'virtual failure of UNCTAD-3 to wring any positive action from the richer countries'.[49] They argued that enlargement of the EC would lead to 'an increasingly self-sufficient, interdependent, but exclusive, club for rich nations'.[50] Christian Aid again renewed calls for international commodity agreements, as well as limits on the operations of MNCs and reform of the Common Agricultural Policy. But ultimately rather than a government led response, Christian Aid looked to European consumers. The concluding section of the petition stated that, 'unless people of the European Community are prepared to sacrifice the unrestricted advance in their own standard of living and increasing consumption of resources, very little progress will be made towards closing the gap between rich and poor nations'.[51]

For many Christian Aid supporters the fact that Europeans, although only one-fifth of the world's population, consumed one-third of the world's food was clear evidence of global economic and social injustice.[52] The Life Style movement, founded in 1972, was seen as a practical response to the excesses of consumer society. Committed to a more equal distribution of the world's resources, the philosophy of the movement was to, 'live more simply that all of us may simply live'.[53] Many converts to the Life Style movement would donate the savings made by their frugal lifestyle to Christian Aid. Although members of the Life Style movement numbered in the hundreds rather than thousands, it still maintained a regional presence through a coordinated network of fifty 'Life Style cells' across the country and gained national coverage through the Christian media. But by 1978, some within Christian Aid were questioning the introspective philosophy of the Life Style movement with its focus on personal ethics. Kate Philips, a correspondent for *Christian Aid News* argued that 'If we seriously want to create a fairer world, then it is the structures of production and distribution that have first to be changed. This means action on a national and international scale, pressing governmental and public opinion towards fairer trade.'[54]

Launched in March 1976, Christian Aid's 'A Fair Slice of the Cake for Tea' represented the first real attempt to positively engage with consumers. Rather than a general critique of consumer society, Christian Aid recognised that if consumers were willing to pay more for every day items then conditions for producers in developing countries could be improved. Christian Aid argued that 'After years of living on the cheap we'll have to get used to paying more. Whether for a cotton shirt or a quarter pound of Quickbrew.'[55] Christian Aid's initiative was run as part of a wider campaign for fair tea prices that had brought together a number of NGOs including War on Want, World Development Movement and Oxfam.[56]

The conditions on tea plantations had been exposed by a World in Action television programme 'Cost of a Cup of Tea'.[57] The programme stated that, in 1973, tea was about the only item on the shopping list that was still as cheap as in 1970. World in Action set out to 'investigate what it costs others to keep the cost of a packet of tea unchanged'.[58] All of the major household brands including Brooke Bond, Lonrho and the Co-operative Wholesale Society were criticised for failing to improve conditions within the Sri Lankan tea industry. By the late 1970s, thousands of British housewives had signed a petition declaring their willingness to pay, 'a fair price for tea in order to help the poor people in the tea-growing countries'.[59] But it was the activity of NGOs such as Christian Aid that maintained the momentum of this campaign and ensured that the plight of tea workers remained in the media and the public conscience of (some) British shoppers throughout the 1970s and 1980s.

A natural extension of the campaign for fair tea prices was Christian Aid's closer links with ATOs, such as Traidcraft, during the 1980s. In 1983 Christian Aid announced a new trading initiative, Traidfare teas, which was to be run in partnership with Traidcraft. Tea from Sri Lanka and Tanzania was featured alongside handcrafts and food products in a special version of the Traidcraft catalogue that was sent out to the sixty thousand supporters of Christian Aid.[60] In return Traidcraft committed to pay Christian Aid 10 per cent of sales resulting from the distribution of the mail order catalogue to their supporters.[61] In 1983 Christian Aid received £11,734 from sales of World Development Movement (WDM) tea, which was allocated for projects among tea workers.[62] These projects included community centres, mobile clinics and schools. This model of funding community projects would later be adapted by the Fairtrade Foundation and relaunched as the Social Premium.

Through its involvement with fair trade, Christian Aid had success-fully demonstrated to the wider Christian church that 'Third World' development was an issue that the church should actively engage with. Despite initial reluctance, by 1989 the English Church Census included support for 'Third World Community Aid' for the first time as an important indicator of church vitality.[63]

III Alternative trade: tearcraft and traidcraft

With a stake in some of the leading Fairtrade brands and products on the shelves of major supermarkets, Traidcraft's sales of £19.6 million in 2007 represent a significant presence in mainstream markets.[64] In contrast, Tearcraft has prioritised artisan made handcrafts and with relatively modest sales of only £1.2 million has remained an 'alternative' niche.[65] Both of these ATOs developed from trading initiatives launched by the Evangelical Alliance Relief Fund (Tearfund) in the mid-1970s. The markedly different business models that evolved is a reflection of the diverse and sometimes conflicting approaches taken by ATOs as they worked to define the concept of 'fair trade'. Through a comparative ana-lysis of the main features that shaped the historical development of Tearcraft and Traidcraft this section looks to explore the complex nature of the relationship between Christian NGOs and fair trade.

Tearfund itself owes its origins to the World Refugee Year (1959–60). Heightened awareness of the plight of refugees resulted in a flow of unsolicited donations to the British Evangelical Alliance. Many of these donations came with requests that the money be sent to Christian mis-sionaries working with refugees. In January 1960, the Evangelical Alliance Executive Council set up a fund so that, 'gifts could be dis-tributed to evangelical agencies engaged in caring for the material and spiritual needs of refugees'.[66] It was not until 1968, under the leader-ship of Rev George Hoffman, that this relief fund was promoted as a separate activity to the Evangelical Alliance. Initially Alan Brash, head of Christian Aid, was sceptical about the need for another relief agency, when Christian Aid was already established as the official agency of the Churches. This dispute was soon resolved when it was made clear that Tear Fund had no intention of competing with Christian Aid. George Hoffman in the first Tear Times, speaking of Tear Fund's objectives, stated, 'we believe we have an added responsibility – like the Catholic and Quaker agencies to their constituencies – to arrest the attention of Evangelicals in this country, and inform them of the needs, require-ments and the opportunities to help'.[67]

In 1974, in response to the unfolding crisis in Bangladesh, which had been left devastated by civil war and a cyclone, Tear Fund agreed to start importing local handicrafts to sell in Britain.[68] This first cargo of handicrafts led Tear Fund to take the financially risky step of setting up its own ATO. The programme was implemented through the work of Ian Prior, on the Tear Fund staff, and Richard Adams, a greengrocer who had been supporting farmers in the Third World by importing their surplus produce. Richard Adams flew out to Bangladesh and filled a cargo plane, on its return leg to Britain after a Tear Fund relief mission, with £10,000 worth of jute handicrafts from local producers. Tearcraft was then registered as a business on the 23rd December 1974 and the first catalogue went out in February 1975.[69]

Tearcraft was committed to a Christian evangelical approach to international trade. This meant solely working with and through evangelicals. George Hoffman had set out Tear Fund's position in a letter to Richard Adams, 'Ideally, of course we would like to see Tearcraft purchasing solely from groups organised by, or associated with, evangelical Christians'.[70] But in practice about 90 per cent of what Tearcraft sold was made by people of other religions even though their efforts were channelled through church organisations.[71] Some within Tearcraft, including Adams, believed that focussing on handicraft production as a practical mission of the church was overly restrictive and was potentially damaging to the commercial viability of the enterprise. Before long these tensions led to growing disagreements and in 1979 Richard Adams left Tearcraft and established a new ATO called Traidcraft.

Adams believed that Traidcraft should maintain a Christian motivation to its work and its founding principles declared that, 'Traidcraft is a Christian response to poverty.'[72] But unlike Tearcraft, Traidcraft was clear that in its mission to fight against poverty, it would work with 'people of all faiths and none'.[73] Richard Adams, commenting on the influence of Christian faith in the company, stated that there was 'no area of our work where there was not endless scope for applying our faith yet few areas where we could lay claim to a definitive approach'.[74] Although about 85 per cent of Traidcraft's staff were Christian, a Christian message was rarely highlighted in Traidcraft campaigns. As Traidcraft moved towards mainstream markets Adams was 'very conscious of how "Christian language" might alienate people'.[75]

By the time Traidcraft came to produce its second catalogue in 1980 it was already extending its range beyond crafts and for the first time featured WDM Tea from Sri Lanka and Campaign Coffee from Nicaragua and Tanzania. The tea although marketed as WDM Tea was imported directly by Traidcraft from the Waulugala estate in south Sri Lanka. The Waulugala estate was owned by a trust set up by the Dissanayake family. The trust ran homes for orphaned and handicapped children, the elderly and the mentally ill. Half the profits from the tea estate went to the trust and the other half was divided between the tea workers as an annual bonus.[76] The success of tea and coffee meant that by the third catalogue in 1981 Traidcraft sales had reached £800,000 and it was now larger than Tearcraft. By 1985 the range of food products had extended to include spices, dried fruit, pulses and grains, nuts, honey, tinned pineapples and peppermints. In total foodstuffs in 1985 represented 12 per cent of Traidcraft sales and tea and coffee represented a further 29 per cent.[77]

In contrast to Oxfam, Traidcraft only had three directly owned shops in Newcastle, Leeds and Liverpool. The majority of sales came through Traidcraft voluntary representatives. This grassroots network of supporters grew from 120 in 1979 to more than 400 by 1982.[78] These unpaid volunteers committed, on average, five to six hours a week on planning and running Traidcraft activities. These activities ranged from: taking on short-let shops at Christmas, to hiring market stalls, visiting schools, offices and factories and lobbing local council meetings.[79] By 1988, 1,500 Traidcraft representatives were active and were achieving sales worth £1.5 million a year (41 per cent of Traidcraft's total sales).[80]

Launching the FAIRTRADE Mark

In 1989, inspired by the success of the Max Havelaar labelling initiative in the Netherlands, Oxfam, Christian Aid and Traidcraft alongside New Consumer and WDM came together to discuss how to take fair trade in Britain from the 'margins to the mainstream'.[81] These discussions would lead, in July 1992, to the formation of the Fairtrade Foundation as the certifying body of the FAIRTRADE Mark in the UK. During these early years the Fairtrade Foundation relied heavily on its member organisations for personnel, expertise and funding.[82] But as NGOs were to discover their membership of the Fairtrade Foundation would require them to redefine their role in relation to the wider fair trade movement. At times it seemed as if the conflicting pressures of a sceptical Charity Commission and the commercial imperatives being driven by negotiations with MNCs would result in NGOs becoming sidelined within the Fairtrade Foundation.

Although the Fairtrade Foundation was officially formed in July 1992 it did not receive charitable status until 1995. There were moments when it seemed that those organisations with charitable status would have to withdraw support or risk having to repay any grants that had been invested into the Fairtrade Foundation. Initial applications to the Charity Commission had proved unsuccessful. It had claimed that the Fairtrade Foundation did not sufficiently target the stated objective of 'poverty relief'. It was argued that the Fairtrade Foundation's aim was, 'to encourage business prosperity which is a much wider purpose'.[83] Even if it could be shown that in every case the producers were poor, the Charity Commission maintained that the means were 'too remote from the achievement of any such purpose'.[84]

Eventually, charity law solicitor Andrew Phillips succeeded in arguing that the Fairtrade Foundation's charitable objective of 'poverty relief' would be met through the distribution of the 'social premium'. In February 1995, Chief Charity Commissioner Richard Fries officially bestowed the Fairtrade Foundation with charitable status. Fries commented that the Fairtrade Foundation was 'an imaginative scheme for setting up permanent arrangements for helping Third World producers'. He further added that Fairtrade Foundation's registration was an example of the ability of charity law to 'encompass new and better ways of meeting charitable ends'.[85]

It was not just resistance from the Charity Commission that had the potential to undermine the Fairtrade Foundation before it had even launched. The newly formed organisation was brought close to breaking point in September 1992, when talks with Typhoo tea broke down following a controversial newspaper advertisement placed by Christian Aid. The banner line of the advert read, 'You have stopped using eggs from battery hens, but what about tea from battery tea workers.'[86] The advert sparked an immediate reaction from other members of the Fairtrade Foundation. Richard Adams, Director of New Consumer and former head of Traidcraft, conscious of the likely impact of the advert described it as 'the torpedoing of the most promising initiative of the last twenty years'.[87] Paul Johns, Acting Chief Executive of the Fairtrade Foundation, also condemned the advert outright, 'You have opened your campaign against unfair trade by dropping a bomb on your allies.'[88]

The main criticism of Christian Aid's advert was that it stood to undermine the Fairtrade Foundation's strategy of 'consultation, dialogue and a new, positive approach to campaigning', as a throw back to '1970s-style campaigning'.[89] But was this a valid criticism or an overreaction? The campaign was certainly hard hitting, but rather than calling for a boycott of tea Christian Aid appealed to consumers to 'Ask your supermarket to buy goods from sources that provide Third World workers with a decent living.'[90] Although this campaign may have been stretching the limits of 'positive engagement', it was far from a direct attack of Typhoo. The Fairtrade Foundation were desperate not to lose Typhoo because it offered the opportunity of 'a fair trade advertising and point of sale campaign employing massive resources which would reach millions of people who are normally not touched by the agencies'.[91]

The impact of this advertisement on Typhoo's decision not to apply for Fairtrade certification is difficult to judge, but it seems that ultimately it was commercial issues including a failure to agree on the level of the licensee fee, the timing of the launch and a restructuring at Premier Tea that were more significant factors. What this incident demonstrates more clearly is the tensions that existed, from the outset, between those members of the Fairtrade Foundation focussed on developing the mass consumer appeal of the FAIRTRADE Mark and those NGOs working to promote a development focussed agenda.

Conclusions

By investigating the work of Oxfam, Christian Aid, Tearcraft and Traidcraft, this chapter has set out to uncover an often overlooked feature of fair trade in Britain – the role of NGOs. The significance of these case studies is not only in that they provide a detailed assessment of the involvement of individual organisations but also that they allow for a more nuanced understanding of the growth of fair trade in modern Britain. It has demonstrated that it is too simplistic to view the growth of fair trade as the straightforward surge in demand of concerned shoppers. Rather, fair trade has been one tactic among many that established development NGOs have promoted for several decades. Moreover, much of the motivation behind this action lies in the Christian beliefs of the organisations and supporters. They have been able to draw on the religious principles of their members to use their consumer power for wider political ends.

It is clear that ethical consumers did not emerge but were shaped through the campaigns and experience of alternative trade pioneered by NGOs. Fair trade developed as an alternative approach that filled the vacuum left by government and business reluctance to engage consumers on issues of international trade and development. It is perhaps in losing the terminology alternative that we have lost the true concept of fair trade. 'Alternative trade' set out to represent an alternative to existing trading relations imposed by governments and big business. Consumers were involved but this movement was not consumer led.

The Fairtrade Foundation set out to 'empower consumers to take responsibility for the role they play when they buy products from the third world'.[92] The rise of the ethical consumer has proved a mixed blessing. By publishing sales figures of Fairtrade certified products the Fairtrade Foundation were able to demonstrate in a measurable way the impact and growth of Fairtrade, but it also made them ever more reliant on MNCs and supermarkets in order to sustain this growth. The Fairtrade Foundation's relations with supermarkets and MNCs have been surprisingly under-debated within the movement after the initial controversy over Christian Aid's tea advert. It was not until 2005, when Nestlé decided to launch a Fairtrade labelled coffee, 'Partners Blend', that these discussions were reopened. Arguably, this is an issue that the Fairtrade Foundation is yet to fully resolve.

Indeed, tensions remain between these campaigning NGOs and the partnerships they have entered into in order to make Fairtrade a mass consumer phenomenon. This was clearly illustrated in 2003, when Oxfam published *Mugged: Poverty in Your Coffee Cup*, a highly critical report of many of the major brands.[93] So far the Fairtrade Foundation has managed to avoid the type of backlash seen by NGOs and ATOs in the US that believed the labelling organisation Transfair had lost touch with the true values of the movement and was engaging with MNCs at any cost. This should be a lesson to the Fairtrade Foundation to not underestimate the importance of its historical origins. In many ways this constitutes its unique selling point. Other labels may be able to replicate and in some cases surpass the Fairtrade criteria (most notably on environmental standards) but it is the movement's NGO origins and continued involvement that acts as the best reassurance for consumers that what they are buying into is more than a public relations exercise.

Arguably, the omission of NGOs from much of the recent commentary on fair trade is a reflection of the Fairtrade Foundation's own efforts, over the last decade, to cultivate an identity distinct from that of its member organisations. In creating its own identity the Fairtrade Foundation aimed to shake off the 'alternative' label that had defined much of the pioneering work of its founding members. But there are signs that, with a growing number of sceptical consumers looking to question the proliferation of social labels, the Fairtrade Foundation may find it prudent to rediscover the NGO origins of the movement.[94]

Notes

1 H. Lamb, Fairtrade Foundation Press Release, '10 Years of Fairtrade: Sales Reach £100m per Year', www.Fairtrade.org.uk/pr010304.htm (1 March 2004).

2 R. Fletcher and H. Wallop, 'Fairtrade Sales Soar as Shoppers Go Ethical', *Daily Telegraph* (26 February 2007). M. Hickman and K. Attwood, 'Fairtrade Sales Double to £500m as Supermarkets Join Trend', *The Independent* (25 February 2008).

3 L. Jones, 'How Fair Trade Hit the Mainstream', *BBC News* (2 March 2004).

4 T. Macalister, 'How Consumer Power Sparked a Fairtrade Revolution on Our High Streets', *The Guardian* (8 March 2006).

5 G. Fridell, *Fair Trade Coffee: The Prospects and Pitfalls of Market-Driven Social Justice* (Toronto: University of Toronto Press, 2007).

6 The Fair Trade Declaration at the 2004 UNCTAD meeting in São Paulo stated that: 'Fair Trade is a trading partnership, based on dialogue, transparency and respect, that seeks greater equity in international trade. It contributes to sustainable development by offering better trading conditions to, and securing the rights of, marginalised producers and workers – especially in the South. Fair Trade organisations (backed by consumers) are engaged actively in supporting producers, awareness raising, and in campaigning for changes in the rules and practice of conventional international trade.' This definition was agreed by an informal network, known by their initials as FINE: Fairtrade Labelling Organisations International (FLO), International Fair Trade Association (IFAT), Network of European World Shops (NEWS!), European Fair Trade Association (EFTA).

7 A. Nicholls, 'Strategic Options in Fair Trade Retailing', *International Journal of Retail & Distribution Management*, 30(1) (2002), pp. 6–17.

8 A. Iriye, 'A Century of NGOs', *Diplomatic History*, 23(3) (Summer 1999), p. 422.

9 *Ibid*, p. 424.

10 P. Burnell, *Charity, Politics and the Third World* (Hemel Hempstead: Harvester Wheatsheaf, 1991).

11 See Buchanan, this volume.

12 A. Nicholls and C. Opal, *Fair Trade: Market Driven Ethical Consumption* (London: Sage Publications, 2004), p. 13.

13 *Ibid,* p. 31.

14 M.K. Goodman, 'Reading Fair Trade: Political Ecological Imaginary and the Moral Economy of Fair Trade Foods', *Political Geography*, 23 (2004), p. 901.

15 C. Barnett, N. Clarke *et al*, 'The Political Ethics of Consumerism', *Consumer Policy Review*, 15(2) (2005), p. 45.

16 *Ibid*, p. 51.

17 In 1992, these organisations alongside CAFOD, the World Development Movement, New Consumer and later the Women's Institute became the founding members of the Fairtrade Foundation.

18 G. Fridell, *Fair Trade Coffee*, p. 39.
19 *Ibid*, p. 22.
20 *Ibid*, p. 51.
21 *Ibid*, p. 23.
22 L. Pearson, *Partners in Development: Report of the Commission on International Development* (New York: Praeger Publishers, 1969), p. 77.
23 Pearson, *Partners in Development*, p. 45.
24 On January 1st 1971 the ICA launched the Co-operative Development Decade, 'a concerted and intensive campaign for the promotion of Co-operatives in developing countries'. *Report of Congress* (1971), p. 59.
25 OXFAM, BRIDGE HS/5: *Oxfam as an Importer: Why; How. An Explanation for Our Customers* (1973).
26 A. Spandau, *Economic Boycott Against South Africa* (Johannesburg: Juta & Co Ltd., 1979). R. Fieldhouse, *Anti-Apartheid: A History of the Movement in Britain* (London: The Merlin Press Ltd, 2005).
27 Oxfam's network of shops rapidly expanded throughout the 1960s, from only four shops in 1962 to 136 by 1967.
28 OXFAM: Guy Stringer, Directors Report to the Executive Committee (February 1974).
29 *Ibid*.
30 OXFAM, BRIDGE HS/5: report by R. Scott, 'What, Why, How: Bridge Summarized' (1973).
31 *Ibid*.
32 OXFAM, BRIDGE HS/5: report, 'Oxfam as an Importer: Why; How. An Explanation for Our Customers' (1973).
33 OXFAM, BRIDGE HS/5: report by R. Scott, 'Agreed Joint Statement of Conclusions' (January 1973).
34 OXFAM, BRIDGE HS/5: R. Scott, *How Can International Marketing be Best Organised to Give Maximum Opportunities and Benefits to the Participants (Producers & Consumers)?* (24 March 1975).
35 OXFAM, BRIDGE HS/5: G. Stringer & R. Scott, *The Improvement and Development of HbS: a Wider Vision* (November 1973).
36 OXFAM, BRIDGE HS/5: report 'The Purpose, Principles and Motivation of Bridge' (November 1975).
37 OXFAM: Executive Committee Papers, 'Director's Report to the Executive Committee' (16 September 1976).
38 OXFAM, Oxfam Activities board meeting minutes (hereafter OA): G. Stringer, *Bridge Producer Dividend*, (September 1976); E, Harriman, 'There's More to Charity than Faith and Hope', *The Sunday Times* (31 October 1976).
39 The Fairtrade Towns scheme was set up in 2000 to encourage support for Fairtrade at a local level. By 2007 there were 300 Fairtrade Towns and more than 200 areas campaigning towards status.
40 P. Cloke, C. Barnett, N. Clarke and A. Malpass, *Faith in Ethical Consumption*, paper given at Countering Consumerism: Religious and Secular Responses (21 April 2006).
41 D. Gerard, 'Values and Voluntary Work', in M. Abrams, D. Gerard and N. Timms (ed.) *Values and Social Change in Britain* (London: Macmillan Press, 1985).
42 The main Churches in the BCC are Anglican, Presbyterian, Methodist, Baptist, United Reform and Church of Scotland. In 1985 the Methodist

Relief and Development Fund was established, but even then the Methodist Church remained committed to supporting Christian Aid.

43 P.J. Burnell, *Charity politics and the Third World* (Harvester Wheatsheaf 1991), p. 54.

44 *Ibid.*

45 CA2/I/46 Memorandum from Christian Aid, 'The Commonwealth and Economic Development' (January 1969).

46 *Ibid.*

47 *Ibid.*

48 *Ibid.*

49 CA2/D/11 The European Community and the Third World, letter to EC Commissioners (25 April 1973).

50 *Ibid.*

51 *Ibid.*

52 CA/J/2 Christian Aid, 'The Consumer Society: A Christian Harvest Festival Service' (1970).

53 H. Dammers, 'An Experiment in Lifestyle', *Christian Aid News*, No. 19 (April/June 1978).

54 K. Philips, 'Lifestyle – Where Do We Go Now?', *Christian Aid News*, No. 19 (April/June 1978).

55 *Ibid.*

56 War on Want, *The State of Tea* (London, 1974); Cambridge World Development Action Group, *Tea: The Colonial Legacy* (1975); Oxfam, '*A Bitter Taste to Your Cuppa*', in Consumer Affairs Bulletin No. 7 (1977); World Development Movement, *The Tea Trade* (London, 1979).

57 World in Action: *Cost of a Cup of Tea* (Granada, September 24th 1973).

58 *Ibid.*

59 Oxfam, 'A Bitter Taste to Your Cuppa', in *Consumer Affairs Bulletin* (No. 7, 1977).

60 R. Adams, *Who Profits?* (Oxford: Lion Publishing, 1989), p. 97.

61 Traidcraft Company Prospectus: second public share issue (1986).

62 CA/J/5, campaign leaflet, *Broken For Tea* (1984).

63 P. Brierley, *Prospects for the Nineties*, MARC Europe, London 1981.

64 Traidcraft Annual Report (2007).

65 Tearlund Annual Report (2007/8).

66 M. Endersbee, *They Can't Eat Prayer: The Story of Tear Fund* (London: Hodder & Stoughton, 1977), p. 20.

67 *Ibid,* p. 88.

68 T. Chester, *Awakening to a World of Need* (Inter Varsity Press, 1993).

69 M. Symonds, *Love in Action: Celebrating 25 Years of Tear Fund* (Guildford: Eagle, 1993).

70 R. Adams, *Who Profits?*, p. 63.

71 *Ibid,* p. 64

72 http://www.traidcraft.co.uk/about_traidcraft/what_makes_us_different/principles.htm

73 *Ibid.*

74 Adams, *Who Profits?*, p. 155.

75 *Ibid,* p. 159.

76 *Ibid,* p. 82.

77 Traidcraft Catalogue (1985–86), p. 48.
78 Traidcraft Public Share Issue (July 1986).
79 Adams, *Who Profits?*, p. 8.
80 *Ibid*, p. 90.
81 OXFAM, BRIDGE COM: report by B. Yates, 'From the Margins to the Mainstream' (September 1990).
82 From 1990–95 the Fairtrade Foundation received in total the following grants from sponsoring agencies: Oxfam £127,000, Christian Aid £105,000, CAFOD £45,000, Traidcraft £3,500, WDM £3,000, New Consumer £3,000.
83 OXFAM, FTF, R0716: P. White (Charity Commission) letter to M. Hayes (Fairtrade Foundation), (16 March 1992).
84 *Ibid.*
85 CAFOD, Committee Grant Approval Writeup, 'Fairtrade Foundation Running Costs' (23/2/1998).
86 OXFAM, BRIDGE COM: Christian Aid advert, 'You Have Stopped Using Eggs from Battery Hens, but what about Tea from Battery Tea Workers', *The Times* (16 September 1992).
87 OXFAM, BRIDGE COM: R. Adams letter to Nick Isles, Christian Aid (17 September 1992).
88 OXFAM, BRIDGE COM: P. Johns, letter to Jenny Borden, Christian Aid (17 September 1992).
89 OXFAM, BRIDGE COM: R. Adams letter to Nick Isles, Christian Aid (17 September 1992).
90 OXFAM, BRIDGE COM: Christian Aid advert, 'You Have Stopped Using Eggs from Battery Hens, but What about Tea from Battery Tea Workers', *The Times* (16 September 1992).
91 OXFAM, BRIDGE COM: R. Adams letter to Nick Isles, Christian Aid (17 September 1992).
92 Fairtrade Foundation, *Introducing Fairtrade: A Guide to the Fairtrade Mark and the Fairtrade Foundation* (London, 2000).
93 http://publications.oxfam.org.uk/oxfam/display.asp?isbn=0855985275.
94 Consumers International, *From Bean to Cup: How Consumer Choice Impacts on Coffee Producers and the Environment* (London: CI, December 2005), p. 29.

13

Transforming a Divided Civil Society? Governance, Conflict Transformation and NGOs in Northern Ireland, 1970–2006

Audra Mitchell

In recent years, bureaucracy has come under increasing criticism. Branded as rigid, elitist and unresponsive to citizens, there has been a widespread effort to replace it with the apparently fluid, energetic and dynamic qualities of traditional social movements. This is one of the central goals of the public policy paradigm known as 'governance' which has gained considerable influence in the United Kingdom (UK) and European Union (EU).[1] Governance is based, in large part, on fusing the public institutions and the organisations and actors known as 'civil society' within the realm of public service provision. In Northern Ireland, the development of governance was closely intertwined with peace-building policies, in particular the paradigm of conflict transformation.[2] The policies that arose from these paradigms aimed to transform the social movements that were thought to generate conflict into a set of stable, community-based non-governmental organisations (NGOs), integrated firmly within governing structures and supportive of the 'formal' peace process. The marriage of the reforms of governance with conflict transformation is expected to satisfy the need for socio-political change that emerged during the Troubles, whilst the bureaucratic aspects are intended to undergird the formal peace-building process.

The cultivation of these new, fused organisations was based on a specific model of the NGO. This model attributes NGOs with the 'heart and mind' of a social movement (a voluntary base, a dynamic and flexible attitude and a civic ethos) and a bureaucratic 'body' (a defined structure, mechanisms for accountability and the ability to interface with appropriate statutory agencies and representatives). In other words, it should balance the social and bureaucratic ethos, highlighting the best aspects of each and bringing about a transformation of social action and public institutions alike. Proponents of governance assume that this kind of transformation will produce a new form of public institution, based upon its two sources but distinct from them. However, it may also bring about a one-sided transformation, in which one of the two forms of action is transformed to resemble the other.

As the case studies below will seek to demonstrate, the latter was true in Northern Ireland during the 1970s to the early 2000s. The manner in which social movements were transformed into NGOs was intended to infuse bureaucracy with the qualities of social action, creating a new forum that could address governmental aims – including the creation of a lasting peace – whilst acknowledging the unique needs and grievances that these social movements expressed. In reality, the civil society approach to peacebuilding may have helped to consolidate attitudes toward peace and to create the institutional basis needed to support the formal peace process, but it did so by fundamentally changing the nature of public participation in Northern Ireland. Specifically, it created an imbalance within the model of the NGO by overemphasising bureaucratic structures and all but eliminating more 'traditional' social movements as a form of political expression. This, in turn, has deprived citizens of an important means of developing and expressing their beliefs, needs, goals and grievances – necessary to any society, but particularly to one attempting to transcend violent conflict.

Case studies

The following case studies will examine the manner in which two social movements were transformed into NGOs, and the imbalance between bureaucracy and social action that this created. It will do so by exploring how the manner in which organisations expressed their values, goals and attitudes changed during this period. Northern Ireland in the 1970s was replete with traditional social movements – radical, informal networks of collective action whose medium was, quite literally, their message. In other words, the form of action in which they engaged – traditional 'social movement' activity – was closely related to their ability to develop and express political ideas, values and attitudes in and through their activities. Yet by the early 2000s, very few of these movements remained in their original form. They appear to have been transformed almost uniformly into NGOs whose main task is to represent local needs to government bodies and ensure that these needs were acknowledged in formalised processes. Although the latter function is valuable in many ways, it appears to have replaced more traditional forms of social action almost entirely with a model of the NGO that does not adequately reflect its origins in social action.

The women's movement

Margaret Ward suggests that women in the island of Ireland have a history of social action dating back to the 1790s,[3] although the most contemporary wave of the women's movement arose from the Civil Rights movement of the late 1960s.[4] It is difficult to draw boundaries around the women's movement, which has included *ad hoc* protests, discussion groups, women's centres and even mainstream political parties, and has engaged with issues ranging from domestic abuse to prisoners' rights. Catriona Beaumont's chapter in this book provides a discussion of the similarly diverse goals and activities of women's organisations in England during this period.

In the 1970s, the overtly political activities of the movement – largely concerned with raising awareness of women's rights and engaging the public in discussions of these rights – were, in themselves, the primary activity of the movement. For example, the Campaign for Social Justice, a group formed in Dungannon to improve access to public housing, engaged in a variety of protests and even squatted in empty public housing to express their demands.[5] Foyle Women's Aid, a group concerned with domestic violence in the (London)Derry area, also staged a squat with the intention of getting arrested in order to publicise their campaign.[6] Theatrical forms of action were also frequently utilised. The Relatives' Action Committee, a prisoners' rights group composed primarily of women, used the format of a parade to enact a scene depicting the suffering of female relatives of interned or imprisoned men.[7] Furthermore, in response to the removal of free milk from schools, a women's group from the Ormeau Road marched a cow directly into Belfast City Hall as a way of communicating directly with city councilors.[8] In confrontational forms of action such as these, message and medium were one in the same.

During the 1980s, as the state began to engage more directly with social movements, the expression of values or goals and the daily activities of organisations began to diverge. This was marked by the appearance and bifurcation of longer-term, sustained campaigns and the delivery of social services. During this decade, campaigns took a less *ad hoc* and more rationalised form, and were directed more narrowly, towards a governmental audience. For example, the Northern Ireland Abortion Campaign of 1980 secured substantial media coverage by sending 600 coat-hangers to the House of Commons, along with a British Airways ticket and a message stating that these were the only options available to women in Northern Ireland who sought abortions.[9] Here, confrontational messages and the use of the media to gain public attention remained, but the process became significantly more formalised and directed towards a specific audience. This trend is further reflected by the forms of expression used by the Northern Ireland Women's Rights Movement (NIWRM). Although the NIWRM still considered its primary audience to be lower-income women, it actively began to seek political influence by engaging in lobbying efforts. Lobbying included the cultivation of relationships with influential members of statutory departments and members of parliament, although the organisation still viewed itself as 'substantially more than just a pressure group'.[10]

At the same time, constitution-based, formally organised and permanent women's centres became the primary form of organisation within the movement. Amongst these was the Ballybeen Women's Centre, created in response to a recommendation from a community worker employed by the Belfast City Council. From its inception, it was highly structured and oriented towards the delivery of services, including childcare and a wide range of social and educational programmes. Although it began on a low budget with few staff, the Centre devoted a great deal of energy to attracting local resources which allowed it to employ full-time staff and improve its premises.[11] In addition to its services, the group engaged in formal lobbying, along with the Women's Information group (a large umbrella organisation representing a number of women's groups in the region) at Westminster to protest changes in social security provision, receiving considerable press coverage for their efforts. It also undertook extensive research projects regarding the welfare of women and communities as part of the lobbying process.[12] However, lobbying activities and the delivery of services were considered separate functions and a premium was placed upon maintaining the political neutrality of service provision. This trend towards professionalisation and service-delivery intensified in the late 1990s and early 2000s. During this decade, the service-provision function of women's groups was emphasised to the extent that groups were created for the express purpose of stimulating the development of new women's centres. An example of this may be found in the formation of the Rural Women's Development Organisation, which was created on the impetus of the Department of Social Development (DSD) in 2006 with a mandate to create 'grassroots' women's groups in rural areas.[13]

Moreover, during the 1990s and early 2000s, the representative function of organisations became more pronounced as the state and the individuals designing major funding programmes (discussed below) began to rely upon consultation with women's groups as a means for legitimising their decisions. Both the Ballybeen Women's Centre and the Falls Women's Centre were consulted frequently as 'experts' in the field of women's issues. As representative bodies, they were encouraged to express their demands directly to statutory bodies and to develop relationships with key civil servants rather than engaging in public campaigns or even external lobbying.[14] This trend further divorced the expression of values from the daily activities of the organisations. In fact, throughout the 1990s and early 2000s, so much of the expressive effort of women's groups was focussed on lobbying that groups began to experience a sense of disconnection from their participants.[15]

The former prisoners' movement

The (former) prisoners' movement,[16] which arose in reaction to the internment and imprisonment of individuals involved in armed struggle, followed a very similar trajectory. During the periods of internment and criminalisation, politically-motivated prisoners engaged in a dynamic range of actions, including protests and strikes.[17] However, in the 1990s and early 2000s, this movement took a very different form in the emergence of former prisoners' organisations with formalised and distinct lobbying and service-delivery functions.

Much like the women's movement, the prisoners' movement in the late 1970s was characterised by inseparability of action from the expression of goals. Within the prisons, the creation of paramilitary command structures and systems for the distribution of scarce resources such as food 'served as a daily reminder of why the men were in prison, as volunteers of their own chosen group, fighting for their cause'.[18] The blanket strikes, hunger strikes and no-wash protests were extreme examples of expression; they used the body and the space within the prison as mediums for conveying messages in a startling, disturbing manner. Even less extreme forms of action, such as teaching the Irish language and decorating cells with paramilitary paraphernalia, were intended to convey an attitude of resistance to prison staff and the public.[19] Despite their lower numbers, Loyalist prisoners also became involved in direct action such as a roof-top protest against the visiting Minister of State.[20]

During the early 1980s, major changes to the activities undertaken within the prison occurred. At the peak of the 1980 hunger strike, the public was still an important target audience; hunger strikers and other activists made extensive use of the media to inform and engage people within Northern Ireland and internationally.[21] However, at this point, the beginnings of a lobbying capacity emerged through the development of formal negotiations between prison staff and wing Officers in Command (OCs) (the acting heads of each wing), in which OCs acted as intermediaries for prisoners, while prison management, likewise, liaised with state officials to negotiate the concessions which would end the hunger strike. A major turning point occurred during the 1983 campaign by Loyalist and Republican Prisoners for segregation, when the groups were forcibly integrated after a large-scale escape of Republican prisoners. This campaign was viewed as an inside issue; no attempts were made to gain external publicity for this campaign. Rather, re-segregation of Republican and Loyalist prisoners into separate wings was established through direct negotiations with prison staff and the exertion of influence by Republican OCs on their Loyalist counterparts.[22] The use of formalised communications channels and formal documents to express demands to prison officials marked some of the earliest lobbying efforts of the movement. In addition, the substitution of formal, parliamentary politics for prison protest became crucial to Republican prisoners with the election of high-profile MPs, such as hunger striker Bobby Sands and female prisoner Bernadette Devlin, during their incarceration.

At the same time, the activities of prisoners engaged in the movement began to change. Although the hierarchical structures were maintained, these became 'based on collective leadership combined with communal responsibility, input and accountability'.[23] Moreover, these structures cooperated with the new policy of skills development by taking part in courses ranging from English and Maths to Music provided by the prison.[24] In addition, Republican prisoners began to formalise their own 'services'. Although the use of the Irish language and the reading of political texts existed from the first days of the movement, these were standardised as 'courses' under the leadership of OCs and other individuals involved in the movement.[25]

These two trends crystallised in the mid-1990s, as thousands of prisoners were released under the Good Friday Agreement and the first mainstream former prisoners' organisations were developed. At this time, groups such as Tar Anall (for Republican former prisoners) and EPIC (for Loyalist former prisoners) emerged as professionally-staffed and funded organisations and began providing a range of services – from personal counselling to employment training and advice – to former prisoners and to lobby for the rights of this group. Organisations for both communities and various factions focussed on creating employment opportunities for former prisoners, providing them with standardised skills and training, engaging them in 'dialogue' with other former prisoners and organisations, offering emotional support and counselling, and providing advice regarding benefits and statutory services amongst other things.[26]

During this period, these NGOs engaged in targeted communications and networking, direct lobbying, negotiation and consultation with government bodies and funders. For example, throughout the mid-1990s, EPIC began to engage in extensive networking amongst similar organisations within Northern Ireland and abroad.[27] Cross-community contact was also promoted through the organisation of regular meetings and conferences between the members of management committees, former prisoners and their family members.[28] In this sense, former prisoners' organisations began to direct a great deal of their expressive effort towards targeted communications and networking within a relatively exclusive group.

Moreover, direct lobbying and the development of direct relationships with funding bodies and statutory agencies became important for many groups. For example Coiste n-Iarchimi, an umbrella organisation for 'mainstream' Republican former prisoners, places great emphasis on influencing statutory bodies 'in order that the issues which affect [their] client base are eventually internalised by this important sector'.[29] In recent years, Coiste has emphasised the need to target its lobbying by bypassing the civil service and creating lines of communication with the 'top level' of government.[30] In all cases, political activities are undertaken separately from the delivery of services and great pains are taken to separate 'political work' from services.[31] Likewise, the managers of non-mainstream Republican organisations such as Teach na Failte, Ex-Pac and An Eochair[32] all stress the need to separate political activities from their interactions with members, largely as a result of the need to retain legitimacy in the eyes of funding bodies or relevant statutory agencies.[33] The development of formal NGOs, with differentiated capacities for lobbying and service-delivery, is particularly striking in a movement whose initial actions were highly politicised and in which the pursuit of goals was inseparable from extreme forms of direct action.

The civil society approach to peace-building: transforming social movements into NGOs

The case studies above illustrate one way in which the transformation of social movements into a particular model of the NGO manifested itself: in the conversion of radical, populist, confrontational forms of expression into professionalised lobbying and service delivery functions. What was it, then, about the model of the NGO used in these policies, that brought about this change? Moreover, what can it tell us about the relative emphasis given to bureaucracy and social action within this model? This section will argue that social action is given a central role in this model of the NGO – as a representative source of values, ideas and beliefs – but it is overpowered by a strong bureaucratic ethos and structure. Within the model, social action is expected to act as legitimate and democratic source of values, interests, needs and goals. In expressing these – through the specific function of representation – it is expected to reflect and include the viewpoints of all parties affected by and party to the conflict. Bureaucracy, on the other hand, provides the institutional basis for the NGO. Most importantly, it provides a set of structures that could be made subject to design and alteration on the part of political actors, and a corporative ethos to lend unity and stability to these structures. Here, the goal of addressing the needs generated by (and expressed through) conflict whilst engaging in active state-building is clearly reflected. In theory, the social element of NGOs should generate and express the values, needs and goals central to the conflict (as well as more basic issues concerning everyday life) through the medium of stable, integrated institutions. In practice, however, the predominance of these bureaucratic elements had the effect of bureaucratising 'traditional' social movements, and denuding them of much of their radical, critical and normative capacity. It is the relative weight assigned to each element in this model of the NGO, to which we now turn, which resulted in this imbalance.

Social action as a source of values, ideas and beliefs

Within the paradigm of governance, the activities of NGOs are expected to produce and express the values, goals and grievances of communities, which then inform and shape statutory policies, providing their democratic basis. Crucially, they are expected to do so in a robustly democratic manner. Most theories of 'civil society' support the hypothesis that a strong civil sphere creates the necessary conditions for democracy by inculcating individual democratic skills, trust and other civic qualities, enhancing communication and interaction and ingraining desirable moral attitudes. The expectations contingent on these assumptions range from the enhancement of trust in localised communities to the gradual democratisation of society as a whole.[34]

These democratic capacities are, in turn, thought to be conducive to the generation and expression of values – in particular, those favourable to the process of peacebuilding. These include: the creation of stability, the promotion of non-violent activity, the inclusion of marginalised groups, tolerance, exchange and dialogue, confidence in government, and increased contact between conflicting communities, simply to name a few.[35] Ample examples of this assumption may be found in peace-building policies at the local, regional and European levels, including the European Union's Peace and Reconciliation funding schemes (PEACE I and PEACE II). PEACE II places a wide range of expectations upon social entities, including: reconciliation, the empowerment of citizens, the reconstruction of the 'social fabric of communities', the promotion of equality and inclusiveness, 'trust-building and prejudice reduction', social integration and inclusion, and even 'promoting abroad the positive image of a more peaceful society'.[36]

By generating these values in a democratic manner and 'transmitting them' to governing institutions, the 'voluntary sector' is also thought to reinforce the goals of governance. Paul Dixon employs this image, suggesting that the use of civil society to further the peace-building goals of government is based on a 'bottom-up' ethos aimed at underwriting and legitimising governmental peacebuilding processes.[37] Similarly, the EU views the 'sector' as an important contributor to 'good governance' and expects it to adopt and reinforce the principles of this policy, including accountability and openness.[38] Local legislation places similar expectations upon the 'voluntary sector', charging it with the tasks of promoting 'human rights, equality and good relations', delivering 'social, economic cultural and environmental change'[39] and promoting shared values, including pluralism, interdependence, enhanced participation and social justice.[40] The idea of community relations endorsed by these bodies provides a key example. It underscores the creation of 'self-confidence and inclusiveness' within each community, which is expected to increase opportunities for cross-community contact.[41] This, in turn, is expected to rarefy tensions existing between conflicted parties and, simultaneously, to enhance the relationship between the 'communities' and statutory bodies.[42] In each case, it is implicitly assumed that these benefits emanate from social action. The idea, therefore, that civil society is a source for development and change in the realm of values, attitudes and ideas is crucial.

Representation

The second assumption relating to the associational aspects of NGOs is that they are authentic representations of their communities and that their representative capacity can be used to inform policy-making through formal processes of consultation. The principle of consultation is firmly embedded in most policies related to the 'voluntary sector' and peace-building since the 1980s. Importantly, it is embedded in section 75 of the Good Friday Agreement, which requires public bodies to consult on their equality impact statements with representatives of nine categories of people whose rights to equal treatment are enshrined in the legislation. There is, however, considerable controversy over whether a given organisation can be considered representative and what determines this status. The manager of the Falls Women's Centre, who is often called upon to testify to government on behalf of the 'women's sector', expresses concern that statutory bodies often view consultations 'like a ticked box' and assume that consulting with one organisation is tantamount to consulting with 'women' as a whole.[43] Moreover, the kinds of groups that are considered representative is a source of contention; for example, should paramilitary organisations be accorded this status, given the relatively high levels of public support for these organisations within some communities?[44] Regardless of these points of contention, it is assumed that social entities possess a democratic character capable of expressing diverse collective identities and needs.

A heavy emphasis on consultation can be found throughout local, regional and European policy documents. The Wolfenden report set the tone for this discourse, suggesting that NGOs make representations to government 'through the signals sent by [their] activities to the statutory system on the nature of shifts in public interest'.[45] The use of consultation in policy-making entails several important assumptions. First, it assumes that the 'sector' is independent of the state and thus can act as a 'critical friend of Government' by challenging its policies constructively.[46] Secondly, it suggests that the interaction of particular social entities with statutory bodies constitutes a 'civil dialogue'[47] between citizens and these bodies, as if each were a unified party engaged in a participatory form of discourse. The EU in particular stresses the representative nature of the 'sector' and aims to enhance this by 'creating a culture of consultation' by means of 'a code of conduct that sets minimum standards, focusing on what to consult on, when, and whom to consult'.[48] Whether or not NGOs can be considered representative of a given society or community is highly contentious; Darren Halpin's chapter regarding the accountability of NGOs to their members explores this topic in more depth. What I wish to emphasise here is the fact that these policies operate *as if* NGOs are representative. In other words, it focusses on the function of representation – that is, their capacity to convey information about goals, needs and issues deriving from social sources effectively and efficiently to governing bodies. Moreover, because representation is assigned such an important role in policy-making processes and is crucial to the state's justification of its policy within the paradigm of governance, there is an incentive for the state to cultivate more NGOs that seek to present themselves as representative of a certain group of people. In turn, funding programmes tend to favour those NGOs that are assumed to represent a particular constituency from which the state or funding body requires input or legitimation. As a result, many NGOs devote a great deal of energy and resources into developing a specific capacity for lobbying or representation as their main means of expressing values, attitudes, beliefs or needs, as reflected in the case studies above.

The role of bureaucracy

Social action, therefore, is given a constitutive role in this model of the NGO. However, it is responsible only for providing expressions of values, needs and goals. These are embodied and implemented by a particular medium: the bureaucratic structures of most contemporary NGOs.

Structure and design

The institutional element of the NGO model used in transformative governance is based on the concept of structure, which assumes that all forms of social action can be understood in terms of relatively stable patterns of behaviour – that is, institutions or organisations. The attraction of a structural approach to 'civil society' is that it allows theorists to assign functionality to particular structures and then to manipulate these structures in order to produce desired results. This assumption is central to Almond and Verba's approach, which encourages the development of informal, dense groups, and Warren's typologies, which frame 'structure' as a crucial determinant in the benefits produced by association.[49] Thus, it enables theorists and policy-makers to formulate and impose structural designs for the 'type of civil society [that] is most appropriate to a modern democratic polity'.[50]

Within these policies, design principles are applied to two levels of 'structure': micro-structures (at the level of discrete organisations) and macro-structures ('civil society' as a whole). The principles used to design ideal micro-structures emphasise standardisation, 'good practice', professionalism, good governance and consistency. For the most part, designs are based on the normative expectations placed on 'civil society', for example the assumption that the structures of 'civil society' are conducive to 'deal[ing] with problems and protests without recourse to ... violence'.[51] This means privileging forms of action that are non-conflictual and generic, as reflected by the emphasis on the provision of statutory services. The EU also focusses on encouraging the development and reproduction of specific micro-structures, suggesting that a database of suitable organisations should be compiled to act as a model and catalyst for the improvement of those groups wishing to be included in its policies.[52] The Home Office expands upon this approach by aiming to create 'demonstration projects' as examples for new NGOs in order to standardise their goals and activities.[53] Training is another important element of design intended to professionalise, standardise and focus social action towards particular aims. Standardisation of activity through training is crucial to PEACE II, the government's 1998 Compact with the Voluntary Sector, Positive Steps and the Home Office's strategy. This results in the substitution of professionalised, moderate, permanent structures for more radical, fluid forms of action, a process which is explored further in Stephen Brooke's chapter on the Abortion Law Reform Association and Jodi Burkett's analysis of the Campaign for Nuclear Disarmament in this volume.

The attempt to impose specific designs upon the macro-structure of 'civil society' is a projection and amplification of these principles. It focusses on the standardisation, coordination and streamlining of 'civil society'. As far back as 1978, the Wolfenden report notes that, with the increased availability of statutory funding, organisations have tended towards greater specialisation of objectives and membership, concern with influencing state policies and secular/materialist objectives. The DSD's Harbison Report advocates this trend, suggesting that the structure of the entire 'sector' should be remodelled in order to avoid duplication and fragmentation in terms of the delivery of services. It also insists that the creation of 'mergers and strategic alliances', increased links with statutory bodies, targeted funding for 'community infrastructure'[54] – largely intermediary or umbrella bodies intended to liaise with statutory agencies – and the development of 'social capital' by means of extended networks are necessary to maximise the efficacy of the 'sector'.[55] Taking a highly coordinated, holistic approach to the design of macro-structures, 'Positive Steps' suggests that design principles should be applied not only to the 'sector', but to all of the sectors involved in its overall strategy; it aims to 'ensure that voluntary and community organizations are able to operate on a level playing field with other service providers'.[56]

Corporatism

The paradigm of 'civil society' is based on a corporatist model. In fact, the use of this term suggests that theorists view civil society as a single, incorporated entity. Cohen and Arato's vision of 'civil society' exemplifies this assumption. According to these authors, 'civil society' is both internally integrated and incorporated within a larger whole also comprising the state and economy.[57] Warren also adopts a corporative approach to association, suggesting that each act of association is part of a 'democratic ecology of associational life',[58] in which each component performs a specific, complementary function within a broader system.

The emphasis on corporatism in the discourses regarding peace-building is reflected in two concepts: first, the idea of a single voluntary sector and secondly, the closer cooperation of statutory and non-statutory entities. Within statutory policy, the concept of a unified 'voluntary and community sector' emerged from the influential Wolfenden report of 1978, a cross-UK inquiry intended to examine, classify and evaluate the 'sector' as a whole, as a means of guiding funders in their decisions.[59] By the mid-1990s, the idea of a single sector was so powerful within the discourse on civil society in Northern Ireland that social entities were expected to act as a sector and the 'integrating dimension' was seen as 'the hallmark of a voluntary and community sector "beyond violence"'.[60] The DSD suggests that the 'sector' should be approached and managed as a single entity, and prioritises the 'consolidation of delivery mechanisms ... [to avoid] duplication of effort' by means of integration and coordination.[61] This sentiment is echoed in 'Positive Steps', which states that 'the sector' should, 'like the public and private sector ... modernise and adjust to ensure maximum effectiveness and efficiency'.[62] A strong emphasis on closer cooperation and integration between statutory bodies and 'civil society' is again reflected in the development of several quasi-statutory 'umbrella groups' intended to distribute government funding, advocate for 'the sector' in government and standardise the activities of social entities, streamlining statutory and 'community' action. An example of this is the Northern Ireland Council for Voluntary Action, formed in 1938. This trend is further emphasised by the assumption that 'civil society' and government are complementary parts of a larger institution. The Northern Ireland Office (NIO) suggests that 'the work of voluntary and community organisations is central to the Government's mission to make this a Giving Age' and places great emphasis on 'enabling [the sector] to contribute effectively to the attainment of Government objectives'.[63] This is echoed by the DSD's 2003 report, which claims that the 'sector' constitutes a 'substantive resource that complements government services and improves policy-making' and stresses the incorporation of all governmental departments within its strategy of integrating 'voluntary and community' organisations into the delivery of services.[64]

Implications and conclusions

The section above outlined the different roles, contributions and emphases assigned to each element (social and bureaucratic action) within the model of the NGO that became integral to governance and peace-building policies in Northern Ireland. This model attempted to provide a medium for the democratic expression of important – and often controversial – needs, values and goals through formalised, integrated structures. Within it, social action is framed as a crucial source of values, attitudes and beliefs, an authentic representation of their variety and diversity, and the most potent vehicle for changing them in ways that can support the reform of the polity. However, in the model of the NGO used by governance, the contributions of social action are channelled through strongly structural, corporatist institutions that are subject to the design and manipulation of 'higher' governing bodies, including local government, national government and the EU.

These institutional elements can exert a powerful influence on the nature of social action and, as the case studies above discussed, the manner in which ideas, values and attitudes are developed and expressed. An emphasis on corporatism suggests that all 'components' of civil society should be relatively homogenous, or at least compatible, structurally, an assumption which is reinforced by the strict application of standards and best practices. When this trend is combined with the design of specific, structure-function relationships, social action becomes highly rationalised. This contrasts sharply with the form of action found in traditional social movements, in which the 'structure' or patterns of action change and adapt *with* changes in the normative direction of the movement, and are an important causal factor in these changes. Moreover, it became widely accepted that the provision of services should be standardised according to externally-developed rules and guidelines. As a result, the everyday activities of NGOs are not concerned with the development or criticism of the way in which services are delivered; this function falls to the representative capacity of the NGO, which, as discussed above, must be exercised in specific, formalised ways. As a result, the contributions of social action are overpowered by the institutional influence of bureaucracy, and the NGOs in question appear to share more in common with statutory bureaucracies than with the social movements from which they were transformed. Governance, then, has not succeeded in transfusing the state with the qualities of social action; rather, the reverse has occurred.

Perhaps more importantly, in targeting social movements into NGOs, these policies have transformed – that is, removed – almost all traditional social movement activity in the region. Whilst NGOs are in many ways beneficial to the polity, they should not become the only form of social action within a polity; this deprives citizens of important venues for participation and the development of political ideas, values and beliefs. Moreover, due to the imbalanced role of bureaucracy in the model of the NGO, these policies have rendered the 'voluntary and community sector' less accessible to citizens by professionalising social action, crowding out or delegitimising organisations that do not meet funding criteria and circumscribing the kinds of activity in which citizens can engage. This, in turn, has reduced opportunities for citizens to engage in traditional forms of collective action, an important source of social change. In a society transitioning from violent conflict and engaged in the development of a new political identity, the loss of opportunities for popular normative engagement may impede the creation of the responsive, inclusive and authentic governing structures promised by the paradigm of governance. Thus, whilst the civil society approach to peacebuilding has helped to consolidate formal, parliamentary peace processes and to create the institutional basis needed to support the formal peace processes, it has also deprived citizens of avenues for expressive action and, ultimately, an important source of social change.

Notes

1 For a summary of the paradigm of governance, see J. Kooiman, *Governing as Governance* (London: Sage, 2003) and J. Pierre (ed.), *Debating Governance: Authority, Steering and Democracy* (Oxford: Oxford University Press, 2000).

2 J. Galtung, *Peace By Peaceful Means* (London: Sage; Oxford, Blackwell, 1996).

3 M. Ward, '"Ulster was Different"? Women, Feminism and Nationalism in the North of Ireland', in Y. Galligan, E. Ward and R. Wilford (eds), *Contesting Politics: Women in Ireland, North and South* (Westview Press, 1999), p. 220.

4 M. McWilliams, 'Struggling for Peace and Justice: Reflections on Women's Activism in Northern Ireland', *Journal of Women's History* 6, 1995, p. 18.

5 *Ibid*, p. 19.

6 J. Hegarty, 'An Analysis of the Development of Derry Women's Aid', PHD Dissertation (University of Ulster, 2006), p. 199.

7 McWilliams, *Struggling*, 19.

8 E. Evason, *Against the Grain: The Contemporary Women's Movement in Northern Ireland* (Attic Press, 1991), p. 6.

9 Evason, *Against*, 27.

10 *Ibid*.

11 Ann Walker, Programme Officer for Ballybeen Women's Centre, Personal Interview, 17 March 2007.

12 R. Taillon (1993) *An Evaluation of the Ballybeen Women's Centre* ([n.p.]: Charities Evaluation Services), p. 21.

13 Karin Eybin, Research Director of the RWDA, Personal Interview, 10 October 2006.

14 Pauline (surname withheld), Director of the Fall's Women's Centre, Personal Interview, 16 March 2007.

15 C. Roulston and M. Whittock, 'We Are These Women ... Self-Conscious Structures for a Women's Centre', in Roulston, Carmel and Celia Davies (eds), *Gender, Democracy and Inclusion in Northern Ireland* (Basingstoke: Palgrave Macmillan, 2000), p. 55.

16 Like the women's movement, this 'movement' consisted of a large and diverse group of people. For the sake of brevity – and due to the much larger number of individuals involved – I shall focus primarily on the activities Republican prisoners. Moreover, although the paramilitary groups and related social movements outside the prison were a crucial factor in the development of this movement, I shall focus exclusively on the actions of male prisoners who became involved in former prisoners' organisations following their release.

17 The 'political' status of internees was revoked and they were referred to, legally and publicly, as normal criminals; during criminalisation, those

prisoners granted a distinct political status saw this status removed and were treated as regular criminals.

18 C. Crawford, *Defenders or Criminals? Loyalist Prisoners and Criminalisation* (Belfast: Blackstaff, 1999), p. 32.

19 K. McEvoy, *Paramilitary Imprisonment in Northern Ireland* (Oxford: Oxford University Press, 2001), p. 33.

20 M. Green, *The Prison Experience – A Loyalist Perspective.* Epic Research Document No. 1 (EPIC, 1998), p. 22.

21 P. O'Malley, *Biting at the Grave: The Hunger Strike and the Politics of Despair* (Belfast: Blackstaff, 1990), p. 73.

22 O'Malley, *Biting*, pp. 95–7.

23 McKeown, *Out*, p. xii.

24 *Ibid*, p. 7.

25 *Ibid*, pp. 180–93.

26 P. Shirlow, B. Graham, K. McEvoy, F. OhAdhmaill and D. Purvis, *Politically Motivated Former Prisoner Groups: Community Activism and Conflict Transformation* (Belfast: Northern Ireland Community Relations Council, 2005), p. 37.

27 J. Crothers, *Reintegration – The Problems and the Issues* (Belfast: Epic, 1998), p. 38.

28 Coiste Na na-Iarchimi, *When the Gates Open* (Coiste n-Iarchimi, 1999).

29 *Ibid*, p. 13.

30 R. Dugdale, *Building the Future in Ireland* (Belfast: Coiste na n-Iarchimi, 2001), p. 27.

31 Mike Ritchie, Director of Coiste, Personal Interview, 13 June, 2007.

32 These groups are representative of the Irish National Liberation Army (INLA)/ Irish Republican Socialist Party, Official IRA (OIRA) and non-aligned Republican prisoners respectively, as opposed to the 'mainstream' (Provisional IRA) Coiste ni-Iarchimi.

33 F. Halligan, Manager of Teach na Failte (representing the official IRA), Personal Interview, 23 March, 2007; T. McKearney, Manager of Ex-Pac, Personal Interview, 26th June, 2007.

34 See G.A. Almond and S. Verba, *The Civic Culture: Political Attitudes and Democracy in Five Nations* (London: SAGE Publications, 1989). See R.D. Putnam, *Bowling Alone: The Collapse and Revival of American Community* (New York: Simon and Schuster, 2000); N. Rosenblum, *Membership and Morals: The Personal Uses of Pluralism in America* (Princeton, N.J.: Princeton University Press); J.L. Cohen and A. Arato, *Civil Society and Political Theory* (Cambridge, MA: The MIT Press, 1994), p. 142. See Mark Warren, *Democracy and Association* (Princeton, N.J.: Princeton University Press, 2001).

35 F. Cochrane, 'Two Cheers for the NGOs: Building Peace from Below in Northern Ireland', in M. Cox, A. Guelke and F. Stephen, eds, *A Farewell To Arms? Beyond the Good Friday Agreement* (Manchester: Manchester University Press, 2006), pp. 254, 257; Belloni, Roberto, 'Civil Society and Peacebuilding in Bosnia and Herzegovina', *Journal of Peace Research* (38) 2001, p. 154; M. Hayes, *Community Relations: A Historical Perspective* (Belfast: SACHR, 1987), p. 13; J. Lampen, *Building the Peace: Good Practice in Community Relations Work in Northern Ireland* (Belfast: Community Relations Council, 1995), p. 13.

36 European Union, *EU Programme for Peace and Reconciliation in Northern Ireland and the Border Region of Ireland, 2000–2004 – Operational Programme* (Brussels: European Union, 2000), pp. 22, 91, 92, 108, 123, 31, 32.

37 Dixon, *Democratization*, p. 3.

38 European Union, *European Governance: A White Paper* (Brussels: European Union, 2001), p. 15.

39 Department of Social Development (Northern Ireland), *Positive Steps: The Government's Response to Investing Together: Report of the Task Force on Resourcing the Voluntary and Community Sector* (Belfast: Department of Social Development, 2004), p. 4.

40 Northern Ireland Office, *Building Real Partnership: Compact Between Government and the Voluntary and Community Sector in Northern Ireland* (Belfast: NIO, 1998), pp. 11, 15.

41 Community Development Review Group, *Community Development in Northern Ireland: A Perspective for the Nineties* (Belfast: Community Development Review Group, 1991), p. 15; Central Community Relations Unit [n.d.]. *Community Relations in Northern Ireland* (Belfast: Central Community Relations Unit), p. 2.

42 Hayes, *Community Relations*, p. 13.

43 Pauline, *Interview*.

44 H. Griffiths (1975), 'Paramilitary Groups and Other Community Action Groups in Northern Ireland Today', *International Review of Community Development*, 33, pp. 193–5.

45 Wolfenden Committee, *The Future of Voluntary Organisations: Report of the Voluntary Organisations* (London: Croom Helm, 1978), p. 29.

46 Department of Social Development, *Positive*, p. 18.

47 EU, *Operational*, p. 1.

48 EU, *White Paper*, p. 16.

49 Almond and Verba, *Civic Culture*, pp. 148–9. See Warren, *Democracy*.

50 Cohen and Arato, *Civil Society*, p. vii.

51 M. Hayes, *Community Relations and the role of the Community Relations Commission in Northern Ireland* (Belfast: Runnymede Trust, 1972), p. 13.

52 EU, *White Paper*, p. 15.

53 Home Office, *Efficiency Scrutiny of Government Funding of the Voluntary Sector: Profiting from Partnership* (London: Home Office, 1990), p. 6.

54 *Ibid*, p. 19.

55 *Ibid*.

56 Department of Social Development, *Positive*, p. 15.

57 Cohen and Arato, *Civil Society*.

58 Warren , *Democracy*, p. 13.

59 Wolfenden Committee, *Future*, p. 28.

60 D. Morrow and D. Wilson, 'Voluntary Action Toward Sustainable Peace', in A. Williamson *Beyond Violence: The Role of Voluntary and Community Action in Building a Sustainable Peace in Northern Ireland* (Belfast: Community Relations Council and Centre for Voluntary Action Studies, University of Ulster), p. 78.

61 Department of Social Development (Northern Ireland). *Partners for Change: Government's Strategy for Support of the Voluntary and Community Sector, 2001–2004* (Belfast: Department of Social Development: 2003), p. 21.

62   Department of Social Development, *Positive*, p. 13.
63   North Ireland Office, *Building Real Partnership*, p. 12.
64   Department of Social Development, *Partners*, p. 3.

14
NGOs and Democratisation: Assessing Variation in the Internal Democratic Practices of NGOs[1]

Darren Halpin

Introduction

In recent times the study of 'groups' has become a much more fashionable form of scholarship. This is particularly evident if one broadens the terminology from simply interest groups to encompass civil society organisations (CSOs), social movement organisations (SMOs) or non-governmental organisations (NGOs). The study of 'groups' is again prominent amongst social scientific scholarship.

Much of the renewed attention given to 'groups' centres on their role in addressing democratic deficits in advanced western democracies, such as the United Kingdom. The problem of 'democratic deficit' is diagnosed in most western democracies; typically on the back of declining voter turnout, falling party memberships and indicators that citizens have lost trust in politicians.[2] In the face of failing political parties some see groups as potentially able to forge new linkages between citizen and state.[3] Not only are parties hollowed out, but electoral systems point to citizen disillusionment and disengagement evidenced by poor turnout in elections and a lack of trust in formal political institutions.[4] Important groups and constituencies lack presence and/or voice in party and parliamentary forums, which make them less than satisfactory as mechanisms for formulating inclusive public policy programmes. In the face of such challenges some look to groups, or the group system, to provide a link between the governed and those doing the governing: they look to groups as potential *agents of democracy*.

Recasting groups as democratic agents leaves group practice open to scrutiny. And critics have been quick to point out the democratic limits of groups. Perhaps the most strident criticism of the democratic credentials of groups has been their lack of internal democracies. It has been argued that the asserted democratic dividends from engaging with groups relies on groups being voluntary, internally democratic, accountable to members and providing arenas for member deliberation.[5] Studies of groups at global,[6] European[7] and domestic levels[8] have consistently observed poorly functioning internal democratic practices among groups. Empirical analyses find members largely disengaged from group life and separate from professionalised secretariats. Accounts of groups as 'campaign businesses'[9] encourages a view of groups as largely elite enterprises. Scholars now talk of the 'hollowing out' of group internal democracies, arguing that 'traditional' group life – generous in participative opportunities and democratic engagement – is giving way to 'mail order' styles of group life.[10]

In the UK context, this general narrative is perhaps best captured in a series of contributions by Wyn Grant. He states unequivocally that, among groups, 'internal democracy is often entirely lacking or heavily constrained'.[11] Further, he says, 'Most pressure groups are not very democratic internally. Where leaderships are elected, it is often through processes that lack transparency ... While there may be elaborate networks of committees to discuss policy, direct consultation of the membership may be limited to an occasional questionnaire or internet poll'.[12] For Grant, these findings go directly to the question of group legitimacy; 'if groups fail to offer at least an opportunity to participate in decision-making, their representative legitimacy may increasingly be called into question'.[13] This chapter asks whether such a conclusion is warranted in all cases of group practice (and if not all then which ones?).

Grant is also concerned about what could be called the 'authenticity' of some groups. The group system, he argues, is biased towards those that are presently well represented by 'well resourced and politically sophisticated organisations'.[14] While this 'political exclusion' is in practice addressed by others speaking for excluded groups, he argues, 'however well-intentioned they are, they are not the authentic voice of the excluded groups themselves'.[15] Internally democratic or not, such groups do not speak in the 'voice' of the constituency advocated for. Grant is questioning the legitimacy of self-appointed advocates speaking for others.

Grant argues that there is the need for a 'wider debate about the democratic legitimacy of pressure groups', in order to create 'a greater transparency about both the representativeness of groups and their relations with government'.[16] An outcome of such a debate could include 'a code of conduct requiring non-governmental organisations to meet certain standards before they are recognised. The standards might include mechanisms for reporting membership; transparency about the source of funds and how they are used; proper procedures for the election of group leadership; and regular and systematic arrangements for consulting membership about policy'.[17] He concludes elsewhere 'at some point there will have to be some consideration of the accountability of non-governmental organisations to their own members. Organisations that seek to represent should be able to demonstrate whom they represent and how they represent them'.[18] This call resonates with the conclusions of European scholars.[19] It also reflects the sentiment of debates within supranational governmental bodies about the need to regulate group access.

This chapter does not dispute the finding that groups often lack internal democratic processes. As will become evident, groups vary remarkably with respect to their democratic practices. The more controversial issue, and that pursued here, is how to interpret the finding. What metrics should be used to adjudicate over the democratic potential and practice of groups? The implicit orthodox test applied to groups is a representation test: accountability and authorisation between a group's leaders and members. Evidence is usually of an organisational nature; specifically, whether active internal democracies exist and whether individuals are affiliated in such a way as to allow them control over group agendas (as members rather than supporters). As exemplified by Grant above, the absence of such organisational practices is interpreted as democratic deficiency. But is this approach relevant to all groups, and, if not, to which groups should it apply? Moreover, what other forms of legitimacy are relevant? What are we to do in the case that groups are unable (rather than unwilling) to operationalise forms of accountability and authorisation that are demanded under the representation test? Should they be excluded as is implied?

An additional area of group critique is around 'authenticity'. The question is not whether they are internally democratic but 'are groups advocating for a constituency affiliating individuals from the very same constituency they seek to help?' What would be the consequences of applying the 'authenticity' test pursued by Wyn Grant? How would one resolve conflict between concerns over the exclusion of social groups from the political system and the desire expressed by Grant for authentic advocates? Would authenticity come at the cost of political exclusion of marginalised constituencies? Is there some middle road?

These questions do not often emerge when examining the 'orthodox' fodder of traditional group studies – trade associations, unions and employer groups. Here the usual critique is of a membership simply remote and disinterested from a professionalising leadership. However, the salience of such questions becomes apparent when one talks about the environment, ethnicities, the disabled, mentally ill and the homeless – constituencies for which internal structures that would satisfy the 'representation' and 'authenticity' tests are tricky to construct. It is precisely groups advocating for these constituencies that are typically studied in NGO studies, and in the Database of Archives of UK Non-Governmental Organisations (DANGO) project.[20] As such, these types of 'thorny', but interesting, questions are perhaps more crucial for scholars identifying with NGO studies.

The chapter makes several propositions. Firstly, borrowing from O'Neill's discussion of representing nature and future generations, it is argued that advocacy by groups for some constituencies simply cannot be pursued through representation style behaviour; it can only be pursued through a form of solidarity. Secondly, in turn, it is argued that solidarity style advocacy by groups does not require (indeed does not benefit from) internal democratic structures. That is, some group advocacy can only be founded on other – non-democratic – forms of legitimacy; that these same groups have affiliates does not imply the need to engage democratically with them ('authenticity' is not possible). Thirdly, by deploying the representation-solidarity categories as a type of continuum, the article demonstrates how it is possible to calibrate democratic expectations of groups and contrast them against group practices (and changes thereof).

Labels and definitions: What is a 'group'? What is an NGO?

A necessary precursor to any examination of the democratic potential and practice of 'groups' is to settle upon a suitable definition. That is, when we say 'group' to what type of political organisation do we refer? The difficulty is that many political organisations conduct-ing the same activities are attributed different labels. The orthodox political science term 'interest group' has to some extent become eclipsed by social movement organisation or non-governmental organisation. To SMO and NGO, add civil society organisations, voluntary sector organisations (VSOs)[21] and third sector organisations.[22] Claims for democratic agency are often made for 'groups' under these labels.

The labelling of groups using interchangeable terms makes it difficult to be certain that we are talking about and analysing the same thing. In the NGO area, it is conceded that 'There is no generally accepted definition of an NGO and the term carries different connotations in different circumstances.'[23] Martens makes a similar observation, explaining that 'it makes comparisons of single NGO studies difficult, if not impossible'.[24] A similar degree of dissatisfaction over the lack of terminological specificity is evident in other sub-literatures.[25] In sorting out labelling, there is a temptation to defend the pre-eminence of one label, such as interest group over NGO or SMO.[26] But the overriding issue is commensurability: do they have equivalence?

Part of the solution with respect to terminology is to decide what type of democratic 'goods' we are most interested in. Rossteutscher[27] identified the following varied assertions as to what democratic 'goods' groups are said to provide, and the contingent relationship with theoretical position:

> identity, cohesion and a sense of belonging (communitarianism); trust and sociability (social capital); mediation and social embeddedness (civil society); efficiency and effectiveness of governance (associative governance)

It is unlikely that all 'groups' would be able to deliver all of the above. Thus the types of democratic contribution we seek to assess will necessarily guide which set of 'groups' we would logically want to include in our analysis. For example, if by democratic contribution one refers solely to generating trust in a community or fostering social skills (political socialisation broadly conceived), then any group that facilitates face-to-face contact between individuals is likely to be of relevance. If however, as is the task of this chapter, we are concerned more specifically with the capacity for groups to 'link' citizens with public policy and formal political processes – by providing political advocacy – then groups ought to have some explicit political focus and collectively engage or organise individuals.[28] The emphasis on organisations whose primary purpose is political advocacy strips out recreational, social and sporting groups whose primary function is other than political. In addition, the insistence that a group organises or affiliates individuals, and, as such, has to contend with collective action problems, removes non-collective actors such as lobbyists and governmental agencies.[29] This approach is defensible as these omitted organisations are by definition incapable of the sustained linkage of individuals with political processes: they are by definition not democratic agents.

While there is no authoritative labelling approach, this direction fortunately finds some consistency across extant literatures. Willets[30] identifies some core features of an NGO. He says 'Clearly an NGO must be independent from the direct control of any government. In addition, there are three other generally accepted characteristics that exclude particular types of bodies from consideration. An NGO will not be constituted as a political party; it will be non-profit-making and it will not be a criminal group, in particular it will be non-violent'. On this basis, he says, 'interest group, pressure group, lobby and private voluntary organisation – could *all* be applied legitimately to most NGOs'.[31] This reflects definitions of interest groups as groups that voluntarily mobilise individuals,[32] are formal organisations, are non-profit and have a primary focus on political advocacy.[33] Influential scholars assign a similar set of features to non-profit organisations, CSOs and SMOs.[34]

Analysis here focusses on 'groups' that are explicitly dedicated political actors and that facilitate some form of collective action (as the introduction to this volume defines them, 'socio-political actors'). There appears to be the basis for some consensus across literatures for a focus on this type of group. But while 'we' may accept the interchangeable nature of terms like NGO, interest group, and CSO, on the basis that they all describe a particular type of 'group' or political organisation, there is no way to stop deployment of labels for different types of political endeavour. But the use of explicit (and non-normative) definitions that inform empirical data collection – much as DANGO is doing – will serve as an incentive for consistency.

Legitimating NGO advocacy: What is the democratic potential of groups?

The 'representative' narrative of NGOs would approve of those organisations practising 'membership' along with robust internal democracies. This chapter questions the logic of such a view. It is argued that expectations of 'democratic' behaviour ought to be calibrated by the *type of advocacy* possible by different groups (on a continuum from representation to solidarity); itself shaped by the types of constituencies groups advocate for.

Are NGOs about representation or solidarity?

To see why the 'representation' narrative alone is insufficient as a heuristic device for analysing group life, it is necessary to step back and consider what representation implies more generally. According to Hannah Pitkin, representation is about 'acting in the interest of the represented, in a manner responsive to them'.[35] Claims to representativeness are underpinned and legitimated by reference to indicators of responsiveness. Yet, Pitkin accepts that 'what is being represented' will shape what type of responsiveness is required (or possible). She distinguishes between 'interests' that are 'unattached' and those that are 'attached'. She says unattached interests are 'interests to which no particular persons were so specially related that they could claim to be privileged to define the interests. But when people are being represented, their claim to have a say in their interest becomes relevant'.[36] The point here is that if interests are unattached then responsiveness becomes difficult to achieve; to whom precisely – to what constituency or client group – is the representative to be responsive to?

In helping to answer this question, the work of O'Neill is useful.[37] He approaches the issue of representation through a discussion of types of constituencies. He argues that some constituencies are simply unable to utilise democratic responsiveness as a way to legitimate representatives. Human constituencies can, for the most part, according to O'Neill, speak in their own voice and be present. As such, they can authorise representatives to speak for them or at least keep unauthorised representatives accountable (by dissenting from their advocacy). These constituencies require the style of representation Pitkin called for in the case of attached interests. This is not the case for other constituencies. O'Neill says that the difficulty in representing nature, future generations and non-humans is that 'two central features of legitimisation – authorisation and presence – are absent. Indeed for nonhumans and future generations there is no possibility of those conditions being met. Neither nonhumans nor future generations can be directly present in decision-making. Clearly, representation can neither be authorised by nonhumans or future generations nor can it be rendered accountable to them'.[38] For O'Neill this denies those advocating for such constituencies usual representative forms of legitimation. In the absence of the usual forms of legitimation available to those advocating for human constituencies, he argues that 'the remaining source of legitimacy to claim to speak is epistemic. Those who claim to speak on behalf of those without voice do so by an appeal to their having knowledge of objective interests of those groups [read constituencies], often combined with special care for them.'[39]

The practical impossibility of advocates for non-humans and future generations actually engaging directly with their constituencies removes any potential for the responsiveness Pitkin identified as central to acts of political representation (and any possibility for producing 'authenticity'). A narrative for legitimating advocacy, separate from representation, is surely needed. O'Neill concludes that we can distinguish between '"acting in solidarity with" and "acting as a representative of"'.[40] For O'Neill, those advocating for such constituencies engage, by necessity, in solidarity and not representation.

Calibrating democratic potential of NGOs?

The above discussion provides the basis for two ideal types of group legitimation, each embodying different expectations about the relationship between the constituency being advocated for and the affiliates of the group: a solidarity and a representation narrative. These ideal types provide a way to calibrate the democratic potential of NGO types, from which we can usefully analyse practice – locating under or over achievement.

Solidarity

NGOs that advocate for constituencies of non-humans and future generations – those constituencies that lack entirely the potential for representation – embody a promise to pursue solidarity. NGOs that advocate for these types of constituencies cannot physically affiliate those constituencies. As O'Neill put it, their beneficiary group lacks the basic capacity to be present, and is not able to be affiliated to the group or to exercise accountability and authorisation; the central components of responsiveness and therefore representation. These NGOs, and those who affiliate with them, are acting 'in solidarity with' constituencies rather than being representatives of the constituency. Thus, even if leaders may consult affiliates, the views of the affiliates to such NGOs are not crucial to legitimating the advocacy of such groups.[41] To be clear, the argument is that solidarity by definition groups – those advocating for constituencies that cannot be made present – do not enhance their democratic legitimacy by virtue of engaging with affiliates. Such solidarity groups may in fact develop internal democracies. But it is not in order to use representation to democratically legitimate advocacy.[42]

Such NGOs legitimate advocacy in other ways: they make epistemic claims. A group pursuing the interests of nature may use, for example, scientific analysis of an ecosystem to legitimate its claims that an increase in intensive land-use would be harmful to the systems' integrity. The views of the groups' affiliates are not relevant in terms of legitimacy. For instance, they are unlikely to take a survey of individuals affiliated to them to enhance their influence, nor are policy-makers likely to seek any reassurance that the position advocated by the group accords with the will of affiliated individuals. As Van Rooy[43] argues they are likely to invoke other 'legitimacy rules' such as 'victimhood', 'expertise', 'experiential evidence', or 'moral authority'. An individual joining this type of NGO is showing solidarity with a separate constituency. In short, groups with potential only to pursue solidarity need only engage in supportership as an affiliation style; with its implications for very shallow internal democratic practices and limited responsiveness to affiliates.[44]

Representation

NGOs that advocate for a constituency that can be present and affiliate individuals from that same constituency to the NGO embody a *promise* to pursue representation. These NGOs have the *potential* for representation as they can by definition affiliate those whom they advocate for. Their beneficiaries and affiliates can be the same people, and these individuals are able to be involved in internal democratic processes. Individuals can form part of a sectional or categoric[45] constituency by virtue of their formal economic role (doctor, lawyer, mechanic, etc) or social/cultural identity (religion, ethnicity, etc.) or experience (e.g. prisoner, asylum seeker, unemployed person). It is the specific economic function/identity/experience that individuals fulfil that forms the criteria for their inclusion in any constituency. In Pitkin's terms, these NGOs advocate for the interests *attached* to human constituencies.

This has implications for the expectations of NGOs advocating for such constituencies. Individuals may decide not to join 'their' NGO(s), yet they are still involuntarily part of the constituency from which the NGO(s) must draw members/supporters and claim to represent. Individuals cannot easily 'exit' from the constituency, as they are not often given an opportunity by the political system to 'voluntarily' join the constituency (unless of course the political system comes over time to recognise a new sub-constituency, e.g. single mothers vs. mothers). Therefore, such groups have an exclusive set of individuals from which to recruit, and cannot easily refuse affiliation from those individuals that fit the definition. These interest groups represent constituencies that are made up of individuals who can speak in their own voice.

Claims to speak for sectional or categoric constituencies are, therefore, legitimated by the accountability of leaders to their constituency and the authorisation of leaders by their constituency. There is an expectation, or more accurately a presumption, therefore, that these groups affiliate with the individuals they organise in a manner that resembles 'membership': membership style affiliations and internal democratic procedures would enhance the legitimacy of their advocacy activities.

By way of a summary, Table 14.1 elaborates the generalised types of advocacy possible by interest groups; contingent largely on the type of constituency being advocated for. The calibration of *expectations* for groups in relation to linkage and internal democracy is, as has been argued, contingent on whether they implicitly promise to pursue solidarity of representation. These are summarised in Table 14.2. This set of ideal types allows one to identify participatory potential against which practice can be contrasted. As will become evident, such a process raises interesting questions about why NGOs develop the democratic practices they do, and challenges the idea that NGOs are necessarily becoming less internally democratic.

Making sense of variation in UK NGO democratic practice

This final section reviews the internal democratic practices of NGOs in the UK. Cases are drawn from within the literature and from the

Table 14.1   What generalised type of advocacy is promised/possible?

	Solidarity	Representation
Sorting questions ...	←――――――――――――――→	
Constituency being advocated for?	Non-Human/ Future Generations	Human
Is an overlap between (i) those 'affiliated' with the NGO, and (ii) the 'constituency' being advocated for <u>possible</u>?	No	Yes
<u>Can</u> the constituency potentially speak in its own voice?	No chance of speaking in own voice	Can speak in own voice

Source: Adapted from D. Halpin, 'The participatory and democratic potential and practice of interest groups: Between solidarity and representation', *Public Administration*, 84(4) (2006), pp. 919–40.

Table 14.2 Summary of expectations for group democratic practices

	Solidarity	Representation
Implications ...	⬅———————————➡	
Implied type of 'linkage'	Supportership	Membership
Implied extent of internal democracy	• Because those affiliated with the NGO are not the beneficiary group they advocate for they need not be consulted in determining positions.	• Because those affiliated with the NGO are the beneficiary group they need to be consulted with.
Implied source of legitimacy	• Epistemic source: Question of expertise or strength of solidarity (experiences) or empathy with beneficiary group	• Question of representatives being responsive to the epresented; rare processes in place for authorisation and accountability?

Source: Adapted from Halpin, 'Participatory and democratic potential and practice of interest groups: Between solidarity and representation', *Public Administration,* 84(4) (2006), pp. 919–40.

authors own empirical studies. Empirical evidence of practice is contrasted with potential (as calibrated by the analytical categories above), capturing the diverse way in which these theoretical labels find their way into practice.

At the two ends of the continuum, we find NGOs that largely approximate in practice their potential for representation or solidarity. As is evident below, group life does not simply 'fit' into either of these conceptual 'ideal type' boxes; however, these concepts provide one way to gain purchase on the promises and potential of NGOs with affiliates with respect to democratising and participatory potential.

Where promise equals practice ...

In many cases, NGO potential for representation or solidarity matches up with practice.

Organisations, like the UK National Union of Students, are representation by definition type NGOs. Responsiveness is possible between representatives and the represented, and structures are in place to make that possible. The literature is replete with cases where such practices, while formally available, are used infrequently. However, following Pitkin's point above, the key is that internal democratic practices are there and responsiveness is possible. If nothing else, these groups are (to borrow Hirschman's terms) vulnerable to 'exit with voice'; there is an inbuilt imperative for leaders to ensure some degree of fit between the interests they pursue and those of their membership lest they risk losing the trust and status ascribed to them by government (and other actors).

The other end of the representation-solidarity continuum is an environment NGO like the World Wide Fund for Nature (WWF) Scotland. It is a solidarity by definition type NGO. Its claim is that it takes action for a living planet. It advocates for nature: it promises solidarity and delivers it. It offers a very open type of affiliation; recruiting through direct mail and internet strategies, seeking up to £10 per month. While the language of 'member' is used, the internal participatory and democratic opportunities are minimal. It is more concerned with the sentiment and sympathy of the groups' 'attentive public'. The route of public opinion and science – not the predispositions of a majority of WWF affiliates – is used to drive home advocacy.

Groups such as the WWF Scotland match a potential for solidarity with equivalent practice.[46] The literature consistently finds that groups advocating for constituencies such as non-humans and the environment operate bereft of opportunities for political engagement by supporters and seek to maximise supporter revenues.[47] This chapter accepts the empirical veracity of this image. But is this a 'natural' mode to organise advocacy for such constituencies or is it an unwelcome development eroding an otherwise more democratic and participatory alternative? This chapter errs towards the former. How could it reproduce the 'authentic representation' of the environment?

Representation by potential, solidarity by practice: an authenticity deficit?

Spotting groups that unambiguously fit the two ends of the continuum – where theoretical potential equates largely with practice – is not difficult. However, apart from environmental NGOs, the usual groups considered by NGO scholars are those organising or speaking for disadvantaged, underprivileged or otherwise politically marginalised human constituencies in society.[48] For most, they are representational groups by definition: they seek to advocate for human constituencies which have the potential for voice and presence. Yet, the evidence is that many struggle to replicate accountability and authorisation structures necessary to fulfil the potential for representation.

Some NGOs find participatory promises very hard to fulfil largely because the constituencies they seek to advocate for – their beneficiary group – are difficult to mobilise. This is most obvious in the case of advocates for constituencies that are politically or economically marginalised (e.g. unemployed, prisoners, asylum seekers). The example of Amnesty International (AI) – a NGO formed in the UK, examined by Jordan and Maloney, is just such a case. They cite Ennals, who observed that the focus of AI's work was defined by the answer to the question 'what will be the most beneficial to the interests of the prisoners involved?'.[49] AI is not pretending to represent its members but to act in the interests – to act for – prisoners held unjustly. They go on to cite Ennal's description of AI as run by a secretariat somewhat remote from the concerns of supporters; AGMs and annual elections exist, but these are under attended and largely divorced from strategic decision-making. Leaders decide which 'prisoners' are to be championed and how to proceed in protecting their interests. But the absence of internal democracy seems appropriate; after all it is the input of prisoners that would enhance democratic legitimacy. The argument for AI to be democratically accountable to affiliates is weak, yet to criticise it for not engaging better with the political prisoners they advocate for is clearly implausible. Scholars and observers may be able to easily spot the potential for representation, but the challenges for group leaders to put potential into practice are often immense.

To the example of AI, one could add NGOs working for the homeless where locating and mobilising such constituencies is itself difficult.[50] Work on patient/user groups has highlighted the difficulties in organising some constituencies along representational lines.[51] Some note the difficulty in, for example, engaging the terminally ill in NGO activities.[52] Variation in democratic practice among NGOs advocating for such constituencies attests to the possibility, but one should not overlook the barriers.

From solidarity to representation: addressing the 'authenticity' critique?

The case of The Royal National Institute of the Blind (RNIB) is revealing. It shows that some NGOs can shift; redefining both potential and practice. There is recognition that the absence of practises necessary to claim representation risks criticism around NGO 'authenticity'. Groups that at one time practiced solidarity may shift to a representation style of operation: over time they have redefined their practice to fulfil potential.

RNIB is a UK NGO that pursues the interests of the blind. Since 2002 it has affiliated the blind into membership; in part a reaction to the type of criticism about authenticity cited above. It offers 'full membership' to those who are blind and partially sighted their families and carers. Associate membership is offered to 'well-wishers' and to 'related professionals'. Its structure is a recent development. Its website explains:

> We began recruiting to our new mass membership in 2002 ... because: We want to give a say to a greater proportion of blind and partially sighted people on how we are run and how we deliver our services. Many blind and partially sighted people have had no input into our decision making until now. Membership will give people that, by involving them in consultations and giving them a chance to vote and stand for election.

There is also an apparent appreciation of the increased status that membership brings. It continues, 'a large membership will give RNIB a stronger voice when we negotiate on behalf of blind and partially sighted people with Government and other organisations'.

The RNIB has turned away from a solidarity style in order to fulfil its implicit promise as a representative group (a contrast to the turn towards solidarity style practices by many business NGOs).[53] Scholarship among 'patient' NGOs in the UK suggests this may be part a broader trend involving the democratic modernisation of groups that were initially formed (often in late 1800s or early 1900s) in a 'philanthropic tradition of providing services for clients'.[54] This type of change of group *modus operandi* is what the authenticity critics would no doubt like to see across the board. But clearly, as the Amnesty International example above attests, some such transformations are easier to make than others.

Defending the authenticity deficit?

In short, for many NGOs it is very difficult, for whatever reason, to effectively establish a system of responsiveness with the constituencies they advocate for. Potential exists but serious (perhaps insurmountable) impediments thwart internal democratic practice. This leaves them open to criticism that they are undemocratic and unrepresentative; that they lack authenticity. The concern with 'authenticity' emerges from the observation that some marginalised constituencies do not often exercise presence or speak in their own voice; but, crucially, they have the potential for both. This chapter does not dispute the principle as set out by Pitkin that attached interests should be represented by those the interests are attached to: the basis of Grant's 'authenticity' position. But practice poses some thorny questions for scholars.

In practice, there are limits to what is popularly accepted in relation to representing attached interests as though they were unattached. Anne Phillips notes that the importance of this requirement for presence surely fluctuates between constituencies: 'some experiences are more detachable than others'.[55] For example, she says that it appears less problematic to have an agricultural expert represent the interests of farmers than it would for a male expert on gender to represent women given that the experiences of the former constituency are more 'objectively' accessible than those of the latter. This type of pragmatic principle – 'objective accessibility' – points to possible ways of policing the boundaries of authenticity. These types of considerations point to how NGOs who have representative potential, yet practice solidarity can defend their practise.

It is precisely at this point that ambitions for political inclusion rub up against arguments for representative democratic legitimacy. For many, groups are valuable precisely because they compensate for the flaws in majoritarian democracy – the views of the electorally unpalatable and marginalised are unheard or unrepresented. But, the difficulty is that many NGOs that would play such a role are themselves not democratic practitioners, which prompts some to argue that they are less legitimate political actors. If a hard line were taken, then the advocates for marginalised constituencies would be excluded. Would that assist the legitimacy of the UK political system as a whole?

As O'Neill has noted, the basis for 'any particular individual or group making public claims to speak on behalf of the interests of others' rely on 'authorisation, accountability or shared identity [presence]'.[56] But, there are many and varied mechanisms to legitimate advocacy outside of internal democratic arrangements. And these are being explored as a way to defend criticism of authenticity deficits in NGO practice. For instance, some argue that the public voices of NGOs constitute a deliberative form of democracy.[57] They develop a concept of external accountability which argues that supporters keep advocates to account by monitoring NGO behaviour, and by withdrawing support when dissatisfied. They argue this is a more pertinent form of accountability than internal democratic processes. Others maintain that groups which lack representativeness and authenticity – for whatever reason – should be free to voice claims, but should be kept away from policy-making on the basis that they do not bring representative democratic legitimacy with them.[58] This debate is important for NGO scholars – and NGOs themselves – to engage in.

Conclusion

This chapter has suggested that internal democracies – even if they could be established – are less important for legitimating the advocacy of NGOs pursuing the interests of non-humans and future generations than NGOs pursuing the interests of humans. These NGOs can only pursue solidarity with constituencies – not their representation. Some NGOs – those that pursue the interests of constituencies without the prospects of 'presence' or 'voice' – cannot bring into membership those they advocate for. Groups for the environment, and future generations, cannot be representative. Their affiliates' views are not helpful in legitimating the advocacy in representative democratic terms (although such internal democratic arrangements may exist and serve other valuable functions). From this perspective, excluding or downgrading the advocacy of *some* NGOs on the basis of absent or poor internal democracies would be problematic. It would lead to the many NGOs advocating for future generations and the environment being excluded from formal politics.

The chapter accepts the theoretical argument around 'authenticity': that attached interests ought to be represented by those to which the interests are attached. Yet, it constrains this argument only to groups capable of representation. But, NGOs that could at least in principle draw their constituency into membership, but do not, would be excluded under the more narrow definition of representation defined above. This would put projects of political exclusion at cross purposes with projects for democratisation. Many politically marginalised and unpopular social groups lack the resources to effectively mobilise collectively. While there is rightly some caution over 'benevolent advocacy' on their behalf, insisting on internal democracy and participation as a pre-requisite to access would simply remove a large number of NGOs from formalised political forums. Balancing the political inclusion and voice for the marginalised and less powerful in society with concerns over 'authenticity' seems a core debate for NGO scholars.

The approach developed herein sets out variations in democratic potential. However, significant puzzles remain. While potential is easy enough to set out, many groups do not find a neat fit between practice and potential. This raises the question 'why?'. This chapter points to factors that make the representational model hard to emulate. However, democratic practices vary even within NGOs advocating for the very same constituency. And, as the RNIB example illustrates, NGOs are able to change practices. Whereas generalised narratives of NGOs 'hollowing out' make attractive arguments, the reality of group practice is far more varied. It is argued here that there is evidence of changing democratic practice – both in terms of 'hollowing out' *and* in terms of 're-democratising'. This means that individual groups may vary their democratic practices over time in either direction; a finding which strongly suggests a need for group case study analysis which is both historical and organisational in focus. This observation should give further impetus to the work of DANGO. Emphasis is perhaps more productively put on NGOs as changing over time as opposed to assumptions of stasis; and on emphasising group agency in addition to the 'shaping' role attributed to environmental changes implied in 'hollowing out' narratives.

Notes

1 This chapter constitutes part of a broader research agenda on group organisational evolution (funded by a Leverhulme Trust Research Fellowship 2007–8). Parts of this chapter have appeared as D. Halpin, 'The Participatory and Democratic Potential and Practice of Interest Groups: Between Solidarity and Representation', *Public Administration*, 84(4) (2006), 919–40. An expanded version will appear as part of D. Halpin, *Interest Groups and Democratisation: Promises and Practice* (Manchester: Manchester University Press, 2009).

2 R.J. Dalton, *Democratic Challenges Democratic Choices* (Oxford: Oxford University Press, 2004); C. Pattie, P. Seyd. and P. Whiteley *Citizenship in Britain: Values, Participation and Democracy* (Cambridge: Cambridge University Press, 2004).

3 See K. Lawson and P. Merkl, 'Alternative Organizations: Environmental, Supplementary, Communitarian and Antiauthoritarian', in Lawson, K. and Merkl, P.H. (eds) *When Parties Fail: Emerging Alternative Organizations* (Princeton: Princeton University Press, 1988), pp. 3–12; R.J. Dalton and M.P. Wattenberg (2000), 'Partisan Change and the Democratic Process', in R.J. Dalton and M.P. Wattenberg (eds), *Parties without Partisans* (Oxford: Oxford University Press, 2000), pp. 261–84; B. Cain, R. Dalton and S. Scarrow (eds) *Democracy Transformed?: Expanding Political Opportunities in Advanced Industrial Democracies* (Oxford: Oxford University Press, 2003).

4 Dalton and Wattenberg, *Parties without Partisans*, pp. 261–84.

5 See discussion by P. Perczynski (2000), 'Active Citizenship and Associative Democracy', in Saward (ed) *Democratic Innovation: Deliberation, Representation, and Association* (London: Routledge, 2000).

6   J.A. Scholte, 'Global Civil Society', in Woods, N. (ed), *The Political Economy of Globalization* (New York: St Martins, 2000), pp. 173–201.

7   A. Warleigh, '"Europeanizing" Civil Society: NGOs as Agents of Political Socialization', *Journal of Common Market Studies*, 39(4) (2001), pp. 19–639.

8   M. Lyons, *Third Sector: The Contribution of Nonprofit and Co-operative Enterprise in Australia* (St Leonards: Allen and Unwin, 2001).

9   G. Jordan and W. Maloney, *The Protest Business* (Manchester: Manchester University Press, 1997).

10   R. Putnam, *Bowling Alone* (New York: Simon and Schuster, 2000); T. Skocpol 'Advocates without Members: The Recent Transformation of American Civic Life', in T. Skocpol and M.P. Fiorina (eds) *Civic Engagement in American democracy* (Washington: Brookings Institution, 1999), pp. 461–509.

11   W. Grant, 'Pressure Politics: The Challenges for Democracy', *Parliamentary Affairs*, 56 (2003), p. 297.

12   W. Grant 'The Challenges for Democracy', p. 301.

13   W. Grant, 'Pressure Politics: From "Insider" Politics to Direct Action?', *Parliamentary Affairs*, 54 (2001), p. 345.

14   W. Grant 'From "Insider" Politics', p. 346.

15   W. Grant 'From "Insider" Politics', p. 346.

16   W. Grant 'From "Insider" Politics', p. 348.

17   W. Grant 'From "Insider" Politics', p. 347.

18   W. Grant 'The Challenges for Democracy', pp. 307–8.

19   See A. Warleigh, '"Europeanizing" Civil Society'.

20   Database of Archives of UK Non-Governmental Organisations since 1945, www.dango.bham.ac.uk, the project behind the conference from which this volume emerged.

21   Normally limited to the voluntary sector, such as those working in charities and social services.

22   Often used interchangeably with VSO.

23   P. Willets 'What is a Non-Governmental Organisation?' (2005), Download at http://www.staff.city.ac.uk/p.willetts/CS-NTWKS/NGO-ART.HTM

24   K. Martens 'Mission Impossible? Defining Nongovernmental Organizations', *Voluntas*, 13(3) (2002), p. 272.

25   See V.F. Heinrich 'Studying Civil Society Across the World: Exploring the Thorny Issue of Conceptualisation and Measurement', *Journal of Civil Society*, 1(3) (2005) pp. 211–28; G. Jordan, D. Halpin and W. Maloney 'Defining Interests: Disambiguation and the Need for New Distinctions?', *British Journal of Politics and International Relations*, 6(2) (2004), pp. 195–212; S. Morris 'Defining the Non-Profit Sector: Some Lessons from History', Civil Society Working Paper 3, Centre for Civil Society (London: London School of Economics, 2000).

26   See W. Grant 'From "Insider" Politics', G. Jordan and W. Maloney, *The Protest Business*.

27   Rossteutscher, S. 'The Lure of the Associative Elixir', in S. Rossteutscher (ed.), *Democracy and the Role of Associations* (London: Routledge, 2005), p. 5.

28   In this chapter democratic contribution is viewed in an explicitly formal political manner. The democratic deficit we focus upon is the direct matter of political linkage: Do groups assist in repairing deficits in formal political

institutions such as to constitute political linkage? Do they provide for avenues of participation or representation in formal political life?

29 Interest group scholars preserve the term 'interest group' for collective actors and 'policy participants' for the unitary actors. NGO scholars may seek to create another term for these unitary actors as well.

30 P. Willets, 'What is a Non-Governmental Organisation?'.

31 P. Willets, 'What is a Non-Governmental Organisation?.

32 They accept affiliation of individual institutions, e.g. businesses.

33 See G. Jordan, D. Halpin and W. Maloney, 'Defining Interests'.

34 See L.M. Salamon and H.K. Anheier, *The Emerging Nonprofit Sector: An Overview* (Manchester: Manchester University Press, 1996); J.A. Scholte, 'Global Civil Society'; M. Diani, 'Networks and Social Movements: A Research Programme', in M. Diani and D. McAdam (eds) *Social Movements and Networks* (Oxford: Oxford University Press, 2003), pp. 299–319.

35 H.F. Pitkin, *The Concept of Representation* (Berkeley: University of California Press, 1967), p. 209.

36 H.F. Pitkin, *The Concept of Representation*, p. 210. This is the basis of the 'authenticity' position. As Hannah Pitkin suggests, if voice is possible then it *should* be expressed.

37 J. O'Neill, 'Representing People, Representing Nature, Representing the World', *Environment and Planning C: Government and Policy*, 19 (2001), pp. 483–500.

38 J. O'Neill, 'Representing people', p. 494.

39 J. O'Neill, 'Representing people', p. 496.

40 J. O'Neill, 'Representing people', p. 492, fn. 18.

41 For an opposing view see R. Eckersley, 'The Discourse Ethics and the Problem of Representing Nature', *Environmental Politics*, 8(2) (1999), pp. 24–49.

42 J. O'Neill, 'Representing People', fn. 12.

43 A. Van Rooy, *The Global Legitimacy Game: Civil Society, Globalization and Protest* (Basingstoke: Palgrave Macmillan, 2004).

44 Why some groups that organise these types of constituencies do practice a membership style affiliation and internal democratic procedures may be unconnected to representation. One could imagine other positive impacts from membership practices by groups that rightly pursue solidarity. Close contact with individuals affiliated with a solidarity group may be useful in establishing transparency over the group's expenditure of supporters' funds and in managing its public image. It may be an important organisational incentive for recruiting those who like to be 'active'. It may be to maximise political power, to increase funding, and to satisfy affiliates that their money and support is being used for the ends the group leaders claimed (even if affiliates themselves are not involved in setting the group goals).

45 Y. Yishai, *Land of Paradoxes: Interest Politics in Israel* (Albany: State University of New York Press, 1991).

46 The solidarity versus representation distinction is also helpful in separating out, for example, professional NGOs organised around the environment from environmental advocates. The Australian Conservation Foundation (ACF) for instance, started life as a group of professional ecologists concerned with environment; its legitimacy arising from the democratically

derived view of its professional membership. It has ended as a group pursuing affiliations with supporters and generating an attentive mass public to show solidarity with nature. It started as a representational group for ecologists, and shifted to a solidarity group for the environment.

47　See Jordan and Maloney *Protest Business* for discussion of FoE and Greenpeace.

48　While this chapter (and other scholars – see Grant 2001 and Willetts 2005) would accept business and trade associations among NGOs, the convention is to employ a public interest or 'benevolence' test which views such groups as out with the voluntary, third or civil society sectors. In turn such tests promote a tendency to examine NGOs that pursue the interests of the marginalised. Such tests with implicit normative dimensions are, however, unhelpful in informing empirical research.

49　*op. cit.* Jordan and Maloney, *Protest Business*, p. 32.

50　See P.F. Whiteley and S.J. Winyward, *Pressure for the Poor: The Poverty Lobby and Policy Making* (London and New York: Methuen, 1987).

51　R. Baggott, J. Allsop and K. Jones, *Speaking for Patients and Carers* (Basingstoke: Palgrave, 2005).

52　N. Small and P. Rhodes, *Too Ill To Talk? User Involvement in Palliative Care*, (London: Routledge, 2000), p. 63.

53　See G. Jordan and D. Halpin, 'Olson Triumphant? Explaining the Growth of a Small Business Organisation', *Political Studies*, 52(3) (2004), pp. 431–49.

54　R. Baggott *et al.*, *Speaking for Patients and Carers*.

55　A. Phillips, 'Representation Renewed', in M. Sawer and G. Zappala (eds), *Speaking for the People: Representation in Australian Politics* (Melbourne: Melbourne University Press, 2001), p. 26.

56　J. O'Neill, 'Representing People', p. 496.

57　See T. Risse, 'Transnational Governance and Legitimacy', in Benz, A. and Papadopoulos, Y. (eds), *Governance and Democracy* (Oxon: Routledge, 2006), pp. 179–99.

58　See Edwards and Zadek (2002), *op. cit.* Van Rooy, *Legitimacy Game*, p. 138.

Index